THE LOEB CLASSICAL LIBRARY

FOUNDED BY JAMES LOEB, LL.D.

EDITED BY

† T. E. PAGE, C.H., LITT.D.

E. CAPPS, PH.D., LL.D.   W. H. D. ROUSE, LITT.D.

L. A. POST, M.A.   E. H. WARMINGTON, M.A.

OVID

THE ART OF LOVE, AND OTHER POEMS

OVID

THE ART OF LOVE, AND
OTHER POEMS

WITH AN ENGLISH TRANSLATION BY

J. H. MOZLEY

SOMETIME SCHOLAR OF KING'S COLLEGE, CAMBRIDGE,
LECTURER IN CLASSICS, UNIVERSITY OF LONDON

DE MEDICAMINE FACIEI   ARTIS AMATORIAE
I–III   REMEDIORUM AMORIS   NUX   IBIS
HALIEUTICON   CONSOLATIO AD LIVIAM
APPENDIX TO IBIS

LONDON
WILLIAM HEINEMANN LTD
CAMBRIDGE, MASSACHUSETTS
HARVARD UNIVERSITY PRESS
MCMXLVII

First printed 1929
Revised and Reprinted 1939
Reprinted 1947

Printed in Great Britain

CONTENTS

INTRODUCTION

The poems here translated consist of (i) the didactic
poems on love, namely, the fragment *On Painting the
Face*, the *Art of Love*, and the *Remedies for Love*;
(ii) four miscellaneous pieces, the fragment on sea-
fishing, the *Ibis*, the *Walnut-tree* and the *Consolation
to Livia*, of which the last two are generally considered
spurious.

I. *The Didactic Love-poems.*

These mark the final stage of Ovid's first poetical
period, his previous achievements in love-poetry being
the *Amores*, which describe his own experiences, and
the *Letters of the Heroines*.[1] It seems to have been
an original idea of the poet's to include love-making
among the subjects of didactic poetry, examples of
which are to be found in the philosophical poems
of Empedocles or Lucretius, and the treatises of a
Macer on herbs or of a Manilius on astronomy. It
was perhaps suggested by some of the poems in the
Amores; for example, i. 4, in which he gives advice
to his mistress how to behave in her husband's
presence, or ii. 2, in which a eunuch is instructed
how to relax his watch over his charge, or i. 8, in

---

[1] The lost tragedy of *Medea* also belongs to this period.

which he retails the advice given by a procuress to a courtesan.

First, we have a fragment on cosmetics, probably a mere versification of a catalogue of recipes, preceded by a comparison of the smartness of modern times with the rude fashions of the past, which serves as an introduction and also to explain the importance of the subject. Gaps have been suspected after ll. 26 and 50, and the work as we have it is unfinished. It was written some time before the *Ars* (*A. A.* iii. 205).

The *Art of Love* was written just at the turn of the eras.[1] In broad outline the scheme of the work is as follows: in Book I the poet gives advice as to where the lover may find a mistress to his taste (1–264), and then as to how she is to be won (265–end); in Book II he gives a number of precepts for the retaining of her affections; Book III is devoted to the women in their turn, and they too receive advice how to capture and to retain a lover's affections. It need hardly be said that the *Ars* has enjoyed uninterrupted popularity; Ovid's knowledge of human, particularly of feminine, nature, the brilliant picture of the social life of Rome, the studied artlessness of the comparisons he draws from animals and from pursuits such as hunting, farming or sailing, the narratives that he cannot resist interweaving with his teaching from time to time—all these elements, together with a considerable degree of humour, his cool flippancy and irresistible wit, have combined to give the work a unique attractiveness.

[1] He refers to the naval sham fight exhibited by Augustus in 2 B.C. and to the expedition of the young Gaius Caesar to the East in 1 B.C.

INTRODUCTION

It was a worthy product of the brilliant and reckless society of Augustan Rome, and it is hardly surprising that, though not the cause of the poet's banishment, it was looked upon with disapproval by the Emperor.[1] And Ovid's plea that he was not damaging the moral life of Rome cannot be taken very seriously; it is true that there was a very clearly marked difference between the respectable "matrona" or "virgo" and the "libertinae," and that Ovid's precepts must be taken as being concerned only with the latter class; intrigues with them, whether they were married or unmarried, were regarded in quite a different light, and Ovid makes the most of this distinction; still, one feels that his protestations are rather too earnest to be really ingenuous.

Ovid, however, is anything but an indiscriminate sensualist; the mere harlot he will have none of (ii. 685 sqq.); he even insists on a high standard of culture in the mistress of his choice. She must be a "culta," even a "docta puella," and that such cultivation of the mind was seriously aimed at by the "libertinae" may be gathered from his remark (ii. 281–2), that though many aimed at being "doctae," few succeeded in their aim. His standard is certainly high, for she must be accomplished in arts and languages, and have read Callimachus, Philetas, Anacreon, Menander, Sappho, besides contemporary Latin verse. Less exacting requirements are that she should be tasteful, elegant,

[1] The real cause seems to have been some discreditable event in which Ovid was concerned (cf. "cur aliquid vidi? cur noxia lumina feci"? etc., *Trist.* 2. 103, and *Trist.* 3. 5. 49); it has been conjectured that it was some escapade of the Princess Julia.

scrupulously clean and *soignée* in dress and person, know how to walk and laugh, etc. Culture to Ovid was the mark of the age, that age into which he rejoiced that he was born (iii. 121), and he delighted in being fastidious; at least, so he would have his readers believe.

In the *Remedies for Love*, precepts are given for the falling *out of* love, if that is required, mainly to men, though it is to be understood that his precepts apply to women too (l. 49). Rival occupations are recommended (there is a long description of country life, l. 169), and the teachings of the *Ars* are reversed, *e.g.* avoid theatres, mark the other's bad points, etc.

II. *Miscellaneous Pieces.*

The *Ibis* was written during the poet's exile at Tomi on the Black Sea; its name is borrowed from a poem written by the Alexandrian poet Callimachus against Apollonius, who, though a native of Rhodes, was apparently a citizen of Naucratis, a town connected with the cult of the Egyptian god Theuth and with the Ibis, a bird sacred to him; hence Apollonius is attacked under that name. Ovid's poem is apparently much longer than that of Callimachus; the real name of the enemy whom he attacks is unknown, though various conjectures have been made. The greater part of the work consists in a long series of imprecations, in the course of which the whole of mythology is ransacked for instances of violent deaths, which the poet prays may be his enemy's lot. (Either Ovid had an extraordinarily retentive memory, or he took a compendium of mythology with him into exile).[1]

The fragment on *Sea-fishing* must also have been written at Tomi, where he could join direct observation, or perhaps rather gossip with fishermen, to information found in hand-books, probably Greek, as there seems to be a source common to this work and to the later works of Oppian and Plutarch on the subject. The fragment falls into three parts: (i) how fishes resist being caught, 1–48, (ii) contrast between fishing and hunting, 49–81, (iii) some rules for catching fish, with a list of various fishes and their haunts, 82–end. Its authorship has been doubted, but in view of Pliny's explicit statement that Ovid wrote it, together with his paraphrase of the opening lines, it seems a little unreasonable to do so. Housman doubts it on the grounds of prosody (*Class. Quarterly,* 1907).

The poem on the *Walnut-tree* is sometimes considered spurious; strong arguments, however, have been adduced by C. Ganzenmuller (*Die Elegie Nux und ihr Verfasser*, Tubingen, 1910) for holding it to be a genuine work of Ovid, written in the last period of his exile; the poet's fate is like that of the tree, for both have enemies who ill-treat them without cause. In form the piece is an expansion of a Greek epigram, *Anthol. Pal.* ix 3.

The *Consolation to Livia* is almost as certainly un-Ovidian as any piece can well be, both in its prosody (*e.g.* ll. 307, 379) and in its heaviness of treatment (contrast the Lament for Tibullus, *Am.*

[1] The student may be referred to C. Zipfel, " Quomodo Ovidius Callimachum aliosque fontes imprimis defixiones secutus sit " (Leipzig, 1910), and to Rostagni's *Ibis* (Florence, 1920).

iii. 9).[1] It has also been remarked that had Ovid
written it he would surely have mentioned it in his
entreaties to Augustus for recall from exile.
Drusus, son of Livia and stepson of the Emperor,
died prematurely while on a campaign in Germany
(9 B.C.); his brother Tiberius, the future Emperor,
brought the body back to Rome.

The *Epicedion,* or Poem of Consolation, became
a favourite literary type in the Flavian age, and
examples of it are to be found among the *Silvae* of
Statius.[2] Such poems seem to our taste insincere
and overwrought, and certainly too long, but the
subject of death and bereavement was one on which
ancient sentiment expressed itself in a different way
from ours; a good example will be found in the
exchange of letters between Cicero and his friend
Servius Sulpicius Rufus on the death of Cicero's
daughter Tullia (*ad Fam.* iv. 5, 6).

THE MANUSCRIPTS

De Medicamine Faciei.

M: Florentinus (Marcianus 223), 11th–12th cent.
L: Lugdunensis, 15th cent.
There are also one or two other late MSS.

---

[1] There are also a number of phrases apparently imitated
from Ovid's writings (*e.g.* 39 = *Fast.* 5. 459, 46 = *Fast.* 1. 299,
104 = *Trist.* 5. 5. 24, 165 = *Her.* 14. 67, etc.); cf. Vollmer's
edn. in *Poetae Latini Minores,* ii., 1911.
[2] The present poem seems to have been imitated by
Statius in his *Thebaid,* e.g. Livia's own lament (l. 121) is
paralleled by that of Ide (*Theb.* iii. 151 ff.), Tiber (l. 221) by
Ismenus (*Theb.* ix. 404), though he has elaborated in both
cases; cf. also a verbal borrowing in the *Silvae* (5. 5. 60, l. 7).

INTRODUCTION

Ars Amatoria.

O: Oxoniensis (Bodl. Auct. F. iv. 32), 9th cent. (Bk. I only).
R: Parisinus (Regius) 7311, 10th cent.

Remedia Amoris.

R: Parisinus (Regius) 7311, 10th cent.
E: Etonensis, 11th cent.

Nux.

M: Florentinus (Marcianus 223), 11th–12th cent.
G: Lentiensis, 12th–13th cent.

Ibis.

There are a number of 12th and 13th cent. MSS. at Frankfurt (F), Berlin (P), Tours (T), Vienna (V), Holkham Hall (H), Trinity Coll., Cambridge (G), Paris (X).

Halieuticon.

V: Vindobonensis (Sannazarianus) 277, 9th cent.

Consolatio ad Liviam.

Various 15th cent. MSS. (see Vollmer, *Poet. Lat. Min.* ii., 1911).

Note—" MSS." in the critical notes signifies either MSS. as opposed to editors, or *other* MSS. as opposed to particular MS. readings.

INTRODUCTION

Note on Editions, etc.

The "Ars" was edited with commentary by
P. Brandt, Leipzig, 1902, and the "Ibis" by
Robinson Ellis, Oxford, 1881. For the numerous
articles, dissertations, etc., the student is referred to
Schanz, Römische Litteraturgeschichte, vol. II, Pt. i.

ON PAINTING THE FACE

DE MEDICAMINE FACIEI LIBER

Discite, quae faciem commendet cura, puellae,
  Et quo sit vobis forma tuenda modo.
Cultus humum sterilem Cerealia pendere iussit
  Munera, mordaces interiere rubi.
Cultus et in pomis succos emendat acerbos,   5
  Fissaque adoptivas accipit arbor opes.
Culta placent.   auro sublimia tecta linuntur,
  Nigra sub imposito marmore terra latet:
Vellera saepe eadem Tyrio medicantur aëno:
  Sectile deliciis India praebet ebur.   10
Forsitan antiquae Tatio sub rege Sabinae
  Maluerint, quam se, rura paterna coli:
Cum matrona, premens altum rubicunda sedile,
  Assiduum duro pollice nebat opus,
Ipsaque claudebat quos filia paverat agnos,   15
  Ipsa dabat virgas caesaque ligna foco.
At vestrae matres teneras peperere puellas:
  Vultis inaurata corpora veste tegi,
Vultis odoratos positu variare capillos,
  Conspicuas gemmis vultis habere manus: 20
Induitis collo lapides oriente petitos,
  Et quantos onus est aure tulisse duos.
Nec tamen indignum, si vobis cura placendi,
  Cum comptos habeant saecula nostra viros.

14 assiduum duro *edd.* : assiduo durum *M.*

ON PAINTING THE FACE

Learn, O women, what pains can enhance your looks, and how your beauty may be preserved. By cultivation was the sterile ground bidden render bounty of wheat, and the devouring briers slain. Cultivation improves the bitter juice of fruit, and the cleft[1] tree gains adopted richness. What is cultivated gives pleasure. Lofty halls are plated with gold, the black earth lies hid under marble buildings. The same fleeces are many times steeped in cauldrons of Tyrian dye : India gives its ivory to be carved into choice figures. The Sabine dames of old under king Tatius would perchance have wished to cultivate their paternal acres rather than themselves : when the matron, sitting rubicund in her high seat, span assiduously with hardened thumb, and herself penned up the lambs her daughter had pastured, herself set the twigs and cleft logs upon the hearth. But your mothers have borne delicate girls. You wish your bodies to be covered with gold-embroidered gowns, you wish to vary the dressing of your perfumed locks, you wish to have hands that shine with gems : you adorn your necks with stones sought from the East, and so large that the ear finds two a burden to bear. Nor is that a fault, if you are anxious to please, for men love elegance in

---

[1] *i.e.* for grafting.

Feminea vestri poliuntur lege mariti,   25
    Et vix ad cultus nupta, quod addat, habet.
Cui se quaeque parent quos et venentur amores,
    Refert; munditia crimina nulla merent.
Rure latent finguntque comas; licet arduus illas
    Celet Athos, cultas altus habebit Athos.   30
Est etiam placuisse sibi cuicumque voluptas;
    Virginibus cordi grataque forma sua est.
Laudatas homini volucris Iunonia pennas
    Explicat, et forma multa superbit avis.
Sic potius nos uret amor quam fortibus herbis,   35
    Quas maga terribili subsecat arte manus.
Nec vos graminibus nec mixto credite succo,
    Nec temptate nocens virus amantis equae;
Nec mediae Marsis finduntur cantibus angues,
    Nec redit in fontes unda supina suos;   40
Et quamvis aliquis Temeseïa moverit aera,
    Numquam Luna suis excutietur equis.

Prima sit in vobis morum tutela, puellae.
    Ingenio facies conciliante placet.
Certus amor morum est: formam populabitur aetas,   45
    Et placitus rugis vultus aratus erit.
Tempus erit, quo vos speculum vidisse pigebit,
    Et veniet rugis altera causa dolor.
Sufficit et longum probitas perdurat in aevum,
    Perque suos annos hinc bene pendet amor.   50

27 pro se quaeque . . . et quos venerentur *M*: cui *Postgate*.
31 cuicumque *Marius*: quaecumque *MSS*.
35 nos uret *Heinsius*: vos urget *MSS*.

4

these times of ours. In feminine wise are your husbands made trim, and the bride has scarce aught to add to their smartness. It makes a difference for whom each prepares herself, and what lover may be the quarry; but by being spruce they will never be wrong. They bury themselves in the country, and yet are trimming their locks; though lofty Athos hid them, lofty Athos would find them smart. There is pleasure, too, in self-satisfaction, whoe'er one may be; dear to the heart of girls is their own beauty. The bird of Juno spreads out the feathers praised by man, and in its own beauty many a bird exults. Thus will love inflame us rather than by strong herbs, which the hand of the sorceress gathers as she plies her terrible craft. Trust not to grasses nor to mixture of juices, nor attempt the noxious venom of an infatuated mare; snakes are not split in twain by Marsian spells,[1] nor does the wave stream backward to its fount; and though one has clashed the bronze of Temese,[2] the Moon will never be shaken from out her car.

Think first, ye women, to look to your behaviour. The face pleases when character commends. Love of character is lasting: beauty will be ravaged by age, and the face that charmed will be ploughed by wrinkles. The time will come, when it will vex you to look at a mirror, and grief will prove a second cause of wrinkles. Goodness endures and lasts for many a day, and throughout its years love securely rests thereon.

[1] The tribe of the Marsians, who lived in central Italy, were famous for their witches, cf. *Ars. Amat.* 2.102.
[2] Temese was a town famous for copper-mines, on the west coast of Italy in Bruttii.

Discite, cum teneros somnus dimiserit artus,
  Candida quo possint ora nitere modo.
Hordea, quae Libyci ratibus misere coloni,
  Exue de palea tegminibusque suis.
Par ervi mensura decem madefiat ab ovis :   55
  Sed cumulent libras hordea nuda duas.
Haec ubi ventosas fuerint siccata per auras,
  Lenta iube scabra frangat asella mola :
Et quae prima cadunt vivaci cornua cervo,
  Contere in haec (solidi sexta face assis eat).   60
Iamque ubi pulvereae fuerint confusa farinae,
  Protinus in cumeris omnia cerne cavis.
Adice narcissi bis sex sine cortice bulbos,
  Strenua quos puro marmore dextra terat.
Sextantemque trahat gummi cum semine Tusco :   65
  Huc novies tanto plus tibi mellis eat.
Quaecumque afficiet tali medicamine vultum
  Fulgebit speculo levior ipsa suo.
Nec tu pallentes dubita torrere lupinos,
  Et simul inflantes corpora frige fabas ;   70
Utraque sex habeant aequo discrimine libras,
  Utraque da nigris comminuenda molis.
Nec cerussa tibi nec nitri spuma rubentis
  Desit et Illyrica quae venit iris humo.
Da validis iuvenum pariter subigenda lacertis :   75
  Sed iustum tritis uncia pondus erit.
Addita de querulo volucrum medicamina nido
  Ore fugant maculas : alcyonea vocant.

ON PAINTING THE FACE

Learn now in what manner, when sleep has let go your tender limbs, your faces can shine bright and fair. Strip from its covering of chaff the barley which Libyan husbandmen have sent in ships. Let an equal measure of vetch be moistened in ten eggs, but let the skinned barley weigh two pounds. When this has dried in the blowing breezes, bid the slow she-ass break it on the rough millstone: grind therewith too the first horns that fall from a nimble stag (let the sixth part of a solid as [1] be added). And now when it is mixed with the dusty grain, sift it all straightway in hollow sieves. Add twelve narcissus-bulbs [2] without their skins, and let a strenuous hand pound them on pure marble. Let gum and Tuscan seed weigh a sixth part of a pound, and let nine times as much honey go to that. Whoever shall treat her face with such a prescription will shine smoother than her own mirror. Nor hesitate to roast pale lupin-seeds, and therewith fry beans that puff out the body; with fair discernment let each have six pounds' weight, give each to the black millstones to be pounded small. Nor let white lead nor foam of red nitre be lacking, nor the iris that comes from Illyrian soil. [3] Give them all alike to be subdued by the strong arms of youths, but when ground their right weight will be one ounce. Spots on the face are banished by a remedy taken from the querulous nest of birds: halcyon-

---

[1] *i.e.* of a pound; it should be remembered that the Roman pound weighed only 12 oz. The scruple (1. 92) was $\frac{1}{24}$th part of an ounce.

[2] cf. Pliny, *N.H.* 21, 75, where it is said to be good for removing blemishes and softening hardnesses.

[3] cf. Pliny, *N.H.* 21, 19, *iris . . . unguentis et medicinae nascens. Laudatissima in Illyrico.*

Pondere, si quaeris, quo sim contentus in illis,
  Quod trahit in partes uncia secta duas.   80
Ut coeant apteque lini per corpora possint,
  Adice de flavis Attica mella favis.
Quamvis tura deos irataque numina placent,
  Non tamen accensis omnia danda focis.
Tus ubi miscueris radenti tubera nitro,   85
  Ponderibus iustis fac sit utrimque triens.
Parte minus quarta dereptum cortice gummi,
  Et modicum e myrrhis pinguibus adde cubum.
Haec ubi contriris, per densa foramina cerne :
  Pulvis ab infuso melle premendus erit.   90
Profuit et marathros bene olentibus addere myrrhis,
  (Quinque trahant marathri scrupula, myrrha novem)
Arentisque rosae quantum manus una prehendat,
  Cumque Ammoniaco mascula tura sale.
Hordea quem faciunt, illis infunde cremorem :   95
  Aequent expensas cum sale tura rosas.
Tempore sint parvo molli licet illita vultu,
  Haerebit toto multus in ore color.
Vidi quae gelida madefacta papavera lympha
  Contereret, teneris illineretque genis.   100

          85 tubera *L and edd.* : corpora *MSS.*
          92 trahant *Muretus* : parent *MSS.*

cream they call it. If you ask with what weight
thereof I am content, it is that which an ounce
divided into two parts weighs. That they may mix
and be properly smeared upon the body, add Attic
honey from its yellow combs. Although incense
appeases the gods and angered powers, it must not
all be offered upon kindled altars. When you have
mixed incense with nitre that scrapes off warts, see
that on either side the balance there is a third
of a pound exact. Add a pound, less its fourth part,
of gum stripped of its bark, and a moderate cube of
juicy myrrh. When you have pounded these up,
sift them in close-set meshes : the powder must be
settled by pouring honey on it. It has been found
useful to add fennel to the fragrant myrrh (let the
fennel weigh five scruples, the myrrh nine), and of
dry rose-leaves as much as the hand can grasp, and
frankincense with salt of Ammon.[1] Thereon pour
the juice that barley makes ;[2] let rose-leaves and
salt together equal the incense in weight. Though
it be smeared but for a short time on your soft
countenance, a fine colour will remain on all your
face. I have seen one who pounded poppies
moistened with cool water, and rubbed them on her
tender cheeks.

---

[1] *i.e.* salt found in the Libyan desert, not "sal ammoniac,"
which is chloride of ammonium.

[2] cf. Pliny, *N.H.* 22, 65, *asperso sale et melle candorem
intibus et suavitatem oris facit.*

THE ART OF LOVE

ARTIS AMATORIAE

LIBER PRIMUS

Siquis in hoc artem populo non novit amandi,
  Hoc legat et lecto carmine doctus amet.
Arte citae veloque rates remoque moventur,
  Arte leves currus : arte regendus amor.
Curribus Automedon lentisque erat aptus habenis,   5
  Tiphys in Haemonia puppe magister erat :
Me Venus artificem tenero praefecit Amori ;
  Tiphys et Automedon dicar Amoris ego.
Ille quidem ferus est et qui mihi saepe repugnet :
  Sed puer est, aetas mollis et apta regi.   10
Phillyrides puerum cithara perfecit Achillem,
  Atque animos placida contudit arte feros.
Qui totiens socios, totiens exterruit hostes,
  Creditur annosum pertimuisse senem.
Quas Hector sensurus erat, poscente magistro   15
  Verberibus iussas praebuit ille manus.
Aeacidae Chiron, ego sum praeceptor Amoris :
  Saevus uterque puer, natus uterque dea.
Sed tamen et tauri cervix oneratur aratro,
  Frenaque magnanimi dente teruntur equi ;   20
Et mihi cedet Amor, quamvis mea vulneret arcu
  Pectora, iactatas excutiatque faces.
Quo me fixit Amor, quo me violentius ussit,
  Hoc melior facti vulneris ultor ero :

---

[1] Charioteer of Achilles and helmsman of the Argo respectively ; Jason came from Thessaly (Haemonia).

THE ART OF LOVE

BOOK I

If anyone among this people knows not the art of loving, let him read my poem, and having read be skilled in love. By skill swift ships are sailed and rowed, by skill nimble chariots are driven: by skill must Love be guided. Well fitted for chariots and pliant reins was Automedon, and Tiphys was the helmsman of the Haemonian ship:[1] me hath Venus set over tender Love as master in the art; I shall be called the Tiphys and Automedon of Love. Wild indeed is he, and apt often to fight against me; but he is a boy, tender his age and easily controlled. The son of Philyra[2] made the boy Achilles accomplished on the lyre, and by his peaceful art subdued those savage passions. He who terrified his friends so often and so often his foes, cowered, we are told, before an aged man. Those hands that Hector was to feel, he held out to the lash obediently, when his master bade. Chiron taught Aeacides, I am Love's teacher: a fierce lad each, and each born of a goddess. Yet even the bull's neck is burdened by the plough, and the high-mettled steed champs the bridle with his teeth; and to me Love shall yield, though he wound my breast with his bow, and whirl aloft his brandished torch. The more violently Love has pierced and branded me, the better shall I avenge the wound that he has made: I will not

[2] Chiron.

13

Non ego, Phoebe, datas a te mihi mentiar artes,   25
   Nec nos aëriae voce monemur avis,
Nec mihi sunt visae Clio Cliusque sorores
   Servanti pecudes vallibus, Ascra, tuis:
Usus opus movet hoc: vati parete perito;
   Vera canam: coeptis, mater Amoris, ades!   30
Este procul, vittae tenues, insigne pudoris,
   Quaeque tegis medios instita longa pedes.
Nos venerem tutam concessaque furta canemus,
   Inque meo nullum carmine crimen erit.

Principio quod amare velis, reperire labora,   35
   Qui nova nunc primum miles in arma venis.
Proximus huic labor est placitam exorare puellam:
   Tertius, ut longo tempore duret amor.
Hic modus, haec nostro signabitur area curru:
   Haec erit admissa meta premenda rota.   40

Dum licet, et loris passim potes ire solutis,
   Elige cui dicas "tu mihi sola places."
Haec tibi non tenues veniet delapsa per auras:
   Quaerenda est oculis apta puella tuis.
Scit bene venator cervis ubi retia tendat,   45
   Scit bene qua frendens valle moretur aper;
Aucupibus noti frutices; qui sustinet hamos,
   Novit quae multo pisce natentur aquae:
Tu quoque, materiam longo qui quaeris amori,
   Ante frequens quo sit disce puella loco.   50
Non ego quaerentem vento dare vela iubebo,
   Nec tibi, ut invenias, longa terenda via est.

---

[1] As they did to Hesiod, see *Theogony*, ll. 22 sqq.
[2] The fillet, or hair-band, was worn only by women of good character; the flounce ("instita") made the skirt reach down to the feet, and was sewn on to it, as in Hor. *Sat.* 1. 2. 28:

falsely claim that my art is thy gift, O Phoebus, nor am I taught by the voice of a bird of the air, neither did Clio and Clio's sisters appear to me while I kept flocks in thy vale, O Ascra:[1] experience inspires this work: give ear to an experienced bard; true will be my song: favour my enterprise, O mother of Love. Keep far away, ye slender fillets, emblems of modesty, and the long skirt that hides the feet in its folds.[2] Of safe love-making do I sing, and permitted secrecy, and in my verse shall be no wrong-doing.

First, strive to find an object for your love, you who now for the first time come to fight in warfare new. The next task is, to win the girl that takes your fancy; the third, to make love long endure. This is my limit, this the field whose bound my chariot shall mark, this the goal my flying wheel shall graze.

While yet you are at liberty and can go at large with loosened rein, choose to whom you will say, "You alone please me." She will not come floating down to you through the tenuous air, she must be sought, the girl whom your glance approves. Well knows the hunter where to spread his nets for the stag, well knows he in what glen the boar with gnashing teeth abides; familiar are the copses to fowlers, and he who holds the hook is aware in what waters many fish are swimming; you too, who seek the object of a lasting passion, learn first what places the maidens haunt. I will not bid you in your search set sails before the wind, nor, that you may find, need a long road be travelled. Though Perseus

"quarum subsuta talos tegat instita veste"; it, too, marked the woman of good character.

Andromedan Perseus nigris portarit ab Indis,
    Raptaque sit Phrygio Graia puella viro,
Tot tibi tamque dabit formosas Roma puellas,   55
    " Haec habet" ut dicas " quicquid in orbe fuit."
Gargara quot segetes, quot habet Methymna racemos,
    Aequore quot pisces, fronde teguntur aves,
Quot caelum stellas, tot habet tua Roma puellas :
    Mater et Aeneae constat in urbe sui.   60
Seu caperis primis et adhuc crescentibus annis,
    Ante oculos veniet vera puella tuos :
Sive cupis iuvenem, iuvenes tibi mille placebunt,
    Cogeris et voti nescius esse tui :
Seu te forte iuvat sera et sapientior aetas,   65
    Hoc quoque, crede mihi, plenius agmen erit.

Tu modo Pompeia lentus spatiare sub umbra,
    Cum sol Herculei terga leonis adit :
Aut ubi muneribus nati sua munera mater
    Addidit, externo marmore dives opus.   70
Nec tibi vitetur quae, priscis sparsa tabellis,
    Porticus auctoris Livia nomen habet :
Quaque parare necem miseris patruelibus ausae
    Belides et stricto stat ferus ense pater.
Nec te praetereat Veneri ploratus Adonis,   75
    Cultaque Iudaeo septima sacra Syro.

---

[1] Probably here the Aethiopians, though the scene is usually placed in Syria. It is implied that Andromeda is "fusca" in 3. 191. The contrast is between the toils that Perseus had to undergo and the ease of finding maidens in Rome.

[2] Gargara is on Mt. Ida in the Troad, and Methymna in the island of Lesbos.

[3] The reference is to the Portico of Pompey, near to the theatre called after him, adorned by plane trees and fountains.

[4] The Portico of Octavia, sister of Augustus, dedicated by her to the memory of her son Marcellus ; she also built a

brought Andromeda from the dusky Indians,[1] though
the Phrygian lover carried off a Grecian girl, yet
Rome will give you so many maidens and so fair
that, " Here," you will say, " is all the beauty of the
world." As numerous as the crops upon Gargara,
as the grape-bunches of Methymna,[2] as the fishes
that lurk within the sea, or the birds among the
leaves, as many as are the stars of heaven, so many
maidens doth thine own Rome contain : the mother
of Aeneas still dwells in the city of her son. Are you
attracted by early and still ripening years? a real
maid will come before your eyes. Would you have a
full-grown beauty? a thousand such will please you,
and, try as you will, you know not which to choose.
Or do you perchance prefer a later and staider age?
still more numerous, believe me, will be their array.

Only walk leisurely beneath the Pompeian shade,[3]
when the sun draws nigh to Hercules' shaggy lion,
or where the mother has added her own gifts to her
son's,[4] a work rich with marble coating. Nor should
you avoid the Livian colonnade which, scattered o'er
with ancient paintings keeps its founder's name,[5] or
where the daughters of Belus dare to plot death for
their wretched cousins, and their fierce sire stands
with drawn sword.[6] Nor let Adonis bewailed of
Venus escape you, nor the seventh day that the

library to his honour, and Augustus named a theatre after
him.

[5] It was called after Livia, the wife of Augustus (cf.
Propertius, 2. 23. 3).

[6] The Portico of the Danaids, in the temple of Apollo on
the Palatine ; there were statues representing the fifty
daughters of Danaus, about to slay the cousins whom they
were forced to marry ; they were the grand-daughters of
Belus, king of Egypt.

17

Nec fuge linigerae Memphitica templa iuvencae :
    Multas illa facit, quod fuit ipsa Iovi.
Et fora conveniunt (quis credere possit ?) amori :
    Flammaque in arguto saepe reperta foro :   80
Subdita qua Veneris facto de marmore templo
    Appias expressis aëra pulsat aquis,
Illo saepe loco capitur consultus Amori,
    Quique aliis cavit, non cavet ipse sibi :
Illo saepe loco desunt sua verba diserto,   85
    Resque novae veniunt, causaque agenda sua est.
Hunc Venus e templis, quae sunt confinia, ridet:
    Qui modo patronus, nunc cupit esse cliens.

Sed tu praecipue curvis venare theatris :
    Haec loca sunt voto fertiliora tuo.   90
Illic invenies quod ames, quod ludere possis,
    Quodque semel tangas, quodque tenere velis.
Ut redit itque frequens longum formica per agmen,
    Granifero solitum cum vehit ore cibum,
Aut ut apes saltusque suos et olentia nactae   95
    Pascua per flores et thyma summa volant,
Sic ruit in celebres cultissima femina ludos :
    Copia iudicium saepe morata meum est.
Spectatum veniunt, veniunt spectentur ut ipsae :
    Ille locus casti damna pudoris habet.   100
Primus sollicitos fecisti, Romule, ludos,
    Cum iuvit viduos rapta Sabina viros.

---

[1] The worship of Adonis was connected with the temple of
Venus, and his festival was very popular with the courtesans
of Rome ; "Syrian" covers most of the near East ; there were
many Jews in Rome since the capture of Jerusalem by Pompey
in 63 B.C.

Syrian Jew holds sacred.[1]   Avoid not the Memphian
shrine of the linen-clothed heifer: many a maid does
she make what she was herself to Jove.[2]   Even the
law-courts (who could believe it ?) are suitable to
love, often has its flame been found in the shrill-
tongued court: where set beneath the marble shrine
of Venus, the Appian nymph strikes the air with her
upspringing waters,[3] there often is the lawyer cheated
by Love, and he who was careful for others is not
careful for himself: often there does the glib speaker
fail for words: a new case comes on and his own
cause must be pleaded.   Venus laughs at him from
her neighbouring shrine: he who was of late an
advocate would fain be a client now.

But specially do your hunting in the round theatres:
more bountifully do these repay your vows.   There
will you find an object for passion or for dalliance,
something to taste but once, or to keep, if so you
wish.   As crowded ants pass and repass in a long
train, bearing in grain-burdened mouth their wonted
food, or as bees, having gained their dells and fragrant
pastures, flit o'er the blossoms and hover o'er the
thyme : so hasten the smartest women to the crowded
games ; many a time have their numbers made my
judgment falter.   They come to see, they come that
they may be seen: to chastity that place is fatal.
Thou first, Romulus, didst disturb the games, when
the rape of Sabine women consoled the widowed men.

---

[2] Isis is often identified with Io in Latin poetry.   The
temple of the former stood in the Campus Martius.

[3] There was a temple of Venus Genetrix in the Forum
Julium, and near it the fountain of the Aqua Appia (so
called because the water was brought by the aqueduct built
by the censor, Appius Claudius).

OVID

Tunc neque marmoreo pendebant vela theatro,
  Nec fuerant liquido pulpita rubra croco ;
Illic quas tulerant nemorosa Palatia, frondes   105
  Simpliciter positae, scaena sine arte fuit ;
In gradibus sedit populus de caespite factis,
  Qualibet hirsutas fronde tegente comas.
Respiciunt, oculisque notant sibi quisque puellam
  Quam velit, et tacito pectore multa movent.   110
Dumque, rudem praebente modum tibicine Tusco,
  Ludius aequatam ter pede pulsat humum,
In medio plausu (plausus tunc arte carebant)
  Rex populo praedae signa petita dedit.
Protinus exiliunt, animum clamore fatentes,   115
  Virginibus cupidas iniciuntque manus.
Ut fugiunt aquilas, timidissima turba, columbae,
  Utque fugit visos agna novella lupos :
Sic illae timuere viros sine more ruentes ;
  Constitit in nulla qui fuit ante color.   120
Nam timor unus erat, facies non una timoris :
  Pars laniat crines, pars sine mente sedet ;
Altera maesta silet, frustra vocat altera matrem :
  Haec queritur, stupet haec ; haec manet, illa fugit ;
Ducuntur raptae, genialis praeda, puellae,   125
  Et potuit multas ipse decere timor.
Siqua repugnarat nimium comitemque negabat,
  Sublatam cupido vir tulit ipse sinu,
Atque ita " quid teneros lacrimis corrumpis ocellos?
  Quod matri pater est, hoc tibi " dixit " ero."   130
Romule, militibus scisti dare commoda solus !
  Haec mihi si dederis commoda, miles ero.
Scilicet ex illo sollemnia more theatra
  Nunc quoque formosis insidiosa manent.

114 petita *Bentley, Madvig*: petenda *MSS.*

20

No awnings then hung o'er a marble theatre, nor was
the platform ruddy with crocus-spray; there, artlessly
arranged, were garlands which the leafy Palatine had
borne; the stage was unadorned; the people sat on
steps of turf, any chance leaves covering their un-
kempt hair. They look about them, and each notes
with his glance the woman he desires, and they brood
much in their secret hearts. And while to the Tuscan
flute-player's rude strains the dancer struck thrice
with his foot the levelled floor, in the midst of the
applause (the applause then was rough and rude) the
king gave to the people the expected sign of rape.
Straightway they leap forth, by their shouts betraying
their eagerness, and lay lustful hand upon the
maidens. As doves, most timorous of birds, flee
from the eagles, and the weanling lamb when it spies
the wolf, so feared they the men rushing wildly on
them; in none remained her former colour. For
their fear was one, but not one was the appearance of
their fear: some tear their hair, some sit crazed;
one is silent in dismay, one calls in vain upon her
mother; this one bewails, that one is struck dumb;
this one remains, that one flees. The captured
women are led off, spoil for the marriage-couch, and
to many their very fear had power to lend grace. If
any struggled overmuch and resisted her mate, up-
borne on his eager breast he carried her off himself,
saying: "Why do you spoil those tender eyes with
tears? What your sire was to your mother that will
I be to you." Ah, Romulus, thou only didst know how
to bestow bounty on thy warriors; so thou but bestow
such bounty upon me, I will be a warrior. And,
mark you, in accord with that tradition our theatres
now too are fraught with danger to the fair.

Nec te nobilium fugiat certamen equorum ;   135
   Multa capax populi commoda Circus habet.
Nil opus est digitis, per quos arcana loquaris,
   Nec tibi per nutus accipienda nota est:
Proximus a domina, nullo prohibente, sedeto,
   Iunge tuum lateri qua potes usque latus ;   140
Et bene, quod cogit, si nolit, linea iungi,
   Quod tibi tangenda est lege puella loci.
Hic tibi quaeratur socii sermonis origo,
   Et moveant primos publica verba sonos.
Cuius equi veniant, facito, studiose, requiras :   145
   Nec mora, quisquis erit, cui favet illa, fave.
At cum pompa frequens certantibus ibit ephebis,
   Tu Veneri dominae plaude favente manu ;
Utque fit, in gremium pulvis si forte puellae
   Deciderit, digitis excutiendus erit :   150
Et si nullus erit pulvis, tamen excute nullum :
   Quaelibet officio causa sit apta tuo.
Pallia si terra nimium demissa iacebunt,
   Collige, et inmunda sedulus effer humo ;
Protinus, officii pretium, patiente puella   155
   Contingent oculis crura videnda tuis.
Respice praeterea, post vos quicumque sedebit,
   Ne premat opposito mollia terga genu.
Parva leves capiunt animos : fuit utile multis
   Pulvinum facili composuisse manu.   160
Profuit et tenui ventos movisse tabella,
   Et cava sub tenerum scamna dedisse pedem.

Hos aditus Circusque novo praebebit amori,
   Sparsaque sollicito tristis harena foro.

141 nolit *O*: nolis *R*.
147 certantibus . . . ephebis *R*: caelestibus . . . eburnis *O*.
161 ventos . . . tabella *MSS.*: vento . . . tabellam *RO*.

Nor let the contest of noble steeds escape you; the spacious Circus holds many opportunities. No need is there of fingers for secret speech, nor need you receive a signal by means of nods. Sit next to your lady, none will prevent you; sit side by side as close as you can; and that is easy, for the rows compel closeness, if she be unwilling, and by the rule of the place you must touch your comrade. Here seek an opening for friendly talk, and begin with words that all may hear. Mind you are zealous in asking whose horses are entering, and quick! whomsoever she favours be sure to favour too. But when the long procession of competing youths passes by applaud Queen Venus with favouring hand.[1] And if perchance, as will happen, a speck of dust falls on your lady's lap, flick it off with your fingers; and if none fall, then flick off—none; let any pretext serve to show your attentiveness. If her cloak hangs low and trails upon the ground, gather it up and lift it carefully from the defiling earth; straightway, a reward for your service, with the girl's permission your eyes will catch a glimpse of her ankles. Then again look round to see that whoever is sitting behind you is not pressing his knee against her tender back. Frivolous minds are won by trifles: many have found useful the deft arranging of a cushion. It has helped too to stir the air with a light fan, or to set a stool beneath a dainty foot.

Such openings will the Circus afford to a new courtship, and the melancholy sand scattered on the busy

---

[1] This procession is described in *Amores*, 3. 2. 43 ff. It started from the Capitol, and came by the Forum and the Forum Boarium to the Circus, of which it traversed the whole length. Ivory statues of gods were carried, and would be applauded by those most sympathetic to them; Mars by soldiers, Venus by lovers, etc.

Illa saepe puer Veneris pugnavit harena, 165
  Et qui spectavit vulnera, vulnus habet.
Dum loquitur tangitque manum poscitque libellum
  Et quaerit posito pignore, vincat uter,
Saucius ingemuit telumque volatile sensit,
  Et pars spectati muneris ipse fuit. 170

Quid, modo cum belli navalis imagine Caesar
  Persidas induxit Cecropiasque rates?
Nempe ab utroque mari iuvenes, ab utroque puellae
  Venere, atque ingens orbis in Urbe fuit.
Quis non invenit turba quod amaret in illa? 175
  Eheu, quam multos advena torsit amor!

Ecce, parat Caesar domito quod defuit orbi
  Addere: nunc, oriens ultime, noster eris.
Parthe, dabis poenas: Crassi gaudete sepulti,
  Signaque barbaricas non bene passa manus. 180
Ultor adest, primisque ducem profitetur in annis,
  Bellaque non puero tractat agenda puer.
Parcite natales timidi numerare deorum:
  Caesaribus virtus contigit ante diem.
Ingenium caeleste suis velocius annis 185
  Surgit, et ignavae fert male damna morae.
Parvus erat, manibusque duos Tirynthius angues
  Pressit, et in cunis iam Iove dignus erat.

181 annis *RO*: armis *MSS*.

---

[1] Gladiatorial shows were sometimes given there.
[2] When a gladiator had received a wound, the people would cry "habet!"
[3] Augustus staged the battle of Salamis on a lake excavated for that purpose at the foot of the Janiculum, in 2 B.C.
[4] A rather abrupt digression, suggested by the idea of a triumph as a suitable occasion for courtship; he only returns to this theme in l. 219; hence, while the vocative in l. 213

Forum.[1] Often has Venus' Boy fought upon that sand, and he who watched the wounds has himself been wounded.[2] While he is speaking and touching her hand and asking for the book, and inquiring which is winning as he lays his stake, he feels the winged barb and groans with the wound, and is himself part of the show which he is watching.

What when Caesar of late brought on Persian and Cecropian vessels under the fashion of a naval fight?[3] Why, youths and maidens came from either sea : the mighty world was in our city. Who found not in that crowd some object for his passion? alas! how many did a foreign love o'erthrow!

Lo![4] Caesar is preparing to add what was lacking to the conquered world : now, farthest East, shalt thou be ours. Parthian, thou shalt pay penalty; rejoice, ye buried Crassi,[5] and ye standards that shamefully endured barbarian violence. Your avenger[6] is at hand, and, though his years be few, proclaims his captaincy, and, though a boy, handles wars that no boy should handle. Cease, timid ones, to count the birthdays of the gods; valour falls early to the lot of Caesars. Heavenly power grows more swiftly than its years, and ill brooks the penalties of slow delay. Small was the Tirynthian when in his hands he crushed two snakes, and already in his cradle he was worthy

refers to Gaius Caesar, in l. 221 he addresses the young lover again.

[5] The battle of Carrhae is referred to (53 B.C.), at which Crassus and his son were slain, and the Roman standards captured by the Parthians.

[6] Gaius Caesar was the young son of Agrippa and Julia, daughter of Augustus ; he was just being sent out to lead a campaign against Phraates, king of the Parthians ; in this war he died of a wound, and so failed to fulfil the prophecy of l. 194.

Nunc quoque qui puer es, quantus tum, Bacche, fuisti,
   Cum timuit thyrsos India victa tuos ?   190
Auspiciis animisque patris, puer, arma movebis,
   Et vinces animis auspiciisque patris :
Tale rudimentum tanto sub nomine debes,
   Nunc iuvenum princeps, deinde future senum ;
Cum tibi sint fratres, fratres ulciscere laesos :   195
   Cumque pater tibi sit, iura tuere patris.
Induit arma tibi genitor patriaeque tuusque :
   Hostis ab invito regna parente rapit ;
Tu pia tela feres, sceleratas ille sagittas :
   Stabit pro signis iusque piumque tuis.   200
Vincuntur causa Parthi : vincantur et armis ;
   Eoas Latio dux meus addat opes.
Marsque pater Caesarque pater, date numen eunti :
   Nam deus e vobis alter es, alter eris.
Auguror, en, vinces ; votivaque carmina reddam,   205
   Et magno nobis ore sonandus eris.
Consistes, aciemque meis hortabere verbis ;
   O desint animis ne mea verba tuis !
Tergaque Parthorum Romanaque pectora dicam,
   Telaque, ab averso quae iacit hostis equo.   210
Qui fugis ut vincas, quid victo, Parthe, relinquis ?
   Parthe, malum iam nunc Mars tuus omen habet.
Ergo erit illa dies, qua tu, pulcherrime rerum,
   Quattuor in niveis aureus ibis equis.

191, 192 animis *MSS* : annis *RO*.

---

[1] *i.e.* being a Caesar his first essay in warfare should bring
victory.

[2] A title which conferred the right to ride at the head of the
annual procession of the Equites.

[3] Actually he only had one, Lucius Caesar ; by the " sire "
Augustus, who had adopted them, is perhaps meant.

of Jove. And thou who even now art a youth, how big then wert thou, O Bacchus, when conquered India feared thy wands? With the auspices and courage of thy sire shalt thou, O youth, make war, and with the auspices and courage of thy sire shalt thou conquer: such, bearing so great a name, should be thy earliest exploit,[1] prince now of the youth,[2] but one day of the elders; since thou hast brothers,[3] avenge thy brothers' wrongs, and since thou hast a sire, guard the rights of thy sire. Thy father and the father of thy country hath girded thee with arms: an enemy snatches a realm from thy unwilling sire; rightful weapons shalt thou bear, dastardly arrows, he; right and duty shall stand to defend thy cause. The Parthians are defeated in their cause: let them be defeated in battle also; let my prince add to Latium the riches of the East. Father Mars and father Caesar, vouchsafe him your presence as he goes; for one of you is, and one will be, a god. Lo! I prophesy: victory shall be thine, and I shall duly pay my votive song, and owe thee loud utterance of praise. Thou wilt stand and in my own words exhort thy warriors; O let not my words fall short of thy valour. I shall tell of Parthian backs and Roman breasts, and of the weapons which the foe shoots from his retreating steed. Thou who dost flee to conquer, what, O Parthian, dost thou leave the conquered?[4] Already, O Parthian, hath thy warfare an evil omen. Therefore that day shall dawn whereon thou, fairest of beings, shalt ride all golden behind four snow-white steeds. Chieftains shall go

---

[4] *i.e.* if flight is your only means of gaining victory, what is there left to you to do when you are defeated?

Ibunt ante duces onerati colla catenis,   215
  Ne possint tuti, qua prius, esse fuga.
Spectabunt laeti iuvenes mixtaeque puellae,
  Diffundetque animos omnibus ista dies.
Atque aliqua ex illis cum regum nomina quaeret,
  Quae loca, qui montes, quaeve ferantur aquae,   220
Omnia responde, nec tantum siqua rogabit;
  Et quae nescieris, ut bene nota refer.
Hic est Euphrates, praecinctus arundine frontem :
  Cui coma dependet caerula, Tigris erit.
Hos facito Armenios; haec est Danaëia Persis :   225
  Urbs in Achaemeniis vallibus ista fuit.
Ille vel ille, duces ; et erunt quae nomina dicas,
  Si poteris, vere, si minus, apta tamen.

Dant etiam positis aditum convivia mensis :
  Est aliquid praeter vina, quod inde petas.   230
Saepe illic positi teneris adducta lacertis
  Purpureus Bacchi cornua pressit Amor :
Vinaque cum bibulas sparsere Cupidinis alas,
  Permanet et capto stat gravis ille loco.
Ille quidem pennas velociter excutit udas :   235
  Sed tamen et spargi pectus amore nocet.
Vina parant animos faciuntque caloribus aptos :
  Cura fugit multo diluiturque mero.
Tunc veniunt risus, tum pauper cornua sumit,
  Tum dolor et curae rugaque frontis abit.   240
Tunc aperit mentes aevo rarissima nostro
  Simplicitas, artes excutiente deo.
Illic saepe animos iuvenum rapuere puellae,
  Et Venus in vinis ignis in igne fuit.

225 facito *Heinsius*: facit *O*: facis *R*.

---

[1] Through Perses, son of Perseus and Andromeda. Ovid seems to have some picture in mind : Cupid is coaxing Bacchus, but the wine makes his wings wet, and he is forced to stop.

before thee, their necks laden with chains, lest they
be able to save themselves by the flight they used
before. Joyous youths shall look on and maidens
with them, and that day shall make all hearts o'er-
flow. And when some girl among them asks the
names of the monarchs, or what places, what
mountains, what rivers are borne along, do you
answer everything, nor only if she ask you; ay, even
if you know not, tell her as if you knew it well.
That is Euphrates, his forehead fringed with reeds; he
with the dark blue locks down-hanging will be Tigris
These, say, are Armenians, here is Persia, sprung
from Danae;[1] that was a city in the Achaemenian
valleys. That one, or that, are chieftains; and you
will have names to give them, correct, if you can,
but if not, yet names that are fitting.

Banquets too give openings, when the tables are
set; somewhat beside wine may you find there.
Often has bright-hued Love with soft arms drawn to
him and embraced the horns of Bacchus as he there
reclined: and when wine has sprinkled Cupid's
thirsty wings, he abides and stands o'erburdened,
where he has taken his place. He indeed quickly
shakes out his dripping plumes, yet does it hurt even
to be sprinkled on the breast with love. Wine gives
courage and makes men apt for passion; care flees
and is drowned in much wine. Then laughter
comes, then even the poor find vigour,[1] then sorrow
and care and the wrinkles of the brow depart. Then
simplicity, most rare in our age, lays bare the mind,
when the god dispels all craftiness. At such time
often have women bewitched the minds of men,
and Venus in the wine has been fire in fire. Trust

[2] A borrowing from Horace, *Odes*, 3. 21. 18.

Hic tu fallaci nimium ne crede lucernae : 245
  Iudicio formae noxque merumque nocent.
Luce deas caeloque Paris spectavit aperto,
  Cum dixit Veneri "vincis utramque, Venus."
Nocte latent mendae. vitioque ignoscitur omni,
  Horaque formosam quamlibet illa facit. 250
Consule de gemmis, de tincta murice lana,
  Consule de facie corporibusque diem.

Quid tibi femineos coetus venatibus aptos
  Enumerem? numero cedet harena meo.
Quid referam Baias praetextaque litora Baiis, 255
  Et quae de calido sulpure fumat, aquam?
Hinc aliquis vulnus referens in pectore dixit
  "Non haec, ut fama est, unda salubris erat."
Ecce suburbanae templum nemorale Dianae
  Partaque per gladios regna nocente manu : 260
Illa quod est virgo, quod tela Cupidinis odit,
  Multa dedit populo vulnera, multa dabit.

Hactenus, unde legas quod ames, ubi retia ponas,
  Praecipit imparibus vecta Thalia rotis.
Nunc tibi, quae placuit, quas sit capienda per artes, 265
  Dicere praecipuae molior artis opus.
Quisquis ubique, viri, dociles advertite mentes,
  Pollicitisque favens, vulgus, adeste meis.

Prima tuae menti veniat fiducia, cunctas
  Posse capi ; capies, tu modo tende plagas. 270
Vere prius volucres taceant, aestate cicadae,
  Maenalius lepori det sua terga canis,

---

[1] The shrine of Diana Nemorensis by the lake of Nemi, near
Rome, where the priest was a runaway slave who had slain

not at such a time o'ermuch to the treacherous lamp; darkness and drink impair your judgment of beauty. It was in heaven's light unveiled that Paris beheld the goddesses, when he said to Venus, "Venus, thou dost surpass the other two." By night are blemishes hid, and every fault is forgiven: that hour makes any woman fair. Consult the daylight for jewels, for wool dyed in purple, consult it too for the face and bodily form.

Why should I recount to you all the gatherings of women, fit occasions for hunting? the sand would yield to my counting. Why tell of Baiae and Baiae's fringe of shore, and the water that smokes with hot sulphur? Someone came hence with a wound in his heart, and said: "Those waters were not, as fame reports them, healthy." Lo! hard by the city is Dian's woodland shrine,[1] and the realm won by the sword and guilty hand: because she is a maid and hates the darts of Cupid, she has given and will give to our people many a wound.

So far Thalia, borne upon unequal wheels,[2] teaches you where to select an object for your love, and where to spread your nets. Now do I essay a task of pre-eminent skill, to tell you by what arts to catch her whom you have chosen. Ye men, whoever, wherever ye may be, attend with docile minds; and, common folk, lend favouring presence to my enterprise.

First let assurance come to your minds, that all women can be caught; spread but your nets and you will catch them. Sooner would birds be silent in spring, or grasshoppers in summer, or the hound of Maenalus flee before the hare than a woman

his predecessor. This grove, too, was much resorted to by lovers.

[2] *i.e.* of the elegiac couplet.

Femina quam iuveni blande temptata repugnet :
   Haec quoque, quam poteris credere nolle, volet.
Utque viro furtiva venus, sic grata puellae :   275
   Vir male dissimulat : tectius illa cupit.
Conveniat maribus, nequam nos ante rogemus,
   Femina iam partes victa rogantis agat.
Mollibus in pratis admugit femina tauro :
   Femina cornipedi semper adhinnit equo.   280
Parcior in nobis nec tam furiosa libido :
   Legitimum finem flamma virilis habet.
Byblida quid referam, vetito quae fratris amore
   Arsit et est laqueo fortiter ulta nefas ?
Myrrha patrem, sed non qua filia debet, amavit,   285
   Et nunc obducto cortice pressa latet :
Illius lacrimis, quas arbore fundit odora,
   Unguimur, et dominae nomina gutta tenet.
Forte sub umbrosis nemorosae vallibus Idae
   Candidus, armenti gloria, taurus erat,   290
Signatus tenui media inter cornua nigro :
   Una fuit labes, cetera lactis erant.
Illum Gnosiadesque Cydoneaeque iuvencae
   Optarunt tergo sustinuisse suo.
Pasiphaë fieri gaudebat adultera tauri ;   295
   Invida formosas oderat illa boves.
Nota cano : non hoc, centum quae sustinet urbes,
   Quamvis sit mendax, Creta negare potest.
Ipsa novas frondes et prata tenerrima tauro
   Fertur inadsueta subsecuisse manu.   300
It comes armentis, nec ituram cura moratur
   Coniugis, et Minos a bove victus erat.

---

[1] Caunus, for whom see *Metamorphoses*, 9. 453.
[2] Crete had a bad reputation in the ancient world for lying ;

persuasively wooed resist a lover: nay, even she, whom you will think cruel, will be kind. And as stolen love is pleasant to a man, so is it also to a woman; the man dissembles badly: she conceals desire better. Did it suit us males not to ask any woman first, the woman, already won, would play the asker. In soft meads the heifer lows to the bull, the mare always whinnies to the horn-footed steed. In us desire is weaker and not so frantic: the manly flame knows a lawful bound. Why should I speak of Byblis, who burnt with a forbidden passion for her brother,[1] and with a rope's noose bravely atoned her sin? Myrrha loved her father, but not as a daughter should, and now lies imprisoned in the confining bark: with her tears, poured forth from the fragrant tree, are we anointed: the drops preserve their mistress' name. Once in the shady vales of woody Ida there was a white bull, the glory of the herd; marked was he by a spot of black between his horns; that was the only blemish, the rest was white as milk. Him would the Gnosian and Cydonian heifers fain have borne upon their backs: Pasiphaë rejoiced to become the leman of a bull, and regarded with envious hate the comely cows. Well known is that I sing of: Crete, that holds a hundred cities, cannot deny this, liar though she be.[2] Herself she is said to have plucked new leaves and tenderest meadow-grass for the bull with unaccustomed hand. She goes in company with the herds, nor does thought of her lord delay her going, and a bull triumphed over Minos. What gain to thee,

cf. Epimenides, quoted in St. Paul's Ep. to Titus, i. 12. Κρῆτες ἀεὶ ψεῦσται.

C

Quo tibi, Pasiphaë, pretiosas sumere vestes?
    Ille tuus nullas sentit adulter opes.
Quid tibi cum speculo, montana armenta petenti?   305
    Quid totiens positas fingis, inepta, comas?
Crede tamen speculo, quod te negat esse iuvencam.
    Quam cuperes fronti cornua nata tuae!
Sive placet Minos, nullus quaeratur adulter:
    Sive virum mavis fallere, falle viro!   310
In nemus et saltus thalamo regina relicto
    Fertur, ut Aonio concita Baccha deo.
A, quotiens vaccam vultu spectavit iniquo,
    Et dixit " domino cur placet ista meo?
Aspice, ut ante ipsum teneris exultet in herbis: 315
    Nec dubito, quin se stulta decere putet."
Dixit, et ingenti iamdudum de grege duci
    Iussit et inmeritam sub iuga curva trahi,
Aut cadere ante aras commentaque sacra coegit,
    Et tenuit laeta paelicis exta manu.   320
Paelicibus quotiens placavit numina caesis,
    Atque ait, exta tenens " ite, placete meo!"
Et modo se Europen fieri, modo postulat Io,
    Altera quod bos est, altera vecta bove.
Hanc tamen implevit, vacca deceptus acerna,   325
    Dux gregis, et partu proditus auctor erat.
Cressa Thyesteo si se abstinuisset amore,
    (Et quantum est, uni posse placere viro!)
Non medium rupisset iter, curruque retorto
    Auroram versis Phoebus adisset equis.   330
Filia purpureos Niso furata capillos
    Pube premit rabidos inguinibusque canes.

---

[1] Aerope, wife of Atreus, brother of Thyestes. The crimes that
followed her adultery made the sun hide his face from Mycenae.
   [2] Scylla; who is here confused with the monster of that name,
as also by Virgil, *Ecl.* vi. 74.

Pasiphaë, to wear thy purple gowns? that lover of thine recks not of any splendour. What dost thou with a mirror, seeking the herds upon the mountains? Why so oft, foolish one, dost thou dress thy braided hair? Nay, believe thy mirror when it tells thee thou art no heifer. How hadst thou wished that horns grew on thy brow! If 'tis Minos pleases thee, seek no adulterer; or if thou wilt deceive thy man, with a man deceive him! Leaving her bower the queen hies her to the woods and glens, like a Bacchanal sped by the Aonian god. Ah, how oft did she look askance upon a cow, and say, "Why does she find favour with my lord? See how she sports before him on the tender grass: nor doubt I but the foolish thing imagines she is comely." She spoke, and straightway ordered her to be taken from the mighty herd, and undeserving to be dragged beneath the curving yoke, or forced her to fall before the altar in a feigned sacrifice, and held in exultant hands her rival's entrails. How oft with her rivals' bodies did she appease the gods, and say, as she held their entrails, "Now go and find favour with my lord!" And now she craves to be Europa and now to be Io, for the one was a cow, and the other was borne by a cow's mate. Her none the less did the leader of the herd make pregnant, deceived by a cow of maple-wood, and by her offspring was the sire betrayed. Had the Cretan woman [1] abstained from love for Thyestes (how great a boon to be able to please one man alone!), Phoebus had not broken off in mid-career, and wresting his car about turned round his steeds to face the dawn. From Nisus his daughter [2] stole the purple hairs, and now holds raving hounds within her womb and loins. The son of

35

Qui Martem terra, Neptunum effugit in undis,
   Coniugis Atrides victima dira fuit.
Cui non defleta est Ephyraeae flamma Creüsae,   335
   Et nece natorum sanguinolenta parens?
Flevit Amyntorides per inania lumina Phoenix:
   Hippolytum pavidi diripuistis equi.
Quid fodis inmeritis, Phineu, sua lumina natis?
   Poena reversura est in caput ista tuum.   340
Omnia feminea sunt ista libidine mota;
   Acrior est nostra, plusque furoris habet.
Ergo age, ne dubita cunctas sperare puellas;
   Vix erit e multis quae neget una tibi.
Quae dant quaeque negant, gaudent tamen esse rogatae:
   Ut iam fallaris, tuta repulsa tua est.   346
Sed cur fallaris, cum sit nova grata voluptas
   Et capiant animos plus aliena suis?
Fertilior seges est alienis semper in agris,
   Vicinumque pecus grandius uber habet.   350

Sed prius ancillam captandae nosse puellae
   Cura sit: accessus molliet illa tuos.
Proxima consiliis dominae sit ut illa, videto,
   Neve parum tacitis conscia fida iocis.
Hanc tu pollicitis, hanc tu corrumpe rogando: 355
   Quod petis, ex facili, si volet illa, feres.
Illa leget tempus (medici quoque tempora servant)
   Quo facilis dominae mens sit et apta capi.
Mens erit apta capi tum, cum laetissima rerum
   Ut seges in pingui luxuriabit humo.   360
Pectora dum gaudent nec sunt adstricta dolore,
   Ipsa patent, blanda tum subit arte Venus.

---

[1] They were falsely accused to Phineus by their stepmother
Idaea.
[2] Cf. *Amores*, 1. 11, 2. 8.

Atreus, who escaped Mars on land and Neptune on the deep, was the dire victim of his wife. Who has not bewailed the flames of Creusa of Ephyre, and the mother stained with her children's blood? Phoenix, son of Amyntor, shed tears from empty eyes; ye frightened horses, ye tore Hippolytus in pieces. Why piercest thou, O Phineus, the eyes of thine innocent sons?[1] upon thine own head will the punishment fall. All those crimes were prompted by women's lust; keener is it than ours, and has more of madness. Come then, doubt not that you may win all women; scarce one out of many will there be to say you nay. And, grant they or deny, yet are they pleased to have been asked: suppose, say, you are mistaken, your rejection brings no danger. But why should you be mistaken, since 'tis new delights that win welcome, and what is not ours charms more than our own? In fields not ours the crops are ever more bounteous, and the neighbouring herd has richer udders.

But take care first to know the handmaid[2] of the woman you would win; she will make your approach easy. See that she be nearest the counsels of her mistress, and one who may be trusted with the secret of your stolen sport. Corrupt her with promises, corrupt her with prayers; if she be willing, you will gain your end with ease. She will choose a time (physicians also observe times) when her mistress is in an easy mood and apt for winning. Then will her mind be apt for winning when in the fulness of joy she grows wanton like the corn crop in a rich soil.[3] When hearts are glad, and not fast bound by grief, then do they lie open, and Venus steals in

[3] *luxurio* is used both of crops which grow very vigorously and of persons who are inclined to "run riot."

37

Tum, cum tristis erat, defensa est Ilios armis :
    Militibus gravidum laeta recepit equum.
Tum quoque temptanda est, cum paelice laesa dolebit :
    Tum facies opera, ne sit inulta, tua.   366
Hanc matutinos pectens ancilla capillos
    Incitet, et velo remigis addat opem,
Et secum tenui suspirans murmure dicat
    "At, puto, non poteris ipsa referre vicem."   370
Tum de te narret, tum persuadentia verba
    Addat, et insano iuret amore mori.
Sed propera, ne vela cadant auraeque residant :
    Ut fragilis glacies, interit ira mora.
Quaeris, an hanc ipsam prosit violare ministram ?   375
    Talibus admissis alea grandis inest.
Haec a concubitu fit sedula, tardior illa ;
    Haec dominae munus te parat, illa sibi.
Casus in eventu est : licet hic indulgeat ausis,
    Consilium tamen est abstinuisse meum.   380
Non ego per praeceps et acuta cacumina vadam,
    Nec iuvenum quisquam me duce captus erit.
Si tamen illa tibi, dum dat recipitque tabellas,
    Corpore, non tantum sedulitate placet,
Fac domina potiare prius, comes illa sequatur :   385
    Non tibi ab ancilla est incipienda venus.
Hoc unum moneo, siquid modo creditur arti,
    Nec mea dicta rapax per mare ventus agit :
Aut non temptaris, aut perfice ; tollitur index,
    Cum semel in partem criminis ipsa venit.   390
Non avis utiliter viscatis effugit alis ;
    Non bene de laxis cassibus exit aper.

370 at *Lachmann* : ut *RO* : poteris *O* : poteras *R.*
373 auraeque *Heinsius* : iraeque *MSS.*
389 non temptaris *Heinsius* : non temptasses *O* : non quam
temptas *R.*

with persuasive art. Ilios, when sad, was defended
by its hosts; rejoicing, it received the warrior-
burdened horse. Then too may she be tried, when
she grieves beneath a rival's smart; see then that
by your efforts she lack not vengeance. Let her
maid incite her, as she combs her tresses in the
morning, and add the help of an oarsman to the
sail, and let her say, sighing softly to herself, " But,
methinks, you will not be able to pay him back
yourself." [1] Then let her speak of you, then add
persuasive words, and swear that you are dying of
frantic love. But be speedy, lest the sails sink and
the breezes fail: like brittle ice, so perishes anger
by delaying. You will ask, whether it profits to
seduce the maid herself; such an enterprise involves
much hazard. An intrigue makes one more eager,
another more sluggish; this one wins you for her
mistress, that one for herself. It may turn out well or
ill; though the issue favour the hazard, yet my counsel
is, abstain. I am not the man to go by precipitous
paths and rocky heights; no youth under my leader-
ship will be captured. Yet while she gives and
takes your letters, should her figure and not her
services alone find favour, see that you gain the
mistress first, and let the servant follow: do not
begin your wooing with the maid. This only do I
urge (if you but trust my art, and the rapacious
breeze blows not my words across the sea): either
make no venture or be successful; the informer
vanishes when once she shares the guilt. The bird
cannot make good its escape when once its wings
are limed; the boar issues not easily from the

---

[1] *i.e.* your husband has been unfaithful; what a pity you
could not pay him back in his own coin !

Saucius arrepto piscis teneatur ab hamo :
   Perprime temptatam, nec nisi victor abi.
Tunc neque te prodet communi noxia culpa,   395
   Factaque erunt dominae dictaque nota tibi.
Sed bene celetur : bene si celabitur index,
   Notitiae suberit semper amica tuae.

Tempora qui solis operosa colentibus arva,
   Fallitur, et nautis aspicienda putat ;   400
Nec semper credenda ceres fallacibus arvis,
   Nec semper viridi concava puppis aquae,
Nec teneras semper tutum captare puellas :
   Saepe dato melius tempore fiet idem.
Sive dies suberit natalis, sive Kalendae,   405
   Quas Venerem Marti continuasse iuvat,
Sive erit ornatus non ut fuit ante sigillis,
   Sed regum positas Circus habebit opes,
Differ opus : tunc tristis hiems, tunc Pliades instant,
   Tunc tener aequorea mergitur Haedus aqua ;   410
Tunc bene desinitur : tunc siquis creditur alto,
   Vix tenuit lacerae naufraga membra ratis.
Tu licet incipias qua flebilis Allia luce
   Vulneribus Latiis sanguinolenta fluit,
Quaque die redeunt, rebus minus apta gerendis,   415
   Culta Palaestino septima festa Syro.
Magna superstitio tibi sit natalis amicae :
   Quaque aliquid dandum est, illa sit atra dies.

---

[1] Do not press your suit on days when it is customary to give presents ; too much will be expected of you. Such days were birthdays, April 1st, which was the feast of Venus, and therefore a festival popular with the demi-mondaine, though we are not told elsewhere that it was a day for presents (the more usual interpretation is March 1st, the feast of the Matronalia, when gifts were certainly given), and the days referred to in ll. 407–8 which, according to Brandt, are those of the Saturnalia, when

entangling nets. Let the fish be held that is wounded from seizing the hook; once you assail her, press the attack, nor depart unless victorious. Then, sharing a common guilt, she will not betray you, you will know her mistress' words and deeds. But keep her secret well; if the informer's secret be well kept, she will always gladly foster your intimacy.

He errs who thinks that seasons are to be marked by sailors only, and by those who till the toilsome fields; not always must the corn be entrusted to the treacherous fields, nor always the hollow bark to the green main, nor always is it safe to angle for young girls; the same thing often goes better at the appointed season. Whether it is her birthday, or the Kalends which delight to join Venus to Mars,[1] or whether the Circus is adorned not, as before, by images, but holds the wealth of kings displayed, put off your attempt: the storm is lowering then, and the Pleiads threaten, the tender Kid is merged in the watery waves: then it is wise to stop; then, if any entrusts him to the deep, scarce has he saved his torn bark's shattered wreck. You may begin on the day on which woeful Allia flows stained with the blood of Latian wounds,[2] or on that day, less fit for business, whereon returns the seventh-day feast that the Syrian of Palestine observes. But hold in awful dread your lady's birthday; let that be a black day whereon a present must be given. Shun it as you

there was probably a display of gifts for sale in the Circus Maximus; when there was an unusually costly display, and not the usual show of trivialities (" sigilla,") the lover would be well advised to keep away. On the other hand, he may make an appearance when the shops are shut on the " dies nefasti" (ll. 413–6), and there can be no idea of buying.

[2] July 18th.

Cum bene vitaris, tamen auferet ; invenit artem
    Femina, qua cupidi carpat amantis opes.   420
Institor ad dominam veniet discinctus emacem,
    Expediet merces teque sedente suas :
Quas illa, inspicias, sapere ut videare, rogabit :
    Oscula deinde dabit ; deinde rogabit, emas.
Hoc fore contentam multos iurabit in annos,   425
    Nunc opus esse sibi, nunc bene dicet emi.
Si non esse domi, quos des, causabere nummos,
    Littera poscetur—ne didicisse iuvet.
Quid, quasi natali cum poscit munera libo,
    Et quotiens opus est, nascitur illa sibi ?   430
Quid, cum mendaci damno maestissima plorat,
    Elapsusque cava fingitur aure lapis ?
Multa rogant utenda dari, data reddere nolunt :
    Perdis, et in damno gratia nulla tuo.
Non mihi, sacrilegas meretricum ut persequar artes, 435
    Cum totidem linguis sint satis ora decem.

Cera vadum temptet, rasis infusa tabellis :
    Cera tuae primum nuntia mentis eat.
Blanditias ferat illa tuas imitataque amantum
    Verba ; nec exiguas, quisquis es, adde preces.   440
Hectora donavit Priamo prece motus Achilles ;
    Flectitur iratus voce rogante deus.
Promittas facito : quid enim promittere laedit ?
    Pollicitis dives quilibet esse potest.
Spes tenet in tempus, semel est si credita, longum : 445
    Illa quidem fallax, sed tamen apta dea est.
Si dederis aliquid, poteris ratione relinqui :
    Praeteritum tulerit, perdideritque nihil.

438 nuntia *O* : conscia *MSS*.

may, yet she will carry off the spoil; a woman knows the way to fleece an eager lover of his wealth. A lewd pedlar will come to your mistress when in buying mood, and will spread his wares before her, while you sit by in misery; and she, that you may fancy yourself a judge, will ask you to inspect them; then she will kiss you; then she will ask you to buy. She will swear that this will satisfy her for many a long year, that she needs it now, that now is a good time to buy it. If you make excuse that you have not the cash at home she will ask for a note of hand —lest you should be glad you ever learned to write. What, when she claims a gift to buy, as she says, a birthday cake, and has a birthday as often as she requires? What when she weeps for a feigned loss in deepest sorrow, and pretends a jewel has slipped from the shell of her ear? Many things do they beg to borrow, but, once borrowed, they will not give them back: you have lost them, but gain no credit for your loss. Ten mouths and as many tongues would not suffice me to tell the unholy ruses of the fair.

Let wax, spread on smooth tablets, attempt the crossing; let wax go first to show your mind. Let that carry your flatteries and words that play the lover; and, whoever you are, add earnest entreaties. Entreaty moved Achilles to give Hector back to Priam; a god when angry is moved by the voice of prayer. See that you promise: what harm is there in promises? In promises anyone can be rich. Hope, once conceived, endures for long; a treacherous goddess is she, but a timely one. Once you have given, you may be abandoned with good reason: your gift is gone, she will have taken it and lost nothing her-

At quod non dederis, semper videare daturus :
   Sic dominum sterilis saepe fefellit ager :   450
Sic, ne perdiderit, non cessat perdere lusor,
   Et revocat cupidas alea saepe manus.
Hoc opus, hic labor est, primo sine munere iungi ;
   Ne dederit gratis quae dedit, usque dabit.
Ergo eat et blandis peraretur littera verbis,   455
   Exploretque animos, primaque temptet iter.
Littera Cydippen pomo perlata fefellit,
   Insciaque est verbis capta puella suis.

Disce bonas artes, moneo, Romana iuventus,
   Non tantum trepidos ut tueare reos ;   460
Quam populus iudexque gravis lectusque senatus,
   Tam dabit eloquio victa puella manus.
Sed lateant vires, nec sis in fronte disertus ;
   Effugiant voces verba molesta tuae.
Quis, nisi mentis inops, tenerae declamat amicae ? 465
   Saepe valens odii littera causa fuit.
Sit tibi credibilis sermo consuetaque verba,
   Blanda tamen, praesens ut videare loqui.
Si non accipiet scriptum, inlectumque remittet,
   Lecturam spera, propositumque tene.   470
Tempore difficiles veniunt ad aratra iuvenci,
   Tempore lenta pati frena docentur equi :
Ferreus adsiduo consumitur anulus usu,
   Interit adsidua vomer aduncus humo.
Quid magis est saxo durum, quid mollius unda ? 475
   Dura tamen molli saxa cavantur aqua.
Penelopen ipsam, persta modo, tempore vinces :
   Capta vides sero Pergama, capta tamen.

---

[1] He is quoting from Virgil, *Aen.* vi. 129.
[2] Acontius, her lover, wrote on an apple, "I swear by Diana

self. But what you have not given you may seem always on the point of giving : thus many a time has a barren field deceived its owner ; thus, lest he shall have lost, the gambler ceases not to lose, and often do the dice recall his greedy hands. " Herein the task, herein the toil " [1]—to win her favour with no preceding gift ; lest what she has given be given for nothing, she will give yet more. Therefore let a letter speed, traced with persuasive words, and explore her feelings, and be the first to try the path. A letter carried in an apple betrayed Cydippe, and the maid was deceived unawares by her own words.[2]

Learn noble arts, I counsel you, young men of Rome, not only that you may defend trembling clients : a woman, no less than populace, grave judge or chosen senate, will surrender, defeated, to eloquence. But hide your powers, nor put on a learned brow ; let your pleading avoid troublesome words. Who, save an idiot, would declaim to his tender sweetheart ? often has a letter been a potent cause of hate.[3] Your language should inspire trust and your words be familiar, yet coaxing too, so that you seem to be speaking in her presence. If she does not receive your message and sends it back unread, hope that one day she will read, and hold to your purpose. In time refractory oxen come to the plough, in time horses are taught to bear the pliant reins ; an iron ring is worn by constant use, a curved share wastes by constant ploughing of the ground. What is harder than rock, what softer than water ? yet soft water hollows out hard rock. Only persevere ; you will overcome Penelope herself ; late, as you see, did Pergamus fall, yet fall it did. Suppose she has

to marry Acontius " ; Cydippe read it aloud, and so was bound by the vow.   [3] *i.e.* if written in declamatory style.

Legerit, et nolit rescribere? cogere noli:
    Tu modo blanditias fac legat usque tuas.   480
Quae voluit legisse, volet rescribere lectis:
    Per numeros venient ista gradusque suos.
Forsitan et primo veniet tibi littera tristis,
    Quaeque roget, ne se sollicitare velis.
Quod rogat illa, timet; quod non rogat, optat, ut instes;
    Insequere, et voti postmodo compos eris.   486

Interea sive illa toro resupina feretur,
    Lecticam dominae dissimulanter adi,
Neve aliquis verbis odiosas offerat auris,
    Quam potes ambiguis callidus abde notis.   490
Seu pedibus vacuis illi spatiosa teretur
    Porticus, hic socias tu quoque iunge moras:
Et modo praecedas facito, modo terga sequaris,
    Et modo festines, et modo lentus eas:
Nec tibi de mediis aliquot transire columnas   495
    Sit pudor, aut lateri continuasse latus;
Nec sine te curvo sedeat speciosa theatro:
    Quod spectes, umeris adferet illa suis.
Illam respicias, illam mirere licebit:
    Multa supercilio, multa loquare notis.   500
Et plaudas, aliquam mimo saltante puellam:
    Et faveas illi, quisquis agatur amans.
Cum surgit, surges; donec sedet illa, sedebis;
    Arbitrio dominae tempora perde tuae.

Sed tibi nec ferro placeat torquere capillos,   505
    Nec tua mordaci pumice crura teras.
Ista iube faciant, quorum Cybeleïa mater
    Concinitur Phrygiis exululata modis.
Forma viros neglecta decet; Minoida Theseus
    Abstulit, a nulla tempora comptus acu.   510

read, but will not write back: compel her not; only see that she is ever reading your flatteries. She who has consented to read will consent to answer what she has read; that will come by its own stages and degrees. Perhaps even an angry letter will first come to you, asking you to be pleased not to vex her. What she asks, she fears; what she does not ask, she desires—that you will continue; press on, then, and soon you will have gained your wish.

Meanwhile, whether she be borne reclining on her cushions, approach your mistress' litter in dissembling fashion, and lest someone intrude hateful ears to your words, hide them, so far as you may, in cunning ambiguities; or whether the spacious colonnade be trodden by her leisurely feet, do you also make friendly dalliance there; and contrive now to go before her, now to follow behind, now hurry, now go slowly. Neither hesitate to slip past some of the columns that part you, nor to join your side to hers; nor let her sit in the round theatre, her fair looks by you unheeded: something worth looking at she will bring on her shoulders. On her you may turn your looks, her you may admire: much let your eyebrows, much let your gestures say. Applaud when an actor portrays some woman in his dance, and favour whoever be the lover that is played. When she rises you will rise; while she sits you will sit too; waste time at your mistress' will.

But take no pleasure in curling your hair with the iron, or in scraping your legs with biting pumice-stone. Bid them do that by whom mother Cybele is sung in howling chorus of Phrygian measures. An uncared-for beauty is becoming to men; Theseus carried off Minos' daughter, though no clasp decked

Hippolytum Phaedra, nec erat bene cultus, amavit;
    Cura deae silvis aptus Adonis erat.
Munditie placeant, fuscentur corpora Campo:
    Sit bene conveniens et sine labe toga:
Lingula ne ruget, careant rubigine dentes,   515
    Nec vagus in laxa pes tibi pelle natet:
Nec male deformet rigidos tonsura capillos:
    Sit coma, sit docta barba resecta manu.
Et nihil emineant, et sint sine sordibus ungues:
    Inque cava nullus stet tibi nare pilus.   520
Nec male odorati sit tristis anhelitus oris:
    Nec laedat naris virque paterque gregis.
Cetera lascivae faciant, concede, puellae,
    Et siquis male vir quaerit habere virum.

Ecce, suum vatem Liber vocat; hic quoque amantes
    Adiuvat, et flammae, qua calet ipse, favet.   526
Gnosis in ignotis amens errabat harenis,
    Qua brevis aequoreis Dia feritur aquis.
Utque erat e somno tunica velata recincta,
    Nuda pedem, croceas inreligata comas,   530
Thesea crudelem surdas clamabat ad undas,
    Indigno teneras imbre rigante genas.
Clamabat, flebatque simul, sed utrumque decebat;
    Non facta est lacrimis turpior illa suis.
Iamque iterum tundens mollissima pectora palmis   535
    "Perfidus ille abiit; quid mihi fiet?" ait.
"Quid mihi fiet?" ait: sonuerunt cymbala toto
    Littore, et adtonita tympana pulsa manu.

---

513 munditie *R*: munditiae *MSS.*
515 lingula ne ruget *Palmer* (cf. iii. 444): lingua ne rigeat *R*
(linguam *O*): linguam ne pigeat *Housman.*
518 docta *Merkel* (*from a MS.*): tuta *RO*: scita *Heinsius*: trita
Housman.

48

his temples.   Phaedra loved Hippolytus, nor yet was
he a dandy ; Adonis, born to the woodland, was a
goddess' care.   Let your person please by cleanliness,
and be made swarthy by the Campus ; let your toga
fit, and be spotless ; do not let your shoe-strap be
wrinkled ; let your teeth be clear of rust, and your
foot not float about, lost in too large a shoe ; nor
let your stubborn locks be spoilt by bad cutting ; let
hair and beard be dressed by a skilled hand.   Do
not let your nails project, and let them be free of dirt ;
nor let any hair be in the hollow of your nostrils.
Let not the breath of your mouth be sour and
unpleasing, nor let the lord and master of the
herd offend the nose.   All else let wanton women
practise, and such men as basely seek to please a
man.

Lo ! Liber summons his bard ; he too helps lovers,
and favours the flame wherewith he burns himself.
The Gnosian maid wandered distractedly on the
unknown sand, where little Dia is lashed by the sea
waves.[1]   Just as she came from sleep, clad in an un-
girt tunic, barefoot, with yellow hair unbound, she
cried upon Theseus over the deaf waters, while an
innocent shower bedewed her tender cheeks.   She
clamoured and wept together, but both became her ;
nor was she made less comely by her tears.   Again
she beats her soft bosom with her hands, and
cries, " He is gone, the faithless one ; what
will become of me ? "   " What will become of
me ? " she cries : then o'er all the shore cymbals
resounded and drums beaten by frenzied hands.

---

[1] Ariadne was the daughter of Minos, King of Crete ; Dia
was the old name of the island of Naxos.

Excidit illa metu, rupitque novissima verba ;
   Nullus in exanimi corpore sanguis erat.   540
Ecce Mimallonides sparsis in terga capillis :
   Ecce leves satyri, praevia turba dei :
Ebrius, ecce, senex pando Silenus asello
   Vix sedet, et pressas continet ante iubas.
Dum sequitur Bacchas, Bacchae fugiuntque petuntque
   Quadrupedem ferula dum malus urget eques,   546
In caput aurito cecidit delapsus asello :
   Clamarunt satyri "surge age, surge, pater."
Iam deus in curru, quem summum texerat uvis,
   Tigribus adiunctis aurea lora dabat :   550
Et color et Theseus et vox abiere puellae :
   Terque fugam petiit, terque retenta metu est.
Horruit, ut steriles agitat quas ventus aristas,
   Ut levis in madida canna palude tremit.
Cui deus "en, adsum tibi cura fidelior" inquit :   555
   "Pone metum : Bacchi, Gnosias, uxor eris.
Munus habe caelum ; caelo spectabere sidus ;
   Saepe reget dubiam Cressa Corona ratem."
Dixit, et e curru, ne tigres illa timeret,
   Desilit ; inposito cessit harena pede :   560
Implicitamque sinu (neque enim pugnare valebat)
   Abstulit ; in facili est omnia posse deo.
Pars "Hymenaee" canunt, pars clamant Euhion
   "euhoe ! "
Sic coeunt sacro nupta deusque toro.

Ergo ubi contigerint positi tibi munera Bacchi,   565
   Atque erit in socii femina parte tori,
Nycteliumque patrem nocturnaque sacra precare,
   Ne iubeant capiti vina nocere tuo.

<hr>

544 ante *Merkel* : arte *MSS.*

<hr>

[1] The name in the text, more commonly Mimallones, was the
Macedonian name for them.
  [2] The epithet of Bacchus derived from the cry of the Bacchanals.

She fainted for fear, and broke off her latest words;
no blood was there in her lifeless frame. Lo!
Bacchanals [1] with tresses streaming behind them, lo!
wanton Satyrs, the god's forerunning band; lo!
drunken old Silenus scarce sits his crookbacked ass,
and leaning clings to the mane before him. While
he pursues the Bacchanals, and the Bacchanals flee
and again attack, and while the unskilful horseman
urges his beast with a rod, he falls off the long-eared
ass and topples head-foremost and the Satyrs cry,
"Come, get up, father, get up!" And now on his
car, that he had covered with grape-clusters, the
god was giving the golden reins to his yoked tigers:
voice, colour—and Theseus, all were gone from the
girl; thrice did she essay flight, thrice did fear
restrain her. She shuddered, as when dry stalks are
shaken by the wind, as when the light rush trembles
in the watery marsh. "Lo, here am I," said the
god to her, "a more faithful lover; have no fear,
Gnosian maid, thou shalt be the spouse of Bacchus.
For thy gift take the sky; as a star in the sky thou
shalt be gazed at; the Cretan Crown shall often
guide the doubtful bark." He spoke, and lest she
should fear the tigers leapt down from the chariot;
the sand gave place to his alighting foot; and
clasping her to his bosom (for she had no strength
to fight) he bore her away; easy is it for a god to be
all-powerful. Some chant "Hail, Hymenaeus!"
some shout "Euhoe!" to the Euhian; [2] so do the
bride and the god meet on the sacred couch.

Therefore when the bounty of Bacchus set before
you falls to your lot, and a woman shares your con-
vivial couch, beseech the Nyctelian [3] sire and the
spirits of the night that they bid not the wines to

[3] *i.e.* god of nocturnal rites and orgies.

51

Hic tibi multa licet sermone latentia tecto
    Dicere, quae dici sentiat illa sibi :   570
Blanditiasque leves tenui perscribere vino,
    Ut dominam in mensa se legat illa tuam :
Atque oculos oculis spectare fatentibus ignem :
    Saepe tacens vocem verbaque vultus habet.
Fac primus rapias illius tacta labellis   575
    Pocula, quaque bibit parte puella, bibas :
Et quemcumque cibum digitis libaverit illa,
    Tu pete, dumque petes, sit tibi tacta manus.
Sint etiam tua vota, viro placuisse puellae :
    Utilior vobis factus amicus erit.   580
Huic, si sorte bibes, sortem concede priorem :
    Huic detur capiti missa corona tuo.
Sive erit inferior, seu par, prior omnia sumat :
    Nec dubites illi verba secunda loqui.
Tuta frequensque via est, per amici fallere nomen : 585
    Tuta frequensque licet sit via, crimen habet.
Inde procurator nimium quoque multa procurat,
    Et sibi mandatis plura videnda putat.

Certa tibi a nobis dabitur mensura bibendi :
    Officium praestent mensque pedesque suum.   590
Iurgia praecipue vino stimulata caveto,
    Et nimium faciles ad fera bella manus.
Occidit Eurytion stulte data vina bibendo ;
    Aptior est dulci mensa merumque ioco.

---

[1] The order of drinking was often decided by lot; it is not clear whether the husband is to be given the first *turn* as a compliment, or to be allowed to *throw* first. Or it may refer to the choosing by lot of a master of the banquet, the "arbiter bibendi."

hurt your head. Here may you say many things lurking in covered speech, so that she may feel they are said to her, and you may trace light flatteries in thin characters of wine, that on the table she may read herself your mistress ; you may gaze at her eyes with eyes that confess their flame : there are often voice and words in a silent look. See that you are the first to seize the cup her lips have touched, and drink at that part where she has drunk ; and whatever food she has touched with her fingers see that you ask for, and while you ask contrive to touch her hand. Let it also be your aim to please your lady's husband ; he will be more useful to you, if made a friend. To him, if you drink by lot, concede the first turn ;[1] give him the garland tossed from your own head. Whether he be below you or hold an equal place, let him take of all before you ; nor hesitate to yield him place in talk. 'Tis a safe and oft-trodden path, to deceive under the name of friend ; safe and oft-trodden though it be, 'tis the path of guilt. Thus too an agent pursues his agency too far and looks after more than was committed to his charge.[2]

I will give you a sure measure of drinking : let mind and feet perform their duty. Especially beware of quarrels caused by wine, and of hands too quick to brutal fight. Eurytion[3] fell by stupidly drinking the liquor set before him ; the table and the wine-cup are fitter for mirthful jests. Sing, if

[2] This awkward couplet seems to mean that as a friend may abuse friendship, so the husband's steward or manager may take to "looking after" his wife.

[3] A Centaur, made drunk at the feast of the Lapiths ; cf. Hom. *Od.* 21. 295.

Si vox est, canta: si mollia brachia, salta: 595
   Et quacumque potes dote placere, place.
Ebrietas ut vera nocet, sic ficta iuvabit:
   Fac tibubet blaeso subdola lingua sono,
Ut, quicquid facias dicasve protervius aequo,
   Credatur nimium causa fuisse merum.   600
Et bene dic dominae, bene, cum quo dormiat illa;
   Sed, male sit, tacita mente precare, viro.
At cum discedet mensa conviva remota,
   Ipsa tibi accessus turba locumque dabit.
Insere te turbae, leviterque admotus eunti   605
   Velle latus digitis, et pede tange pedem.
Conloquii iam tempus adest; fuge rustice longe
   Hinc pudor; audentem Forsque Venusque iuvat.
Non tua sub nostras veniat facundia leges:
   Fac tantum incipias, sponte disertus eris.   610
Est tibi agendus amans, imitandaque vulnera verbis;
   Haec tibi quaeratur qualibet arte fides.
Nec credi labor est: sibi quaeque videtur amanda;
   Pessima sit, nulli non sua forma placet.
Saepe tamen vere coepit simulator amare,   615
   Saepe, quod incipiens finxerat esse, fuit.
Quo magis, o, faciles imitantibus este, puellae:
   Fiet amor verus, qui modo falsus erat.
Blanditiis animum furtim deprendere nunc sit,
   Ut pendens liquida ripa subitur aqua.   620
Nec faciem, nec te pigeat laudare capillos
   Et teretes digitos exiguumque pedem:
Delectant etiam castas praeconia formae;
   Virginibus curae grataque forma sua est.
Nam cur in Phrygiis Iunonem et Pallada silvis   625
   Nunc quoque iudicium non tenuisse pudet?

you have a voice; if your arms are lithe, dance;
please by whatever gifts you can. As real drunken-
ness does harm, so will feigned bring profit: make
your crafty tongue stumble in stammering talk, so
that, whatever you do or say more freely than you
should, may be put down to too much wine. And
" Here's luck," say, " to the lady," and " Luck to
him who sleeps with her ! " : but in your silent soul
let the prayer be " Deuce take the husband." But
when the tables are removed and the company depart,
and the crowd itself gives you chance of access, join
the crowd, and gently drawing nigh to her as she
goes pull her sleeve with your fingers, and let your
foot touch hers. Now is the time for talk with her ;
away with you, rustic shame ! Chance and Venus
help the brave. Let not your eloquence submit to
our poets' laws; see but that you make a start :
your eloquence will come of itself. You must play
the lover, and counterfeit heartache with words : her
belief in that you must win by any device. Nor is it
hard to be believed : each woman thinks herself
lovable; hideous though she be, there is none her
own looks do not please. Yet often the pretender
begins to love truly after all, and often becomes what
he has feigned to be. Wherefore, you women, be
more compliant to pretenders; one day will the love
be true which but now was false. Now be the time
to ensnare the mind with crafty flatteries, as the
water undermines an overhanging bank. Nor be
weary of praising her looks, her hair, her shapely
fingers, her small foot : even honest maids love to
hear their charms extolled ; even to the chaste their
beauty is a care and a delight. For why even now
are Juno and Pallas ashamed that they won not the
judgment in the Phrygian woods? When you

Laudatas ostendit avis Iunonia pinnas :
　Si tacitus spectes, illa recondit opes.
Quadrupedes inter rapidi certamina cursus
　Depexaeque iubae plausaque colla iuvant.　　　　630

Nec timide promitte : trahunt promissa puellas ;
　Pollicito testes quoslibet adde deos.
Iuppiter ex alto periuria ridet amantum,
　Et iubet Aeolios inrita ferre notos.
Per Styga Iunoni falsum iurare solebat　　　　635
　Iuppiter ; exemplo nunc favet ipse suo.
Expedit esse deos, et, ut expedit, esse.putemus ;
　Dentur in antiquos tura merumque focos ;
Nec secura quies illos similisque sopori
　Detinet ; innocue vivite : numen adest ;　　　　640
Reddite depositum ; pietas sua foedera servet :
　Fraus absit ; vacuas caedis habete manus.
Ludite, si sapitis, solas impune puellas :
　Hac minus est una fraude tuenda fides.
Fallite fallentes : ex magna parte profanum　　　　645
　Sunt genus : in laqueos quos posuere, cadant.
Dicitur Aegyptos caruisse iuvantibus arva
　Imbribus, atque annos sicca fuisse novem,
Cum Thrasius Busirin adit, monstratque piari
　Hospitis adfuso sanguine posse Iovem.　　　　650
Illi Busiris "fies Iovis hostia primus,"
　Inquit "et Aegypto tu dabis hospes aquam."
Et Phalaris tauro violenti membra Perilli
　Torruit : infelix inbuit auctor opus.
Iustus uterque fuit : neque enim lex aequior ulla est,
　Quam necis artifices arte perire sua.　　　　656
Ergo ut periuras merito periuria fallant,
　Exemplo doleat femina laesa suo.

644 minus . . . tuenda *Heinsius* (*from MSS.*): magis , , ,
pudenda *RO*.

praise her the bird of Juno displays her plumes :
should you gaze in silence she hides away her wealth.
Even steeds, amid the contests of the rapid course,
delight to have their manes combed and their necks
patted.

Nor be timid in your promises ; by promises women
are betrayed ; call as witnesses what gods you please.
Jupiter from on high smiles at the perjuries of lovers,
and bids the winds of Aeolus carry them unfulfilled
away. Jupiter was wont to swear falsely by Styx to
Juno ; now he favours his own example. It is
expedient there should be gods, and as it is ex-
pedient let us deem that gods exist ; let incense and
wine be poured on the ancient hearths ; nor does
careless quiet like unto slumber hold them ; live
innocently, gods are nigh ; return what is given to
your keeping ; let duty keep her covenant ; let fraud
be absent ; keep your hands clean of blood. If you
are wise, cheat women only, and avoid trouble ; keep
faith save for this one deceitfulness. Deceive the
deceivers ; they are mostly an unrighteous sort ; let
them fall into the snare which they have laid.
Egypt is said to have lacked the rains that bless
its fields, and to have been parched for nine years,
when Thrasius approached Busiris, and showed that
Jove could be propitiated by the outpoured blood of
a stranger. To him said Busiris, " Thou shalt be
Jove's first victim, and as a stranger give water unto
Egypt." Phalaris too roasted in his fierce bull the
limbs of Perillus ; its maker first made trial of his
ill-omened work. Both were just ; for there is no
juster law than that contrivers of death should
perish by their own contrivances. Therefore, that
perjuries may rightly cheat the perjured, let the
woman feel the smart of a wound she first inflicted.

Et lacrimae prosunt : lacrimis adamanta movebis :
    Fac madidas videat, si potes, illa genas.   660
Si lacrimae (neque enim veniunt in tempore semper)
    Deficient, uda lumina tange manu.
Quis sapiens blandis non misceat oscula verbis ?
    Illa licet non det, non data sume tamen.
Pugnabit primo fortassis, et " improbe " dicet :   665
    Pugnando vinci se tamen illa volet.
Tantum ne noceant teneris male rapta labellis,
    Neve queri possit dura fuisse, cave.
Oscula qui sumpsit, si non et cetera sumet,
    Haec quoque, quae data sunt, perdere dignus erit. 670
Quantum defuerat pleno post oscula voto ?
    Ei mihi, rusticitas, non pudor ille fuit.
Vim licet appelles : grata est vis ista puellis :
    Quod iuvat, invitae saepe dedisse volunt.
Quaecumque est veneris subita violata rapina,   675
    Gaudet, et inprobitas muneris instar habet.
At quae cum posset cogi, non tacta recessit,
    Ut simulet vultu gaudia, tristis erit.
Vim passa est Phoebe : vis est allata sorori ;
    Et gratus raptae raptor uterque fuit.   680
Fabula nota quidem, sed non indigna referri,
    Scyrias Haemonio iuncta puella viro.
Iam dea laudatae dederat sua praemia formae
    Colle sub Idaeo vincere digna duas :
Iam nurus ad Priamum diverso venerat orbe,   685
    Graiaque in Iliacis moenibus uxor erat :
Iurabant omnes in laesi verba mariti :
    Nam dolor unius publica causa fuit.

662 uda *MSS.* : uncta *Heinsius.*

---

[1] Phoebe and Hilaira, daughters of Leucippus, were ravished by Castor and Pollux ; see Ov. *Fasti,* 5. 699.

Tears too are useful; with tears you can move iron; let her see, if possible, your moistened cheeks. If tears fail (for they do not always come at need), touch your eyes with a wet hand. Who that is wise would not mingle kisses with coaxing words? Though she give them not, yet take the kisses she does not give. Perhaps she will struggle at first, and cry "You villain!" yet she will wish to be beaten in the struggle. Only beware lest snatching them rudely you hurt her tender lips, and she be able to complain of your roughness. He who has taken kisses, if he take not the rest beside, will deserve to lose even what was granted. After kisses how much was lacking to your vow's fulfilment? ah! that was awkwardness, not modesty. You may use force; women like you to use it; they often wish to give unwillingly what they like to give. She whom a sudden assault has taken by storm is pleased, and counts the audacity as a compliment. But she who, when she might have been compelled, departs untouched, though her looks feign joy, will yet be sad. Phoebe suffered violence, violence was used against her sister:[1] each ravisher found favour with the ravished. Well-known, yet not undeserving of mention, is the tale of the Scyrian maid and her Haemonian lover.[2] Already had the goddess given her own reward for her beauty's praising, she who won triumph o'er the twain 'neath Ida's mount; already from distant lands his daughter-in-law had come to Priam, and a Grecian wife was within the walls of Troy; all were swearing allegiance to the injured spouse, for the grief of one became the

[2] The maid is Deidamia and the lover Achilles. Lines 683–689 describe when the story happened, viz. after the carrying off of Helen, who is the "gift" (*sua praemia*) that Venus bestows on Paris.

Turpe, nisi hoc matris precibus tribuisset, Achilles
   Veste virum longa dissimulatus erat.   690
Quid facis, Aeacide? non sunt tua munera lanae;
   Tu titulos alia Palladis arte petas.
Quid tibi cum calathis? clipeo manus apta ferendo est:
   Pensa quid in dextra, qua cadet Hector, habes?
Reïce succinctos operoso stamine fusos!   695
   Quassanda est ista Pelias hasta manu.
Forte erat in thalamo virgo regalis eodem;
   Haec illum stupro comperit esse virum.
Viribus illa quidem victa est, ita credere oportet:
   Sed voluit vinci viribus illa tamen.   700
Saepe "mane!" dixit, cum iam properaret Achilles;
   Fortia nam posito sumpserat arma colo.
Vis ubi nunc illa est? Quid blanda voce moraris
   Auctorem stupri, Deïdamia, tui?
Scilicet ut pudor est quaedam coepisse priorem,   705
   Sic alio gratum est incipiente pati.
A! nimia est iuveni propriae fiducia formae,
   Expectat siquis, dum prior illa roget.
Vir prior accedat, vir verba precantia dicat:
   Excipiat blandas comiter illa preces.   710
Ut potiare, roga: tantum cupit illa rogari;
   Da causam voti principiumque tui.
Iuppiter ad veteres supplex heroïdas ibat:
   Corrupit magnum nulla puella Iovem.
Si tamen a precibus tumidos accedere fastus   715
   Senseris, incepto parce referque pedem.
Quod refugit, multae cupiunt: odere quod instat;
   Lenius instando taedia tolle tui.
Nec semper veneris spes est profitenda roganti:
   Intret amicitiae nomine tectus amor.   720

people's cause. Basely, had he not so far yielded
to his mother's prayers, Achilles had disguised
his manhood in a woman's robe. What dost thou,
Aeacides? wools are not thy business; by another
art of Pallas do thou seek fame. What hast thou to
do with baskets? thy arm is fitted to bear a shield.
Why holdest thou a skein in the hand by which
Hector shall die? Cast away the spindle girt
about with toilsome windings! That hand must
shake the Pelian spear. It chanced that in the
same chamber was the royal maid; by her rape
she found him to be a man. By force indeed was she
vanquished, so one must believe; yet by force did
she wish to be vanquished all the same. Often
cried she, "Stay," when already Achilles was hasting
from her; for, the distaff put away, he had taken
valiant arms. Where is that violence now? Why
with coaxing words, Deidamia, dost thou make to tarry
the author of thy rape? In truth, just as there is shame
sometimes in beginning first, so when another begins
it is pleasant to submit. Ah, too confident in his own
charms is a lover, if he wait until she ask him first.
Let the man take the first step, let the man speak
entreating words; she will listen kindly to coaxing
entreaties. That you may gain her, ask: she only
wishes to be asked; provide the cause and starting-
point of your desire. Jupiter went a suppliant to
the heroines of old: no woman seduced the mighty
Jove. Yet if you find that your prayers cause swollen
pride, stop what you have begun, draw back a pace.
Many women desire what flees them; they hate
what is too forward; moderate your advance, and
save them from getting tired of you. Nor must the
hope of possession be always proclaimed in your en-
treaties; let love find entrance veiled in friendship's

Hoc aditu vidi tetricae data verba puellae :
  Qui fuerat cultor, factus amator erat.

Candidus in nauta turpis color, aequoris unda
  Debet et a radiis sideris esse niger :
Turpis et agricolae, qui vomere semper adunco   725
  Et gravibus rastris sub Iove versat humum.
Et tibi, Palladiae petitur cui palma coronae,
  Candida si fuerint corpora, turpis eris.
Palleat omnis amans : hic est color aptus amanti ;
  Hoc decet, hoc stulti non valuisse putent.   730
Pallidus in Dirces silvis errabat Orion,
  Pallidus in lenta naïde Daphnis erat.
Arguat et macies animum : nec turpe putaris
  Palliolum nitidis inposuisse comis.
Attenuant iuvenum vigilatae corpora noctes   735
  Curaque et e magno qui fit amore dolor.
Ut voto potiare tuo, miserabilis esto,
  Ut qui te videat, dicere possit " amas."
Conquerar, an moneam mixtum fas omne nefasque ?
  Nomen amicitia est, nomen inane fides.   740
Ei mihi, non tutum est, quod ames, laudare sodali ;
  Cum tibi laudanti credidit, ipse subit.
At non Actorides lectum temeravit Achillis :
  Quantum ad Pirithoum, Phaedra pudica fuit.
Hermionam Pylades quo Pallada Phoebus, amabat,   745
  Quodque tibi geminus, Tyndari, Castor, erat.
Siquis idem sperat, iacturas poma myricas
  Speret, et e medio flumine mella petat.

730 stulti *Herzberg* : multi *R* : nulli *Mueller*.
731 Dirces *Heinsius* : linces *R* : Orion *MSS.* : Arion *R*.
747 iacturas *RO* : laturas *MSS*.

name. I have seen an unwilling mistress deluded by
this approach; he who had been an admirer became a
lover.

White is a shameful colour in a sailor; swarthy
should he be, both from the sea-waves and from
heaven's beams; shameful too in a husbandman,
who ever beneath the sky turns up the ground with
curved ploughshare and heavy harrows. Thou too
who seekest the prize of Pallas' garland [1] art shamed
if thy body be white. But let every lover be pale;
this is the lover's hue. Such looks become him;
let fools think that such looks avail not. Pale
did Orion wander in Dirce's glades, pale was Daphnis
when the naiad proved unkind. Let leanness
also prove your feelings; nor deem it base to set
a hood on your bright locks. Nights of vigil make
thin the bodies of lovers, and anxiety and the
distress that a great passion brings. That you may
gain your desire be pitiable, so that whoso sees you
may say, "You are in love." Shall I complain, or
warn you, that right and wrong are all confounded?
Friendship is but a name, faith is an empty name.
Alas, it is not safe to praise to a friend the object of
your love; so soon as he believes your praises, he slips
into your place. But, you will say, the son of Actor [2]
stained not Achilles' couch, and as concerned Piri-
thous, Phaedra was chaste. Pylades loved Hermione
as Phoebus Pallas, and as twin Castor was to thee,
O Tyndaris. If anyone has this hope, let him hope
that tamarisks will drop apples, let him seek honey
in the middle of a river. Naught pleases but what

---

[1] *i.e.* the athlete, who contended for a crown of olive in
the games.
[2] Patroclus, grandson of Actor. Hermione was the wife of
Orestes, the friend of Pylades.

Nil nisi turpe iuvat : curae sua cuique voluptas :
　　Haec quoque ab alterius grata dolore venit.　　　　750
Heu facinus ! non est hostis metuendus amanti ;
　　Quos credis fidos, effuge, tutus eris.
Cognatum fratremque cave carumque sodalem :
　　Praebebit veros haec tibi turba metus.

Finiturus eram, sed sunt diversa puellis　　　　　　755
　　Pectora : mille animos excipe mille modis.
Nec tellus eadem parit omnia ; vitibus illa
　　Convenit, haec oleis ; hac bene farra virent.
Pectoribus mores tot sunt, quot in orbe figurae ;
　　Qui sapit, innumeris moribus aptus erit,　　　　760
Utque leves Proteus modo se tenuabit in undas,
　　Nunc leo, nunc arbor, nunc erit hirtus apēr.
Hic iaculo pisces, illa capiuntur ab hamis :
　　Hic cava contento retia fune trahunt.
Nec tibi conveniet cunctos modus unus ad annos :　　765
　　Longius insidias cerva videbit anus.
Si doctus videare rudi, petulansve pudenti,
　　Diffidet miserae protinus illa sibi.
Inde fit, ut quae se timuit committere honesto,
　　Vilis ad amplexus inferioris eat.　　　　　　770

Pars superat coepti, pars est exhausta laboris.
　　Hic teneat nostras ancora iacta rates.

is shameful, none cares but for his own pleasure, and
sweet is that when it springs from another's pain.
Ah, the reproach of it! no foe need a lover fear;
fly those whom you deem faithful, and you will be
safe. Kinsman, brother—beware of them and of
thy boon companion; they will cause you real fears.

I was about to end, but various are the hearts of
women; use a thousand means to waylay as many
hearts. The same earth bears not everything; this
soil suits vines, that olives; in that, wheat thrives.
Hearts have as many fashions as the world has
shapes; the wise man will suit himself to countless
fashions, and like Proteus will now resolve himself
into light waves, and now will be a lion, now a tree,
now a shaggy boar. Here fish are caught with
spears, there with hooks; here they are dragged with
taut ropes in hollow nets. Nor let one method suit
all ages; a grown hind will regard the snare from
further away. Should you seem learned to the
simple, or wanton to the prude, she will straightway
feel a pitiful self-distrust. And so comes it that she
who has feared to commit herself to an honourable
lover degrades herself to the embraces of a mean
one.

Part of my enterprise remains, part is now finished.
Here let the anchor be thrown, and hold my bark
secure.

D

LIBER SECUNDUS

Dicite "io Paean!" et "io" bis dicite "Paean!"
    Decidit in casses praeda petita meos ;
Laetus amans donat viridi mea carmina palma,
    Praelata Ascraeo Maeonioque seni.
Talis ab armiferis Priameïus hospes Amyclis   5
    Candida cum rapta coniuge vela dedit;
Talis erat qui te curru victore ferebat,
    Vecta peregrinis Hippodamia rotis.
Quid properas, iuvenis? mediis tua pinus in undis
    Navigat, et longe quem peto portus abest.   10
Non satis est venisse tibi me vate puellam :
    Arte mea capta est, arte tenenda mea est.
Nec minor est virtus, quam quaerere, parta tueri :
    Casus inest illic ; hoc erit artis opus.
Nunc mihi, siquando, puer et Cytherea, favete,   15
    Nunc Erato, nam tu nomen amoris habes.
Magna paro, quas possit Amor remanere per artes,
    Dicere, tam vasto pervagus orbe puer.
Et levis est, et habet geminas, quibus avolet, alas :
    Difficile est illis inposuisse modum.   20

Hospitis effugio praestruxerat omnia Minos :
    Audacem pinnis repperit ille viam.
Daedalus ut clausit conceptum crimine matris
    Semibovemque virum semivirumque bovem,

---

[1] Pelops, who came from Phrygia to Elis, the home of
Hippodamia, and there won her by his victory in a chariot race.
[2] cf. ἔρως, ἐρᾶν.
[3] Daedalus had fled from Athens, and taking refuge in Crete
had constructed a prison (the labyrinth) for the Minotaur ; when
66

BOOK II

CRY "Hurrah! Triumph!" and "Hurrah! Triumph!" cry once more : the prey I sought has fallen into my toils; joyously does the lover crown my poem with green palm-leaves, and prefer it to the Maeonian and Ascraean sages. In such mood did the stranger, Priam's son, spread his gleaming sails from warlike Amyclae in the company of his stolen bride; in such mood was he who bore thee in victorious car, O Hippodamia, conveyed upon his foreign wheels. [1] Why do you hasten, O youth? your bark sails in mid-ocean, and the harbour I seek is far away. It is not enough that through my strains you have won your mistress; by my art you gained her, by my art she must be kept. Nor is there less prowess in guarding what is won than in seeking; in that there is chance, but this task demands skill. Now, if ever, favour me, Cytherea and thy Boy! and thou, Erato, for thy name is a name of Love. [2] Great things am I planning—to tell by what arts Love can be made to tarry, the boy that wanders over the wide world. Fickle is he, and he has two wings, wherewith to fly away ; hard is it to restrain them.

Every way had Minos barred his guest's escape, yet he by means of feathers found a daring path. [3] When Daedalus imprisoned him whom his mother wrongfully conceived, the man half-bull and the bull

he wished to return to his native land, Minos refused to let him go.

"Sit modus exilio," dixit "iustissime Minos :   25
    Accipiat cineres terra paterna meos.
Et quoniam in patria, fatis agitatus iniquis,
    Vivere non potui, da mihi posse mori.
Da reditum puero, senis est si gratia vilis :
    Si non vis puero parcere, parce seni."   30
Dixerat haec ; sed et haec et multo plura licebat
    Dicere : regressus non dabat ille viro.
Quod simul ut sensit, "nunc, nunc, o Daedale,"
    dixit :
    "Materiam, qua sis ingeniosus, habes.
Possidet et terras et possidet aequora Minos :   35
    Nec tellus nostrae nec patet unda fugae.
Restat iter caeli : caelo temptabimus ire.
    Da veniam coepto, Iupiter alte, meo :
Non ego sidereas adfecto tangere sedes :
    Qua fugiam dominum, nulla, nisi ista, via est.   40
Per Styga detur iter, Stygias transnabimus undas ;
    Sunt mihi naturae iura novanda meae."
Ingenium mala saepe movent : quis crederet umquam
    Aërias hominem carpere posse vias ?
Remigium volucrum disponit in ordine pinnas,   45
    Et leve per lini vincula nectit opus,
Imaque pars ceris adstringitur igne solutis,
    Finitusque novae iam labor artis erat.
Tractabat ceramque puer pinnasque renidens,
    Nescius haec umeris arma parata suis.   50
Cui pater "his" inquit "patria est adeunda carinis,
    Hac nobis Minos effugiendus ope.
Aëra non potuit Minos, alia omnia clausit ;
    Quem licet, inventis aëra rumpe meis.
Sed tibi non virgo Tegeaea comesque Bootae   55
    Ensiger Orion aspiciendus erit :

half-man, " Let my exile have an end, most righteous Minos," said he, " let my father's land receive my ashes. And because, pursued by unjust fate, I could not live in my own country, let me be able to die there. Grant my boy his return, if you hold cheap your gratitude to his sire ; spare the sire, if you will not spare the boy." So spake he ; but this and much more might he speak : the other gave not the hero his return. Which when he knew, he said, " Now, Daedalus, now is your chance to show your wit. Lo ! Minos possesses the earth and also the seas : nor land nor wave is free for our escape. The way of the sky remains : by the sky we will essay to go ; pardon my enterprise, Jupiter on high. I endeavour not to touch thy starry dwellings ; no way but this have I to escape my master. Should a way be given me by Styx, o'er the Stygian waters we will swim ; I must devise new laws for my nature." Ills often stir the wits ; who would e'er have believed that man could sail the paths of air ? He arranges in order feathers, the oarage of the birds, and inter- weaves the frail fabric with linen fastenings ; the base is bound with wax softened in the fire, and already the toil of the wondrous work was over. With beaming face the boy handled the feathers and the wax, not knowing that the harness was prepared for his own shoulders. "These are the ships," said his father, " whereon we must sail home ; by their aid must we flee from Minos. The air Minos could not close, though he had closed all else ; break through the air (for there thou canst) by my device. But not on the Tegean maid [1] nor on sword-bearing Orion, comrade of Bootes, must thou fix thy gaze : me do

---

[1] Callisto, *i.e.* the constellation of the Bear.

OVID

Me pinnis sectare datis; ego praevius ibo:
  Sit tua cura sequi; me duce tutus eris.
Nam sive aetherias vicino sole per auras
  Ibimus, impatiens cera caloris erit:　　　　　　　　60
Sive humiles propiore freto iactabimus alas,
  Mobilis aequoreis pinna madescet aquis.
Inter utrumque vola; ventos quoque, nate, timeto,
  Quaque ferent aurae, vela secunda dato."
Dum monet, aptat opus puero, monstratque moveri,　65
  Erudit infirmas ut sua mater aves.
Inde sibi factas umeris accommodat alas,
  Perque novum timide corpora librat iter.
Iamque volaturus parvo dedit oscula nato,
  Nec patriae lacrimas continuere genae.　　　　　70
Monte minor collis, campis erat altior aequis:
  Hinc data sunt miserae corpora bina fugae.
Et movet ipse suas, et nati respicit alas
  Daedalus, et cursus sustinet usque suos.
Iamque novum delectat iter, positoque timore　　75
  Icarus audaci fortius arte volat.
Hos aliquis, tremula dum captat arundine pisces,
  Vidit, et inceptum dextra reliquit opus.
Iam Samos a laeva (fuerant Naxosque relictae
  Et Paros et Clario Delos amata deo)　　　　　　80
Dextra Lebynthos erat silvisque umbrosa Calymne
  Cinctaque piscosis Astypalaea vadis,
Cum puer, incautis nimium temerarius annis,
  Altius egit iter, deseruitque patrem.
Vincla labant, et cera deo propiore liquescit,　　85
  Nec tenues ventos brachia mota tenent.

---

[1] From Claros, an Ionian town, where Apollo had an oracle.

thou follow on the wings that I shall give thee; I will lead the way, let it be thine to follow; under my leadership thou wilt be safe. For if we go nigh the sun through the upper air, the wax will be impatient of the heat; or if we beat our low-flying wings too near the sea, the nimble feathers will be wet with watery spray. Fly between the two; and the winds also hold in awe, my son, and where the breezes carry thee, spread thy sails to the breeze." While he counsels, he fits his handiwork on the boy, and shows him how to move, as their mother instructs the tender fledglings. Then he fastens on his shoulders the wings he has made for himself, and cautiously poises his body for its new journey. And now on the verge of flight he kissed his little son, nor could the father's eyes restrain the tears. There was a hill smaller than a mountain, but rising above the level plains; from this the bodies of the twain were launched on their hapless flight. Daedalus, while he plies his own, looks back at his son's wings, and ever keeps on his own course. And now the wondrous voyage delights them, and forgetting his fear Icarus flies more courageously with daring skill. One who was angling for fish with tremulous line beheld them, and his right hand left the task he had begun. Already was Samos on their left, (Naxos and Paros had been passed, and Delos loved by the Clarian [1] god): on their right was Lebynthos and Calymne shady with forests, and Astypalaea girt with fish-haunted seas; when the boy, too bold in his youthful daring, deserted his sire and winged his way too high. The fastenings give way, and the wax, too near the god, is melted; nor do his moving arms keep their hold on the frail

Territus a summo despexit in aequora caelo:
  Nox oculis pavido venit oborta metu.
Tabuerant cerae: nudos quatit ille lacertos,
  Et trepidat, nec quo sustineatur, habet.   90
Decidit, atque cadens " pater, o pater, auferor !" inquit,
  Clauserunt virides ora loquentis aquae.
At pater infelix, nec iam pater, " Icare !" clamat,
  " Icare," clamat " ubi es, quove sub axe volas ? "
" Icare" clamabat, pinnas aspexit in undis.   95
  Ossa tegit tellus : aequora nomen habent.

Non potuit Minos hominis conpescere pinnas
  Ipse deum volucrem detinuisse paro.
Fallitur, Haemonias siquis decurrit ad artes,
  Datque quod a teneri fronte revellit equi.   100
Non facient, ut vivat amor, Medeïdes herbae
  Mixtaque cum magicis naenia Marsa sonis.
Phasias Aesoniden, Circe tenuisset Ulixem,
  Si modo servari carmine posset amor.
Nec data profuerint pallentia philtra puellis :   105
  Philtra nocent animis, vimque furoris habent.
Sit procul omne nefas ; ut ameris, amabilis esto :
  Quod tibi non facies solave forma dabit :
Sis licet antiquo Nireus adamatus Homero,
  Naïadumque tener crimine raptus Hylas,   110
Ut dominam teneas, nec te mirere relictum,
  Ingenii dotes corporis adde bonis.

87 despexit *MSS.*: dispexit *R*.
109 sis *Heinsius*: sit *MSS.*

---

[1] *i.e.* of Thessaly, famed for magic, as was also the mountain
district of the Marsi in Central Italy.
[2] The "hippomanes" was said to be a growth upon the
forehead of a foal, which was bitten off by the mare imme-

airs. Terrified, he gazed down at the water from
the height of heaven; in his panic fear darkness
came flooding upon his eyes. The wax had melted:
bare are the arms he shakes; he shudders, nor has
he aught that may sustain him. Down he falls, and
falling cries, " Father, O father, I am borne away ";
the green waters choked the words upon his lips.
But his hapless sire, a sire no longer, calls, " Icarus!"
" Icarus!" he cries, " where art thou? where beneath
heaven art thou flying?" " Icarus!" he was cry-
ing—he saw the feathers in the water. The earth
covers his bones: the waters bear his name.

Minos could not control the wings of a man; I
am planning to hold fast the winged god. Deceived
is he whoever has recourse to Haemonian arts,[1] and
gives what he tears from the forehead of a foal.[2]
Medean herbs will not keep love alive, nor Marsian
charm united to magic sounds. The Phasian had
kept the son of Aeson,[3] Circe had kept Ulysses, if
love could be saved by spells alone. Nor will pale
philtres given to girls profit: philtres affect the mind
and have power to madden. Far hence be all un-
holy deeds! that you may be loved, be lovable; and
this nor face nor figure alone will bring you; though
you be Nireus, loved by Homer of old, or young
Hylas, stolen by wicked Naiads, that you may
keep your mistress, nor marvel to find yourself
abandoned, add gifts of mind to bodily advantages.

diately after giving birth, and which had the power of a
love-potion (cf. Plin. N.H 8. 165); elsewhere it is described
as a poison that dripped from the genitals of mares (Virg. G.
3. 280; Tib. 2. 4. 57; Prop. 4. 5. 18); or as an Arcadian plant
(Theocr. 2. 48).

[3] Medea and Jason.

Forma bonum fragile est, quantumque accedit ad annos
    Fit minor, et spatio carpitur ipsa suo.
Nec violae semper nec hiantia lilia florent,   115
    Et riget amissa spina relicta rosa.
Et tibi iam venient cani, formose, capilli,
    Iam venient rugae, quae tibi corpus arent.
Iam molire animum, qui duret, et adstrue formae :
    Solus ad extremos permanet ille rogos.   120
Nec levis ingenuas pectus coluisse per artes
    Cura sit et linguas edidicisse duas.
Non formosus erat, sed erat facundus Ulixes,
    Et tamen aequoreas torsit amore deas.
O quotiens illum doluit properare Calypso,   125
    Remigioque aptas esse negavit aquas !
Haec Troiae casus iterumque iterumque rogabat :
    Ille referre aliter saepe solebat idem.
Littore constiterant : illic quoque pulchra Calypso
    Exigit Odrysii fata cruenta ducis.   130
Ille levi virga (virgam nam forte tenebat)
    Quod rogat, in spisso littore pingit opus.
" Haec " inquit " Troia est," muros in littore fecit :
    " Hic tibi sit Simois ; haec mea castra puta.
Campus erat," (campumque facit) " quem caede Dolonis
    Sparsimus, Haemonios dum vigil optat equos.   136
Illic Sithonii fuerant tentoria Rhesi :
    Hac ego sum captis nocte revectus equis."
Pluraque pingebat, subitus cum Pergama fluctus
    Abstulit et Rhesi cum duce castra suo.   140
Tum dea " quas " inquit " fidas tibi credis ituro,
    Perdiderint undae nomina quanta, vides ? "

115 semper nec hiantia *some MSS.* ianthina *conj. Brandt :*
semperve hyacinthia *Heinsius* (nec hyaccintia *with* hyac *erased
and* Apollinea *written over R*).

A frail advantage is beauty, that grows less as time draws on, and is devoured by its own years. Violets do not bloom for ever, nor lilies open-mouthed; when the rose is perished, the hard thorn is left behind. And to thee, O handsome youth, will soon come hoary hairs, soon will come wrinkles to make furrows in your body. Now make thee a soul that will abide, and add it to thy beauty; only that endures to the ultimate pyre. Nor let it be a slight care to cultivate your mind in liberal arts, or to learn the two languages well. Ulysses was not comely, but he was eloquent; yet he fired two goddesses of the sea with love. Ah, how oft did Calypso grieve that he was hasting, and say that the waters were not fit for oars. Again and again did she ask to hear the fate of Troy; often would he tell the same tale in other words. They stood upon the shore; there also fair Calypso inquired the cruel fate of the Odrysian chief.[1] He with a light staff (for by chance he carried a staff) draws in the deep sand the tale of which she asks. "Here," says he "is Troy" (he made walls upon the beach), "and here, suppose, is Simois; imagine this to be my camp. There was a plain" (and he draws a plain) "which we sprinkled with Dolon's blood, while he watched and yearned for the Haemonian steeds. There were the tents of Sithonian Rhesus; on that night I rode back on the captured horses." More was he portraying, when a sudden wave washed Pergamus away, and the camp of Rhesus with its chief. Then said the goddess, "Those waters which thou thinkest will be favourable to thy voyage, dost see what great names they have destroyed?"

[1] The Thracian king Rhesus.

Ergo age, fallaci timide confide figurae,
    Quisquis es, aut aliquid corpore pluris habe.
Dextera praecipue capit indulgentia mentes ;   145
    Asperitas odium saevaque bella movet.
Odimus accipitrem, quia vivit semper in armis,
    Et pavidum solitos in pecus ire lupos.
At caret insidiis hominum, quia mitis, hirundo,
    Quasque colat turres, Chaonis ales habet.   150
Este procul, lites et amarae proelia linguae :
    Dulcibus est verbis mollis alendus amor.
Lite fugent nuptaeque viros nuptasque mariti,
    Inque vicem credant res sibi semper agi ;
Hoc decet uxores ; dos est uxoria lites :   155
    Audiat optatos semper amica sonos.
Non legis iussu lectum venistis in unum :
    Fungitur in vobis munere legis amor.
Blanditias molles auremque iuvantia verba
    Adfer, ut adventu laeta sit illa tuo.   160
Non ego divitibus venio praeceptor amandi :
    Nil opus est illi, qui dabit, arte mea ;
Secum habet ingenium, qui, cum libet, " accipe " dicit ;
    Cedimus : inventis plus placet ille meis.
Pauperibus vates ego sum, quia pauper amavi ;   165
    Cum dare non possem munera, verba dabam.
Pauper amet caute : timeat maledicere pauper,
    Multaque divitibus non patienda ferat.
Me memini iratum dominae turbasse capillos :
    Haec mihi quam multos abstulit ira dies !   170
Nec puto, nec sensi tunicam laniasse ; sed ipsa
    Dixerat, et pretio est illa redempta meo.

Come then, trust but timidly, whoever you are, to treacherous beauty; or possess something worth more than outward shape. Chief above all does tactful indulgence win the mind; harshness causes hatred and angry wars. We hate the hawk because he ever lives in arms, and the wolves that are wont to go against the timorous flock. But the swallow is free from men's attack because he is gentle, and the Chaonian bird [1] has towers he may inhabit. Keep far away, quarrels and bitter-tongued affrays; with soft words must love be fostered. With quarrels let wives pursue husbands and husbands wives, and deem that they are ever at issue with each other; this befits wives; the dowry of a wife is quarrelling: but let your mistress ever hear welcome sounds. Not by the law's command have you come into one bed; for you love performs the work of law. Bring soft blandishments and words that soothe the ear, that your coming may make her glad. I come not to teach the rich to love: he who will give has no need of my art; he who when he pleases says "Accept" has wit enough of his own; I give place: my devices will not please so much as he. I am the poet of the poor, because I was poor when I loved; since I could not give gifts, I gave words. Let the poor man love with caution; let the poor man fear to speak harshly; let him bear much that the rich would not endure. I remember how once in anger I disarranged my lady's hair; of how many days did that anger rob me! I do not think nor did I notice that I tore her vest; but she said so, and it was paid for at my expense. But do you, if

---

[1] The dove, from the doves that revealed the future in the oaks of Dodona in Chaonia.

At vos, si sapitis, vestri peccata magistri
    Effugite, et culpae damna timete meae.
Proelia cum Parthis, cum culta pax sit amica,   175
    Et iocus, et causas quicquid amoris habet.

Si nec blanda satis, nec erit tibi comis amanti,
    Perfer et obdura : postmodo mitis erit.
Flectitur obsequio curvatus ab arbore ramus :
    Frangis, si vires experiere tuas.   180
Obsequio tranantur aquae : nec vincere possis
    Flumina, si contra, quam rapit unda, nates.
Obsequium tigresque domat Numidasque leones ;
    Rustica paulatim taurus aratra subit.
Quid fuit asperius Nonacrina Atalanta ?   185
    Succubuit meritis trux tamen illa viri.
Saepe suos casus nec mitia facta puellae
    Flesse sub arboribus Milaniona ferunt ;
Saepe tulit iusso fallacia retia collo,
    Saepe fera torvos cuspide fixit apros :   190
Sensit et Hylaei contentum saucius arcum :
    Sed tamen hoc arcu notior alter erat.
Non te Maenalias armatum scandere silvas,
    Nec iubeo collo retia ferre tuo :
Pectora nec missis iubeo praebere sagittis ;   195
    Artis erunt cautae mollia iussa meae.
Cede repugnanti : cedendo victor abibis :
    Fac modo, quas partes illa iubebit, agas.
Arguet, arguito ; quicquid probat illa, probato ;
    Quod dicet, dicas ; quod negat illa, neges.   200
Riserit, adride ; si flebit, flere memento ;
    Imponat leges vultibus illa tuis.

you are wise, avoid your master's errors, and fear
the loss my fault incurred. Battle with Parthians,
but with a cultured mistress have peace and mirth
and whatever is the cause of love.

Should she be neither kindly nor courteous to
your wooing, persist and steel your resolve; one day
she will be kind. By compliance is the curved
bough bent away from the tree; you will break it if
you try your strength. By compliance are waters
swum; nor can you conquer rivers if you swim
against the current's flow. Compliance tames tigers
and Numidian lions; little by little the bull submits
to the rustic plough. What could be more stern
than Nonacrian Atalanta? yet stubborn as she was
she yielded to a hero's prowess. Often, they say,
beneath the trees Milanion bewailed his lot and the
maiden's cruelty; often did he bear the crafty nets
on his obedient neck, often with ruthless spear trans-
fixed the grisly boars; from the bow too that Hylaeus
strung did he feel the wound—and yet another bow [1]
was still more known than this. I do not bid you
arm and climb the forests of Maenalus, nor carry
nets upon your neck; nor do I bid you offer your
breast to flying arrows; easy will be the precepts of
my cautious art. Yield if she resists; by yielding
you will depart the victor; only play the part she
bids you play. Blame if she blames; approve what-
ever she approves. Affirm what she affirms and
deny what she denies. If she laughs, laugh with
her; if she weeps, remember to weep; let her
impose her laws upon your countenance. If she be

[1] The bow of Hylaeus (a Centaur who made an attempt
upon Atalanta) marked the extreme point of Milanion's
endurance on her behalf: yet Cupid's bow (l. 192) was even
more effective in making her love him.

Seu ludet, numerosque manu iactabit eburnos,
    Tu male iactato, tu male iacta dato:
Seu iacies talos, victam ne poena sequatur,   205
    Damnosi facito stent tibi saepe canes:
Sive latrocinii sub imagine calculus ibit,
    Fac pereat vitreo miles ab hoste tuus.
Ipse tene distenta suis umbracula virgis,
    Ipse fac in turba, qua venit illa, locum.   210
Nec dubita tereti scamnum producere lecto,
    Et tenero soleam deme vel adde pedi.
Saepe etiam dominae, quamvis horrebis et ipse,
    Algenti manus est calfacienda sinu.
Nec tibi turpe puta (quamvis sit turpe, placebit),   215
    Ingenua speculum sustinuisse manu.
Ille, fatigata praebendo monstra noverca
    Qui meruit caelum, quod prior ipse tulit,
Inter Ioniacas calathum tenuisse puellas
    Creditur, et lanas excoluisse rudes.   220
Paruit imperio dominae Tirynthius heros:
    I nunc et dubita ferre, quod ille tulit.
Iussus adesse foro, iussa maturius hora
    Fac semper venias, nec nisi serus abi.
Occurras aliquo, tibi dixerit, omnia differ,   225
    Curre, nec inceptum turba moretur iter.
Nocte domum repetens epulis perfuncta redibit:
    Tunc quoque pro servo, si vocat illa, veni.
Rure erit, et dicet "venias": Amor odit inertes:
    Si rota defuerit, tu pede carpe viam.   230

217 fatigata . . . noverca *Madvig*: -ae . . . -ae *MSS.*: prae-
bendo *R*: perdendo *MSS.*

---

[1] "numeri" could be used either in the sense of "tali," the
large dice marked on four sides, or of "tesserae," the smaller
ones, marked on six sides. As "dare" can mean to move a
piece, the first couplet may refer to a game where pieces were

gaming, and throwing with her hand the ivory dice,[1]
do you throw amiss and move your throws amiss;
or if it is the large dice you are throwing, let no
forfeit follow if she lose; see that the ruinous dogs
often fall to you; or if the piece be marching under
the semblance of a robbers' band, let your warrior
fall before his glassy foe. Do you yourself hold her
parasol outstretched upon its rods, yourself make
room for her in the crowd, where she is coming.
Nor hesitate to place the footstool for her trim
couch; take off her slipper from her dainty foot, or
put it on. Often too when she is cold, though you
are shivering too, you must warm your lady's hand
in your own lap. Nor think it base (though base, it
will give pleasure) to hold a mirror in your freeborn
hand. He who won the heaven which first he bore
himself, when his step-mother was wearied of sending
monsters, is believed to have held a basket among
Ionian maidens, and to have spun fine the unworked
wool. The Tirynthian hero obeyed a mistress'
command: go, shrink from enduring what he en-
dured! Bidden meet her at the Forum, go earlier
than the hour of bidding, nor leave till it be late.
She has told you to join her somewhere: put off
everything, run! let not the crowd delay your
passage. At night she will return to her house, the
banquet finished: then too come in the slave's stead,
if she calls. You are in the country, and she says
"Come!" Love hates the sluggish: if wheels fail,
make the journey on foot. Let neither the fatal

moved as well as dice thrown, and the second to throwing
merely. The third couplet refers to the game of "robbers,"
the "ludus latrunculorum," which seems to have taken
different forms. "Canes," the name given to a bad throw,
the opposite being called "Venus," as in Prop. 4. 8. 45.

Nec grave te tempus sitiensque Canicula tardet,
　　Nec via per iactas candida facta nives.

Militiae species amor est; discedite, segnes:
　　Non sunt haec timidis signa tuenda viris.
Nox et hiems longaeque viae saevique dolores　　235
　　Mollibus his castris et labor omnis inest.
Saepe feres imbrem caelesti nube solutum,
　　Frigidus et nuda saepe iacebis humo.
Cynthius Admeti vaccas pavisse Pheraei
　　Fertur, et in parva delituisse casa.　　240
Quod Phoebum decuit, quem non decet? exue fastus,
　　Curam mansuri quisquis amoris habes.
Si tibi per tutum planumque negabitur ire,
　　Atque erit opposita ianua fulta sera,
At tu per praeceps tecto delabere aperto:　　245
　　Det quoque furtivas alta fenestra vias.
Laeta erit, et causam tibi se sciet esse pericli;
　　Hoc dominae certi pignus amoris erit.
Saepe tua poteras, Leandre, carere puella:
　　Transnabas, animum nosset ut illa tuum.　　250

Nec pudor ancillas, ut quaeque erit ordine prima,
　　Nec tibi sit servos demeruisse pudor.
Nomine quemque suo (nulla est iactura) saluta,
　　Iunge tuis humiles, ambitiose, manus.
Sed tamen et servo (levis est inpensa) roganti　　255
　　Porrige Fortunae munera parva die:
Porrige et ancillae, qua poenas luce pependit
　　Lusa maritali Gallica veste manus.

---

　　[1] This would be the skylight in the roof of the "atrium,"
usually called the "compluvium."
　　[2] The day, July 7th, was called by the Romans Nonae
Caprotinae, and on it women sacrificed to Juno Caprotina
("sub caprifico," under a wild fig tree) in memory of the

heat and the thirsty Dogstar delay you, nor a road
made white by fallen snow.

Love is a kind of warfare; avaunt, ye laggards!
these banners are not for timid men to guard.
Night, storm, long journeys, cruel pains, all kinds
of toil are in this dainty camp. Oft will you put up
with rain from melting clouds of heaven, and oft
will you lie cold on the bare ground. The Cynthian
is said to have pastured the kine of Admetus king of
Pherae, and to have made a humble cot his lodging.
Whom does that not become which became Phoebus?
put off your pride, whoever you are that care for an
enduring love. If it is denied you to go by a safe
and easy road, and if the door be held by a fastened
bolt, yet slip down headlong through an opening in
the roof;[1] or let a high window afford a secret path.
She will rejoice, and know herself the cause of peril
to you; this will be a pledge of your lady's sure
affection. Oft was it in your power, Leander, to be
absent from your mistress : you swam across that
she might know your passion.

Blush not to win over handmaidens, as each stands
first in rank, nor blush to win over slaves. Salute
each one by name : you lose nothing thereby ; clasp
low-born hands, ambitious one, in yours. Ay, even
to a slave, should he ask you (the cost is trivial),
offer some small gift on the day of Fortune ; offer it
to a handmaid also, on the day that the Gallic band
paid penalty, tricked by the marriage-robe.[2] Believe

handmaidens who were given up to the Gauls in place of and
disguised as the Roman matrons and virgins whom they
demanded. According to Plutarch (*Romulus* 29, *Camillus*
33) it was not Gauls but Latins on whom the trick was
played. The handmaidens signalled to the Romans from a
fig tree, and they thereupon fell on the enemy.

Fac plebem, mihi crede, tuam; sit semper in illa
    Ianitor et thalami qui iacet ante fores.   260
Nec dominam iubeo pretioso munere dones:
    Parva, sed e parvis callidus apta dato.
Dum bene dives ager, dum rami pondere nutant,
    Adferat in calatho rustica dona puer.
Rure suburbano poteris tibi dicere missa,   265
    Illa vel in Sacra sint licet empta via.
Adferat aut uvas, aut quas Amaryllis amabat—
    At nunc castaneas non amat illa nuces.
Quin etiam turdoque licet missaque columba
    Te memorem dominae testificere tuae.   270
Turpiter his emitur spes mortis et orba senectus.
    A, pereant, per quos munera crimen habent!

Quid tibi praecipiam teneros quoque mittere versus?
    Ei mihi, non multum carmen honoris habet.
Carmina laudantur, sed munera magna petuntur: 275
    Dummodo sit dives, barbarus ipse placet.
Aurea sunt vere nunc saecula: plurimus auro
    Venit honos: auro conciliatur amor.
Ipse licet venias Musis comitatus, Homere,
    Si nihil attuleris, ibis, Homere, foras.   280
Sunt tamen et doctae, rarissima turba, puellae;
    Altera non doctae turba, sed esse volunt.
Utraque laudetur per carmina: carmina lector
    Commendet dulci qualiacumque sono;
His ergo aut illis vigilatum carmen in ipsas   285
    Forsitan exigui muneris instar erit.

269 columba *MSS*: corona *R.*

---

[1] Cf. *Amores*, 1. 11, 2. 2, 2. 8, etc.
[2] Because she has more extravagant tastes nowadays. The

me, make the humble folk your own; let the gate-
keeper ever be one of them, and him who lies be-
fore her chamber-door.[1] Nor do I bid you give
your mistress costly gifts: let them be small, but
choose your small gifts cunningly and well. While
lands are fertile, while your branches droop with
their burden, let a slave bring rustic tributes in a
basket. You can say they were sent to you from
your suburban property, though you bought them in
the Sacred Way. Let him bring either grapes or
the nuts "that Amaryllis loved"—but chestnuts she
loves not now.[2] Nay too by sending a thrush or a
pigeon[3] you may witness that you are mindful of
your lady. Dishonourable is it when such gifts
produce the hope of death and a childless old age;
ah, perish they by whom gifts bear reproach!

Shall I bid you send tender verses also? Alas, a
poem is not much honoured. Poems are praised,
but costly gifts are sought; so he be wealthy, even
a barbarian pleases. Now truly is the age of gold:
by gold comes many an honour, by gold is affection
gained. Though you come, Homer, and all the
Muses with you, if you bring nothing, Homer, out
you go! Yet there are learned women too, a scanty
number; and others are not learned, but wish to be
so. Let either sort be praised in poems; his verses,
whate'er their quality, let the reader commend by
the charm of his recital; and thus to learned and
unlearned the poem fashioned in their praise will
perchance seem like a little gift.

reference is to Virg. *Ecl.* 2. 52: "Castaneasque nuces mea
quas Amaryllis amabat."
[3] Birds were frequently used as pets: thrushes were also a
delicacy.

At quod eris per te facturus, et utile credis,
　　Id tua te facito semper amica roget.
Libertas alicui fuerit promissa tuorum:
　　Hanc tamen a domina fac petat ille tua:　　　　290
Si poenam servo, si vincula saeva remittis,
　　Quod facturus eras, debeat illa tibi:
Utilitas tua sit, titulus donetur amicae:
　　Perde nihil, partes illa potentis agat.
Sed te, cuicumque est retinendae cura puellae,　　295
　　Attonitum forma fac putet esse sua.
Sive erit in Tyriis, Tyrios laudabis amictus:
　　Sive erit in Cois, Coa decere puta.
Aurata est? ipso tibi sit pretiosior auro;
　　Gausapa si sumpsit, gausapa sumpta proba.　　300
Astiterit tunicata, "moves incendia" clama,
　　Sed timida, caveat frigora, voce roga.
Conpositum discrimen erit, discrimina lauda:
　　Torserit igne comam, torte capille, place.
Brachia saltantis, vocem mirare canentis,　　　305
　　Et, quod desierit, verba querentis habe.
Ipsos concubitus, ipsum venerere licebit
　　Quod iuvat, et laudi gaudia noctis habe.
Ut fuerit torva violentior illa Medusa,
　　Fiet amatori lenis et aequa suo.　　　　　　310
Tantum, ne pateas verbis simulator in illis,
　　Effice, nec vultu destrue dicta tuo.
Si latet ars, prodest: adfert deprensa pudorem,
　　Atque adimit merito tempus in omne fidem.

Saepe sub autumnum, cum formosissimus annus,　　315
　　Plenaque purpureo subrubet uva mero,
Cum modo frigoribus premitur, modo solvitur aestu,
　　Aëre non certo, corpora languor habet.

308 laudi *Housman*: quaedam *R*: praedam *Merkel.*

86

But what you are going to do of yourself and
deem to be useful, see that your mistress always
begs you do. One of your slaves has been promised
his liberty; see that he asks it nevertheless from
your mistress: if you release a slave from punishment
or cruel chains, make her your debtor for what you
were about to do: be yours the gain; make your
mistress a present of the glory: waste nothing; let
her play the powerful lady. But whoever you are who
are anxious to keep your mistress, be sure she thinks
you spellbound by her beauty. If she be in Tyrian
attire, then praise her Tyrian gown; or in Coan,
then find the Coan style becoming. Is her raiment
golden? let her be to you more precious than gold
itself; if she wear woollens, then approve the woollens
that she wears. Should she stand by you in her shift,
cry "You inflame me!" but with timid voice beg
her to mind the cold. Has she arranged her parting?
praise it. Has she curled her hair with the irons?
curled tress, find favour. Admire her arms as she
dances, her voice as she sings; and find words of
complaint that she has stopped. Your actual union
and moment of bliss you may adore, and praise the
pleasures of the night. Though she be more violent
than grim Medusa, she will be mild and gentle to
her lover. Only while so talking take care not to
show you are feigning, nor let your looks undo your
words. Art, if hidden, avails; if detected, it brings
shame, and deservedly discredits you for ever.

Often in autumn, when the season is most fair,
and the grape begins to blush with the purple wine,
when at one time we are stiffened with cold, at
another melted with heat, then in the uncertain air
a languor holds the body. May she indeed keep

Illa quidem valeat; sed si male firma cubabit,
    Et vitium caeli senserit aegra sui,   320
Tunc amor et pietas tua sit manifesta puellae,
    Tum sere, quod plena postmodo falce metas.
Nec tibi morosi veniant fastidia morbi,
    Perque tuas fiant quae sinet ipsa. manus.
Et videat flentem, nec taedeat oscula ferre,   325
    Et sicco lacrimas conbibat ore tuas.
Multa vove, sed cuncta palam; quotiesque libebit,
    Quae referas illi, somnia laeta vide.
Et veniat, quae lustret anus lectumque locumque,
    Praeferat et tremula sulpur et ova manu.   330
Omnibus his inerunt gratae vestigia curae:
    In tabulas multis haec via fecit iter.
Nec tamen officiis odium quaeratur ab aegra:
    Sit suus in blanda sedulitate modus:
Neve cibo prohibe, nec amari pocula suci   335
    Porrige: rivalis misceat illa tuus.

Sed non quo dederas a litore carbasa vento,
    Utendum, medio cum potiere freto.
Dum novus errat amor, vires sibi colligat usu:
    Si bene nutrieris, tempore firmus erit.   340
Quem taurum metuis, vitulum mulcere solebas:
    Sub qua nunc recubas arbore, virga fuit:
Nascitur exiguus, sed opes adquirit eundo,
    Quaque venit, multas accipit amnis aquas.
Fac tibi consuescat: nil adsuetudine maius: 345
    Quam tu dum capias, taedia nulla fuge.
Te semper videat, tibi semper praebeat aures;
    Exhibeat vultus noxque diesque tuos.

---

[1] Eggs and sulphur are frequently referred to, as means of
purification in sickness, in cases of unrequited love, in the

her health! but should she ail, and in sickness suffer
from the inclement sky, then let your love and
affection be manifest to the girl, then sow what
afterwards you may reap with a full sickle. Nor
let impatience with fretful sickness come upon you;
let yours be the hands that do what she will allow.
And let her see you weeping, and be not weary of
giving her kisses; let her drink your tears with
parched mouth. Make many vows, and all aloud;
and whenever you wish, have joyful dreams to tell
her. And let an old woman come to purify her
bed and chamber, and to bring sulphur[1] and eggs
with trembling hand. All this will show signs of
willing care; this path has led many to a legacy.
Yet incur not by your services the displeasure of
the sick one; flattering zeal in service should
keep its proper limits: debar her not from food,
nor offer cups of bitter juices; them let your rival
mingle.

But the wind to which you spread your sails when
leaving the shore should not be used when once
you have won the open sea. While love wanders in
its youth let it gather strength by experience; so
but you nurture it well, in time it will be strong.
The bull you fear, you were wont to stroke as a calf;
the tree under which you lie was once a sapling: a
river at birth is small, but acquires force by flowing;
wherever it fares, it receives many waters. See that
she grows used to you: than use and wont naught is
mightier: till you secure that, shun no weariness. Let
her be always seeing you, always giving you her ear;
let night and day show her your features. When you

worship of Isis; cf. also Juv. 6. 518 for their use in September,
and Ov. *Fast*. 4. 739, at the Parilia.

Cum tibi maior erit fiducia, posse requiri,
    Cum procul absenti cura futurus eris,   350
Da requiem : requietus ager bene credita reddit,
    Terraque caelestes arida sorbet aquas.
Phyllida Demophoon praesens moderatius ussit :
    Exarsit velis acrius illa datis.
Penelopen absens sollers torquebat Ulixes ;   355
    Phylacides aberat, Laodamia, tuus.
Sed mora tuta brevis : lentescunt tempore curae,
    Vanescitque absens et novus intrat amor.
Dum Menelaus abest, Helene, ne sola iaceret,
    Hospitis est tepido nocte recepta sinu.   360
Qui stupor hic, Menelaë, fuit ? tu solus abibas,
    Isdem sub tectis hospes et uxor erant.
Accipitri timidas credis, furiose, columbas ?
    Plenum montano credis ovile lupo ?
Nil Helene peccat, nihil hic committit adulter :   365
    Quod tu, quod faceret quilibet, ille facit.
Cogis adulterium dando tempusque locumque ;
    Quid nisi consilio est usa puella tuo ?
Quid faciat ? vir abest, et adest non rusticus hospes,
    Et timet in vacuo sola cubare toro.   370
Viderit Atrides : Helenen ego crimine solvo :
    Usa est humani commoditate viri.

Sed neque fulvus aper media tam saevus in ira est,
    Fulmineo rabidos cum rotat ore canes,
Nec lea, cum catulis lactantibus ubera praebet,   375
    Nec brevis ignaro vipera laesa pede,
Femina quam socii deprensa paelice lecti
    Ardet, et in vultu pignora mentis habet.

are quite confident that you can be missed, when your
absence is likely to be regretted, suffer her to rest:
a field that is rested well repays its trust, and a dry
soil drinks up heaven's rain. Demophoon's presence
fired in Phyllis but a moderate flame: when his sails
were set she burned more fiercely. In the absence
of crafty Ulysses was Penelope racked; absent too,
Laodamia, was thy Phyllacides. But a short so-
journing is safest: affection wanes with lapse of
time: an absent love vanishes, and a new one
takes its place. While Menelaus was away, Helen,
that she should not lie alone, was welcomed at night
by the warm bosom of her guest. What folly was
this, Menelaus? you went away alone; your wife
and her guest were beneath the selfsame roof.
Madman, do you trust timid doves to a hawk? do
you trust a full sheepfold to a mountain wolf? In
naught does Helen sin; in naught is that adulterer
to blame: he does what you, what anyone would
have done. By giving time and place you are
compelling adultery; the woman has but used your
own counsel. What could she do? her husband is
away; a guest, and no rustic one, is present; and
she fears to sleep in an empty bed alone. Let the
son of Atreus see to it; Helen I absolve from
blame: she used the opportunity a courteous lover
gave.

But neither is the red boar so savage at his fury's
height, when with lightning jaw he o'erturns the
raging hounds, nor the lioness when she is giving
the udder to her unweaned cubs, nor the tiny adder
hurt by a careless foot, as is a woman set aflame
when a rival is taken in the bed she shares; on her
face she bears the tokens of her feelings. She rushes

In ferrum flammasque ruit, positoque decore
    Fertur, ut Aonii cornibus icta dei.   380
Coniugis admissum violataque iura marita est
    Barbara per natos Phasias ulta suos.
Altera dira parens haec est, quam cernis, hirundo :
    Aspice, signatum sanguine pectus habet.
Hoc bene compositos, hoc firmos solvit amores ;   385
    Crimina sunt cautis ista timenda viris.
Nec mea vos uni damnat censura puellae :
    Di melius ! vix hoc nupta tenere potest.
Ludite, sed furto celetur culpa modesto :
    Gloria peccati nulla petenda sui est.   390
Nec dederis munus, cognosse quod altera possit,
    Nec sint nequitiae tempora certa tuae.
Et, ne te capiat latebris sibi femina notis,
    Non uno est omnis convenienda loco ;
Et quotiens scribes, totas prius ipse tabellas   395
    Inspice : plus multae quam sibi missa legunt.
Laesa Venus iusta arma movet, telumque remittit,
    Et, modo quod questa est, ipse querare, facit.
Dum fuit Atrides una contentus, et illa
    Casta fuit : vitio est improba facta viri.   400
Audierat laurumque manu vittasque ferentem
    Pro nata Chrysen non valuisse sua :
Audierat, Lyrnesi, tuos, abducta, dolores,
    Bellaque per turpis longius isse moras.

381 marita est *R* : maritae *MSS.*

---

[1] *i.e.* the Bacchic frenzy, Bacchus being commonly represented
with horns ; Aonian, *i.e.* Boeotian, from the close connection of
Bacchus with Thebes.

[2] The references are to Medea of Phasis, the river of Colchis,
and to Procne, daughter of Pandion, and wife of Tereus ; both
took vengeance (by slaying their offspring) on the unfaithfulness
of their husbands. Procne was turned into a swallow.

to seize fire and steel and, her modesty flung aside,
rages as though struck by the horns of the Aonian
god.[1] The barbarous Phasian by means of her own
children avenged the crime of her spouse and wed-
lock's broken law. Another terrible parent is this
swallow that you behold: look, her breast is stained
with blood.[2] This it is loosens loves that are well
compact and strong; these are sins to be feared by
cautious husbands. Yet my ruling does not condemn
you to one woman alone: heaven forfend! even a
young bride can hardly secure this. Have your
sport, but let modest deception veil the fault; seek
no vainglory from your sin. Give no gift whereof
the other might learn, and have no fixed seasons for
your wantonness. And lest the lady catch you in
some well-known retreat, meet not every mistress in
one spot; and whenever you write, examine the whole
letter first yourself; many read more than the message
sent to them.[3] Venus when injured wages righteous
war, and flings the weapon back; and she makes you
complain yourself of what she complained of but now.
While Atrides was content with one, she was chaste
also; she was made wicked by her husband's sin.
She had heard that Chryses, wearing the fillets and
with laurel in his hand, had not availed for his
daughter; she had heard of thy sorrows, stolen
Lyrnesian maid,[4] and how shameful tarrying had

[3] She may see traces in the wax of a former love-letter,
cf. iii. 496.

[4] Agamemnon refused to give up Chryseis, daughter of
Chryses, until a plague was sent on the Greek army; he
then took away Briseis, whom Achilles had taken as spoil
from Lyrnesos; this made Achilles withdraw from the fight-
ing. Agamemnon also took Cassandra, Priam's daughter, as
part of the spoil of Troy. Clytemnestra took revenge by
plotting his death with her lover Aegisthus, son of Thyestes.

Haec tamen audierat: Priameïda viderat ipsa: 405
  Victor erat praedae praeda pudenda suae.
Inde Thyestiaden animo thalamoque recepit,
  Et male peccantem Tyndaris ulta virum.

Quae bene celaris, siquae tamen acta patebunt,
  Illa, licet pateant, tu tamen usque nega.   410
Tum neque subiectus, solito nec blandior esto:
  Haec animi multum signa nocentis habent:
Sed lateri ne parce tuo: pax omnis in uno est;
  Concubitu prior est infitianda venus.
Sunt, qui praecipiant herbas, satureia, nocentes   415
  Sumere; iudiciis ista venena meis;
Aut piper urticae mordacis semine miscent,
  Tritaque in annoso flava pyrethra mero;
Sed dea non patitur sic ad sua gaudia cogi,
  Colle sub umbroso quam tenet altus Eryx.   420
Candidus, Alcathoi qui mittitur urbe Pelasga,
  Bulbus, et, ex horto quae venit herba salax,
Ovaque sumantur, sumantur Hymettia mella,
  Quasque tulit folio pinus acuta nuces.

Docta, quid ad magicas, Erato, deverteris artes?   425
  Interior curru meta terenda meo est.
Qui modo celabas monitu tua crimina nostro,
  Flecte iter, et monitu detege furta meo.
Nec levitas culpanda mea est: non semper eodem
  Impositos vento panda carina vehit.   430
Nam modo Threïcio Borea, modo currimus Euro,
  Saepe tument Zephyro lintea, saepe Noto.

425 magicas *MSS.*: medicas *Heinsius.*

---

[1] A similar mixture is recommended by Pliny.
[2] Megara.   [3] *i.e. eruca*, rocket.

drawn out the war. Yet this she had but heard:
Priam's daughter she herself had seen; the victor
was his own captive's shameful prey. Then did she
welcome Thyestes' son to her heart and to her
bower: and Tyndareus' daughter avenged her hus-
band's heinous sin.

Should what you have well concealed be neverthe-
less made manifest, manifest though it be yet deny
it ever. Be not submissive then, nor more flattering
than of wont; such signs point overmuch to guilt;
but spare no efforts; peace is centred in one thing:
by caresses must the former passion be disproved.
Some counsel the taking of savory, noxious herb; it
is poison, in my judgment; or they mingle pepper
with the seed of biting nettle,[1] and yellow camomile
ground up in old wine; but the goddess whom lofty
Eryx holds upon his shady hill will not thus be driven
to her joys. Let white onions, sent from the Pelas-
gian city of Alcathous,[2] be eaten, and the salacious
plant which comes from the garden,[3] eggs too and
Hymettian honey, and the nuts that the sharp-leaved
pine tree bears.

Why turnest thou, learned Erato, to magical arts?
my chariot must graze the inner goal.[4] You who
were but now concealing your fault by my ad-
vice, turn your path, and by my advice uncover
your deceit. And blame me not for fickleness: not
always with the same wind does the curved bark
bear its crew. For now we run before Thracian
Boreas, now before Eurus; often our sails swell with
the Zephyr, often with the south wind. See how the

---

[4] *i.e.* the true (but more esoteric) doctrine must be re-
vealed; it is contrasted with the remedies just mentioned.
Heinsius' suggestion *medicas* makes the passage clearer: there
is a more subtle way, *e.g.* a skilful use of jealousy (l. 445).

Aspice, ut in curru modo det fluitantia rector
   Lora, modo admissos arte retentet equos.
Sunt quibus ingrate timida indulgentia servit,   435
   Et, si nulla subest aemula, languet amor.
Luxuriant animi rebus plerumque secundis,
   Nec facile est aequa commoda mente pati.
Ut levis absumptis paulatim viribus ignis
   Ipse latet, summo canet in igne cinis,   440
Sed tamen extinctas admoto sulpure flammas
   Invenit, et lumen quod fuit ante, redit :
Sic, ubi pigra situ securaque pectora torpent,
   Acribus est stimulis eliciendus amor.
Fac timeat de te, tepidamque recalface mentem :   445
   Palleat indicio criminis illa tui ;
O quater et quotiens numero conprendere non est
   Felicem, de quo laesa puella dolet :
Quae, simul invitas crimen pervenit ad aures,
   Excidit, et miserae voxque colorque fugit.   450
Ille ego sim, cuius laniet furiosa capillos :
   Ille ego sim, teneras cui petat ungue genas,
Quem videat lacrimans, quem torvis spectet ocellis,
   Quo sine non possit vivere, posse velit.
Si spatium quaeras, breve sit, quod laesa queratur,   455
   Ne lenta vires colligat ira mora ;
Candida iamdudum cingantur colla lacertis,
   Inque tuos flens est accipienda sinus.
Oscula da flenti, Veneris da gaudia flenti,
   Pax erit : hoc uno solvitur ira modo.   460
Cum bene saevierit, cum certa videbitur hostis,
   Tum pete concubitus foedera, mitis erit.
Illic depositis habitat Concordia telis :
   Illo, crede mihi, Gratia nata loco est.

driver in his car now lets the reins float loose, now skilfully holds back the galloping steeds. Some women are there whom timid indulgence serves without reward, and, when no rival exists, their passion wanes. Often pride waxes in prosperity, nor is it easy to bear good fortune with equal mind. Just as a fire, growing frail as its forces gradually abate, itself lies hid, while the cinders grow grey on the surface of the fire; but add sulphur, and it finds its extinguished flames, and the light that once was there returns—so when hearts grow torpid in dull repose and freedom from all care, sharp goads must call forth love. See that she has fears about you, and fire anew her cooling thoughts; let her grow pale at hearing of your guilt; O four times and unnumbered times happy is he over whom an injured woman grieves; who, as soon as the charge has reached her unwilling ears, faints away, and voice and colour leave her unhappy frame. May I be he whose hair she furiously rends! may I be he whose tender cheeks her nails attack! whom weeping she regards, at whom she glares with angry eyes, without whom she could not live, though fain she would! Should you ask how long, let the time for her to lament her injuries be short, lest anger gather strength by slow delay; long ere this let your arms encircle her white neck, and gather her weeping to your bosom. Kiss her as she weeps, give her as she weeps the joys of Venus; then there will be peace, in this way alone will anger be dispelled. When she has raged her fill, when she seems your certain foe, then seek the treaty of a love embrace: that will make her gentle. Therein dwells Concord when the fight is o'er; there, believe me, was Reconciliation born.

E

OVID

Quae modo pugnarunt, iungunt sua rostra columbae, 465
  Quarum blanditias verbaque murmur habet.

Prima fuit rerum confusa sine ordine moles,
  Unaque erat facies sidera, terra, fretum ;
Mox caelum impositum terris, humus aequore cincta est
  Inque suas partes cessit inane chaos ;   470
Silva feras, volucres aer accepit habendas,
  In liquida pisces delituistis aqua.
Tum genus humanum solis errabat in agris,
  Idque merae vires et rude corpus erat ;
Silva domus fuerat, cibus herba, cubilia frondes :   475
  Iamque diu nulli cognitus alter erat.
Blanda truces animos fertur mollisse voluptas :
  Constiterant uno femina virque loco ;
Quid facerent, ipsi nullo didicere magistro :
  Arte Venus nulla dulce peregit opus.   480
Ales habet, quod amet ; cum quo sua gaudia iungat,
  Invenit in media femina piscis aqua ;
Cerva parem sequitur, serpens serpente tenetur,
  Haeret adulterio cum cane nexa canis ;
Laeta salitur ovis : tauro quoque laeta iuvenca est : 485
  Sustinet inmundum sima capella marem ;
In furias agitantur equae, spatioque remota
  Per loca dividuos amne sequuntur equos.
Ergo age et iratae medicamina fortia praebe :
  Illa feri requiem sola doloris habent :   490
Illa Machaonios superant medicamina sucos :
  His, ubi peccaris, restituendus eris.

Haec ego cum canerem, subito manifestus Apollo
  Movit inauratae pollice fila lyrae.

---

[1] He and Podalirius were the physicians of the Greek army
before Troy ; they were sons of Asclepius.

The doves who lately fought now join bill to bill; words of blandishment are in their cooing.

First there was a confused mass of things without order, and stars and earth and sea had but one appearance; presently the sky was set over the earth, the land was ringed by the sea, and empty void retired to its own place; the forest received wild beasts to keep, and the air birds; ye lurked, ye fishes, in the liquid waters. Then mankind wandered in the lonely fields; brute strength was theirs and forms uncouth; woodland was their home, their food grass, their bedding leaves; and for long none knew his fellow. Beguiling pleasure is said to have softened those fierce spirits: a man and a woman had tarried together in one spot; what were they to do, they learnt themselves with none to teach them: artlessly did Venus accomplish the sweet act. The bird has one he may love; in mid-sea the female fish finds one with whom to unite in pleasure; the hind follows her mate, serpent is clasped by serpent, the hound is joined in clinging lechery to the bitch; gladly the ewe endures the leap, the heifer rejoices in the bull, the snub-nosed goat supports her unclean lord; mares are excited to frenzy, and through regions far removed follow the stallions, though streams divide them. Come then, and for an angry woman bring powerful medicines; they alone give repose to savage wrath; those medicines surpass the juices of Machaon,[1] by them, when you have erred, must you be restored to favour.[2]

While I was singing thus, Apollo suddenly appeared and moved with his thumb the strings of his

[2] For the "medicamina fortia" that he recommends see ll. 457 *sqq.*

In manibus laurus, sacris inducta capillis   495
  Laurus erat; vates ille videndus adit.
Is mihi " Lascivi " dixit " praeceptor Amoris,
  Duc, age, discipulos ad mea templa tuos,
Est ubi diversum fama celebrata per orbem
  Littera, cognosci quae sibi quemque iubet.   500
Qui sibi notus erit, solus sapienter amabit,
  Atque opus ad vires exiget omne suas.
Cui faciem natura dedit, spectetur ab illa :
  Cui color est, umero saepe patente cubet :
Qui sermone placet, taciturna silentia vitet :   505
  Qui canit arte, canat ; qui bibit arte, bibat.
Sed neque declament medio sermone diserti,
  Nec sua non sanus scripta poeta legat ! "
Sic monuit Phoebus : Phoebo parete monenti ;
  Certa dei sacro est huius in ore fides.   510

Ad propiora vocor.   Quisquis sapienter amabit
  Vincet, et e nostra, quod petet, arte feret.
Credita non semper sulci cum foenore reddunt,
  Nec semper dubias adiuvat aura rates ;
Quod iuvat, exiguum, plus est, quod laedat amantes ; 515
  Proponant animo multa ferenda suo.
Quot lepores in Atho, quot apes pascuntur in Hybla,
  Caerula quot bacas Palladis arbor habet,
Littore quot conchae, tot sunt in amore dolores ;
  Quae patimur, multo spicula felle madent.   520
Dicta erit isse foras, quam tu fortasse videbis :
  Isse foras, et te falsa videre puta.
Clausa tibi fuerit promissa ianua nocte :
  Perfer et inmunda ponere corpus humo.

     496 adit *MSS.* : abit *R* : agit *Heinsius.*

golden lyre. In his hand was bay, with bay his
sacred locks were veiled; he draws nigh, a poet
worthy to behold. "Preceptor of wanton love,"
said he to me, "come, lead thy pupils to my shrine,
where there is a saying renowned in fame o'er all the
world, which bids each be known by himself.[1] Only
he who knows himself will love with wisdom, and
perform all his task according to his powers. Let
him to whom nature has given beauty be looked at
for that; he who has a fair skin, let him oft lie with
shoulder visible; let him who pleases by his talk
break the still silence; who sings well, let him sing,
who drinks well, let him drink. But neither let the
eloquent declaim in the midst of talk, nor the
frenzied poet recite his verses." So Phoebus coun-
selled: obey ye Phoebus' counsels; in the sacred
mouth of that god is sure warrant.

To nearer matters am I called. Whoso loves
wisely will be victorious, and by my art will gain
his end. Not always do the furrows repay their
trust with interest, not always does the wind assist
perplexed vessels; what aids lovers is but little,
more there is to thwart them; let them make up
their minds to many a trial. As many as the hares
that feed on Athos, or the bees on Hybla, as many
as the berries that the blue-grey tree of Pallas
bears, or the shells that are on the shore, so many
are the pains of love; the darts that wound us are
steeped in much poison. She will be said to have
gone abroad, though you perchance will see her:
believe she has gone, and that your eyes deceive you.
On the promised night her door will be shut against
you: endure to lay your body even on unclean

---

[1] The famous γνῶθι σεαυτόν on Apollo's temple at Delphi.

Forsitan et vultu mendax ancilla superbo   525
  Dicet " quid nostras obsidet iste fores? "
Postibus et durae supplex blandire puellae,
  Et capiti demptas in fore pone rosas.
Cum volet, accedes : cum te vitabit, abibis ;
  Dedecet ingenuos taedia ferre sui.   530
" Effugere hunc non est " quare tibi possit amica
  Dicere ? non omni tempore sensus adest.
Nec maledicta puta, nec verbera ferre puellae
  Turpe, nec ad teneros oscula ferre pedes.

Quid moror in parvis ?   Animus maioribus instat ;   535
  Magna canam : toto pectore, vulgus, ades.
Ardua molimur, sed nulla, nisi ardua, virtus :
  Difficilis nostra poscitur arte labor.
Rivalem patienter habe, victoria tecum
  Stabit : eris magni victor in arce Iovis.   540
Haec tibi non hominem, sed quercus crede Pelasgas
  Dicere : nil istis ars mea maius habet.
Innuet illa, feras ; scribet, ne tange tabellas :
  Unde volet, veniat ; quoque libebit, eat.
Hoc in legitima praestant uxore mariti,   545
  Cum, tener, ad partes tu quoque, somne, venis.
Hac ego, confiteor, non sum perfectus in arte ;
  Quid faciam ? monitis sum minor ipse meis.
Mene palam nostrae det quisquam signa puellae,
  Et patiar, nec me quolibet ira ferat ?   550
Oscula vir dederat, memini, suus : oscula questus
  Sum data ; barbaria noster abundat amor.

532 adest *Heinsius* : obest *R.*
540 in arce *MSS.* : in orbe *R.*

---

[1] *i.e.* you cannot on every occasion rely on your physical attractiveness.

ground. Perhaps some lying, proud-faced maid will say, "Why does this fellow besiege our door?" Supplicate and coax both door and cruel damsel, take the roses from your head and hang them on the doorpost. When she is willing, go to her; when she shuns you, depart; the well-bred man should not bear to become a bore. Why should your mistress be able to say, "I cannot escape from this fellow?" the senses are not always present to aid.[1] Think it not shameful to endure a woman's abuse or blows, nor to give kisses to her tender feet.

Why do I tarry over small matters? my spirit ventures greater themes: of great things will I sing: ye people, give all your mind. I attempt a difficult task; but what is meritorious must needs be difficult: stern toil is demanded by my art. Endure a rival patiently: victory will be on your side; you will stand a victor on the citadel of great Jove.[2] Think that no man, but the Pelasgian oaks[3] are saying this: naught of greater import than this does my art contain. Does she beckon? bear it; does she write? touch not her tablets[4]; let her come whence she will; let her go whither she pleases. Husbands afford this liberty to their lawful wives, when thou, soft sleep, comest to their aid. In this art, I confess, I am not perfect; what am I to do? I fall short of my own counsels. Shall anyone in my presence make signs to my own mistress? shall I endure it? shall wrath not drive me where it will? Her own husband, I remember, had kissed her: I complained of the kisses; my love is full of savagery. Not once only

---

[2] *i.e.* like a triumphing Consul on the Capitol.
[3] The oracle of Dodona, sacred to Pelasgian Zeus.
[4] *i.e.* when she is writing to a rival.

Non semel hoc vitium nocuit mihi : doctior ille,
    Quo veniunt alii conciliante viri.
Sed melius nescisse fuit : sine furta tegantur,   555
    Ne fugiat ficto fassus ab ore pudor.
Quo magis, o iuvenes, deprendere parcite vestras :
    Peccent, peccantes verba dedisse putent.
Crescit amor prensis ; ubi par fortuna duorum est,
    In causa damni perstat uterque sui.   560
Fabula narratur toto notissima caelo,
    Mulciberis capti Marsque Venusque dolis.
Mars pater, insano Veneris turbatus amore,
    De duce terribili factus amator erat.
Nec Venus oranti (neque enim dea mollior ulla est) 565
    Rustica Gradivo difficilisque fuit.
A, quotiens lasciva pedes risisse mariti
    Dicitur, et duras igne vel arte manus.
Marte palam simul est Vulcanum imitata, decebat,
    Multaque cum forma gratia mixta fuit.   570
Sed bene concubitus primos celare solebant.
    Plena verecundi culpa pudoris erat.
Indicio Solis (quis Solem fallere possit ?)
    Cognita Vulcano coniugis acta suae.
Quam mala, Sol, exempla moves ! Pete munus ab ipsa
    Et tibi, si taceas, quod dare possit, habet.   576
Mulciber obscuros lectum circaque superque
    Disponit laqueos : lumina fallit opus.
Fingit iter Lemnum ; veniunt ad foedus amantes :
    Impliciti laqueis nudus uterque iacent.   580
Convocat ille deos ; praebent spectacula capti :
    Vix lacrimas Venerem continuisse putant.
Non vultus texisse suos, non denique possunt
    Partibus obscenis opposuisse manus.

556 ficto *Madvig* : victo *MSS.* : fassus *R* : laesus *MSS.* (*and
correction in R*).

has this fault done me harm: wiser he by whose complaisance other men come to his mistress. But ignorance were better: allow deceptions to be hid, lest the shame of confession fly from her dissembling countenance.[1] Wherefore all the more, O lovers, detecting your mistresses; let them err, and erring think they have deceived. Detection fans the flame of passion; where two have shared misfortune, each persists in the cause of his own fall. There is a story, most famous over all the world, of Mars and Venus caught by Mulciber's guile. Father Mars, plagued by frenzied love of Venus, from a terrible captain became a lover. Nor was Venus bashful (for no goddess has a tenderer heart), nor unresponsive to Gradivus' prayers. Ah, how oft is she said to have laughed, the wanton, at her husband's legs, and at his hands hardened by fire and workmanship! In Mars' presence she had but to imitate Vulcan, and it became her: and much charm was mingled with her beauty. But at first they concealed their meetings well, and full of shamefast modesty was their sinning. By the Sun's evidence (who could deceive the Sun?) the doings of his wife were made known to Vulcan. How bad an example, Sun, you are giving! Request a privilege from her: you too she will oblige, if you will but hold your tongue. Mulciber disposes hidden snares around and above the couch; the device baffles the eye. He feigns a voyage to Lemnos; the lovers meet as arranged; caught in the snares the two lie naked. He summons the gods; the captured pair afford a spectacle; scarce did Venus, they say, restrain her tears. They cannot cover their faces, nor even veil their lewd parts

---

[1] *i.e.* lest she no longer blush to confess, but do so shamelessly.

OVID

Hic aliquis ridens "in me, fortissime Mavors,   585
  Si tibi sunt oneri, vincula transfer ! " ait.
Vix precibus, Neptune, tuis captiva resolvit
  Corpora : Mars Threcen occupat, illa Paphum.
Hoc tibi perfecto, Vulcane, quod ante tegebant,
  Liberius faciunt, ut pudor omnis abest: 590
Saepe tamen demens stulte fecisse fateris,
  Teque ferunt artis paenituisse tuae.
Hoc vetiti vos este ; vetat deprensa Dione
  Insidias illas, quas tulit ipsa, dare.
Nec vos rivali laqueos disponite, nec vos   595
  Excipite arcana verba notata manu.
Ista viri captent, si iam captanda putabunt,
  Quos faciet iustos ignis et unda viros.
En, iterum testor : nihil hic, nisi lege remissum
  Luditur : in nostris instita nulla iocis.   600

Quis Cereris ritus ausit vulgare profanis,
  Magnaque Threïcia sacra reperta Samo?
Exigua est virtus praestare silentia rebus :
  At contra gravis est culpa tacenda loqui.
O bene, quod frustra captatis arbore pomis   605
  Garrulus in media Tantalus aret aqua!
Praecipue Cytherea iubet sua sacra taceri :
  Admoneo, veniat nequis ad illa loquax.
Condita si non sunt Veneris mysteria cistis,
  Nec cava vesanis ictibus aera sonant,   610
Attamen inter nos medio versantur in usu,
  Sed sic, inter nos ut latuisse velint.

589 perfecto *R* : profectum *Heinsius.*
593 vetiti vos esse (este *Ehwald*) *R* : vetui . . . vos ecce *MSS.*

---

[1] *i.e.* this is a pursuit for husbands, not for lovers. Fire and
water, as symbols of the home life, or, according to some, of
purification, were presented to the new bride by her husband

with their hands. Then someone laughs and says,
"Most valiant Mars, if they burden you, transfer
your chains to me!" Scarce at thy prayer, O
Neptune, does he set their bodies free: Mars
hurries to Thrace, and she to Paphos. After this
feat of thine, O Vulcan, what they before concealed
they do more freely, since all shame is absent: yet
often, mad fool, dost thou confess that thou didst
act stupidly, and they say thou hast repented of
thine own skill. Do you be warned of this; Dione's
detection warns you not to set those snares that she
endured. Devise no toils for your rival, nor lie in
wait for letters written in a secret hand. Them let
those men try to catch (if they think them worth
the catching) whom fire and water will make lawful
husbands.[1] Lo! again do I bear witness: there is
here no sport save what the law allows: no long
skirt figures in my mirth.

Who would dare to publish to the profane the
rites of Ceres, or the great ceremonies devised in
Samothrace?[2] Keeping silence is but a small virtue,
but to speak what should not be uttered is a heinous
crime. Well is it that garrulous Tantalus clutches
in vain at the apples on the tree, and parches in the
water's midst! Cytherea above all forbids her rites
to be told of; I give warning that no talkative person
approach them. Even if the mysteries of Venus are
not hidden in chests,[3] nor does the hollow bronze re-
sound to frenzied blows,[4] yet among us they are met
with in common use, but only so that among us they

on first entering her new home. The words therefore mean
"those properly married."

[2] The Eleusinian mysteries of Ceres and those at Samo-
thrace were famous in the ancient world.

[3] As were certain mysterious objects in the worship of Ceres.

[4] *i.e.* to warn the profane to hold aloof.

OVID

Ipsa Venus pubem, quotiens velamina ponit,
    Protegitur laeva semireducta manu.
In medio passimque coit pecus: hoc quoque viso   615
    Avertit vultus saepe puella suos.
Conveniunt thalami furtis et ianua nostris,
    Parsque sub iniecta veste pudenda latet :
Et si non tenebras, ad quiddam nubis opacae
    Quaerimus, atque aliquid luce patente minus.   620
Tunc quoque, cum solem nondum prohibebat et imbrem
    Tegula, sed quercus tecta cibumque dabat,
In nemore atque antris, non sub Iove, iuncta voluptas ;
    Tanta rudi populo cura pudoris erat.
At nunc nocturnis titulos inponimus actis,   625
    Atque emitur magno nil, nisi posse loqui !
Scilicet excuties omnes ubicumque puellas,
    Cuilibet ut dicas "haec quoque nostra fuit,"
Ne desint, quas tu digitis ostendere possis ?
    Ut quamque adtigeris, fabula turpis erit ?   630
Parva queror . fingunt quidam, quae vera negarent,
    Et nulli non se concubuisse ferunt.
Corpora si nequeunt, quae possunt, nomina tangunt,
    Famaque non tacto corpore crimen habet.
I nunc, claude fores, custos odiose puellae,   635
    Et centum duris postibus obde seras !
Quid tuti superest, cum nominis extat adulter,
    Et credi quod non contigit esse, cupit ?
Nos etiam veros parce profitemur amores,
    Tectaque sunt solida mystica furta fide.   640

---

[1] The Cnidian Aphrodite of Praxiteles has this attitude,
except that it is the right hand; it became a recognised

would fain be hidden. Venus herself,[1] as oft as she lays aside her robes, half stooping covers with her left hand her secret parts. Beasts unite everywhere and in public view; and oft at the sight a maiden turns her face aside. Chambers and a locked door beseem our secret doings, the parts of shame are hid 'neath a covering garment, and we seek, if not darkness, at least dim shadow and somewhat less than open daylight. In those days too when sun and rain were not yet kept out by a roof, but an oak gave food and covering alike, pleasure was shared in forest and cave, not in the open air: so strong was the thought of shame in a simple folk. But now we make our nightly exploits a title to renown, and purchase at a high price naught but the power to brag! What! shall you make trial of all women everywhere, so that you may say to no matter who, "She too was mine," and never lack girls to point to with your finger? As you touch upon each, shall there be a tale of shame? I lament but trifles[2]: some make up tales which if true they would deny, and say there is no woman with whom they have not lain. If bodies escape them, they take hold of names, and though the body escape, the name retains the charge. Go now, hateful guardian, bar the lady's door, and add a hundred bolts to the sturdy posts. What remains secure, when the dishonourer of her name abides, and would have what ne'er befell believed? As for me I recount even true amours but sparely, and a solid secrecy hides my dark intrigues.

type, as in the Venus de Medicis; cf. also Apuleius, *Met.* 2. 17, 10. 31.

  [2] *i.e.* in comparison with what follows.

Parcite praecipue vitia exprobrare puellis,
  Utile quae multis dissimulasse fuit.
Nec suus Andromedae color est obiectus ab illo,
  Mobilis in gemino cui pede pinna fuit.
Omnibus Andromache visa est spatiosior aequo :   645
  Unus, qui modicam diceret, Hector erat.
Quod male fers, adsuesce, feres bene ; multa vetustas
  Lenit : at incipiens omnia sentit amor.
Dum novus in viridi coalescit cortice ramus,
  Concutiat tenerum quaelibet aura, cadet :   650
Mox eadem ventis, spatio durata, resistet,
  Firmaque adoptivas arbor habebit opes.
Eximit ipsa dies omnes e corpore mendas,
  Quodque fuit vitium, desinit esse mora.
Ferre novae nares taurorum terga recusant :   655
  Adsiduo domitas tempore fallit odor.
Nominibus mollire licet mala : fusca vocetur,
  Nigrior Illyrica cui pice sanguis erit :
Si paeta est, Veneris similis : si flava, Minervae :
  Sit gracilis, macie quae male viva sua est ;   660
Dic habilem, quaecumque brevis, quae turgida, plenam,
  Et lateat vitium proximitate boni.

Nec quotus annus eat, nec quo sit nata, require,
  Consule, quae rigidus munera Censor habet :
Praecipue si flore caret, meliusque peractum   665
  Tempus, et albentes iam legit illa comas.
Utilis, o iuvenes, aut haec, aut serior aetas :
  Iste feret segetes, iste serendus ager.
Dum vires annique sinunt, tolerate labores :
  Iam veniet tacito curva senecta pede.   670

  659 paeta *MSS.* : crassa *Merkel* : flava *R* (*in marg.*) : rava
Heinsius : parva *R* : torva *Merkel*.

Particularly forbear to reproach a woman with her faults, faults which many have found it useful to feign otherwise. Her complexion was not made a reproach against Andromeda by him on whose either foot was a swift moving pinion. All thought Andromache too big: Hector alone deemed her of moderate size. Grow used to what you bear ill : you will bear it well; age eases many a smart, but love feels everything at first. While the graft is newly growing in the green bark, let any breeze but shake the weakling shoot, 'twill fall; soon, strengthened by time, this same tree will withstand the winds, and stoutly bear its adopted fruits. Time itself removes all faults from the body, and what was a blemish ceases to be a hindrance. Nostrils in youth cannot bear the hides of bulls; when years of habit have tamed them the odour is not noticed. With names [1] you can soften shortcomings; let her be called swarthy, whose blood is blacker than Illyrian pitch; if cross-eyed, she is like Venus : yellow-haired, like Minerva; call her slender whose thinness impairs her health; if short, call her trim; if stout, of full body; let its nearness to a virtue conceal a fault.

Ask not how old she be, nor under what consul she was born; these are the duties of the stern Censor : particularly so, if she is past her prime, if the flower of her age is over, and already she is plucking out the whitening hairs. Profitable, ye lovers, is that or even a later age; that field will bear, that field must be sown. Endure the toil, while your strength and years permit; soon bent old age will come with silent

[1] Well-known parallels to this advice are Lucretius, 4. 1160 sqq. ; Horace, *Sat*. 1. 3. 38 sqq.

Aut mare remigiis, aut vomere findite terras,
   Aut fera belligeras addite in arma manus,
Aut latus et vires operamque adferte puellis:
   Hoc quoque militia est, hoc quoque quaerit opes.
Adde, quod est illis operum prudentia maior,   675
   Solus et artifices qui facit, usus adest:
Illae munditiis annorum damna rependunt,
   Et faciunt cura, ne videantur anus.
Utque velis, venerem iungunt per mille figuras:
   Invenit plures nulla tabella modos.   680
Illis sentitur non inritata voluptas:
   Quod iuvet, ex aequo femina virque ferant.
Odi concubitus, qui non utrumque resolvunt;
   Hoc est, cur pueri tangar amore minus.
Odi quae praebet, quia sit praebere necesse,   685
   Siccaque de lana cogitat ipsa sua.
Quae datur officio, non est mihi grata voluptas:
   Officium faciat nulla puella mihi.
Me voces audire iuvat sua gaudia fassas:
   Utque morer memet sustineamque roget.   690
Aspiciam dominae victos amentis ocellos:
   Langueat, et tangi se vetet illa diu.
Haec bona non primae tribuit natura iuventae,
   Quae cito post septem lustra venire solent.
Qui properant, nova musta bibant: mihi fundat avitum
   Consulibus priscis condita testa merum.   696
Nec platanus, nisi sera, potest obsistere Phoebo,
   Et laedunt nudos prata novella pedes.
Scilicet Hermionen Helenae praeponere posses,
   Et melior Gorge, quam sua mater, erat?   700
At venerem quicumque voles adtingere seram,
   Si modo duraris, praemia digna feres.

---

[1] Daughter of Althaea and Oeneus, king of Aetolia.

foot. Cleave the sea with oars, or the earth with the plough, or exert your warlike hands in savage battle, or bring to women's service your bodily strength and vigour and diligence: this too is warfare, this too calls for your powers. Add this, that they have greater acquaintance with their business, and they have experience, which alone gives skill, upon their side: they make good the waste of years by elegance, and by their pains contrive not to seem old. According to your taste they will embrace you in a thousand ways; no picture could devise more modes than they. They need no spur to enjoy their pleasure: let both man and woman feel what delights them equally. I hate embraces which leave not each outworn; that is why a boy's love appeals to me but little. I hate her who gives because she must, and who, herself unmoved, is thinking of her wool. Pleasure given as a duty has no charms for me; for me let no woman be dutiful. I like to hear the words that confess rapture, that beg me hold back and stay awhile. May I see my mistress in frenzy, with eyes that confess defeat; may she be languid, and long refuse to be embraced. These joys, which come quickly after seven lustres, nature has not granted to early youth. Let those who hasten drink new liquor; for me let a jar put down under ancient consuls pour forth its ancestral wine. Neither can the plane tree, save it be mature, resist the sun, and new-sprung meads injure naked feet. What? would you be able to prefer Hermione to Helen, and was Gorge[1] fairer than her mother? whoever you are that wish to approach charms that are mature, if you will play your part, you will win a fitting reward.

Conscius, ecce, duos accepit lectus amantes :
    Ad thalami clausas, Musa, resiste fores.
Sponte sua sine te celeberrima verba loquentur,   705
    Nec manus in lecto laeva iacebit iners.
Invenient digiti, quod agant in partibus illis,
    In quibus occulte spicula figit Amor.
Fecit in Andromache prius hoc fortissimus Hector,
    Nec solum bellis utilis ille fuit.   710
Fecit et in capta Lyrneside magnus Achilles,
    Cum premeret mollem lassus ab hoste torum.
Illis te manibus tangi, Briseï, sinebas,
    Imbutae Phrygia quae nece semper erant.
An fuit hoc ipsum, quod te, lasciva, iuvaret,   715
    Ad tua victrices membra venire manus?
Crede mihi, non est veneris properanda voluptas,
    Sed sensim tarda prolicienda mora.
Cum loca reppereris, quae tangi femina gaudet,
    Non obstet, tangas quo minus illa, pudor.   720
Aspicies oculos tremulo fulgore micantes,
    Ut sol a liquida saepe refulget aqua.
Accedent questus, accedet amabile murmur,
    Et dulces gemitus aptaque verba ioco.
Sed neque tu dominam velis maioribus usus   725
    Desine, nec cursus anteat illa tuos ;
Ad metam properate simul : tum plena voluptas,
    Cum pariter victi femina virque iacent.
Hic tibi versandus tenor est, cum libera dantur
    Otia, furtivum nec timor urget opus.   730
Cum mora non tuta est, totis incumbere remis
    Utile, et admisso subdere calcar equo.

Finis adest operi : palmam date, grata iuventus,
    Sertaque odoratae myrtea ferte comae.
Quantus apud Danaos Podalirius arte medendi,   735
    Aeacides dextra, pectore Nestor erat,

Lo! the conscious couch has received two lovers: tarry, O Muse, at the closed door of their chamber. Of their own accord, without your aid, they will utter eloquent speech, nor will the left hand lie idle on the bed. Their fingers will find what to do in those parts where Love plies his weapons unperceived. Most valiant Hector of old did thus with Andromache, nor in war alone did he avail. Thus did the great Achilles with the Lyrnesian captive, when weary from the foe he burdened the soft couch. By those hands didst thou suffer thyself to be touched, Briseis, that were ever imbued in Phrygian blood; was it this very thing, wanton one, that delighted thee, that a conqueror's hands should caress thy limbs? Believe me, love's bliss must not be hastened, but gradually lured on by slow delay. When you have found the place where a woman loves to be touched, let not shame prevent you from touching it. You will see her eyes shooting tremulous gleams, as the sun often glitters in clear water. Then she will complain, then she will lovingly murmur, and sweetly sigh, and utter words that fit the sport. But neither do you, spreading too full sail, leave your mistress behind, nor let her outstrip your speed; haste side by side to the goal: then is pleasure full, when man and woman lie vanquished both together. This is the tenor you must keep, when dallying is free, and no fear urges on the secret work. When delay is dangerous, it is best to press on with all oars, and to spur the galloping horse.

My task is finished: give me the palm, ye grateful lovers, and bring wreaths of myrtle for my scented locks. As great as was Podalirius among the Greeks in the art of healing, or Aeacides in might of hand,

Quantus erat Calchas extis, Telamonius armis,
    Automedon curru, tantus amator ego.
Me vatem celebrate, viri, mihi dicite laudes,
    Cantetur toto nomen in orbe meum.   740
Arma dedi vobis : dederat Vulcanus Achilli ;
    Vincite muneribus, vicit ut ille, datis.
Sed quicumque meo superarit Amazona ferro,
    Inscribat spoliis " Naso magister erat."

Ecce, rogant tenerae, sibi dem praecepta, puellae :   745
    Vos eritis chartae proxima cura meae !

or Nestor in understanding, as great as was Calchas at the sacrifice, or Telamon's son in arms, or Automedon in the chariot, so great a lover am I. Celebrate me, the prophet, O ye men; sing my praises, let my name be sung in all the world. I have given you armour; Vulcan gave armour to Achilles; do ye conquer, as he conquered, by virtue of the gift. But whosoever shall by my steel lay low the Amazon, let him inscribe upon his spoils "NASO WAS MY MASTER."

Lo! the young women are begging me to give them counsel: you will be my poetry's next care.

LIBER TERTIUS

Arma dedi Danais in Amazonas ; arma supersunt,
  Quae tibi dem et turmae, Penthesilea, tuae.
Ite in bella pares ; vincant, quibus alma Dione
  Faverit et toto qui volat orbe puer.
Non erat armatis aequum concurrere nudas ;   5
  Sic etiam vobis vincere turpe, viri.
Dixerit e multis aliquis " quid virus in angues
  Adicis, et rabidae tradis ovile lupae ? "
Parcite paucarum diffundere crimen in omnes ;
  Spectetur meritis quaeque puella suis.   10
Si minor Atrides Helenen, Helenesque sororem
  Quo premat Atrides crimine maior habet,
Si scelere Oeclides Talaioniae Eriphylae
  Vivus et in vivis ad Styga venit equis,
Est pia Penelope lustris errante duobus   15
  Et totidem lustris bella gerente viro.
Respice Phylaciden et quae comes isse marito
  Fertur et ante annos occubuisse suos.
Fata Pheretiadae coniunx Pagasaea redemit :
  Proque viro est uxor funere lata viri.   20
" Accipe me, Capaneu ! cineres miscebimus " inquit
  Iphias, in medios desiluitque rogos.
Ipsa quoque et cultu est et nomine femina Virtus :
  Non mirum, populo si placet illa suo.

---

[1] Eriphyle was bribed by the gift of a necklace to send her
husband Amphiaraus to the war against Thebes, in which he
was swallowed up alive.

[2] Protesilaus and Laodamia.

[3] Alcestis and Admetus.

BOOK III

I HAVE armed the Danai against the Amazons; there remain arms which I must give to thee, Penthesilea, and to thy troop. Go into battle on equal terms; let those conquer whom kind Dione favours, and the boy who flies o'er all the world. It were not just that defenceless maids should fight with armed men; such a victory, O men, would be shameful for you also. Some one or other may say to me, "Why do you add gall to serpents, and betray the sheepfold to the mad she-wolf?" Forbear to spread over all the reproach of a few; let each woman be judged on her own merits. If the younger son of Atreus has a charge to bring against Helen, and the elder against Helen's sister, if by the crime of Talaonian Eriphyle Oeclides went to Styx alive and drawn by living steeds,[1] yet Penelope is chaste, though for ten years her lord was wandering, and fighting for as many years. Consider Phylacides and her who is said to have accompanied her spouse, and to have died before her time.[2] The Pagasaean consort of Pheretiades redeemed his fate, and in her husband's funeral his wife was borne in her husband's stead.[3] "Take me, Capaneus; we will mingle our ashes," cried the daughter of Iphis,[4] and leapt into the middle of the pyre. Virtue too herself is by dress[5] and name a woman; no wonder if she please her own

---

[4] Evadne.

[5] Virtue is commonly represented as modestly dressed in white, as in Xenophon, *Mem.* 2. 1. 22.

Nec tamen hae mentes nostra poscuntur ab arte :   25
  Conveniunt cumbae vela minora meae.
Nil nisi lascivi per me discuntur amores ;
  Femina praecipiam quo sit amanda modo.
Femina nec flammas nec saevos excutit arcus ;
  Parcius haec video tela nocere viris.   30
Saepe viri fallunt : tenerae non saepe puellae,
  Paucaque, si quaeras, crimina fraudis habent.
Phasida iam matrem fallax dimisit Iaso :
  Venit in Aesonios altera nupta sinus.
Quantum in te, Theseu, volucres Ariadna marinas   35
  Pavit, in ignoto sola relicta loco !
Quaere, novem cur una viae dicantur, et audi
  Depositis silvas Phyllida flesse comis.
Et famam pietatis habet, tamen hospes et ensem
  Praebuit et causam mortis, Elissa, tuae.   40
Quid vos perdiderit, dicam ? nescistis amare :
  Defuit ars vobis ; arte perennat amor.
Nunc quoque nescirent : sed me Cytherea docere
  Iussit, et ante oculos constitit ipsa meos.
Tum mihi " Quid miserae " dixit " meruere puellae ?   45
  Traditur armatis vulgus inerme viris.
Illos artifices gemini fecere libelli :
  Haec quoque pars monitis erudienda tuis.
Probra Therapnaeae qui dixerat ante maritae,
  Mox cecinit laudes prosperiore lyra.   50
Si bene te novi (cultas ne laede puellas !)
  Gratia, dum vives, ista petenda tibi est."

33 Phasida iam *edd*.: Phasideam *MSS*.
37 una viae *Heinsius*: una vice *R* : isse vias dicatur *MSS*.

---

¹ Jason deserted Medea for Creusa.

folk. Yet such minds are not demanded by my art,
smaller sails become my bark. Naught save wanton
loves are learnt through me; I will teach in what
way a woman is to be loved. A woman wields
neither flames nor savage bows: seldom do I see
these weapons hurting men. Often do men deceive,
tender maids not often; should you inquire, they
are rarely charged with deceit. Perfidious Jason
sent away the Phasian, already a mother; another
bride came to the bosom of Aeson's son.[1] So far as
concerned thee, O Theseus, Ariadne fell a prey to
the sea-birds, left desolate in an unknown spot! Ask
why one way is called Nine Ways,[2] and hear how
the woods shed their leaves and wailed for Phyllis.
Famed too is he [3] for piety, yet thy guest, Elissa, gave
thee both a sword and the cause of thy destruction.
Shall I tell what led you all to ruin? ye knew not
how to love; it was skill ye lacked; skill makes love
unending. Would that now too they knew not!
but Cytherea bade me teach them, and stood her-
self before my eyes. Then she said, "What have
poor women deserved? their defenceless throng is
surrendered to armed men. These have two poems
taught the craft: those too must be instructed by
your counsels. He who first abused the Therapnean
consort soon sang her praises on a more prosperous
lyre; [4] if I know you well (harm not the cultured fair!),
so long as you live you must seek their favour." She

---

[2] Phyllis ran nine times to the sea when Demophoon did
not come to her. Hence the name of the place Ἐννέα ὁδοί,
afterwards Amphipolis.
[3] *i.e.* Aeneas.
[4] Stesichorus is referred to: Therapnae was the birthplace
of Helen.

OVID

Dixit, et e myrto (myrto nam vincta capillos
    Constiterat) folium granaque pauca dedit;
Sensimus acceptis numen quoque : purior aether   55
    Fulsit, et e toto pectore cessit onus.
Dum facit ingenium, petite hinc praecepta, puellae,
    Quas pudor et leges et sua iura sinunt.
Venturae memores iam nunc estote senectae :
    Sic nullum vobis tempus abibit iners.   60
Dum licet, et vernos etiamnum educitis annos,
    Ludite : eunt anni more fluentis aquae ;
Nec quae praeteriit, iterum revocabitur unda,
    Nec quae praeteriit, hora redire potest.
Utendum est aetate : cito pede labitur aetas,   65
    Nec bona tam sequitur, quam bona prima fuit.
Hos ego, qui canent, frutices violaria vidi :
    Hac mihi de spina grata corona data est.
Tempus erit, quo tu, quae nunc excludis amantes,
    Frigida deserta nocte iacebis anus,   70
Nec tua frangetur nocturna ianua rixa,
    Sparsa nec invenies limina mane rosa.
Quam cito (me miserum !) laxantur corpora rugis,
    Et perit in nitido qui fuit ore color.
Quasque fuisse tibi canas a virgine iuras,   75
    Spargentur subito per caput omne comae.
Anguibus exuitur tenui cum pelle vetustas,
    Nec faciunt cervos cornua iacta senes :
Nostra sine auxilio fugiunt bona ; carpite florem,
    Qui, nisi carptus erit, turpiter ipse cadet.   80
Adde, quod et partus faciunt breviora iuventae
    Tempora : continua messe senescit ager.

61 vernos *Heinsius* : veros *R* : educitis *Housman* : editis *MSS.*
(*with* etiamnunc).

---

[1] The phrase seems to imply that only women of a certain

spoke, and from her myrtle (for she stood with myrtle binding her hair) she gave me a leaf and a few berries; as I took them I felt too their power divine, heaven shone with purer light, and my heart was relieved of all its burden.   While she inspires me, seek precepts here, O women, whom propriety and the laws and your own rights permit.[1] Now already be mindful of the old age which is to come; thus no hour will slip wasted from you. While you can, and still are in your spring-time, have your sport; for the years pass like flowing water; the wave that has gone by cannot be called back, the hour that has gone by cannot return.   You must employ your time: time glides on with speedy foot, nor is that which follows so good as that which went before.   These plants, now withering, I saw as violet-beds; from this thorn was a pleasing garland given me.   That day will come when you, who now shut out your lovers, will lie, a cold and lonely old woman, through the night; nor will your door be broken in a nightly brawl, nor will you find your threshold strewn with roses in the morning.   How quickly, ah, me! is the body furrowed by wrinkles, and the colour fled that once was in that lovely face! And the white hairs that you swear have been there since maidenhood will suddenly be scattered over all your head.   Serpents put off their age with their frail skins, nor are stags made old by casting their horns: our charms flee without our aid; pluck the flower, which save it be plucked will basely wither.   Besides, childbirth shortens the period of youth: a field grows old by continual harvesting.   Latmian [2] Endy-

class are meant, *i.e.* the demi-monde, to whom the law allowed certain recognised privileges.

[2] Latmus was a mountain in Caria.

OVID

Latmius Endymion non est tibi, Luna, rubori,
  Nec Cephalus roseae praeda pudenda deae.
Ut Veneri, quem luget adhuc, donetur Adonis :   85
  Unde habet Aenean Harmoniamque suos ?
Ite per exemplum, genus o mortale, dearum,
  Gaudia nec cupidis vestra negate viris.
Ut iam decipiant, quid perditis ? omnia constant ;
  Mille licet sumant, deperit inde nihil.   90
Conteritur ferrum, silices tenuantur ab usu :
  Sufficit et damni pars caret illa metu.
Quis vetet adposito lumen de lumine sumi ?
  Quisve cavo vastas in mare servet aquas ?
Et tamen ulla viro mulier " non expedit " inquit ?   95
  Quid, nisi quam sumes, dic mihi, perdis aquam ?
Nec vos prostituit mea vox, sed vana timere
  Damna vetat : damnis munera vestra carent.
Sed me flaminibus venti maioris iturum,
  Dum sumus in portu, provehat aura levis.   100

Ordior a cultu ; cultis bene Liber ab uvis
  Provenit, et culto stat seges alta solo.
Forma dei munus : forma quota quaeque superbit ?
  Pars vestrum tali munere magna caret.
Cura dabit faciem ; facies neglecta peribit,   105
  Idaliae similis sit licet illa deae.
Corpora si veteres non sic coluere puellae,
  Nec veteres cultos sic habuere viros ;
Si fuit Andromache tunicas induta valentes,
  Quid mirum ? duri militis uxor erat.   110
Scilicet Aiaci coniunx ornata venires,
  Cui tegumen septem terga fuere boum ?

---

[1] Aurora, by whom he was the father of Tithonus.
[2] Anchises was the father of Aeneas : Mars, of Harmonia.

mion brings no blush to thee, O Moon, nor is Cepha-
lus a prize that shames the roseate goddess [1]; though
Adonis, whom she mourns, be granted to Venus,
whence has she her Aeneas and Harmonia? [2] Study,
ye mortal folk, the examples of the goddesses, nor
deny your joys to hungry lovers. Though they at
last deceive you, what do you lose? those joys abide;
though they take a thousand pleasures, naught is lost
therefrom. Iron is worn away, and flints are dimi-
nished by use; that part endures, and has no fear of
loss. What forbids to take light from a light that is
set before you, or who would guard vast waters upon
the cavernous deep? And yet does any woman say
to a man, "It is not expedient"? [3] tell me, what are
you doing, save wasting the water that you will
draw? Nor do my words make you vile, but forbid
you to fear unreal loss; there is no loss in your
giving. But though the blasts of a stronger wind
will soon impel me, while I am still in harbour, let
a light breeze bear me on.

I begin with the body's care: from grapes well
cared for Liber gives good vintage, on well-cared-for
soil the crops stand high. Beauty is heaven's gift:
how few can boast of beauty! A great part of you
lack a gift so precious. Care will give good looks:
looks neglected go to waste though they resemble
the Idalian goddess. If women of old did not so
cultivate their bodies, the women of old had not
lovers so cultivated; if Andromache was clad in a
stout tunic, what wonder? she was a hardy soldier's
wife. Were you his spouse, forsooth, would you come
dressed up to Ajax, whose protection was seven oxen's

[3] For a woman to give herself to a man is no more
wasteful than taking a light from a torch, or using water
when it is needed. In fact, not to do so is itself a waste.

OVID

Simplicitas rudis ante fuit: nunc aurea Roma est,
  Et domiti magnas possidet orbis opes.
Aspice quae nunc sunt Capitolia, quaeque fuerunt: 115
  Alterius dices illa fuisse Iovis.
Curia concilio nunc est dignissima tanto:
  De stipula Tatio regna tenente fuit.
Quae nunc sub Phoebo ducibusque Palatia fulgent,
  Quid nisi araturis pascua bubus erant? 120
Prisca iuvent alios: ego me nunc denique natum
  Gratulor: haec aetas moribus apta meis.
Non quia nunc terrae lentum subducitur aurum,
  Lectaque diverso littore concha venit:
Nec quia decrescunt effosso marmore montes, 125
  Nec quia caeruleae mole fugantur aquae:
Sed quia cultus adest, nec nostros mansit in annos
  Rusticitas, priscis illa superstes avis.

Vos quoque non caris aures onerate lapillis,
  Quos legit in viridi decolor Indus aqua, 130
Nec prodite graves insuto vestibus auro,
  Per quas nos petitis, saepe fugatis, opes.
Munditiis capimur: non sint sine lege capilli:
  Admotae formam dantque negantque manus.
Nec genus ornatus unum est: quod quamque decebit
  Elegat, et speculum consulat ante suum. 136
Longa probat facies capitis discrimina puri:
  Sic erat ornatis Laodamia comis.
Exiguum summa nodum sibi fronte relinqui,
  Ut pateant aures, ora rotunda volunt. 140

---

[1] The Temple of Apollo on the Palatine and the palace of
Augustus himself there are alluded to.
[2] It is not luxury or the rage for building, both highly

hides? There was rude simplicity of old, but now golden Rome possesses the vast wealth of the conquered world. See what the Capitol is now, and what it was : you would say they belonged to different Jupiters. The senate-house now is most worthy of so august a gathering : when Tatius held the rule it was made of wattles. The Palatine [1] whereon now Phoebus and our chieftains are set in splendour, what was it save the pasture of oxen destined to the plough? Let ancient times delight other folk : I congratulate myself that I was not born till now ; this age fits my nature well. Not because now stubborn gold is drawn from out the earth, and shells come gathered from divers shores, nor because mountains diminish as the marble is dug from them, nor because masonry puts to flight the dark-blue waters; but because culture [2] is with us, and rusticity, which survived until our grandsires, has not lasted to our days.

You too burden not your ears with precious stones, which the discoloured Indian gathers from the green water, and come not forth weighed down with the gold sewn upon your garments; the wealth wherewith you seek us ofttimes repels. 'Tis with elegance we are caught: let not your locks be lawless: a touch of the hand can give or deny beauty. Nor is there but one form of adornment : let each choose what becomes her, and take counsel before her own mirror. An oval face prefers a parting upon the head left unadorned: the tresses of Laodamia were so arranged. Round faces would fain have a small knot left on top of the head, so that the ears show.

characteristic of the time, that Ovid admires, but "culture," *i.e.* refinement, manners, cultivated society.

Alterius crines umero iactentur utroque :
    Talis es adsumpta, Phoebe canore, lyra.
Altera succinctae religetur more Dianae,
    Ut solet, attonitas cum petit illa feras.
Huic decet inflatos laxe iacuisse capillos :   145
    Illa sit adstrictis impedienda comis ;
Hanc placet ornari testudine Cyllenea :
    Sustineat similes fluctibus illa sinus.
Sed neque ramosa numerabis in ilice glandes,
    Nec quot apes Hyblae, nec quot in Alpe ferae, 150
Nec mihi tot positus numero conprendere fas est :
    Adicit ornatus proxima quaeque dies.
Et neglecta decet multas coma ; saepe iacere
    Hesternam credas ; illa repexa modo est.
Ars casu similis ; sic capta vidit ut urbe   155
    Alcides Iolen, " hanc ego " dixit "amo."
Talem te Bacchus Satyris clamantibus euhoe
    Sustulit in currus, Gnosi relicta, suos.
O quantum indulget vestro natura decori,
    Quarum sunt multis damna pianda modis ! 160
Nos male detegimur, raptique aetate capilli,
    Ut Borea frondes excutiente, cadunt.
Femina canitiem Germanis inficit herbis,
    Et melior vero quaeritur arte color :
Femina procedit densissima crinibus emptis,   165
    Proque suis alios efficit aere suos.
Nec rubor est emisse ; palam venire videmus
    Herculis ante oculos virgineumque chorum.

---

[1] It was discovered by Mercury, who was born on Mt. Cyllene
in Arcadia, and made into a lyre.
   [2] *i.e.* herbs brought from Germany, where they were used to
make a sort of soap or dye, which dyed the hair a blonde colour ;
cf. Mart. 8. 83. 20, "et mutat Latias spuma Batava comas."

Let one girl's locks hang down on either shoulder;
thus art thou, tuneful Phoebus, when thou hast
taken up thy lyre. Let another braid her hair like
girt-up Dian, as she is wont to be when she hunts
the frightened beasts. This one it beseems to let
her waving locks lie loose; let that one have her
tight-drawn tresses close confined: this one is
pleased by the adornment of the Cyllenian [1] tortoise-
shell; let that one bear folds that resemble waves.
But you will not count the acorns on the oak's
numerous boughs, nor how many bees there are in
Hybla, nor wild beasts upon the Alps; nor can I
enumerate all the fashions that there are: each day
adds more adornments. Even neglected hair is
becoming to many; often you would think it lay
loose from yesterday; this very moment it has been
combed afresh. Art counterfeits chance; when
Alcides beheld Iole thus in the captured city, he
said, "This is the woman I love." Thus wert thou,
deserted Gnosian, when Bacchus lifted thee to his
car, and the Satyrs cried "Hurrah!" Ah, how kind
is nature to your beauty, you whose defects may be
made good in so many ways! We are shamefully
left bare and, carried away by time, our hairs fall, as
when Boreas shakes down the leaves. A woman
stains her whitening locks with German juices,[2] and
by skill seeks a hue better than the real; a woman
walks 'neath a burden of purchased tresses, and
money buys new locks for old. Nor does she blush
to buy: publicly do we see them sold before the
eyes of Hercules and the Virgin band.[3] What shall

[3] Temple of Hercules and the Muses in the Circus, built
by Fulvius Nobilior 189, renewed by Marcius Philippus, the
step-father of Octavia.

Quid de veste loquar ?   Nec nunc segmenta requiro
  Nec quae de Tyrio murice lana rubes.   170
Cum tot prodierint pretio leviore colores,
  Quis furor est census corpore ferre suos !
Aëris, ecce, color, tum cum sine nubibus aër,
  Nec tepidus pluvias concitat auster aquas :
Ecce, tibi similis, quae quondam Phrixon et Hellen 175
  Diceris Inois eripuisse dolis ;
Hic undas imitatur, habet quoque nomen ab undis :
  Crediderim nymphas hac ego veste tegi.
Ille crocum simulat : croceo velatur amictu,
  Roscida luciferos cum dea iungit equos :   180
Hic Paphias myrtos, hic purpureas amethystos,
  Albentesve rosas, Threïciamve gruem ;
Nec glandes, Amarylli, tuae, nec amygdala desunt ;
  Et sua velleribus nomina cera dedit.
Quot nova terra parit flores, cum vere tepenti 185
  Vitis agit gemmas pigraque fugit hiemps,
Lana tot aut plures sucos bibit ; elige certos :
  Nam non conveniens omnibus omnis erit.
Pulla decent niveas : Briseïda pulla decebant :
  Cum rapta est, pulla tum quoque veste fuit. 190
Alba decent fuscas : albis, Cepheï, placebas :
  Sic tibi vestitae pressa Seriphos erat.

Quam paene admonui, ne trux caper iret in alas,
  Neve forent duris aspera crura pilis !

---

  [1] Bands of stuff heavily embroidered or inlaid with gold, and sewn on the dresses.
  [2] The colours seem to be : 173 sky-blue ; 175 golden, the colour of the Ram with the Golden Fleece (though Ovid speaks of it in the feminine gender) ; 177 either green-grey ("glaucus") or water-blue ("cumatilis") ; 179 saffron ; 181 green, amethyst, white, grey ; 183 chestnut-brown, pink (?), yellow like wax ("cerina" means a garment of this colour).

I say of clothes? flounces,[1] I need you not, nor the wool that blushes with Tyrian dye. When so many cheaper colours walk abroad, what madness to carry whole incomes on one's body! Lo![2] there is the colour of the sky, when the sky is cloudless, and warm Auster brings no rainy showers; lo, here is one like thee, who once art said to have rescued Phrixus and Helle from Ino's wiles; this colour imitates water, and from water has its name: in this raiment I could think the Nymphs were clad. That colour counterfeits saffron: in saffron robe is the dewy goddess veiled, when she yokes her light-bringing steeds; this has the hue of Paphian myrtle, that, of purple amethysts, these of white roses and of Thracian cranes; nor, Amaryllis, are thy chestnuts lacking, nor yet almonds; and wax has given to fleeces its own name. As many as are the flowers that the new-born earth produces, when the vine in warm spring urges forth its buds, and sluggish winter is fled, so many dyes and more does the wool drink up; choose those that are sure to please, for not every one suits every woman. Snow-white skins like dark grey colours, dark grey became Briseis; even when she was carried off was her robe dark grey. Those dark of hue like white; in white didst thou please, Cepheis:[3] for thee thus clad was Seriphos oppressed.

How nearly did I warn you that no rude goat find his way beneath your arms, and that your legs be not rough with bristling hairs! But I am not

For Amaryllis cf. Bk. ii. 1. 267, where he quotes from Virgil, Ecl. 2. 52.

[3] Andromeda, because of whose beauty the island of Seriphos was oppressed through the jealousy of the gods.

Sed non Caucasea doceo de rupe puellas,   195
   Quaeque bibant undas, Myse Caice, tuas.
Quid si praecipiam ne fuscet inertia dentes,
   Oraque suscepta mane laventur aqua?
Scitis et inducta candorem quaerere creta :
   Sanguine quae vero non rubet, arte rubet.   200
Arte supercilii confinia nuda repletis,
   Parvaque sinceras velat aluta genas.
Nec pudor est oculos tenui signare favilla,
   Vel prope te nato, lucide Cydne, croco.
Est mihi, quo dixi vestrae medicamina formae,   205
   Parvus, sed cura grande, libellus, opus ;
Hinc quoque praesidium laesae petitote figurae ;
   Non est pro vestris ars mea rebus iners.
Non tamen expositas mensa deprendat amator
   Pyxidas : ars faciem dissimulata iuvat.   210
Quem non offendat toto faex inlita vultu,
   Cum fluit in tepidos pondere lapsa sinus?
Oesypa quid redolent? quamvis mittatur Athenis
   Demptus ab inmundo vellere sucus ovis.
Nec coram mixtas cervae sumpsisse medullas,   215
   Nec coram dentes defricuisse probem ;
Ista dabunt formam, sed erunt deformia visu :
   Multaque, dum fiunt, turpia, facta placent ;
Quae nunc nomen habent operosi signa Myronis
   Pondus iners quondam duraque massa fuit ;   220

---

[1] The reading "creta" is much to be preferred to "cera,"
wax. It is obviously powder he is thinking of. The next line
clearly refers to rouge.

[2] Some ingredients are mentioned by Pliny, *e.g.* bears' fat
and lamp-black (28. 46), ants' eggs and squashed flies (30. 46);
Tertullian mentions soot (*De Cult. Fem.* 1. 2, 2. 5), also
Petronius 126.

[3] For the eyebrows cf. Juv. 2. 93, where soot is spoken of ;

teaching girls from the cliffs of Caucasus, nor such as drink thy waters, Mysian Caicus. Why should I enjoin that no laziness leave the teeth to darken, and that hands should be washed with water in the morning? You know, too, how to gain a bright hue by applying powder:[1] art gives complexion if real blood gives it not. By art[2] you fill up the bare confines of the eyebrow, and a tiny patch veils cheeks without a blemish.[3] Nor are you ashamed to mark your eyes with powdery ash, or with saffron born near thee, O shining Cydnus.[4] I have a book,[5] a small work, but great in the pains it cost me, wherein I have told of the paints that will make you beautiful; from it too seek means to rescue impaired beauty: my art is no sluggard in your behalf. Yet let no lover find the boxes set out upon the table; your looks are aided by dissembled art. Who would not be offended by paint smeared over all the face, when by its weight it glides and falls into your warm bosom? How strong is the smell of oil of wool, though from Athens be sent the juices drawn from a sheep's unwashed fleece![6] Nor should I approve your openly taking the mixed marrow of a hind, or cleaning your teeth for all to see; such things will give beauty, but they will be unseemly to look on: many things, ugly in the doing, please when done; the statues of industrious Myron that now are famous were once a hard mass and lifeless weight; gold

"aluta," skin or leather treated with alum is usually called "splenium."

[4] A river in Cilicia.

[5] *De Medicamine Faciei Femineae.*

[6] "Oesypum" was a cosmetic prepared from the sweat and dirt in the wool of a sheep; the best is said to have come from Attica.

Anulus ut fiat, primo conliditur aurum ;
 Quas geritis vestis, sordida lana fuit ;
Cum fieret, lapis asper erat : nunc, nobile signum,
 Nuda Venus madidas exprimit imbre comas.
Tu quoque dum coleris, nos te dormire putemus ;   225
 Aptius a summa conspiciere manu.
Cur mihi nota tuo causa est candoris in ore ?
 Claude forem thalami ! quid rude prodis opus ?
Multa viros nescire decet ; pars maxima rerum
 Offendat, si non interiora tegas.   230
Aurea quae splendent ornato signa theatro,
 Inspice, quam tenuis bractea ligna tegat :
Sed neque ad illa licet populo, nisi facta, venire,
 Nec nisi summotis forma paranda viris.
At non pectendos coram praebere capillos,   235
 Ut iaceant fusi per tua terga, veto.
Illo praecipue ne sis morosa caveto
 Tempore, nec lapsas saepe resolve comas.
Tuta sit ornatrix ; odi, quae sauciat ora
 Unguibus et rapta brachia figit acu.   240
Devovet ut tangit dominae caput illa, simulque
 Plorat in invisas sanguinolenta comas.
Quae male crinita est, custodem in limine ponat,
 Orneturve Bonae semper in aede deae.
Dictus eram subito cuidam venisse puellae :   245
 Turbida perversas induit illa comas.
Hostibus eveniat tam foedi causa pudoris,
 Inque nurus Parthas dedecus illud eat.
Turpe pecus mutilum, turpis sine gramine campus,
 Et sine fronde frutex, et sine crine caput.   250

     228 prodis *some MSS.* : cogis *R.*
     231 splendent *Burmann* : pendent *MSS.*

---

 [1] The well-known type of Venus Anadyomene, *i.e.* "rising
from the sea."

is first crushed that it may become a ring; the
gowns you wear were once filthy wool; your jewel
was rough when being shaped: now it is a noble
gem, whereon naked Venus is wringing her spray-
drenched tresses.[1] So while you are at your toilet
let us think that you are asleep; it is more fitting
you should be seen when the last touch has been
given. Why must I know the cause of the white-
ness of your cheek? Shut your chamber door: why
show the unfinished work? There is much that it
befits men not to know; most of your doings would
offend, did you not hide them within. Those images
that shine all golden in the decorated theatre, see
how thin the gold leaf that conceals the wood; but
neither may the people come nigh them, till complete,
nor save when men are absent should beauty be con-
trived. Yet I forbid you not to let your locks be
combed before them, so that they lie rippling adown
your back: at that time, especially, beware of being
ill-tempered, nor often unbind your fallen tresses.
Let the tiring-woman be safe; I hate her who tears
with her nails her handmaid's face, or seizing a
needle stabs her arms. That maid curses, as she
touches it, her mistress' head, and weeps the while,
bloodstained, over the hated locks. Let her who
has poor hair set a guard at her door, or always be
tired in the temple of the Good Goddess.[2] My
arrival was suddenly announced to a woman once;
in confusion she put her hair on all awry. Let my
foes endure a cause of shame so fearful! upon
Parthian women let that dishonour fall! Ugly is
a bull without horns; ugly is a field without grass,
a plant without leaves, or a head without hair.

[2] *i.e.* where no men may come.

Non mihi venistis, Semele Ledeve, docendae,
    Perque fretum falso, Sidoni, vecta bove,
Aut Helene, quam non stulte, Menelaë, reposcis,
    Tu quoque non stulte, Troice raptor, habes.
Turba docenda venit, pulchrae turpesque puellae :   255
    Pluraque sunt semper deteriora bonis.
Formosae non artis opem praeceptaque quaerunt :
    Est illis sua dos, forma sine arte potens ;
Cum mare compositum est, securus navita cessat :
    Cum tumet, auxiliis adsidet ille suis.   260
Rara tamen mendo facies caret : occule mendas,
    Quaque potes vitium corporis abde tui.
Si brevis es, sedeas, ne stans videare sedere :
    Inque tuo iaceas quantulacumque toro ;
Hic quoque, ne possit fieri mensura cubantis,   265
    Iniecta lateant fac tibi veste pedes.
Quae nimium gracilis, pleno velamina filo
    Sumat, et ex umeris laxus amictus eat.
Pallida purpureis spargat sua corpora virgis,
    Nigrior ad Pharii confuge piscis opem.   270
Pes malus in nivea semper celetur aluta :
    Arida nec vinclis crura resolve suis.
Conveniunt tenues scapulis analectrides altis :
    Angustum circa fascia pectus eat.
Exiguo signet gestu, quodcumque loquetur,   275
    Cui digiti pingues et scaber unguis erit.
Cui gravis oris odor numquam ieiuna loquatur,
    Et semper spatio distet ab ore viri.
Si niger aut ingens aut non erit ordine natus
    Dens tibi, ridendo maxima damna feres.   280

273 analectrides *Heinsius*: analeptrides (-lecptr- *R*) *MSS.*

---

[1] Garments with bright stripes would set off the pale complexion ; cf. Virg. *Aen.* 8. 660.
[2] Possibly a reference to crocodile's dung, supposed to

136

You have not come to learn from me, Semele and Leda, or thou, Sidonian maid, borne on the false bull o'er the sea; or Helen, whom not foolishly, Menelaus, thou askest back, and whom not foolishly, Trojan ravisher, thou dost keep. It is the crowd that come to learn, women both fair and plain; and ever are the plain more numerous than the fair. The beautiful care not for precepts and the help of art; their dowry have they, beauty that without art is powerful; when the sea is calm the careless sailor takes his ease; when it swells high he implores his helpers. Yet rare is the face that lacks a blemish: hide your blemishes, and so far as you can conceal any fault of body. Sit if you are short, lest standing you seem to be sitting, and recline, small as you are, on your couch; here, too, lest your measure be taken as you lie, let your feet be hidden by a robe thrown across them. Let her that is too slender choose garments of full texture, and let her robe hang loosely from her shoulders. Let a pale woman adorn her person with purple stripes,[1] and one who is swarthy have recourse to the aid of the Pharian fish.[2] Let an ill-formed foot be ever hidden beneath a snow-white sandal; never release lean ankles from their bonds. Small pads suit high shoulder-blades: a band should surround a narrow chest. Let her whose fingers are fat, or nails rough, mark what she says with but little gesture. She whose breath is tainted should never speak before eating, and she should always stand at a distance from her lover's face. If you have a tooth that is black or too large or growing out of place, laughing will cost you dear.

---

impart radiance to the skin; Brandt, however, reads "vestis" here, *i.e.* linen.

Quis credat ? discunt etiam ridere puellae,
    Quaeritur atque illis hac quoque parte decor.
Sint modici rictus, parvaeque utrimque lacunae,
    Et summos dentes ima labella tegant.
Nec sua perpetuo contendant ilia risu,   285
    Sed leve nescio quid femineumque sonent.
Est, quae perverso distorqueat ora cachinno :
    Cum risu laeta est altera, flere putes.
Illa sonat raucum quiddam atque inamabile ridet,
    Ut rudit a scabra turpis asella mola.   290
Quo non ars penetrat ? discunt lacrimare decenter,
    Quoque volunt plorant tempore, quoque modo.
Quid, cum legitima fraudatur littera voce,
    Blaesaque fit iusso lingua coacta sono ?
In vitio decor est, quaedam male reddere verba :   295
    Discunt posse minus, quam potuere, loqui.
Omnibus his, quoniam prosunt, inpendite curam
    Discite femineo corpora ferre gradu.
Est et in incessu pars non contempta decoris :
    Allicit ignotos ille fugatque viros.   300
Haec movet arte latus, tunicisque fluentibus auras
    Accipit, extensos fertque superba pedes :
Illa velut coniunx Umbri rubicunda mariti
    Ambulat, ingentes varica fertque gradus.
Sed sit, ut in multis, modus hic quoque : rusticus alter
    Motus, concesso mollior alter erit.   306
Pars umeri tamen ima tui, pars summa lacerti
    Nuda sit, a laeva conspicienda manu.
Hoc vos praecipue, niveae, decet : hoc ubi vidi,
    Oscula ferre umero, qua patet usque, libet.   310

---

[1] By this he clearly means a too-affected movement, as the
next is too rustic and homely ; he is describing a swaying
motion combined with a haughty pointing of the feet ; something
like the artificial walk of mannequins in a show-room is suggested.

Who would believe it? women learn even how to laugh; here too seemliness is required of them. Let the mouth be but moderately opened, let the dimples on either side be small, and let the bottom of the lip cover the top of the teeth. Nor should they strain their sides with continuous laughter, but laugh with a feminine trill. One woman will distort her face with a hideous guffaw, another, you would think, was weeping, while she is laughing happily. That one's laugh has a strident and unlovely harshness, as when a mean she-ass brays by the rough millstone. How far does art not go? they learn to weep becomingly, and can wail when and how they choose. What, when they defraud letters of their rightful utterance, and the tongue is compelled to lisp at their command? The defect has charm— this uttering some words amiss; they learn the power to mar their power of speech. Give attention to all these things, because they are useful: learn to carry yourself with womanly step. In walk too there is no mean part of charm; it attracts or repels unknown admirers. This woman sways her side with skill, and welcomes the breeze with flowing robe, as she haughtily places her extended feet;[1] that one walks like the sunburnt spouse of an Umbrian lord, and takes long, straddling steps. But, as in many things, let there be moderation here; one motion is rustic, another will be more affected than is allowed. Nevertheless let the lower part of your shoulder and the upper part of your arm be bare and easily seen from the left hand. This becomes you especially, you who have snowy skins; when I see this, fain would I kiss that shoulder, wherever it is exposed.

Monstra maris Sirenes erant, quae voce canora
    Quamlibet admissas detinuere rates.
His sua Sisyphides auditis paene resolvit
    Corpora, nam sociis inlita cera fuit.
Res est blanda canor : discant cantare puellae :   315
    Pro facie multis vox sua lena fuit.
Et modo marmoreis referant audita theatris,
    Et modo Niliacis carmina lusa modis.
Nec plectrum dextra, citharam tenuisse sinistra
    Nesciat arbitrio femina docta meo.   320
Saxa ferasque lyra movit Rhodopeïus Orpheus,
    Tartareosque lacus tergeminumque canem.
Saxa tuo cantu, vindex iustissime matris,
    Fecerunt muros officiosa novos.
Quamvis mutus erat, voci favisse putatur   325
    Piscis, Arioniae fabula nota lyrae.
Disce etiam duplici genialia nablia palma
    Verrere : conveniunt dulcibus illa iocis.

Sit tibi Callimachi, sit Coi nota poetae,
    Sit quoque vinosi Teïa Musa senis ;   330
Nota sit et Sappho (quid enim lascivius illa ?),
    Cuive pater vafri luditur arte Getae.
Et teneri possis carmen legisse Properti,
    Sive aliquid Galli, sive, Tibulle, tuum :
Dictaque Varroni fulvis insignia villis   335
    Vellera, germanae, Phrixe, querenda tuae :

---

[1] A later legend made Ulysses the son of Sisyphus, whose name was proverbial for cunning ; when Ulysses sailed past the Sirens' rock, he bound himself to the mast, and stopped the ears of his crew with wax : see Hom. *Od.* xii. l. 166.

[2] Amphion, who punished Dirce for her cruelty to his mother Antiope.

The Sirens were wondrous creatures of the sea, who with tuneful voice detained vessels, how swift soe'er they sailed. Hearing them the son of Sisyphus[1] all but unloosed his body; for his comrades' ears were stopped with wax. A persuasive thing is song: let women learn to sing; with many voice instead of face has been their procuress. Let them repeat now ditties heard in marble theatres, now songs acted in the fashion of Nile; nor should a woman skilled as I would have her be ignorant how to hold the quill in her right hand and the lyre in her left. With his lyre did Orpheus of Rhodope move rocks and hearts, and the lakes of Tartarus and the three-headed dog. At thy strains, most just avenger of thy mother,[2] the stones with ready service formed new walls. A fish though dumb is believed to have shown favour to the voice in the well-known fable of Arion's lyre. Learn also to sweep with both hands the genial Phoenician harp;[3] suitable is it to merry-making.

Let the Muse of Callimachus and of the Coan bard be known to you, and the old drunkard's Teian strains;[4] let Sappho too be known (for who more wanton than she?), or he whose sire is deceived by the crafty Getan's cunning.[5] And you should be able to read a poem of tender Propertius or something of Gallus or of you, Tibullus; and the fleece that Varro told of, famous for its tawny hairs, a cause of complaint to thy sister, Phrixus; and Aeneas

---

[3] A ten- or twelve-stringed instrument, mentioned in Chronicles i. 15. 16.

[4] Philetas and Anacreon.

[5] Menander, in whose comedies the father is often deceived by the slave (often called Geta).

OVID

Et profugum Aenean, altae primordia Romae,
  Quo nullum Latio clarius extat opus.
Forsitan et nostrum nomen miscebitur istis,
  Nec mea Lethaeis scripta dabuntur aquis :   340
Atque aliquis dicet " nostri lege culta magistri
  Carmina, quis partes instruit ille duas :
Deve tribus libris, titulus quos signat Amorum,
  Elige, quod docili molliter ore legas :
Vel tibi composita cantetur Epistola voce :   345
  Ignotum hoc aliis ille novavit opus."
O ita, Phoebe, velis ! ita vos, pia numina vatum,
  Insignis cornu Bacche, novemque deae !

Quis dubitet, quin scire velim saltare puellam,
  Ut moveat posito brachia iussa mero ?   350
Artifices lateris, scenae spectacula, amantur :
  Tantum mobilitas illa decoris habet.
Parva monere pudet, talorum dicere iactus
  Ut sciat, et vires, tessera missa, tuas :
Et modo tres iactet numeros, modo cogitet, apte   355
  Quam subeat partem callida, quamque vocet.
Cautaque non stulte latronum proelia ludat,
  Unus cum gemino calculus hoste perit,

---

the wanderer, origin of lofty Rome, a work than
which none more famous has appeared in Latium.
Perhaps too my name will be joined to theirs,
nor will my writings be given to Lethe's waters;
and someone will say, "Read the elegant poems
of our master, wherein he instructs the rival
parties;[1] or from the three books marked by the
title of 'Loves' choose out what you may softly
read with docile voice; or let some Letter[2] be read
by you with practised utterance; he first invented
this art, unknown to others." So grant it, O
Phoebus! so grant it, ye blessed souls of poets,
and thou, O horned Bacchus, and ye goddesses
nine!

Who would doubt that I would have a woman
know how to dance,[3] that when the wine is set
she may, when bidden, move her arms. Artists
whom the stage displays win favour as they move
their sides; so great a charm has this easy move-
ment. I am ashamed to advise in little things,
that she should know the throws of the dice, and
thy powers, O flung counter.[4] Now let her throw
three dice, and now reflect which side she may
fitly join in her cunning, and which challenge. Let
her cautiously and not foolishly play the battle of
the brigands, when one piece falls before his double

359–60 the situation seems to be that of a king in chess
trying to avoid checkmate.

The available evidence is considered at length in Pauly-
Wissowa, s.v. *Lusoria tabula*. See also " Roman Board
Games," by R. G. Austin, in *Greece and Rome*, Oct. 1934 and
Feb. 1935. The point of " aemulus " may lie in the fact that
a piece which commonly played with a partner (" compar ")
might lose that partner to the enemy; having lost her he
perhaps had to go back to where he started.

Bellatorque sua prensus sine compare bellat,
    Aemulus et coeptum saepe recurrit iter.   360
Reticuloque pilae leves fundantur aperto,
    Nec, nisi quam tolles, ulla movenda pila est.
Est genus, in totidem tenui ratione redactum
    Scriptula, quot menses lubricus annus habet :
Parva tabella capit ternos utrimque lapillos,   365
    In qua vicisse est continuasse suos.
Mille facesse iocos ; turpe est nescire puellam
    Ludere : ludendo saepe paratur amor.
Sed minimus labor est sapienter iactibus uti :
    Maius opus mores composuisse suos.   370
Tum sumus incauti, studioque aperimur in ipso,
    Nudaque per lusus pectora nostra patent :
Ira subit, deforme malum, lucrique cupido,
    Iurgiaque et rixae sollicitusque dolor :
Crimina dicuntur, resonat clamoribus aether,   375
    Invocat iratos et sibi quisque deos :
Nulla fides, tabulaeque novae per vota petuntur ;
    Et lacrimis vidi saepe madere genas.
Iuppiter a vobis tam turpia crimina pellat,
    In quibus est ulli cura placere viro.   380

Hos ignava iocos tribuit natura puellis ;
    Materia ludunt uberiore viri.
Sunt illis celeresque pilae iaculumque trochique
    Armaque et in gyros ire coactus equus.
Nec vos Campus habet, nec vos gelidissima Virgo,   385
    Nec Tuscus placida devehit amnis aqua.

364 scriptula *Scaliger* : spicula *MSS.*

---

[1] Perhaps putting marbles or other balls into a bag or net, and taking them out one by one without moving any of the rest.

foe, and the warrior caught without his mate fights on, and the enemy retraces many a time the path he has begun. And let the smooth balls be flung into the open net, nor must any ball be moved save that which you will take out.[1] There is a sort of game confined by subtle method into as many lines as the slippery year has months:[2] a small board has three counters on either side, whereon to join your pieces together is to conquer.[3] Make up a thousand games; it is unseemly for a girl to know not how to play; by play love is often won. But the smallest task is to use your throws wisely: more important is it to control one's own behaviour. Then are we incautious and reveal ourselves in our very zest, and in our games our hearts show clear to see; anger steals in, an unsightly evil, and desire for gain, and brawls and quarrels and distressful grief; reproaches are hurled; the air resounds with cries, and each calls angry gods to his aid: none trusts his neighbour, and amid vows new tables are demanded; oft have I seen cheeks wet with tears. May Jupiter keep such foul reproach far from you, who seek to win any man's favour.

These are the games that indolent nature has given to women; men have richer material for their sport. Swift balls have they, and javelins and hoops and armour, and the horse that is trained to go in circles. You the Campus knows not, nor the cool water of the Maiden, nor does the Tuscan river bear you down on its placid stream. But you

[2] Called "duodecim scripta," twelve lines drawn across the board.
[3] This game, also mentioned *Trist.* 2. 481, is a form of the old game called Merels, to which also Noughts and Crosses, Fox and Geese belong.

At licet et prodest Pompeias ire per umbras,
    Virginis aetheriis cum caput ardet equis ;
Visite laurigero sacrata Palatia Phoebo :
    Ille Paraetonicas mersit in alta rates ;   390
Quaeque soror coniunxque ducis monimenta pararunt,
    Navalique gener cinctus honore caput ;
Visite turicremas vaccae Memphitidos aras,
    Visite conspicuis terna theatra locis ;
Spectentur tepido maculosae sanguine harenae,   395
    Metaque ferventi circueunda rota.
Quod latet, ignotum est : ignoti nulla cupido :
    Fructus abest, facies cum bona teste caret.
Tu licet et Thamyram superes et Amoebea cantu,
    Non erit ignotae gratia magna lyrae.   400
Si Venerem Cous nusquam posuisset Apelles,
    Mersa sub aequoreis illa lateret aquis.
Quid petitur sacris, nisi tantum fama, poetis ?
    Hoc votum nostri summa laboris habet.
Cura deum fuerant olim regumque poetae :   405
    Praemiaque antiqui magna tulere chori.
Sanctaque maiestas et erat venerabile nomen
    Vatibus, et largae saepe dabantur opes.

---

[1] The constellation of Virgo, in which the sun is in August.
The "Maiden" of l. 385 is the water of the aqueduct so
called, which was thought the most pleasing to swim in. For
the Pompeian shade see note on i. 67.

[2] "Palatia" covers other buildings on the Palatine besides
the Imperial Palace; e.g. the temple of Apollo built by
Augustus.

[3] Those of Cleopatra. Paraetonium is on the coast west of
the Nile Delta.

may, and with profit, walk through the Pompeian shade, when the head is scorched with the Maiden's [1] celestial steeds. Visit the Palace sacred to laurelled Phoebus: [2] it was he that sank in the deep the Paraetonian barks; [3] and the monuments that the sister and consort of our Chief have won, and his son-in-law whose head is wreathed with naval glory. [4] Visit the incense-burning altars of the Memphian heifer; [5] visit three theatres [6] in conspicuous seats. See the arena stained with warm blood, and the goal [7] that the glowing wheels must round. What is hidden is unknown; what is unknown none desires; naught is gained when a comely face has none to see it. Though in song you may surpass Thamyras and Amoebeus, in an unknown lyre there is no great delight. If Coan Apelles had never painted Venus, she would still be lying hid in the sea's depths. What is sought by the sacred bards save fame alone? toil we ne'er so hard, this is all we ask. Poets once were the care of chieftains and of kings, [8] and choirs of old won great rewards. Sacred was the majesty and venerable the name of the poet; and ofttimes lavish wealth was given them. Ennius,

[4] Agrippa married Julia, daughter of Augustus. He built the "Porticus Argonautarum," so called from the scenes portrayed in it, in 25 B.C., to commemorate the battle of Actium.

[5] Isis, confused with Io, turned into a heifer by Juno.

[6] Those of Pompey (dedicated 55 B.C.), Marcellus (built by Augustus in memory of the young Marcellus) and Balbus (dedicated 13 B.C.) are meant.

[7] The "meta" was the turning-post at the end of the Circus.

[8] *e.g.* Euripides, the guest of Archelaus, king of Macedonia, Anacreon of Polycrates, Pindar and Bacchylides of Hiero.

Ennius emeruit, Calabris in montibus ortus,
    Contiguus poni, Scipio magne, tibi.   410
Nunc ederae sine honore iacent, operataque doctis
    Cura vigil Musis nomen inertis habet.
Sed famae vigilare iuvat : quis nosset Homerum,
    Ilias aeternum si latuisset opus ?
Quis Danaën nosset, si semper clusa fuisset,   415
    Inque sua turri perlatuisset anus ?
Utilis est vobis, formosae, turba, puellae.
    Saepe vagos ultra limina ferte pedes.
Ad multas lupa tendit oves, praedetur ut unam,
    Et Iovis in multas devolat ales aves.   420
Se quoque det populo mulier speciosa videndam :
    Quem trahat, e multis forsitan unus erit.
Omnibus illa locis maneat studiosa placendi,
    Et curam tota mente decoris agat.
Casus ubique valet ; semper tibi pendeat hamus :   425
    Quo minime credas gurgite, piscis erit.
Saepe canes frustra nemorosis montibus errant,
    Inque plagam nullo cervus agente venit.
Quid minus Andromedae fuerat sperare revinctae,
    Quam lacrimas ulli posse placere suas ?   430
Funere saepe viri vir quaeritur ; ire solutis
    Crinibus et fletus non tenuisse decet.

Sed vitate viros cultum formamque professos,
    Quique suas ponunt in statione comas.
Quae vobis dicunt, dixerunt mille puellis :   435
    Errat et in nulla sede moratur amor.
Femina quid faciat, cum sit vir levior ipsa,
    Forsitan et plures possit habere viros ?

sprung from Calabrian hills, won a place, great
Scipio, by thy side; but now the ivy lies un-
honoured, and wakeful toil devoted to the learned
Muses bears the name of sloth. Yet wakeful pursuit
of fame brings reward: who would know of Homer
if the Iliad, an ever-enduring work, had lain hid?
Who would know of Danae, had she always been
a prisoner, and tarried to old womanhood in her
tower? Profitable to you, beauteous damsels, is a
crowd; oft let your wandering feet stray o'er the
threshold. The wolf draws nigh to many sheep
that she may prey on one, and the eagle of Jove
swoops down on many birds. Let the beautiful
woman also offer herself to the people to be seen;
out of many there will be one, perchance, whom
she may attract. Let her that is eager to please
be always everywhere, and give all her mind's
attention to her charms. Chance everywhere has
power; ever let your hook be hanging; where
you least believe it, there will be a fish in the
stream. Often do hounds stray in vain through
mountain glens, and a stag, without any driving it,
falls into the nets. What had fettered Andromeda
less to hope for than that her tears could e'er
find favour? Often a husband is sought for at a
husband's funeral; it is becoming to go with dis-
hevelled hair, and to mourn without restraint.

But avoid men who profess elegance and good
looks, and who arrange their hair in its proper
place. What they tell you they have told a thou-
sand women; their fancy wanders, and has no
fixed abode. What can a woman do when her lover
is smoother than herself, and may perhaps have
more lovers than she? You will hardly believe me,

Vix mihi credetis, sed credite : Troia maneret,
    Praeceptis Priami si foret usa sui.   440
Sunt qui mendaci specie grassentur amoris,
    Perque aditus talis lucra pudenda petant.
Nec coma vos fallat liquido nitidissima nardo,
    Nec brevis in rugas lingula pressa suas :
Nec toga decipiat filo tenuissima, nec si   445
    Anulus in digitis alter et alter erit.
Forsitan ex horum numero cultissimus ille
    Fur sit, et uratur vestis amore tuae.
" Redde meum ! " clamant spoliatae saepe puellae,
    " Redde meum ! " toto voce boante foro.   450
Has, Venus, e templis multo radiantibus auro
    Lenta vides lites Appiadesque tuae.
Sunt quoque non dubia quaedam mala nomina fama :
    Deceptae a ! multi crimen amantis habent.
Discite ab alterius vestris timuisse querellis ;   455
    Ianua fallaci ne sit aperta viro.
Parcite, Cecropides, iuranti credere Theseo :
    Quos faciet testes, fecit et ante, deos.
Et tibi, Demophoon, Theseï criminis heres,
    Phyllide decepta nulla relicta fides.   460
Si bene promittent, totidem promittite verbis :
    Si dederint, et vos gaudia pacta date.
Illa potest vigiles flammas extinguere Vestae,
    Et rapere e templis, Inachi, sacra tuis,
Et dare mixta viro tritis aconita cicutis,   465
    Accepto venerem munere siqua negat.

---

440 Priami . . . sui *MSS.*: Priame . . . tuis *R*: Priamis (*i.e.*
Cassandra) . . . tuis *Housman.*

yet believe: Troy would have survived, had she followed the precepts of her own Priam. Some make their assault under a false appearance of love, and by such approaches seek shameful gains. Let not their hair, sleek with liquid nard, deceive you, nor the tongue of the belt tucked tightly into the creases it makes; let not the toga of finest texture play you false, nor if there be one ring and yet another on their fingers. Perchance out of their number the most elegant will prove a thief, and be inflamed by longing for your robe. "Give me back my own," robbed women often cry; "give me back my own," cry their voices over the whole forum: these quarrels dost thou watch unheeding, O Venus,[1] from temples shining with lavish gold, thou and thy Appian Nymphs.[2] There are, too, certain names[3] of ill fame unquestionable; many, alas, bear the reproach of a deserted mistress. Learn from the complaints of another to fear for yourselves; nor let your door be open to a false lover. Ye maids of Athens, believe not Theseus' oaths: the gods he will call to witness, he has called upon before, and thou too, Demophoon, heir of Theseus' reproach, art no longer trusted since thou didst play Phyllis false. If they make fair promises, promise in as many words; if they give, give also your bargained joys. That woman could extinguish Vesta's watchful flame, and rob thy temple, Inachis,[4] of its sanctities, and give aconite mixed with pounded hemlock to her lover, who receives a gift and then denies her favours.

---

[1] See note on i. 81 ff.   [2] See note on i. 82.
[3] *i.e.* men of as bad repute as Theseus and Demophoon.
[4] See note on 393. Io was daughter of Inachus, king of Argos.

OVID

Fert animus propius consistere : supprime habenas,
    Musa, nec admissis excutiare rotis.
Verba vadum temptent abiegnis scripta tabellis :
    Accipiat missas apta ministra notas.   470
Inspice : quodque leges, ex ipsis collige verbis,
    Fingat, an ex animo sollicitusque roget.
Postque brevem rescribe moram : mora semper amantes
    Incitat, exiguum si modo tempus habet.
Sed neque te facilem iuveni promitte roganti,   475
    Nec tamen e duro quod petit ille nega.
Fac timeat speretque simul, quotiensque remittes,
    Spesque magis veniat certa minorque metus.
Munda, sed e medio consuetaque verba, puellae,
    Scribite : sermonis publica forma placet;   480
A ! quotiens dubius scriptis exarsit amator,
    Et nocuit formae barbara lingua bonae !
Sed quoniam, quamvis vittae careatis honore,
    Est vobis vestros fallere cura viros,
Ancillae puerique manu perarate tabellas,   485
    Pignora nec puero credite vestra novo.
Vidi ego pallentes isto terrore puellas
    Servitium miseras tempus in omne pati.
Perfidus ille quidem, qui talia pignora servat,
    Sed tamen Aetnaei fulminis instar habent.   490
Iudice me fraus est concessa repellere fraudem,
    Armaque in armatos sumere iura sinunt.
Ducere consuescat multas manus una figuras,
    (A ! pereant, per quos ista monenda mihi)

---

485 manu perarate *Bentley*, *Merkel* : manus ferat arte *R.*

---

[1] Apparently he means that he has been getting too discursive
and will now deal more closely with his subject.

My spirit bids me take a closer stand;[1] draw in the
reins, my Muse, nor dash headlong with ungoverned
wheels. Let words written on fir-wood tablets pre-
pare the way: let a suitable handmaid receive the
missive; examine it, and in what you read, gather
from the words themselves whether he is feigning,
or writes from his heart in real distress; after brief
delay write back: delay ever spurns lovers on, if but
its term be brief. But neither promise yourself too
easily to him who entreats you, nor yet deny what
he asks too stubbornly. Cause him to hope and fear
together; and as often as you reply, see that hope
becomes surer and fear diminishes. Dainty, O women,
be the words you write, but customary and in common
use: ordinary speech gives pleasure; ah, how often
has a message inflamed a doubting lover, or some
barbaric phrase done harm to beauteous shape.
But because, though you lack the honour of the
fillet, you too have your lords[2] you are eager to
deceive, write your messages by the hand of slave
or handmaid, and entrust not your pledges to a slave
you know not; I have seen women pale with terror
on that account, suffering in their misery unending
servitude. Perfidious indeed is he who keeps such
pledges, but they hold what is like a thunderbolt of
Aetna. In my judgment fraud may be repelled by
fraud, and the laws allow arms to be taken against
an armed foe.[3] Let one hand be accustomed to
tracing many figures, (ah, perish they who make

---

[2] Though not lawful wives, you are not less eager to
deceive your lords.

[3] As love-letters may be used as evidence against you it is
permissible to return fraud by fraud, and learn to write in
different hands. For l. 496, cf. ii. 396 and note.

OVID

Nec nisi deletis tutum rescribere ceris,   495
  Ne teneat geminas una tabella manus.
Femina dicatur scribenti semper amator :
  Illa sit in vestris, qui fuit ille, notis.

Si licet a parvis animum ad maiora referre,
  Plenaque curvato pandere vela sinu,   500
Pertinet ad faciem rabidos compescere mores :
  Candida pax homines, trux decet ira feras.
Ora tument ira : nigrescunt sanguine venae :
  Lumina Gorgoneo saevius igne micant.
"I procul hinc," dixit "non es mihi, tibia, tanti,"   505
  Ut vidit vultus Pallas in amne suos.
Vos quoque si media speculum spectetis in ira,
  Cognoscat faciem vix satis ulla suam.
Nec minus in vultu damnosa superbia vestro :
  Comibus est oculis alliciendus amor.   510
Odimus inmodicos (experto credite) fastus :
  Saepe tacens odii semina vultus habet.
Spectantem specta, ridenti mollia ride :
  Innuet, acceptas tu quoque redde notas.
Sic ubi prolusit, rudibus puer ille relictis   515
  Spicula de pharetra promit acuta sua.
Odimus et maestas : Tecmessam diligat Aiax ;
  Nos hilarem populum femina laeta capit.
Numquam ego te, Andromache, nec te, Tecmessa,
    rogarem,
  Ut mea de vobis altera amica foret.   520
Credere vix videor, cum cogar credere partu,
  Vos ego cum vestris concubuisse viris.
Scilicet Aiaci mulier maestissima dixit
  "Lux mea" quaeque solent verba iuvare viros ?

---

499 si licet *R* : sed libet *Heinsius and edd.*

this counsel needful!) nor is it safe to write an answer unless the wax is quite smoothed over, lest one tablet hold two hands. Let your lover always be called a woman by the writer: in your messages let what is really " he " be " she."

If I may turn my mind from small things to greater, and spread out full my swelling sails, it is beauty's task to hold mad moods in check; fair peace is becoming to men, fierce anger to beasts. The face becomes swollen with passion; the veins grow black with blood, the eyes flash more savagely than Gorgon fire. "Away with you," said Pallas, "to me, flute, you are not worth the cost," when she saw her countenance in the stream. And you, should you in mid-passion behold a mirror, scarce one of you would know her own features. Not less harmful in your looks is pride; by gentle eyes must love be enticed. I hate immoderate haughtiness (believe one who knows); a silent face oft holds the seeds of hatred. Look at one who is looking at you; return a pleasant smile; if he beckons, acknowledge and return his nod. 'Tis after such prelude that young Cupid, abandoning the foils, draws the sharp arrows from his quiver. Melancholy women too I hate; let Ajax love Tecmessa;[1] we, a mirthful folk, are charmed by cheerful women. Never would I ask you, Andromache, nor you, Tecmessa, to be either of you my mistress. Scarce, methinks, can I believe, though your offspring compel me, that you ever lay with your husbands. What, did that most melancholy of women call Ajax "Darling," or use such words as please a lover?

---

[1] She was a captive woman, and hence melancholy.

Quis vetat a magnis ad res exempla minores   525
   Sumere, nec nomen pertimuisse ducis?
Dux bonus huic centum commisit vite regendos,
   Huic equites, illi signa tuenda dedit:
Vos quoque, de nobis quem quisque erit aptus ad usum,
   Inspicite, et certo ponite quemque loco.   530
Munera det dives: ius qui profitebitur, adsit:
   Facundus causam saepe clientis agat:
Carmina qui facimus, mittamus carmina tantum:
   Hic chorus ante alios aptus amare sumus.
Nos facimus placitae late praeconia formae: 535
   Nomen habet Nemesis, Cynthia nomen habet:
Vesper et Eoae novere Lycorida terrae:
   Et multi, quae sit nostra Corinna, rogant.
Adde, quod insidiae sacris a vatibus absunt,
   Et facit ad mores ars quoque nostra suos.   540
Nec nos ambitio, nec amor nos tangit habendi:
   Contempto colitur lectus et umbra foro.
Sed facile haeremus, validoque perurimur aestu,
   Et nimium certa scimus amare fide.
Scilicet ingenium placida mollitur ab arte,   545
   Et studio mores convenienter eunt.
Vatibus Aoniis faciles estote, puellae:
   Numen inest illis, Pieridesque favent.
Est deus in nobis, et sunt commercia caeli:
   Sedibus aetheriis spiritus ille venit.   550
A doctis pretium scelus est sperare poetis;
   Me miserum! scelus hoc nulla puella timet.
Dissimulate tamen, nec prima fronte rapaces
   Este: novus viso casse resistet amans.

---

[1] The badge of the centurions, symbolising the power to inflict corporal punishment.

Who forbids me to use great things as examples
for little, or to fear the name of leader? To this man
a good leader commits a hundred men to be ruled
by his vinewood staff,[1] to another the care of horse-
men, to another that of the standards: do you
likewise consider the use to which each of us is suited,
and set each in his proper place. Let the rich man
give presents; let him who professes law give legal
aid; let the eloquent often plead his client's cause;
let us who make poems send poems only: we poets
are a band more fitted than the rest for love. 'Tis
we who herald the loved one's beauty far and wide;
renowned is Nemesis,[2] Cynthia is renowned; evening
and Eastern lands know of Lycoris, and many in-
quire who my Corinna may be. Besides, treachery
is alien to sacred bards, and our art too helps to
shape our character.[3] Neither ambition nor love of
gain affects us; the Forum we despise, and cultivate
the couch and the shade. But we are easily caught,
and burn with a strong passion, and know how to
love with a loyalty most sure. 'Tis in truth from the
gentle art that our spirit wins tenderness, and our
behaviour is akin to our pursuit. Be kind, ye women,
to Aonian bards; divinity is in them, and the Muses
show them favour. There is a god in us; we are in
touch with heaven: from celestial places comes our
inspiration. To hope for reward from skilled poets
is a crime: ah, wretched that I am, it is a crime no
woman fears! Yet dissemble, and carry not greed
on your open countenance; a new lover will take
fright if he sees the net. But a rider would not use

---

[2] Nemesis, Cynthia and Lycoris were the loves of Ti-
bullus, Propertius and Gallus respectively.

[3] Explained in ll. 545, 6.

Sed neque vector equum, qui nuper sensit habenas, 555
  Comparibus frenis artificemque reget,
Nec stabiles animos annis viridemque iuventam
  Ut capias, idem limes agendus erit.
Hic rudis et castris nunc primum notus Amoris,
  Qui tetigit thalamos praeda novella tuos, 560
Te solam norit, tibi semper inhaereat uni :
  Cingenda est altis saepibus ista seges.
Effuge rivalem : vinces, dum sola tenebis ;
  Non bene cum sociis regna Venusque manent.
Ille vetus miles sensim et sapienter amabit, 565
  Multaque tironi non patienda feret :
Nec franget postes, nec saevis ignibus uret,
  Nec dominae teneras adpetet ungue genas,
Nec scindet tunicasve suas tunicasve puellae,
  Nec raptus flendi causa capillus erit. 570
Ista decent pueros aetate et amore calentes ;
  Hic fera composita vulnera mente feret.
Ignibus heu lentis uretur, ut umida faena,
  Ut modo montanis silva recisa iugis.
Certior hic amor est : brevis et fecundior ille ; 575
  Quae fugiunt, celeri carpite poma manu.

Omnia tradantur : portas reseravimus hosti ;
  Et sit in infida proditione fides.
Quod datur ex facili, longum male nutrit amorem :
  Miscenda est laetis rara repulsa iocis. 580
Ante fores iaceat, " crudelis ianua ! " dicat,
  Multaque summisse, multa minanter agat.
Dulcia non ferimus : suco renovemur amaro ;
  Saepe perit ventis obruta cumba suis ;
Hoc est, uxores quod non patiatur amari : 585
  Conveniunt illas, cum voluere, viri ;

the same bridle for a horse who but lately felt the reins and for one who knows his paces; nor must the same path be taken to catch discreet age and tender youth. This raw recruit, now first known to Love's campaigning, who has come, a new prey, to your chamber-door—let him know none but you, let him cling to you alone; high is the fence that must guard that tender crop. Avoid a rival: you will prevail, so long as you alone have power; in partnership neither thrones nor love stand sure.[1] But the veteran will come gradually and prudently to love, and will bear much a recruit would not endure; he will not break doors nor burn them with fierce flames, nor attack with his nails the soft cheeks of his mistress, nor rend his own nor his lady's clothes, nor will torn tresses be a cause of weeping. Such doings suit lads aflame with youth and love; but he will bear bitter smarts composedly, he will burn, ah, with slow fires like damp hay, like timber lately cut from the mountain ridge. Such love is surer; the other is richer but brief; pluck with quick hand the fruit that quickly passes.

Let all be revealed: we have flung our gates open to the foe, and in faithless treason let us keep faith. What is easily given ill fosters an enduring love; let an occasional repulse vary your merry sport. Let him lie before your gate; let him cry, "Ah, cruel door!" and play the suppliant oft, and oft the threatener. We cannot bear sweetness; let us be refreshed by bitter juices; oft is a vessel sunk by favouring winds; 'tis this which prevents wives from being loved: to them their husbands come

---

[1] *i.e.* kings and lovers must rule alone, cf. "nulla societas nec fides regni est," Cic. *Off.* i. 8. 26.

Adde forem, et duro dicat tibi ianitor ore
  "Non potes," exclusum te quoque tanget amor.
Ponite iam gladios hebetes : pugnetur acutis ;
  Nec dubito, telis quin petar ipse meis.   590
Dum cadit in laqueos captus quoque nuper amator,
  Solum se thalamos speret habere tuos.
Postmodo rivalem partitaque foedera lecti
  Sentiat : has artes tolle, senescit amor.
Tum bene fortis equus reserato carcere currit,   595
  Cum quos praetereat quosque sequatur habet.
Quamlibet extinctos iniuria suscitat ignes :
  En, ego (confiteor !) non nisi laesus amo.
Causa tamen nimium non sit manifesta doloris,
  Pluraque sollicitus, quam sciet, esse putet.   600
Incitat et ficti tristis custodia servi,
  Et nimium duri cura molesta viri.
Quae venit ex tuto, minus est accepta voluptas :
  Ut sis liberior Thaide, finge metus.
Cum melius foribus possis, admitte fenestra,   605
  Inque tuo vultu signa timentis habe.
Callida prosiliat dicatque ancilla "perimus !"
  Tu iuvenem trepidum quolibet abde loco.
Admiscenda tamen venus est secura timori,
  Ne tanti noctes non putet esse tuas.   610

Qua vafer eludi possit ratione maritus,
  Quaque vigil custos, praeteriturus eram.
Nupta virum timeat : rata sit custodia nuptae ;
  Hoc decet, hoc leges iusque pudorque iubent.
Te quoque servari, modo quam vindicta redemit,   615
  Quis ferat ? Ut fallas, ad mea sacra veni !

---

[1] *i.e.* any husband.   [2] The celebrated Athenian courtesan.
[3] The praetor touched with the rod the slave that was to be
set free. He is addressing "libertinae," emancipated slave-girls.

whenever they will; add but a door, and let a doorkeeper say to you [1] with stubborn mouth, "You cannot;" once shut out, you too, sir, will be touched by love. Throw down the foils now, and fight with sharpened swords; nor do I doubt that I shall be attacked with my own weapons. While a lover lately ensnared is falling into the toils, let him hope that he alone has the right to your chamber; later on let him be aware of a rival and of the shared privilege of your couch; neglect these devices and his love will wane. The valiant horse races best, at the barrier's fall, when he has others to follow and o'erpass. Fires, howe'er extinct, are aroused by injury; lo, myself (I confess) save when hurt, I cannot love. But let the cause of pain be not too manifest, and in his vexation let him fancy more than he knows. The surly guardianship of a pretended slave excites him, and the irksome vigilance of a husband too severe. Pleasure safely enjoyed is less welcome; though you be freer than Thais [2] pretend to fears. Though it were easier by the door, admit him by the window, and show signs of fright upon your face. Let a clever maid hurry in, and cry, "We are undone!" conceal the frightened youth in any hiding-place. Yet with fear must be mingled secure enjoyment, lest he think your nights are not worth while.

How a crafty husband or a vigilant guardian may be deceived I was about to pass by; let the bride fear her spouse, let the guarding of a bride be sure; that is seemly, that the laws and right and modesty command: but that you too should be watched, whom the rod [3] has lately redeemed, who could endure? Attend my rites that you may learn to

Tot licet observent (adsit modo certa voluntas),
　　Quot fuerant Argo lumina, verba dabis.
Scilicet obstabit custos, ne scribere possis,
　　Sumendae detur cum tibi tempus aquae?　　　　620
Conscia cum possit scriptas portare tabellas,
　　Quas tegat in tepido fascia lata sinu?
Cum possit sura chartas celare ligatas,
　　Et vincto blandas sub pede ferre notas?
Caverit haec custos, pro charta conscia tergum　　625
　　Praebeat, inque suo corpore verba ferat.
Tuta quoque est fallitque oculos e lacte recenti
　　Littera: carbonis pulvere tange, leges.
Fallet et umiduli quae fiet acumine lini,
　　Et feret occultas pura tabella notas.　　　　　630
Adfuit Acrisio servandae cura puellae:
　　Hunc tamen illa suo crimine fecit avum.
Quid faciat custos, cum sint tot in urbe theatra,
　　Cum spectet iunctos illa libenter equos,
Cum sedeat Phariae sistris operata iuvencae,　　635
　　Quoque sui comites ire vetantur, eat,
Cum fuget a templis oculos Bona Diva virorum,
　　Praeterquam siquos illa venire iubet?
Cum, custode foris tunicas servante puellae,
　　Celent furtivos balnea multa iocos,　　　　　640
Cum, quotiens opus est, fallax aegrotet amica,
　　Et cedat lecto quamlibet aegra suo,
Nomine cum doceat, quid agamus, adultera clavis,
　　Quasque petas non det ianua sola vias?

---

[1] Sympathetic ink being unknown to the ancients, they used
a sort of "milk" which on being treated with charcoal revealed
the writing; Brandt quotes Pliny (26. 62), who mentions a plant
which had exactly such a power; its name was "tithymalum,"
called by the Romans "herba lactaria" or "lactuca caprina;"
cf. Ausonius, *Ep.* 28. 31. The same effect is produced, according
to Ovid, by writing with a stalk of wet flax.

deceive. Though as many keep watch as Argus had
eyes (so your purpose be but firm), you will deceive
them. Will a guardian forsooth prevent your writing,
when time is allowed you for taking a bath? when a
confidant can carry a written tablet, concealed by a
broad band on her warm bosom? when she can hide
a paper packet in her stocking, and bear your
coaxing message 'twixt foot and sandal? Should the
guardian beware of this, let the confidant offer her
back for your note, and bear your words upon her
body. A letter too is safe and escapes the eye,
when written in new milk:[1] touch it with coal-dust,
and you will read. That too will deceive which is
written with a stalk of moistened flax, and a pure
sheet will bear hidden marks.[2] Acrisius used dili-
gence to guard his daughter: yet by her own crime
she made him a grandsire. What can a guardian
do, when there are so many theatres in the city?
when she delights to watch the teams of horses?
when she sits doing honour with the sistrum to the
Pharian heifer, and goes where her male attendants
are forbidden to go? when the Good Goddess repels
from the temple the eyes of men, except such as she
bids come there herself? when, while the guardian
keeps the girl's clothes without, the numerous baths
hide furtive sport? when, so often as is needful, the
cunning friend falls sick, and, however ailing, with-
draws from her own bed?[3] when by its very name the
adulterate[4] key tells us what to do, and not only the
door permits the passage you demand? Much wine,

---

[2] Perhaps this may refer to wax not written on, but cover-
ing marks on the wood underneath.

[3] *i.e.* to let the lover take her place.

[4] *i.e.* false.

Fallitur et multo custodis cura Lyaeo,   645
  Illa vel Hispano lecta sit uva iugo ;
Sunt quoque, quae faciant altos medicamina somnos,
  Victaque Lethaea lumina nocte premant;
Nec male deliciis odiosum conscia tardis
  Detinet, et longa iungitur ipsa mora.   650
Quid iuvat ambages praeceptaque parva movere,
  Cum minimo custos munere possit emi ?
Munera, crede mihi, capiunt hominesque deosque:
  Placatur donis Iuppiter ipse datis.
Quid sapiens faciet? (stultus quoque munere gaudet;) 655
  Ipse quoque accepto munere mutus erit.
Sed semel est custos longum redimendus in aevum :
  Saepe dabit, dederit quas semel ille manus.
Questus eram, memini, metuendos esse sodales :
  Non tangit solos ista querella viros.   660
Credula si fueris, aliae tua gaudia carpent,
  Et lepus hic aliis exagitatus erit.
Haec quoque, quae praebet lectum studiosa locumque
  Crede mihi, mecum non semel illa fuit.
Nec nimium vobis formosa ancilla ministret :   665
  Saepe vicem dominae praebuit illa mihi.

Quo feror insanus ? quid aperto pectore in hostem
  Mittor, et indicio prodor ab ipse meo ?
Non avis aucupibus monstrat, qua parte petatur :
  Non docet infestos currere cerva canes.   670
Viderit utilitas : ego coepta fideliter edam :
  Lemniasin gladios in mea fata dabo.
Efficite (et facile est), ut nos credamus amari :
  Prona venit cupidis in sua vota fides.

---

[1] Spanish wines were not thought much of at Rome.
[2] *i.e.* the maid who helps her mistress.
[3] *i.e.* will the wise man be found as corruptible as the fool ?
Yes, he will.

too, will baffle a guardian's care, even though the grape be picked on Spanish slopes[1]; there are drugs, too, which induce deep slumber, and steep the vanquished eyes in Lethaean night; easily too does a confidant[2] detain the hateful fellow with tardy dalliance, and keep him by her own side in long delays. What avails it to make a long tale of trivial precepts, when a small bribe will buy the guardian? Bribes, believe me, buy both gods and men; Jupiter himself is appeased by the offering of gifts. What will the wise man do? (for the fool also delights in a bribe;) he too when bribed will hold his tongue.[3] But the guardian must be bought outright for a long time; the service he has given once he will often give. Once I lamented, I remember, that comrades were to be feared: 'tis not men only that my lament touches. If you are too trusting, other women will reap your joys, and that hare[4] will be hunted by others. She too, who eagerly offers bed and room, not once only, believe me, has she been with me.[5] Nor let too pretty a serving-maid attend you: often has she played her mistress' part for me.

Whither am I borne in my frenzy? Why rush I with open breast against the foe, and am betrayed by my own evidence? The bird does not show the fowlers where it may be hunted; the hind does not teach the enemy hounds to run. Let expediency see to itself; I will fulfil my purpose faithfully; I will give the Lemnian women swords to slay me. Make us (and it is easy) believe we are loved; swift comes belief to those whose desires are keen. Let

[4] *i.e.* her lover, whom other women will embrace.
[5] *i.e.* a woman who offers to put up the lover, but gains his affections in place of the mistress.

Spectet amabilius iuvenem, suspiret ab imo   675
    Femina, tam sero cur veniatque roget:
Accedant lacrimae, dolor et de paelice fictus,
    Et laniet digitis illius ora suis:
Iamdudum persuasus erit; miserebitur ultro,
    Et dicet " cura carpitur ista mei."   680
Praecipue si cultus erit speculoque placebit,
    Posse suo tangi credet amore deas.
Sed te, quaecumque est, moderate iniuria turbet,
    Nec sis audita paelice mentis inops.
Nec cito credideris: quantum cito credere laedat,   685
    Exemplum vobis non leve Procris erit.

Est prope purpureos colles florentis Hymetti
    Fons sacer et viridi caespite mollis humus:
Silva nemus non alta facit; tegit arbutus herbam,
    Ros maris et lauri nigraque myrtus olent: 690
Nec densum foliis buxum fragilesque myricae,
    Nec tenues cytisi cultaque pinus abest.
Lenibus inpulsae zephyris auraque salubri
    Tot generum frondes herbaque summa tremit.
Grata quies Cephalo: famulis canibusque relictis   695
    Lassus in hac iuvenis saepe resedit humo,
" Quae " que "meos releves aestus," cantare solebat
    " Accipienda sinu, mobilis aura, veni."
Coniugis ad timidas aliquis male sedulus aures
    Auditos memori detulit ore sonos;   700
Procris ut accepit nomen, quasi paelicis, Aurae,
    Excidit, et subito muta dolore fuit;
Palluit, ut serae lectis de vite racemis
    Pallescunt frondes, quas nova laesit hiemps,
Quaeque suos curvant matura cydonia ramos,   705
    Cornaque adhuc nostris non satis apta cibis.

---

[1] This story is also told in *Metam.* 7. 796 sqq.

the woman regard the youth with more loving looks,
and deeply sigh, and ask why he comes so late : let
tears be added, and feigned wrath about a rival ;
and let her tear his cheeks with her nails : long
since will he have been persuaded ; he will be quick
to pity, and will say, "For love of me is she distressed."
Particularly if he be well dressed and approved
by his glass will he believe that goddesses could fall
in love with him. But, however he wrong you, let it
disturb you but little, nor be put out when you hear
of a rival. Nor be quick to believe : what harm
quick belief can do, Procris will be to you a weighty
warning.

Near the purple hills of flowery Hymettus [1] there
is a sacred spring and ground soft with green turf :
trees of no great height form a grove ; arbutus
covers the grass, and rosemary, bays and dark myrtles
are fragrant ; nor is the thick foliage of the box-tree
lacking, or brittle tamarisks and thin lucerne and
the cultivated pine. Gentle zephyrs and health-
giving breezes sway the varied foliage, and the tips
of the grasses tremble. Sweet sleep was upon
Cephalus ; leaving servants and hounds the youth
often rested in this spot when weary, and, "Come,
wandering Aura," was he wont to sing, "come to my
bosom and refresh my sultriness." To his wife's
timid ears some foolish busy-body reported with
mindful utterance the sounds he had heard ; when
Procris heard the name of Aura, a rival, as she thought,
she fainted, and was speechless with sudden grief :
she paled, as pale the late leaves upon clusters of the
vine, hurt by the first breath of winter, and as ripe
quinces that bend their boughs are pale, and cornel-
berries not yet fit for human food. When her spirits

Ut rediit animus, tenues a pectore vestes
    Rumpit, et indignas sauciat ungue genas ;
Nec mora, per medias passis furibunda capillis
    Evolat, ut thyrso concita Baccha, vias.   710
Ut prope perventum, comites in valle relinquit,
    Ipsa nemus tacito clam pede fortis init.
Quid tibi mentis erat, cum sic male sana lateres,
    Procri ? quis adtoniti pectoris ardor erat ?
Iam iam venturam, quaecumque erat Aura, putabas 715
    Scilicet, atque oculis probra videnda tuis.
Nunc venisse piget (neque enim deprendere velles),
    Nunc iuvat : incertus pectora versat amor.
Credere quae iubeant, locus est et nomen et index,
    Et quia mens semper quod timet, esse putat.   720
Vidit ut oppressa vestigia corporis herba,
    Pulsantur trepidi corde micante sinus.
Iamque dies medius tenues contraxerat umbras,
    Inque pari spatio vesper et ortus erant :
Ecce, redit Cephalus silvis, Cyllenia proles,   725
    Oraque fontana fervida pulsat aqua.
Anxia, Procri, lates : solitas iacet ille per herbas,
    Et " zephyri molles auraque " dixit " ades ! "
Ut patuit miserae iucundus nominis error,
    Et mens et rediit verus in ora color.   730
Surgit, et oppositas agitato corpore frondes
    Movit, in amplexus uxor itura viri :
Ille feram movisse ratus, iuvenaliter artus
    Corripit, in dextra tela fuere manu.
Quid facis, infelix ? non est fera, supprime tela !   735
    Me miserum ! iaculo fixa puella tuo est.

returned, she plucked the frail garment from
her breast, and marred with her nails her innocent
cheeks; and straightway with streaming hair she
flies through the streets in frenzy, like a Bacchant
sped by the thyrsus. When she drew nigh, she left her
comrades in the vale, and herself secretly with silent
step bravely entered the wood. What were thy
feelings, Procris, when thus frantic thou lurkedst
there? What a fire was in thy maddened heart!
Soon would she come, that Aura, whoe'er she might
be (so didst thou think), and thine own eyes would
see the shame. Now dost thou regret thy coming (for
thou could'st not wish to find him guilty), now art
thou glad: this way and that love sways thy heart.
To commend belief there is the name and the place
and the informer, and because the mind ever thinks
its fears are true. When she saw the mark of a body
on the flattened grass, her leaping heart beats within
her fearful bosom. And now midday had drawn
short the unsubstantial shadows, and evening and
morning were equally removed: lo! Cephalus, son of
Cyllene, returns from the woods, and scatters
spring water on his glowing cheeks. Anxiously,
Procris, thou liest hid: he rests on the wonted
grass, and cries, " Come, breeze, come tender
Zephyrs!" When the name's pleasing error was
manifest to the hapless woman, her reason re-
turned, and the true colour to her face. She rises,
and speeding to her lover's embrace stirred with
her hurrying frame the leaves that were in her
way: he thinking he saw a quarry leapt up with
youthful ardour, and his weapon was in his hand.
What dost thou, hapless one? 'tis no beast: drop
thy bow. Woe is me! thy dart has pierced the

" Ei mihi ! " conclamat " fixisti pectus amicum.
  Hic locus a Cephalo vulnera semper habet.
Ante diem morior, sed nulla paelice laesa :
  Hoc faciet positae te mihi, terra, levem.   740
Nomine suspectas iam spiritus exit in auras :
  Labor, io, cara lumina conde manu ! "
Ille sinu dominae morientia corpora maesto
  Sustinet, et lacrimis vulnera saeva lavat :
Exit, et incauto paulatim pectore lapsus   745
  Excipitur miseri spiritus ore viri.

Sed repetamus opus : mihi nudis rebus eundum est,
  Ut tangat portus fessa carina suos.
Sollicite expectas, dum te in convivia ducam,
  Et quaeris monitus hac quoque parte meos.   750
Sera veni, positaque decens incede lucerna :
  Grata mora venies ; maxima lena mora est.
Etsi turpis eris, formosa videbere potis,
  Et latebras vitiis nox dabit ipsa tuis.
Carpe cibos digitis : est quiddam gestus edendi :   755
  Ora nec immunda tota perungue manu.
Neve domi praesume dapes, sed desine citra
  Quam capis ; es paulo quam potes esse minus ;
Priamides Helenen avide si spectet edentem,
  Oderit, et dicat " stulta rapina mea est."   760
Aptius est, deceatque magis potare puellas :
  Cum Veneris puero non male, Bacche, facis.
Hoc quoque, qua patiens caput est, animusque pedesque
  Constant : nec, quae sunt singula, bina vide.

749 sollicite *R and some MSS.* : scilicet *most MSS.* : expectas
MSS.   expectes *R.*
752 venies *MSS.* : veniens *R* : est Veneri *Heinsius.*
757, 8 neve *R* : sive *Heinsius* : sed *R* : seu *Heinsius* : capis es
Heinsius, Madvig : capeis *R.*

maid. "Alas!" she cries, "thou hast pierced a
friendly breast: this spot hath ever a wound from
Cephalus. Untimely I die, yet injured by no rival:
this will make thee, earth, lie lightly on my bones.
Now goes my spirit out upon the air whose name I
once suspected: alas! I am failing; close my eyes
with the hand I love." He raises to his sad bosom
his lady's dying form, and laves the cruel wound in
tears: her spirit passes, and ebbing little by little
from her rash breast is caught upon her unhappy
lover's lips.

But let us back to our work! with unveiled
matters must I deal, if my weary bark is to reach her
haven. Anxiously are you expecting me to lead you
to the feast; here too do you await my counsels.
Come late, and make a graceful entrance when the
lamp has been set: delay will enhance your charm:
a great procuress is delay. Though plain, to the
tipsy you will seem fair: and night herself will hide
your faults. Help yourself with your fingers:
manners in eating count for something; and smear
not all your face with a soiled hand. And do not take
your meal beforehand at home, but stop short of
your appetite; eat somewhat less than you are able;[1]
if Priam's son saw Helen eating greedily, he would
hate her and say, "My prize is a foolish woman."
Better suited is drinking, and were more becoming in a
woman: not badly goest thou, Bacchus, with Venus'
son. This too note, when the head endures, the
mind and feet are also firm; do not see double where

[1] *i.e.* do not eat first at home and so have no appetite, but
(on the other hand) do not indulge the latter to the full.
Reading "sive . . . seu," the sense is "in order not to seem
gluttonous, either have some food at home first, or stop short
of your appetite when at dinner."

Turpe iacens mulier multo madefacta Lyaeo :   765
   Digna est concubitus quoslibet illa pati.
Nec somnis posita tutum succumbere mensa :
   Per somnos fieri multa pudenda solent.

Ulteriora pudet docuisse : sed alma Dione
   "Praecipue nostrum est, quod pudet" inquit "opus."
Nota sibi sint quaeque : modos a corpore certos   771
   Sumite : non omnes una figura decet.
Quae facie praesignis erit, resupina iaceto :
   Spectentur tergo, quis sua terga placent.
Milanion umeris Atalantes crura ferebat :   775
   Si bona sunt, hoc sunt accipienda modo.
Parva vehatur equo : quod erat longissima, numquam
   Thebaïs Hectoreo nupta resedit equo.
Strata premat genibus, paulum cervice reflexa,
   Femina per longum conspicienda latus.   780
Cui femur est iuvenale, carent quoque pectora menda,
   Stet vir, in obliquo fusa sit ipsa toro.
Nec tibi turpe puta crinem, ut Phylleïa mater,
   Solvere, et effusis colla reflecte comis.
Tu quoque, cui rugis uterum Lucina notavit,   785
   Ut celer aversis utere Parthus equis.
Mille modi veneris ; simplex minimique laboris,
   Cum iacet in dextrum semisupina latus.
Sed neque Phoebei tripodes nec corniger Ammon
   Vera magis vobis, quam mea Musa, canet :   790
Siqua fides arti, quam longo fecimus usu,
   Credite : praestabunt carmina nostra fidem.
Sentiat ex imis venerem resoluta medullis
   Femina, et ex aequo res iuvet illa duos.

776 accipienda *Heinsius (from a MS.)*: aspicienda *R.*

---

[1] See Hom. *Il.* vi. 397, Mart. xi. 104. 14.
[2] *i.e.* Thessalian, perhaps Laodamia.

there is but one. A woman lying steeped in wine is an ugly sight; she deserves to endure any union whatever. Nor is it safe when the table is cleared to fall asleep; in sleep much happens that is shameful.

What remains I blush to tell; but kindly Dione says, "What brings a blush is before all else my business." Let each woman know herself; from your own bodies fix your methods; one fashion does not suit all alike. Let her who is fair of face recline upon her back; let those whose backs please them be seen from behind. Milanion bore Atalanta's legs upon his shoulders; if they are comely, let them be taken thus. A small woman should ride astride; because she was tall, his Theban[1] bride never sat Hector like a horse. A woman whose long flanks deserve to be seen should press the coverlets with her knees, her neck bent backward somewhat. If her thighs be youthful and her breasts without blemish, her lover should stand, and she herself lie slantwise on the couch. Nor think it unbecoming to loose your hair, like the Phylleian mother,[2] and bend back your neck amid flowing tresses. And you whose belly Lucina has marked with wrinkles, like the swift Parthian, use a backward-turned steed. There are a thousand modes of love; a simple one, and least fatiguing, is when the woman lies upon her right side, half-reclined. But neither Phoebus' tripods nor horned Ammon will tell you more truth than does my Muse: if an art I have learnt by long experience be trustworthy, give credence: my poems will warrant for its truth. Let the woman feel love's act, unstrung to the very depths of her frame, and let that act delight both alike. Nor let winning

Nec blandae voces iucundaque murmura cessent,   795
   Nec taceant mediis improba verba iocis.
Tu quoque, cui veneris sensum natura negavit,
   Dulcia mendaci gaudia finge sono.
Infelix, cui torpet hebes locus ille, puella,
   Quo pariter debent femina virque frui.   800
Tantum, cum finges, ne sis manifesta, caveto:
   Effice per motum luminaque ipsa fidem.
Quam iuvet, et voces et anhelitus arguat oris ;
   A! pudet, arcanas pars habet ista notas.
Gaudia post Veneris quae poscet munus amantem,   805
   Illa suas nolet pondus habere preces.
Nec lucem in thalamos totis admitte fenestris ;
   Aptius in vestro corpore multa latent.

Lusus habet finem : cygnis descendere tempus,
   Duxerunt collo qui iuga nostra suo.   810
Ut quondam iuvenes, ita nunc, mea turba, puellae
   Inscribant spoliis " Naso magister erat."

sounds and pleasant murmurs be idle, nor in the midst of the play let naughty words be hushed. You to whom nature has denied the sensation of love, counterfeit the sweet bliss with lying sounds. Unhappy the woman for whom that place, whereof man and woman ought to have joy alike, is dull and unfeeling. Only, when you pretend, see that you are not caught: win assurance by your movements and even by your eyes. Let your words and panting breath make clear your pleasure; ah, for shame! that part of your body has its secret signs. She that after love's joys will ask a lover for reward will not wish her prayers to have much weight. And let not light into your room by all the windows; it is better that much of your body should be hidden.

Our sport is ended: it is time to step down from the swans whose necks have drawn my car. As once the youths, so now let the women, my votaries, write upon their spoils, NASO WAS OUR MASTER.

THE REMEDIES OF LOVE

REMEDIA AMORIS

Legerat huius Amor titulum nomenque libelli:
  "Bella mihi, video, bella parantur" ait.
"Parce tuum vatem sceleris damnare, Cupido,
  Tradita qui toties te duce signa tuli.
Non ego Tydides, a quo tua saucia mater   5
  In liquidum rediit aethera Martis equis.
Saepe tepent alii iuvenes: ego semper amavi,
  Et si, quid faciam nunc quoque, quaeris, amo.
Quin etiam docui, qua posses arte parari,
  Et quod nunc ratio est, impetus ante fuit.   10
Nec te, blande puer, nec nostras prodimus artes,
  Nec nova praeteritum Musa retexit opus.
Siquis amat quod amare iuvat, feliciter ardet:
  Gaudeat, et vento naviget ille suo.
At siquis male fert indignae regna puellae,   15
  Ne pereat, nostrae sentiat artis opem.
Cur aliquis laqueo collum nodatus amator
  A trabe sublimi triste pependit onus?
Cur aliquis rigido fodit sua pectora ferro?
  Invidiam caedis, pacis amator, habes.   20
Qui, nisi desierit, misero periturus amore est,
  Desinat; et nulli funeris auctor eris.
Et puer es, nec te quicquam nisi ludere oportet:
  Lude; decent annos mollia regna tuos.
Nam poteras uti nudis ad bella sagittis: 25
  Sed tua mortifero sanguine tela carent.

---

[1] Venus was wounded by Diomede before Troy (Hom., *Il.*
5. 334), and rescued by Ares.
[2] In the three books of the preceding poem.

THE REMEDIES OF LOVE

LOVE read the name and title of this book: "Wars," said he, "wars are in store for me, I perceive." "Ah, Cupid, hold me not guilty of a crime, who am thy poet, and have so often under thy command borne the standards thou didst give me. I am not Tydeus' son, from whom thy mother fled back wounded on Mars' chariot to the pure air of heaven.[1] Other youths are ofttimes cool; I have ever been a lover, and, shouldst thou ask what I am doing now, I love. Nay too, I have taught by what skill thou mightest be gained,[2] and what was impulse then is science now. Neither thee do I betray, O winsome boy, nor mine own craft, nor does the new Muse unravel the old work. If any lover has delight in his love, blest is his passion: let him rejoice and sail on with favouring wind. But if any endures the tyranny of an unworthy mistress, lest he perish, let him learn the help my art can give. Why has some lover cast the noose about his neck, and hung, a sad burden, from a lofty beam? Why has one pierced his breast with the unyielding sword? Lover of peace, thou bearest the reproach of that murder. He who, unless he give o'er, will die of hapless love,—let him give o'er; and thou shalt be the death of none. Thou art a boy, nor does aught save play become thee: play then; a tender rule becomes thy years. For thou wert able to use arrows unsheathed for war: yet thy darts are free from deadly blood. Let thy

Vitricus et gladiis et acuta dimicet hasta,
    Et victor multa caede cruentus eat :
Tu cole maternas, tuto quibus utimur, artes,
    Et quarum vitio nulla fit orba parens.   30
Effice nocturna frangatur ianua rixa,
    Et tegat ornatas multa corona fores :
Fac coeant furtim iuvenes timidaeque puellae,
    Verbaque dent cauto qualibet arte viro :
Et modo blanditias, rigido modo iurgia posti   35
    Dicat et exclusus flebile cantet amans.
His lacrimis contentus eris sine crimine mortis ;
    Non tua fax avidos digna subire rogos."
Haec ego : movit Amor gemmatas aureus alas,
    Et mihi "propositum perfice" dixit "opus."   40

Ad mea, decepti iuvenes, praecepta venite,
    Quos suus ex omni parte fefellit amor.
Discite sanari, per quem didicistis amare :
    Una manus vobis vulnus opemque feret.
Terra salutares herbas, eademque nocentes   45
    Nutrit, et urticae proxima saepe rosa est ;
Vulnus in Herculeo quae quondam fecerat hoste,
    Vulneris auxilium Pelias hasta tulit.
Sed quaecumque viris, vobis quoque dicta, puellae,
    Credite : diversis partibus arma damus,   50
E quibus ad vestros siquid non pertinet usus,
    Attamen exemplo multa docere potest.
Utile propositum est saevas extinguere flammas,
    Nec servum vitii pectus habere sui.
Vixisset Phyllis, si me foret usa magistro,   55
    Et per quod novies, saepius isset iter ;

---

[1] Telephus, son of Hercules, was wounded and healed by the
spear of Achilles.

step-father fight with sword and sharp spear, and go triumphant stained with much shedding of blood: do thou practise thy mother's art, which it is safe to use, and by whose fault no parent is bereaved. Cause the door to be broken in the nightly brawl, and the gates to be hid 'neath the decking of many a garland: make youths and timid girls keep secret tryst, and by whatever art deceive the cautious husband: and let the excluded lover utter now blandishments, now reproaches to the unyielding door-post, and sing in doleful strain. Those tears will content thee, free from the reproach of death; thy torch deserves not to be set to greedy pyres." Thus I, and Love all golden moved his jewelled wings, and, " Finish," said he to me, " thy purposed task."

Come, hearken to my precepts, slighted youths, ye whom your own love has utterly betrayed. Learn healing from him through whom ye learnt to love: one hand alike will wound and succour. The same earth fosters healing herbs and noxious, and oft is the nettle nearest to the rose; the Pelian spear which wounded once its Herculean foe, bore relief also to the wound.[1] But whatever is said to men, deem also said to you, ye women: we give arms to the opposing sides, and if aught thereof concerns not your needs, yet by example it can teach much. A profitable aim it is to extinguish savage flames, and have a heart not enslaved to its own frailty. Phyllis would have lived, had she used my counsels, and taken more often the path she took nine times;[2] nor would

---

[2] See below l, 591 ff. and *Heroides* 2.

OVID

Nec moriens Dido summa vidisset ab arce
    Dardanias vento vela dedisse rates ;
Nec dolor armasset contra sua viscera matrem,
    Quae socii damno sanguinis ulta virum est   60
Arte mea Tereus, quamvis Philomela placeret,
    Per facinus fieri non meruisset avis.
Da mihi Pasiphaën, iam tauri ponet amorem :
    Da Phaedram, Phaedrae turpis abibit amor.
Redde Parim nobis, Helenen Menelaus habebit,   65
    Nec manibus Danais Pergama victa cadent.
Impia si nostros legisset Scylla libellos,
    Haesisset capiti purpura, Nise, tuo.
Me duce damnosas, homines, conpescite curas,
    Rectaque cum sociis me duce navis eat.   70
Naso legendus erat tum, cum didicistis amare :
    Idem nunc vobis Naso legendus erit.
Publicus assertor dominis suppressa levabo
    Pectora : vindictae quisque favete suae.
Te precor incipiens, adsit tua laurea nobis,   75
    Carminis et medicae, Phoebe, repertor opis.
Tu pariter vati, pariter succurre medenti :
    Utraque tutelae subdita cura tua est.

Dum licet, et modici tangunt praecordia motus,
    Si piget, in primo limine siste pedem.   80
Opprime, dum nova sunt, subiti mala semina morbi,
    Et tuus incipiens ire resistat equus.

---

[1] The reference is to Medea's slaying of her own children to
punish Jason.

[2] Tereus ravished Philomela, and was turned into a hoopoe ;
Pasiphae, wife of Minos, loved a bull, and bore the Minotaur ;
Phaedra, wife of Theseus, loved her stepson Hippolytus ; Scylla,
daughter of Nisus, betrayed him to her lover Minos by cutting
off his lock of purple hair.

dying Dido have seen from her citadel's height
the Dardan vessels spread their sails to the wind;
nor would anger have armed against her own off-
spring the mother who took vengeance on her hus-
band with the loss of kindred blood.[1] By my art
Tereus, though Philomel found favour, had not
deserved by crime to become a bird. Give me
Pasiphae: soon will she love the bull no more;
give me Phaedra: Phaedra's shameful love will
disappear. Give Paris to me: Menelaus will keep
Helen, nor will vanquished Pergamum fall by
Danaan hands. Had impious Scylla read my verse,
the purple had stayed on thy head, O Nisus.[2]
Under my guidance, ye men, control your ruinous
passions, and under my guidance let ship and crew
run straight. You should have read Naso then
when you learnt to love: you should read the
same Naso now. A public champion, I shall relieve
hearts that groan beneath their lords: welcome
each of you the rod[3] that liberates. Thee I beseech
at the outset, let thy laurel be nigh to aid me,
O Phoebus, inventor of song and of the healing
art! Succour alike the poet and alike the healer;
the labours of both are under thy patronage.

While it may be, and but moderate feeling moves
your heart, if you dislike it, stay your foot on the
first threshold. Crush, while yet they are new, the
baneful seeds of sudden disease, and let your steed
at the outset check his pace. For delay gives

[3] "assero" was the word used of those who "claimed"
either a slave for freedom or the reverse. "vindicta"
(from "vim dicere," declaration of authority) was the rod,
also called "festuca," with which the claimed man was
touched.

183

Nam mora dat vires, teneras mora percoquit uvas,
    Et validas segetes quae fuit herba, facit.
Quae praebet latas arbor spatiantibus umbras,   85
    Quo posita est primum tempore virga fuit ;
Tum poterat manibus summa tellure revelli :
    Nunc stat in inmensum viribus aucta suis.
Quale sit id, quod amas, celeri circumspice mente,
    Et tua laesuro subtrahe colla iugo.   90
Principiis obsta ; sero medicina paratur,
    Cum mala per longas convaluere moras.
Sed propera, nec te venturas differ in horas ;
    Qui non est hodie, cras minus aptus erit :
Verba dat omnis amor, reperitque alimenta morando ;
    Optima vindictae proxima quaeque dies.   96
Flumina pauca vides de magnis fontibus orta :
    Plurima collectis multiplicantur aquis.
Si cito sensisses, quantum peccare parares,
    Non tegeres vultus cortice, Myrrha, tuos.   100
Vidi ego quod fuerat primo sanabile vulnus,
    Dilatum longae damna tulisse morae.
Sed quia delectat Veneris decerpere fructum,
    Dicimus adsidue " cras quoque fiet idem."
Interea tacitae serpunt in viscera flammae,   105
    Et mala radices altius arbor agit.
Si tamen auxilii perierunt tempora primi,
    Et vetus in capto pectore sedit amor,
Maius opus superest : sed non, quia serior aegro
    Advocor, ille mihi destituendus erit.   110
Quam laesus fuerat partem, Poeantius heros
    Certa debuerat praesecuisse manu ;

---

[1] She was turned into the tree that bears her name for the crime of incest, see *Metam.* 10. 298.

[2] Philoctetes, son of Poeas, who had a diseased foot, and was left by the Greeks on Lemnos. He was destined to end

THE REMEDIES OF LOVE

strength, delay matures the tender grapes, and
makes what is grass into lusty crops. The tree
that gives broad shade to strollers, when first it
was planted, was a tender shoot, then it could
be pulled by the hand from the surface earth:
now it stands firm, grown by its own strength to
unmeasured height. Consider in swift thought
what kind of thing it is you love, and withdraw
your neck from a yoke that may one day gall.
Resist beginnings; too late is the medicine pre-
pared, when the disease has gained strength by
long delay. Ay, and make haste, nor wait on the
coming hours; he who is not ready to-day will be
less so to-morrow: all love deceives and finds
sustenance in delaying; next day is ever the best
for your deliverance. Few rivers do you see that
are born of mighty springs: most are increased by
gathered waters. Hadst thou been quick to know
how great a crime thou wert devising, thou hadst
not, Myrrha, hid thy face in bark.[1] I have seen a
wound, that at first was healable, by tarrying suffer
the penalty of long delay. But because we delight to
pluck the blooms of Venus, ever we repeat, "To-
morrow it will be the same." Meanwhile secret
flames creep into our inmost being, and the evil
tree drives its roots deeper down. Yet if the time
for early succour is lost, and an old love is seated
in the captured heart, a heavier task remains: but,
because I am called late to the patient's side, I
must not leave him to his fate. The Poeantian
hero should have cut away with unfaltering hand
that part where he had been hurt;[2] yet was he

the Trojan war through being the possessor of the bow and
arrows of Hercules.

185

Post tamen hic multos sanatus creditur annos
  Supremam bellis imposuisse manum.
Qui modo nascentes properabam pellere morbos,   115
  Admoveo tardam nunc tibi lentus opem.
Aut nova, si possis, sedare incendia temptes,
  Aut ubi per vires procubuere suas:
Cum furor in cursu est, currenti cede furori;
  Difficiles aditus impetus omnis habet.   120
Stultus, ab obliquo qui cum descendere possit,
  Pugnat in adversas ire natator aquas.
Impatiens animus, nec adhuc tractabilis arte,
  Respuit atque odio verba monentis habet.
Adgrediar melius tum, cum sua vulnera tangi   125
  Iam sinet, et veris vocibus aptus erit.
Quis matrem, nisi mentis inops, in funere nati
  Flere vetet? non hoc illa monenda loco est.
Cum dederit lacrimas animumque impleverit aegrum,
  Ille dolor verbis emoderandus erit.   130
Temporis ars medicina fere est: data tempore prosunt,
  Et data non apto tempore vina nocent.
Quin etiam accendas vitia inritesque vetando,
  Temporibus si non adgrediare suis.

Ergo ubi visus eris nostrae medicabilis arti,   135
  Fac monitis fugias otia prima meis.
Haec, ut ames, faciunt, haec quod fecere, tuentur;
  Haec sunt iucundi causa cibusque mali.
Otia si tollas, periere Cupidinis arcus,
  Contemtaeque iacent et sine luce faces.   140
Quam platanus vino gaudet, quam populus unda,
  Et quam limosa canna palustris humo,

---

¹ You will be swept away if you try to make head against
passion, so go down the stream gently in a zig-zag course.

healed, we believe, after many years, and dealt
the blow that ended all the war. I who of late
was hastening to nip an ailment in the bud now
cautiously apply to you my tardy aid. Either when
'tis new try, if you can, to assuage a fire, or when by
its own force it has collapsed : when its fury is
at full speed, give way to its furious speeding; im-
petuous force is ever hard to face. Foolish is the
swimmer who though he can pass down it in a
slanting course struggles to go against the stream.[1]
The impatient spirit, as yet intractable to skill,
rejects and holds in abhorrence words of counsel.
More wisely shall I then approach when he suffers at
last his wounds to be touched, and is fit for true
admonishment. Who save a fool would forbid a
mother to weep o'er the body of her son? not then
must she be counselled. When she has shed tears
and fulfilled her mind's distress, then may words set
a limit to that grief. The art of being timely is
almost a medicine : wine timely given helps, un-
timely, harms. Nay, you would inflame the malady,
and by forbidding irritate it, should you attack it
at an unfitting time.

When therefore I shall find you amenable to
my skill, obey my counsels and first of all shun
leisure. That makes you love; that guards what
it has done ; that is the cause and sustenance of
the pleasant evil. Take away leisure and Cupid's
bow is broken, and his torch lies extinguished and
despised. As the plane rejoices in wine,[2] or the
poplar in water, or the reed of the mere in marshy

---

[2] Because men plant it to give them shade to drink
under, and sometimes pour water on its roots in libation.

Tam Venus otia amat; qui finem quaeris amoris,
  Cedit amor rebus : res age, tutus eris.
Languor, et inmodici sub nullo vindice somni,   145
  Aleaque, et multo tempora quassa mero
Eripiunt omnes animo sine vulnere nervos :
  Adfluit incautis insidiosus Amor.
Desidiam puer ille sequi solet, odit agentes :
  Da vacuae menti, quo teneatur, opus.   150
Sunt fora, sunt leges, sunt, quos tuearis, amici :
  Vade per urbanae splendida castra togae.
Vel tu sanguinei iuvenalia munera Martis
  Suspice : deliciae iam tibi terga dabunt.
Ecce, fugax Parthus, magni nova causa triumphi,   155
  Iam videt in campis Caesaris arma suis :
Vince Cupidineas pariter Parthasque sagittas,
  Et refer ad patrios bina tropaea deos.
Ut semel Aetola Venus est a cuspide laesa,
  Mandat amatori bella gerenda suo.   160
Quaeritis, Aegisthus quare sit factus adulter ?
  In promptu causa est : desidiosus erat.
Pugnabant alii tardis apud Ilion armis :
  Transtulerat vires Graecia tota suas.
Sive operam bellis vellet dare, nulla gerebat :   165
  Sive foro, vacuum litibus Argos erat.
Quod potuit, ne nil illic ageretur, amavit.
  Sic venit ille puer, sic puer ille manet.

Rura quoque oblectant animos studiumque colendi :
  Quaelibet huic curae cedere cura potest.   170

---

¹ Fighting and glory are to be found in the arts of peace,
cf. l. 166.
² It was a popular delusion of the time that Augustus
contemplated a great Parthian war; in 20 B.C. diplomacy
had resulted in the return of the Roman standards lost at
Carrhae, but in 4 B.C. another expedition, under the young

ground, so does Venus delight in leisure; you who seek an end of love, love yields to business: be busy, and you will be safe. Listlessness, and too much sleep with none to check you, and dicing, and fuddling the temples with much wine, without a wound rob the spirit of all its strength: insidious Love glides into defenceless hearts. Where sloth is, that Boy is wont to follow; he hates the busy: give the empty mind some business to occupy it. There are the courts, there are the laws, there are friends for you to protect: frequent the camps that gleam with the city gown.[1] Or undertake the manly task of blood-stained Mars: you will soon be routing your pleasures. Lo! the fugitive Parthian, fresh cause of glorious triumph, already beholds the arms of Caesar on his plains:[2] defeat alike Cupid's and the Parthian's arrows, and bring home to your country's gods a double trophy. No sooner was Venus hurt by the Aetolian spear than she bids her lover wage her wars.[3] Do you ask why Aegisthus became an adulterer? the reason is near at hand: he was a sluggard. Others were fighting in the lagging war by Ilium: Greece had sent thither all her might. Did he wish to engage in warfare, Argos was waging none: or to the courts? Argos was free from legal strife. All he could do, he did; that he might not there do naught, he fell in love. So comes that Boy, so does that Boy remain.

The country also delights the mind, and the pursuit of husbandry: no care is there but must

Gaius, had been found necessary to re-establish Roman ascendancy; v. *Ars Am.* i. 177.
[3] cf. note on l. 5.

Colla iube domitos oneri supponere tauros,
　　Sauciet ut duram vomer aduncus humum:
Obrue versata Cerialia semina terra,
　　Quae tibi cum multo faenore reddat ager.
Aspice curvatos pomorum pondere ramos,　　175
　　Ut sua, quod peperit, vix ferat arbor onus;
Aspice labentes iucundo murmure rivos;
　　Aspice tondentes fertile gramen oves.
Ecce, petunt rupes praeruptaque saxa capellae:
　　Iam referent haedis ubera plena suis;　　180
Pastor inaequali modulatur arundine carmen,
　　Nec desunt comites, sedula turba, canes;
Parte sonant alia silvae mugitibus altae,
　　Et queritur vitulum mater abesse suum.
Quid, cum suppositos fugiunt examina fumos,　　185
　　Ut relevent dempti vimina curva favi?
Poma dat autumnus: formosa est messibus aestas:
　　Ver praebet flores: igne levatur hiemps.
Temporibus certis maturam rusticus uvam
　　Deligit, et nudo sub pede musta fluunt;　　190
Temporibus certis desectas alligat herbas,
　　Et tonsam raro pectine verrit humum.
Ipse potes riguis plantam deponere in hortis,
　　Ipse potes rivos ducere lenis aquae.
Venerit insitio; fac ramum ramus adoptet,　　195
　　Stetque peregrinis arbor operta comis.
Cum semel haec animum coepit mulcere voluptas,
　　Debilibus pinnis inritus exit Amor.
Vel tu venandi studium cole: saepe recessit
　　Turpiter a Phoebi victa sorore Venus.　　200
Nunc leporem pronum catulo sectare sagaci,
　　Nunc tua frondosis retia tende iugis,

yield to this. Bid the tamed bulls bow their necks to the burden, that the curved share may wound the stubborn ground; bury the seeds of Ceres in the upturned soil, that the earth may restore them to you with lavish usury. Watch your boughs bent with the weight of apples, so that the tree scarce sustains the burden of its produce; watch the streams gliding with cheerful sound; watch the sheep cropping the fertile grass. Lo! the goats make for the rocks and precipitous cliffs: soon they will bring back full udders to their kids; the shepherd plays a ditty on his unequal pipes, nor lacks the company of his faithful dogs; elsewhere the deep glades resound with lowings, and a mother complains that her calf is lost. What of the swarms that flee from the torch-smoke set beneath them, that the taking of the combs may unburden the rounded osiers? Autumn brings fruit: summer is fair with harvest: spring gives flowers: winter is relieved by fire. At fixed seasons the countryman picks the ripened grapes, and the vintage flows beneath his naked foot; at fixed seasons he cuts and binds the grasses, and harrows the shaven earth with wide-toothed comb. You yourself can plant a shoot in a well-watered garden, you yourself can guide the runnels of gentle water. The time of grafting has come: see that bough adopts bough, and that the tree stands covered with leaves that are not its own. When once this pleasure begins to charm the mind, on maimed wings Love flutters hopelessly away. Or cultivate the pleasures of the chase: ofttimes has Venus, vanquished by Phoebus' sister, beaten a base retreat. Now pursue with cunning hound the forward-straining hare, now

Aut pavidos terre varia formidine cervos,
    Aut cadat adversa cuspide fossus aper.
Nocte fatigatum somnus, non cura puellae,   205
    Excipit et pingui membra quiete levat.
Lenius est studium, studium tamen, alite capta
    Aut lino aut calamis praemia parva sequi,
Vel, quae piscis edax avido male devoret ore,
    Abdere suspensis aera recurva cibis.   210
Aut his aut aliis, donec dediscis amare,
    Ipse tibi furtim decipiendus eris.
Tu tantum quamvis firmis retinebere vinclis,
    I procul, et longas carpere perge vias ;
Flebis, et occurret desertae nomen amicae,   215
    Stabit et in media pes tibi saepe via :
Sed quanto minus ire voles, magis ire memento ;
    Perfer, et invitos currere coge pedes.
Nec pluvias opta, nec te peregrina morentur
    Sabbata, nec damnis Allia nota suis.   220
Nec quot transieris, sed quot tibi, quaere, supersint
    Milia ; nec, maneas ut prope, finge moras :
Tempora nec numera, nec crebro respice Romam,
    Sed fuge : tutus adhuc Parthus ab hoste fuga est.

Dura aliquis praecepta vocet mea ; dura fatemur   225
    Esse ; sed ut valeas, multa dolenda feres.
Saepe bibi sucos, quamvis invitus, amaros
    Aeger, et oranti mensa negata mihi.
Ut corpus redimas, ferrum patieris et ignes,
    Arida nec sitiens ora levabis aqua :   230

stretch your nets on leafy ridges; either with varied panic alarm the timid deer, or meet the boar and fell him with your spear-thrust. Tired out, at nightfall sleep, not thoughts of a girl, will await you, and refresh your limbs with healthy repose. 'Tis a milder pleasure (yet a pleasure it is) to seek a humble prize by snaring birds with net or reed, or to hide in the suspended bait the brazen hook, which the greedy fish may swallow to his hurt with ravening mouth. By these or other pursuits, until you unlearn your love, you must craftily deceive yourself. Only go away, though strong be the bonds that hold you, go far, and make a lengthy voyage; you will weep, and the name of your deserted mistress will haunt your mind; and oft will your foot halt in mid-journey: yet the less you wish to go, the more be sure of going; persist, and compel your unwilling feet to run. Hope not for rain, nor let foreign sabbaths stay you, nor Allia well-known for its ill-luck.[1] Ask not how many miles you have covered, nor how many more remain; nor feign delays that you may tarry near at hand. Count not the days, nor be ever looking back at Rome; but flee: by flight the Parthian is still safe from his foe.

Some may call my counsels cruel: cruel I confess they are; but, to recover health, you are willing to bear much pain. Often when ill have I drunk, though unwilling, bitter juices, and the feast was denied to my prayers. To redeem your body you will suffer steel and fire, nor, though thirsty, refresh your parched mouth with water: to be whole in

---

[1] The disastrous defeat of the Romans by the Gauls on the river Allia (July 18, 390 B.C.) was a black date in their Kalendar, and so ill-omened for starting a journey.

Ut valeas animo, quicquam tolerare negabis ?
　At pretium pars haec corpore maius habet.
Sed tamen est artis tristissima ianua nostrae,
　Et labor est unus tempora prima pati.
Aspicis, ut prensos urant iuga prima iuvencos,　235
　Et nova velocem cingula laedat equum ?
Forsitan a laribus patriis exire pigebit :
　Sed tamen exibis : deinde redire voles ;
Nec te Lar patrius, sed amor revocabit amicae,
　Praetendens culpae splendida verba tuae.　240
Cum semel exieris, centum solatia curae
　Et rus et comites et via longa dabit.
Nec satis esse putes discedere ; lentus abesto,
　Dum perdat vires sitque sine igne cinis.
Quod nisi firmata properaris mente reverti,　245
　Inferet arma tibi saeva rebellis Amor.
Quidquid et afueris, avidus sitiensque redibis,
　Et spatium damno cesserit omne tuo.

Viderit, Haemoniae siquis mala pabula terrae
　Et magicas artes posse iuvare putat.　250
Ista veneficii vetus est via ; noster Apollo
　Innocuam sacro carmine monstrat opem.
Me duce non tumulo prodire iubebitur umbra,
　Non anus infami carmine rumpet humum ;
Non seges ex aliis alios transibit in agros,　255
　Nec subito Phoebi pallidus orbis erit.
Ut solet, aequoreas ibit Tiberinus in undas :
　Ut solet, in niveis Luna vehetur equis.
Nulla recantatas deponent pectora curas,
　Nec fugiet vivo sulpure victus amor.　260
Quid te Phasidiae iuverunt gramina terrae,
　Cum cuperes patria, Colchi, manere domo ?

---

¹ *i.e.*, Thessaly, always famed for witchcraft.

mind, is there aught you will refuse to bear? Ah, but this part of you is costlier than the body. Yet the gateway of my art is the severest trial, and your only labour will be to endure the first beginning. Do you see how the first yoke chafes the captured bullocks, how the new saddle hurts the flying steed? Perchance 'twill irk you to leave your home and country; yet leave it you will: and then you will wish to return; but it will not be your home and country, but the love of your mistress that calls you back, cloaking your weakness in grand words. Once you have gone forth, a hundred cares will bring you solace, the country scenes, your comrades, the long road. Nor think it enough to depart; be absent long, till the fuel lose its force and the flame be spent. If you haste to return save with well-steeled mind, Love will renew the fight, and wage fierce war against you. For all your absence you will come back greedy and athirst, and all that time will but have done you harm.

If anyone thinks that the baneful herbs of Haemonia[1] and arts of magic can avail, let him take his own risk. That is the old way of witchcraft; my patron Apollo gives harmless aid in sacred song. Under my guidance no spirit will be bidden issue from the tomb, no witch will cleave the ground with hideous spell; no crops will pass from field to field, nor Phoebus' orb grow suddenly pale. As of wont will Tiber flow to the sea's waters; as of wont will the Moon ride in her snow-white car. No hearts will lay aside their passion by enchantment, nor love flee vanquished by strong sulphur. What availed thee the grasses of thy Phasian land, O Colchian maid, when thou wert fain to stay in thy

Quid tibi profuerunt, Circe, Perseïdes herbae,
    Cum sua Neritias abstulit aura rates?
Omnia fecisti, ne callidus hospes abiret: 265
    Ille dedit certae lintea plena fugae.
Omnia fecisti, ne te ferus ureret ignis:
    Longus et invito pectore sedit amor.
Vertere tu poteras homines in mille figuras,
    Non poteras animi vertere iura tui.   270
Diceris his etiam, cum iam discedere vellet,
    Dulichium verbis detinuisse ducem:
" Non ego, quod primo, memini, sperare solebam,
    Iam precor, ut coniunx tu meus esse velis;
Et tamen, ut coniunx essem tua, digna videbar,   275
    Quod dea, quod magni filia Solis eram.
Ne properes, oro; spatium pro munere posco:
    Quid minus optari per mea vota potest?
Et freta mota vides, et debes illa timere:
    Utilior velis postmodo ventus erit.   280
Quae tibi causa fugae? non hic nova Troia resurgit,
    Non aliquis socios rursus ad arma vocat.
Hic amor et pax est, in qua male vulneror una,
    Totaque sub regno terra futura tuo est."
Illa loquebatur, navem solvebat Ulixes: 285
    Inrita cum velis verba tulere noti.
Ardet et adsuetas Circe decurrit ad artes,
    Nec tamen est illis adtenuatus amor.

Ergo quisquis opem nostra tibi poscis ab arte,
    Deme veneficiis carminibusque fidem.   290

282 rursus *R*: Rhesus *edd.*

native home? What did Persean herbs profit thee,
O Circe, when a breeze that favoured them bore
the Neritian barks away?[1] Thou didst all, that the
cunning stranger should not leave thee: yet he
spread full canvas in unhindered flight. Thou didst
all, that the fierce fire should not burn thee: yet
long abode the passion in thy unwilling breast.
Thou wert able to change men into a thousand
shapes, yet wert unable to change the laws of thine
own soul. In these words even, when already he
was eager to depart, art thou said to have detained
the Dulichian chief: "I pray not now, what first,
I remember, I was wont to hope, that thou wouldst
wish to be my husband; and yet methought I was
worthy to be thy wife, in that I was a goddess,
daughter of the mighty Sun. I beseech thee not to
haste; I crave the boon of time: what less could my
vows pray for? Thou seest the waters roused, and
shouldst fear them: presently the wind will be more
useful to thy sails. What cause hast thou for flight?
no new Troy rises here again, none calls his mates
to arms once more. Love is here, and peace, wherein
I alone am wounded sore, and the land will be
all beneath thy sway." She was yet speaking:
Ulysses loosed his ship; with the sails the winds
bore away her unavailing words. Circe aflame has
recourse to her wonted arts, yet not by them is her
passion calmed.

Therefore, whoever you are that seek aid in my
skill, have no faith in spells and witchcraft. If

[1] Colchian maid: Medea. Neritian: Ithacan, from Mt.
Neritus in that island. Persean: from Perse, mother of
Circe.

Si te causa potens domina retinebit in Urbe,
  Accipe, consilium quod sit in Urbe meum.
Optimus ille sui vindex, laedentia pectus
  Vincula qui rupit, dedoluitque semel.
Sicui tantum animi est, illum mirabor et ipse,   295
  Et dicam "monitis non eget iste meis."
Tu mihi, qui quod amas, aegre dediscis amare,
  Nec potes, et velles posse, docendus eris.
Saepe refer tecum sceleratae facta puellae,
  Et pone ante oculos omnia damna tuos.   300
" Illud et illud habet, nec ea contenta rapina est :
  Sub titulum nostros misit avara lares.
Sic mihi iuravit, sic me iurata fefellit,
  Ante suas quotiens passa iacere fores !
Diligit ipsa alios, a me fastidit amari ;   305
  Institor, heu, noctes, quas mihi non dat, habet !"
Haec tibi per totos inacescant omnia sensus :
  Haec refer, hinc odii semina quaere tui.
Atque utinam possis etiam facundus in illis
  Esse ! dole tantum, sponte disertus eris.   310
Haeserat in quadam nuper mea cura puella :
  Conveniens animo non erat illa meo :
Curabar propriis aeger Podalirius herbis,
  Et, fateor, medicus turpiter aeger eram.
Profuit adsidue vitiis insistere amicae,   315
  Idque mihi factum saepe salubre fuit.
"Quam mala" dicebam "nostrae sunt crura puellae !"
  Nec tamen, ut vere confiteamur, erant.

293 sui *Heinsius* : fuit *R*.

---

[1] "titulus" is literally the notice or placard of sale.

some powerful cause keeps you in imperial Rome, hear what my counsel is in Rome. He best wins freedom for himself who has burst the bonds that hurt his soul, and once for all o'ercome the smart. If any has such fortitude, I, even I, will marvel at him, and say, "That man needs not my precepts." But you who love and with pain unlearn your loving, who cannot and yet wish you could, you must be taught by me. Bring often to your mind what your cursed mistress has done, and set all your loss before your eyes. "This has she, and that, nor is content with so much plunder: the greedy wretch has brought all my house beneath the hammer.[1] Thus did she swear to me, and swearing played me false; how often did she suffer me to lie before her door! She cares for others herself, but scorns my love: a pedlar[2] (curse him!) enjoys the nights she refuses to me!" Let all this steep your feelings in gall: remember that, seek there the seeds of hatred. And would that you could be eloquent too therein! well, only suffer, and eloquence will come. Lately my attentions were paid to a certain girl; she my passion did not favour: a sick Podalirius,[3] I treated myself with my own herbs, and, I confess, I was a shamefully sick physician. It helped me to harp continually on my mistress' faults, and that, when I did it, often brought me relief. "How ugly," would I say, "are my girl's legs!" and yet they were not, to say the

---

[2] These travelling dealers in luxuries were a special danger; cf. Hor. *Od.* 3. 6. 30, "institor dedecorum pretiosus emptor," and *Ars Am.* 1. 421.

[3] The physician of the Greeks in Homer (*Il.* 2. 729, 11. 832).

" Brachia quam non sunt nostrae formosa puellae !"
    Et tamen, ut vere confiteamur, erant.   320
" Quam brevis est !" nec erat; " quam multum poscit
    amantem !"
Haec odio venit maxima causa meo.
Et mala sunt vicina bonis; errore sub illo
    Pro vitio virtus crimina saepe tulit.
Qua potes, in peius dotes deflecte puellae,   325
    Iudiciumque brevi limite falle tuum.
Turgida, si plena est, si fusca est, nigra vocetur :
    In gracili macies crimen habere potest.
Et poterit dici petulans, quae rustica non est:
    Et poterit dici rustica, siqua proba est.   330
Quin etiam, quacumque caret tua femina dote,
    Hanc moveat, blandis usque precare sonis.
Exige quod cantet, siqua est sine voce puella :
    Fac saltet, nescit siqua movere manum.
Barbara sermone est ? fac tecum multa loquatur ;   335
    Non didicit chordas tangere ? posce lyram.
Durius incedit ? fac inambulet ; omne papillae
    Pectus habent tumidae ? fascia nulla tegat.
Si male dentata est, narra, quod rideat, illi ;
    Mollibus est oculis ? quod fleat illa, refer.   340
Proderit et subito, cum se non finxerit ulli,
    Ad dominam celeres mane tulisse gradus.
Auferimur cultu ; gemmis auroque teguntur
    Omnia ; pars minima est ipsa puella sui.
Saepe ubi sit, quod ames, inter tam multa requiras ; 345
    Decipit hac oculos aegide dives Amor.
Improvisus ades, deprendes tutus inermem :
    Infelix vitiis excidet illa suis.
Non tamen huic nimium praecepto credere tutum
    est :
    Fallit enim multos forma sine arte decens.   350

truth. "How far from comely are my girl's arms!" yet comely they were, to say the truth. "How short she is!" though she was not; "how much she asks of her lover!" that proved my chiefest cause of hate. Faults too lie near to charms; by that error virtues oft were blamed for vices. Where you can, turn to the worse your girl's attractions, and by a narrow margin criticise amiss.[1] Call her fat, if she is full-breasted, black, if dark-complexioned; in a slender woman leanness can be made a reproach. If she is not simple, she can be called pert: if she is honest, she can be called simple. Nay more, whatever gift your mistress lacks, ever with coaxing words pray her to employ it. Insist that she sing, if she be without a voice; make her dance, if she know not how to move her arms. Has her speech an accent? make her talk much with you; she has never learnt to touch the strings? call for the lyre. Her gait is awkward? take her for a walk; her breast is all swelling paps? let no bands conceal the fault. If her teeth are ugly, tell her something to make her laugh; are her eyes weak? recount a tearful tale. It will profit, too, of a sudden, when she has not prepared herself for anyone, to speed of a morning to your mistress. We are won by dress; all is concealed by gems and gold; a woman is the least part of herself. Often may you ask, where is there aught to love amid so much; with this aegis wealthy Love deceives the eye. Arrive unexpectedly: safe yourself, you will catch her unarmed: she will fall, hapless woman, by her own defects. Yet 'tis not safe to trust this precept overmuch, for artless beauty deceives many

---

[1] *i.e.*, just get on the wrong side of truth in your criticism.

Tum quoque, compositis cum collinit ora venenis,
    Ad dominae vultus (nec pudor obstet) eas.
Pyxidas invenies et rerum mille colores,
    Et fluere in tepidos oesypa lapsa sinus.
Illa tuas redolent, Phineu, medicamina mensas :   355
    Non semel hinc stomacho nausea facta meo.

Nunc tibi quae medio veneris praestemus in usu,
    Eloquar : ex omni est parte fugandus amor.
Multa quidem ex illis pudor est mihi dicere ; sed tu
    Ingenio verbis concipe plura meis.   360
Nuper enim nostros quidam carpsere libellos,
    Quorum censura Musa proterva mea est.
Dummodo sic placeam, dum toto canter in orbe,
    Quod volet, inpugnent unus et alter opus.
Ingenium magni livor detractat Homeri :   365
    Quisquis es, ex illo, Zoile, nomen habes.
Et tua sacrilegae laniarunt carmina linguae,
    Pertulit huc victos quo duce Troia deos.
Summa petit livor ; perflant altissima venti :
    Summa petunt dextra fulmina missa Iovis.   370
At tu, quicumque es, quem nostra licentia laedit,
    Si sapis, ad numeros exige quidque suos.
Fortia Maeonio gaudent pede bella referri ;
    Deliciis illic quis locus esse potest ?
Grande sonant tragici ; tragicos decet ira cothurnos : 375
    Usibus e mediis soccus habendus erit.
Liber in adversos hostes stringatur iambus,
    Seu celer, extremum seu trahat ille pedem.

351 compositis cum collinit *Riese* : compositis cum linit *R*.

---

[1] Phineus was punished for cruelty to his sons by the
Harpies, who made the food on his table foul and stinking,
cf. Virg., *Aen.* 3. 211.

[2] A severe critic of Homer (hence called Homeromastix) who
lived under Ptolemy Philadelphus, 285–247.

a lover. Then too, when she is painting her cheeks
with concoctions of dyes, go (let not shame hinder
you) and see your mistress' face. Boxes you will
find, and a thousand colours, and juices that melt
and drip into her warm bosom. Such drugs smell
of your table, Phineus;[1] not once only has my
stomach grown queasy at them.

Now I will tell you what I recommend in the
midst of the practice of love: passion must be
repelled on every side. Much of this indeed I am
ashamed to speak; but do you by your wit imagine
more than my words say. For certain folk of late
have found fault with my writings, and brand my
Muse as a wanton. Yet so long as I please thereby,
so long as I am sung in all the world, let this man
or that attack me as he will. Envy disparages great
Homer's genius: whoever you are, Zoilus,[2] you get
your fame from him. You too, under whose guidance
Troy brought hither her vanquished gods—your
poems too irreverent tongues have wounded. What
is highest is Envy's mark; winds sweep the summits,
and thunderbolts sped by Jove's right hand seek out
the heights. But you, whoever you are whom my
freedom hurts, suit each theme, if you are wise, to
its proper numbers. Valiant wars rejoice to be sung
in Maeonian metre;[3] what place can be found there
for lovers' tales? Tragedians sound a noble strain;
anger becomes the tragic buskin: the sock must
be used for common scenes. Let the free iambus
be drawn[4] against the opposing foe, whether it
rapidly advance, or drag its final foot.[5] Let winsome

[3] *i.e.*, hexameters, the metre of Homer, the Maeonian bard.
[4] *i.e.*, like a sword.
[5] "celer" refers to the ordinary iambic, what follows to
the Scazon, or halting iambic, in which the last foot is a
spondee.

Blanda pharetratos elegeia cantet Amores,
    Et levis arbitrio ludat amica suo.   380
Callimachi numeris non est dicendus Achilles,
    Cydippe non est oris, Homere, tui.
Quis feret Andromaches peragentem Thaida partes ?
    Peccat, in Andromache Thaida quisquis agat.
Thais in arte mea est; lascivia libera nostra est ;   385
    Nil mihi cum vitta ; Thais in arte mea est.
Si mea materiae respondet Musa iocosae,
    Vicimus, et falsi criminis acta rea est.
Rumpere, Livor edax : magnum iam nomen habemus ;
    Maius erit, tantum quo pede coepit eat.   390
Sed nimium properas : vivam modo, plura dolebis ;
    Et capiunt animi carmina multa mei.
Nam iuvat et studium famae mihi crevit honore ;
    Principio clivi noster anhelat equus.
Tantum se nobis elegi debere fatentur,   395
    Quantum Vergilio nobile debet epos.

Hactenus invidiae respondimus : attrahe lora
    Fortius, et gyro curre, poeta, tuo.
Ergo ubi concubitus et opus iuvenale petetur,
    Et prope promissae tempora noctis erunt,   400
Gaudia ne dominae, pleno si corpore sumes,
    Te capiant, ineas quamlibet ante, velim ;
Quamlibet invenias, in qua tua prima voluptas
    Desinat : a prima proxima segnis erit.
Sustentata venus gratissima ; frigore soles,   405
    Sole iuvant umbrae, grata fit unda siti.
Et pudet, et dicam : venerem quoque iunge figura,
    Qua minime iungi quamque decere putes.
Nec labor efficere est : rarae sibi vera fatentur,
    Et nihil est, quod se dedecuisse putent.   410

---

[1] The typical courtesan and heroine respectively.   [2] *i.e.* Envy.

Elegy sing of quivered Loves, and lightly sport in
kindly mood at her own pleasure. Achilles must not
be told of in the numbers of Callimachus; Cydippe
suits not thy utterance, Homer. Who could endure
Thais playing Andromache's part?[1] she errs, who
in Andromache plays the part of Thais. Thais is
the subject of my art; unfettered is my love-making:
naught have I to do with fillets; Thais is the
subject of my art. If my Muse meets the charge of
mirthful themes, I have won, and she is accused on
a false charge. Burst thyself, greedy Envy! my
fame is great already; it will be greater still, so it
keep its first good fortune. But you[2] haste over-
much: if I but live, you will grieve the more;
many a song in store has my genius yet. For the
desire of fame delights me, and has grown with my
renown; my steed pants but at the beginning of the
slope. Elegy admits it owes as much to me as the
noble Epic owes to Virgil.

So far I have but made answer to reproach: pull
the rein more strongly, and run, poet, in thy proper
track. When therefore union is sought and the
work of lusty youth, and the time of the promised
night draws nigh, lest your pleasure in your mistress
enthral you, if you take it with full vigour, I would
have you be with someone first; find someone
in whom the first bliss may spend itself: that
which follows will be slow to come. Pleasure
deferred is keenest: in cold we enjoy the sun, in
sunshine shade, in thirst water is welcome. I am
ashamed, yet I will say it: choose also a posture for
your union that you think least helpful and least be-
coming. Nor is that hard to manage: few women
admit the truth, nor is there anything they will think

Tunc etiam iubeo totas aperire fenestras,
  Turpiaque admisso membra notare die.
At simul ad metas venit finita voluptas,
  Lassaque cum tota corpora mente iacent,
Dum piget, et malis nullam tetigisse puellam,   415
  Tacturusque tibi non videare diu,
Tunc animo signa, quodcumque in corpore mendum est,
  Luminaque in vitiis illius usque tene.
Forsitan haec aliquis (nam sunt quoque) parva vocabit,
  Sed quae non prosunt singula, multa iuvant.   420
Parva necat morsu spatiosum vipera taurum :
  A cane non magno saepe tenetur aper.
Tu tantum numero pugna, praeceptaque in unum
  Contrahe : de multis grandis acervus erit.
Sed quoniam mores totidem, totidemque figurae,   425
  Non sunt iudiciis omnia danda meis.
Quo tua non possunt offendi pectora facto,
  Forsitan hoc alio iudice crimen erit.
Ille quod obscenas in aperto corpore partes
  Viderat, in cursu qui fuit, haesit amor :   430
Ille quod a Veneris rebus surgente puella
  Vidit in inmundo signa pudenda toro,
Luditis, o siquos potuerunt ista movere :
  Adflarant tepidae pectora vestra faces.
Adtrahet ille puer contentos fortius arcus ;   435
  Saucia maiorem turba petetis opem.
Quid, qui clam latuit reddente obscena puella,
  Et vidit, quae mos ipse videre vetat ?
Di melius, quam nos moneamus talia quemquam !.
  Ut prosint, non sunt expedienda tamen.   440

has not become them. Then too I bid you open all the windows, and by the admitted light observe unseemly limbs. But as soon as pleasure has reached its goal and is spent, and bodies and minds are utterly weary, while boredom is on you and you wish you had never touched a woman, and you think you will not touch one again for long, then mark well in your mind every blemish her body has, and keep your eye ever on her faults. Someone perchance will call them small (for so they are), but things that avail not singly help when they are many. The tiny viper's bite slays the spacious bull: the boar is often held by a small hound. Only fight with the aid of numbers, and gather my precepts all together; many will make a mighty heap. But since there are so many fashions and so many postures, trust not wholly to my counsels. What cannot offend your feelings, perhaps will be a reproach to another's judgment. One passion was checked, because the lover, in full train, saw the obscene parts exposed; another, because, when the woman arose from the business of love, the couch was seen to be soiled by shameful marks. You are not in earnest, if any there be whom such things have power to influence: your hearts were kindled by feeble fires. More strongly will that Boy bend his taut bow-string; a wounded crowd, you will seek more potent aid.[1] What of him who lurked in hiding while the girl performed her obscenities, and saw what even custom forbids to see? Heaven forfend I should give anyone such counsel! though it may help, 'twere better not to

---

[1] *i.e.*, you have yet to experience what passion really means.

Hortor et, ut pariter binas habeatis amicas :
    Fortior est, plures siquis habere potest ;
Secta bipertito cum mens discurrit utroque,
    Alterius vires subtrahit alter amor.
Grandia per multos tenuantur flumina rivos,   445
    Saevaque diducto stipite flamma perit.
Non satis una tenet ceratas ancora puppes,
    Nec satis est liquidis unicus hamus aquis :
Qui sibi iam pridem solacia bina paravit,
    Iam pridem summa victor in arce fuit.   450
At tibi, qui fueris dominae male creditus uni,
    Nunc saltem novus est inveniendus amor.
Pasiphaës Minos in Procride perdidit ignes :
    Cessit ab Idaea coniuge victa prior.
Amphilochi frater ne Phegida semper amaret,   455
    Callirhoë fecit parte recepta tori.
Et Parin Oenone summos tenuisset ad annos,
    Si non Oebalia paelice laesa foret.
Coniugis Odrysio placuisset forma tyranno :
    Sed melior clausae forma sororis erat.   460
Quid moror exemplis, quorum me turba fatigat ?
    Successore novo vincitur omnis amor.
Fortius e multis mater desiderat unum,
    Quam quae flens clamat "tu mihi solus eras."
Et ne forte putes nova me tibi condere iura   465
    (Atque utinam inventi gloria nostra foret !),
Vidit ut Atrides (quid enim non ille videret,
    Cuius in arbitrio Graecia tota fuit ?)
Marte suo captam Chryseïda, victor amabat :
    At senior stulte flebat ubique pater.   470
Quid lacrimas, odiose senex ? bene convenit illis :
    Officio natam laedis, inepte, tuo.

---

[1] Idaea was the second wife of Phineus, his first wife being
Cleopatra, daughter of Boreas and Oreithyia.

use it. This I do advise, have two mistresses at once; he is yet stronger who can have more; when the attention, parted in twain, shifts from this one to that, one passion saps the other's force. Great rivers are diminished by much channelling, and a fierce flame dies when the fuel is divided. One anchor holds not sufficiently the wax-smeared prows, one hook is not enough in running streams: he who long since procured two consolations for himself, long since was victor in the high citadel. But you, who have wrongly given yourself to one mistress, now at least must find a second love. In Procris Minos lost his passion for Pasiphae; before Idaea, the first wife, vanquished, gave way.[1] Callirhoe, who shared his couch, was the cause that the brother of Amphilochus[2] did not for ever love Phegeus' daughter. Oenone had kept Paris till life was o'er, had she not been harmed by her Oebalian rival. His wife's beauty had pleased the Odrysian tyrant,[3] but superior was the beauty of her imprisoned sister. Why do I waste time on cases whose number wearies me? all love is vanquished by a succeeding love. With better heart does a mother mourn one son out of many than she who cries in tears "thou wert my only one." And lest you think I am giving you new laws (and would that the glory of the discovery were mine), when Atrides saw (for what could he not see, in whose power all Greece lay?) Chryseis the prisoner of his army, he, the conqueror, loved her: but everywhere her old sire wept stupid tears. Why do you weep, hateful old man? it is well with them; you are hurting your daughter, you fool, by your

---

[2] Alcmaeon, who left Alphesiboea for Callirhoe.

[3] Tereus, who ravished Philomela, sister of his wife Procne.

Quam postquam reddi Calchas, ope tutus Achillis,
 Iusserat, et patria est illa recepta domo,
"Est" ait Atrides "illius proxima forma,   475
 Et, si prima sinat syllaba, nomen idem :
Hanc mihi, si sapiat, per se concedat Achilles :
 Si minus, imperium sentiat ille meum.
Quod siquis vestrum factum hoc incusat, Achivi,
 Est aliquid valida sceptra tenere manu.   480
Nam si rex ego sum, nec mecum dormiat ulla,
 In mea Thersites regna, licebit, eat."
Dixit, et hanc habuit solacia magna prioris,
 Et posita est cura cura repulsa nova.
Ergo adsume novas auctore Agamemnone flammas, 485
 Ut tuus in bivio distineatur amor.
Quaeris, ubi invenias ? artes, i, perlege nostras :
 Plena puellarum iam tibi navis erit.

Quod siquid praecepta valent mea, siquid Apollo
 Utile mortales perdocet ore meo,   490
Quamvis infelix media torreberis Aetna,
 Frigidior glacie fac videare tuae :
Et sanum simula, ne, siquid forte dolebis,
 Sentiat ; et ride, cum tibi flendus eris.
Non ego te iubeo medias abrumpere curas : 495
 Non sunt imperii tam fera iussa mei.
Quod non es, simula, positosque imitare furores :
 Sic facies vere quod meditatus eris.
Saepe ego, ne biberem, volui dormire videri :
 Dum videor, somno lumina victa dedi :   500
Deceptum risi, qui se simulabat amare,
 In laqueos auceps decideratque suos.

officiousness. And when Calchas, safe 'neath Achilles' protection, had ordered her to be restored, and she was taken back by her father's house, "There is one," said Atrides, "whose beauty is next to hers, and, but for the first syllable,[1] the name is just the same. Her, were he wise, Achilles would freely yield me; otherwise let him feel my power. If any of you, Achaeans, blames this deed, it is something to hold a sceptre in strong grasp. For if I am king, and no maiden sleep with me, Thersites may sit upon my throne." He spoke, and took her as ample solace for his former love; his passion was allayed, for the new drove out the old. Learn therefore from Agamemnon, and take another flame, that your love may be sundered at the parting of the ways. Do you ask where you may find one? go, read my precepts, your ship will soon be full of women.

But if my counsels avail aught, if Apollo by my mouth teaches men aught useful, though you are miserably scorched in Aetna's midst, yet make yourself seem colder than ice to your mistress; and feign to be heart-whole, lest, if perchance you show your anguish, she notice it; and laugh, when you would mourn your plight. 'Tis not that I bid you break off your passion in mid-career: such cruel commands belong not to my rule. Feign what you are not, and counterfeit an assuaged frenzy; so will you do in fact what you have practised doing.[2] Often have I wished to seem to sleep, that I might not drink: and, while seeming, I have surrendered vanquished eyes to slumber: I have laughed at one deceived, who feigned to love, and fell like a bird-catcher into his own snare.

---

[1] Agamemnon demanded Briseis in exchange for Chryseis, Chryses' daughter.   [2] *i.e.*, you will really assuage it.

Intrat amor mentes usu, dediscitur usu :
    Qui poterit sanum fingere, sanus erit.
Dixerit, ut venias : pacta tibi nocte venito ;   505
    Veneris, et fuerit ianua clausa : feres.
Nec dic blanditias, nec fac convicia posti,
    Nec latus in duro limine pone tuum.
Postera lux aderit : careant tua verba querellis,
    Et nulla in vultu signa dolentis habe.   510
Iam ponet fastus, cum te languere videbit :
    Hoc etiam nostra munus ab arte feres.
Te quoque falle tamen, nec sit tibi finis amandi
    Propositus : frenis saepe repugnat equus.
Utilitas lateat ; quod non profitebere, fiet :   515
    Quae nimis apparent retia, vitat avis.
Nec sibi tam placeat, nec te contemnere possit ;
    Sume animos, animis cedat ut illa tuis.
Ianua forte patet ? quamvis revocabere, transi.
    Est data nox ? dubita nocte venire data.   520
Posse pati facile est, ubi, si patientia desit,
    Protinus ex facili gaudia ferre licet.

Et quisquam praecepta potest mea dura vocare ?
    En, etiam partes conciliantis ago.
Nam quoniam variant animi, variabimus artes ;   525
    Mille mali species, mille salutis erunt.
Corpora vix ferro quaedam sanantur acuto :
    Auxilium multis sucus et herba fuit.
Mollior es, neque abire potes, vinctusque teneris,
    Et tua saevus Amor sub pede colla premit ?   530
Desine luctari : referant tua carbasa venti,
    Quaque vocant fluctus, hac tibi remus eat.

521 si patientia *edd.* : sapientia *R.*

THE REMEDIES OF LOVE

By wont love comes into the mind, by wont is love
unlearnt : he who can counterfeit sanity will be
sane.[1] She has bidden you come: come on the
night arranged for you ; you have come, and the
door is shut: you must bear it. Neither utter
endearments nor hurl abuse at the door, nor lay
your side on the hard threshold. The next day
dawns : let there be no complaining in your words,
no sign of grief upon your face. Soon will she drop
her pride, when she sees your ardour fail : this profit
too will you win from my art. Yet deceive yourself
also, nor think to make an end of loving : the steed
often resists the reins. Conceal your gain ; what
you do not proclaim will come about : the bird avoids
the nets that show too plainly. Let her not please
herself so well, nor be able to despise you : take
courage, that to your courage she may yield. Her
door maybe is open ? pass it by, though she call you
back. She has granted a night? hesitate to come
on the night she grants you. To be able to endure
is easy, when, should endurance fail, you can at once
win the favours of some easy mistress.

And can anyone call my precepts hard? lo ! I
even play the reconciler. For since natures vary,
I will vary my arts; the disease has a thousand
forms, I have a thousand remedies. Some bodies
even sharp steel will scarcely heal; to many juices
and herbs give aid. You are too soft-hearted, and
cannot tear yourself away, but are held fast-bound,
and cruel Love has set his foot upon your neck ?
Cease to struggle : let the winds bear your canvas
backwards; where the waves invite you, there let

---

[1] If he can pretend that the frenzy has left him (*sanum*
being the opposite of *furentem*, cf. l. 493) then he will be
"really cured" (*sanus*).

Explenda est sitis ista tibi, quo perditus ardes;
  Cedimus; e medio iam licet amne bibas:
Sed bibe plus etiam, quam quod praecordia poscunt, 535
  Gutture fac pleno sumpta redundet aqua.
Perfruere usque tua, nullo prohibente, puella:
  Illa tibi noctes auferat, illa dies.
Taedia quaere mali: faciunt et taedia finem.
  Iam quoque, cum credes posse carere, mane,   540
Dum bene te cumules et copia tollat amorem,
  Et fastidita non iuvet esse domo.

Fit quoque longus amor, quem diffidentia nutrit:
  Hunc tu si quaeres ponere, pone metum.
Qui timet, ut sua sit, ne quis sibi detrahat illam,   545
  Ille Machaonia vix ope sanus erit.
Plus amat e natis mater plerumque duobus,
  Pro cuius reditu, quod gerit arma, timet.
Est prope Collinam templum venerabile portam;
  Inposuit templo nomina celsus Eryx: 550
Est illic Lethaeus Amor, qui pectora sanat,
  Inque suas gelidam lampadas addit aquam.
Illic et iuvenes votis oblivia poscunt,
  Et siqua est duro capta puella viro.
Is mihi sic dixit (dubito, verusne Cupido,   555
  An somnus fuerit: sed puto, somnus erat)
" O qui sollicitos modo das, modo demis amores,
  Adice praeceptis hoc quoque, Naso, tuis.
Ad mala quisque animum referat sua, ponet amorem;
  Omnibus illa deus plusve minusve dedit.   560

your oar be plied. You must sate that thirst where-
with you despairingly burn; I give way; now you
may drink from mid-stream: but drink even more
than your heart craves for; see that the water you
quaff overflows from your full throat. Continue,
unchecked, to enjoy your mistress; let hers be your
nights, and hers your days. Seek to be sated with
your complaint: satiety too can make an end.
Still remain, even when you think you could do
without, until you have all your fill, and plenty
destroys passion, and her house, grown distasteful,
causes you no delight.

That passion also lingers long that diffidence
fosters; if you would be rid of this, be rid of fear.
He who fears lest she be his no more, lest some-
one take her from him, will scarce be healed by
Machaon's art.[1] A mother of two sons usually loves
that one more for whose return from the wars she is
afraid. Near the Colline Gate there is a venerable
shrine;[2] lofty Eryx has set his name thereon;
Lethaean Love is there, who makes hearts whole,
and pours cool water upon his torch. There youths
seek oblivion for their vows, and maidens under the
spell of a heartless lover. Thus did he speak to me
(I know not whether it was very Cupid, or a dream:
a dream, I fancy): "O thou who now givest, now
takest away heart-troubling passion, add this too, O
Naso, to thy precepts. Let each give his mind to
his own woes: he will be rid of his love; heaven has
assigned them, more or less, to all. Let him who

[1] Machaon was a brother of Podalirius, son of Asclepius,
see note on l. 313.
[2] A temple of Venus Erycina.

Qui Puteal Ianumque timet celeresque Kalendas,
  Torqueat hunc aeris mutua summa sui;
Cui durus pater est, ut voto caetera cedant,
  Huic pater ante oculos durus habendus erit;
Hic male dotata pauper cum coniuge vivit,   565
  Uxorem fato credat obesse suo.
Est tibi rure bono generosae fertilis uvae
  Vinea?   ne nascens usta sit uva, time.
Ille habet in reditu navim: mare semper iniquum
  Cogitet et damno littora foeda suo.   570
Filius hunc miles, te filia nubilis angat;
  Et quis non causas mille doloris habet?
Ut posses odisse tuam, Pari, funera fratrum
  Debueras oculis substituisse tuis."
Plura loquebatur: placidum puerilis imago   575
  Destituit somnum, si modo somnus erat.
Quid faciam?   media navim Palinurus in unda
  Deserit; ignotas cogor inire vias.

Quisquis amas, loca sola nocent, loca sola caveto!
  Quo fugis? in populo tutior esse potes.   580
Non tibi secretis (augent secreta furores)
  Est opus: auxilio turba futura tibi est.
Tristis eris, si solus eris, dominaeque relictae
  Ante oculos facies stabit, ut ipsa, tuos.
Tristior idcirco nox est quam tempora Phoebi;   585
  Quae relevet luctus, turba sodalis abest.
Nec fuge conloquium, nec sit tibi ianua clausa,
  Nec tenebris vultus flebilis abde tuos.

566 fato . . . obesse suo *edd.*: facto *R*: facito . . . adesse
suam *Madvig.*

---

[1] The Puteal was a circular enclosure in the Comitium at
Rome, sometimes called Puteal Libonis, from a certain Libo
who erected it; it stood near the temple of Janus, and was
the scene of financial transactions. The temple of Janus was

fears the Puteal and Janus and the swift Kalends be tortured by his sum of debt[1]; he who has a cruel sire, though all else be granted to his prayer, must keep that cruel sire before his eyes; here lives a poor man with an ill-dowered wife: let him think his wife stands in the way of his destiny. You have a fruitful estate and a vineyard abundant in fine grapes? fear lest the ripening grapes be scorched. Another has a ship returning home: let him fancy the sea is ever stormy, and the coasts befouled with his fortune's wreck. Let one be distressed for a soldier son, another for a daughter of ripe years; and who has not a thousand causes of worry? To be able to hate your mistress, Paris, you should have placed your brothers' deaths before your eyes." More was he speaking: the boyish image fled from my tranquil sleep, if sleep it was. What am I to do? in mid-waters Palinurus[2] deserts his ship; I am forced to travel ways I know not.

Whoever you are that love, solitary places are dangerous, beware of solitudes. Whither do you flee? you will be safer in a crowd. You have no need for secrecy (secrecy adds to passion); a crowd will give you succour. If alone, you will be sad, and the shape of your deserted mistress will stand, as if herself, before your eyes. Hence night is sadder than the hours of Phoebus; the companions, who might relieve your gloom, are absent. And fly not intercourse, nor let your door be closed, nor hide your tearful countenance in darkness. Ever have

also the place for merchants and money-changers, though the name can also refer to the Kalends of January, when interest was due, or money had to be repaid.

[2] The steersman of Aeneas, who fell into the water and was drowned (*Aen.* 5. 854 sqq.).

Semper habe Pyladen aliquem, qui curet Orestem :
    Hic quoque amicitiae non levis usus erit.   590
Quid, nisi secretae laeserunt Phyllida silvae ?
    Certa necis causa est : incomitata fuit.
Ibat, ut Edono referens trieterica Baccho
    Ire solet fusis barbara turba comis,
Et modo, qua poterat, longum spectabat in aequor, 595
    Nunc in harenosa lassa iacebat humo.
" Perfide Demophoon ! " surdas clamabat ad undas,
    Ruptaque singultu verba loquentis erant.
Limes erat tenuis longa subnubilus umbra,
    Quo tulit illa suos ad mare saepe pedes.   600
Nona terebatur miserae via : " viderit ! " inquit,
    Et spectat zonam pallida facta suam,
Aspicit et ramos ; dubitat, refugitque quod audet
    Et timet, et digitos ad sua colla refert.
Sithoni, tunc certe vellem non sola fuisses :   605
    Non flesset positis Phyllida silva comis.
Phyllidis exemplo nimium secreta timeto,
    Laese vir a domina, laesa puella viro.

Praestiterat iuvenis quidquid mea Musa iubebat,
    Inque suae portu paene salutis erat :   610
Reccidit, ut cupidos inter devenit amantes,
    Et, quae condiderat, tela resumpsit Amor.
Siquis amas, nec vis, facito contagia vites ;
    Haec etiam pecori saepe nocere solent.
Dum spectant laesos oculi, laeduntur et ipsi,   615
    Multaque corporibus transitione nocent.
In loca nonnumquam siccis arentia glebis
    De prope currenti flumine manat aqua :
Manat amor tectus, si non ab amante recedas ;
    Turbaque in hoc omnes ingeniosa sumus.¹   620

    ¹ *i.e.*, we are all cunning in finding ways of letting our
passion renew itself.

some Pylades to care for his Orestes: this too will
prove no small benefit of friendship. What, save the
secret woods, were Phyllis' bane? the cause of her
death is sure: she had no companion. She was
going, as the barbarian throng is wont to go, when
it keeps the triennial feast of Edonian Bacchus,
with hair dishevelled, and now, where she could,
she gazed on the far-flung sea, now weary lay on
the sandy ground. "Faithless Demophoon!" she
cried to the deaf waves, and her sobbing broke the
words she uttered. There was a narrow way o'er-
cast by the long shadows, by which she oft betook
herself to the sea. For the ninth time she trod
her hapless path: "Let him see to it!" she cries,
and turning pale looks at her girdle; she looks at
the branches also; she hesitates, and shrinks from
what she ventures, and is afraid, and sets her fingers
at her neck. Then truly, Sithonian maid, could I
wish thou hadst not been alone: the wood had not
shed its leaves and wept for Phyllis. By example
of Phyllis fear too much secrecy, O lover pained by
thy mistress, O girl pained by thy lover!

A youth had performed whate'er my Muse com-
manded, and was nearly within the haven of his
safety; he fell back, when he came among eager
lovers, and Love resumed the arms he had put
away. If you love, nor wish to love, see that you
shun contagion; even beasts are hurt thereby. The
eyes, in beholding the afflicted, themselves suffer
affliction, and many things harm our bodies through
chance encounter. Sometimes water steals from a
river running near into dry and parching soil: Love
steals in all unseen, if you go not from your lover;
in this we are all cunning folk.[1] Another also

Alter item iam sanus erat; vicinia laesit:
  Occursum dominae non tulit ille suae.
Vulnus in antiquum rediit male firma cicatrix,
  Successumque artes non habuere meae.
Proximus a tectis ignis defenditur aegre;   625
  Utile finitimis abstinuisse locis.
Nec quae ferre solet spatiantem porticus illam,
  Te ferat, officium neve colatur idem.
Quid iuvat admonitu tepidam recalescere mentem?
  Alter, si possis, orbis habendus erit.   630
Non facile esuriens posita retinebere mensa,
  Et multam saliens incitat unda sitim.
Non facile est taurum visa retinere iuvenca,
  Fortis equus visae semper adhinnit equae.
Haec ubi praestiteris, ut tandem littora tangas,   635
  Non ipsam satis est deseruisse tibi.
Et soror et mater valeant et conscia nutrix,
  Et quisquis dominae pars erit ulla tuae.
Nec veniat servus, nec flens ancillula fictum
  Suppliciter dominae nomine dicat have.   640
Nec si scire voles, quid agat, tamen, illa, rogabis;
  Perfer! erit lucro lingua retenta tuo.
Tu quoque, qui causam finiti reddis amoris,
  Deque tua domina multa querenda refers,
Parce queri; melius sic ulciscere tacendo,   645
  Ut desideriis effluat illa tuis.
Et malim taceas quam te desisse loquaris:
  Qui nimium multis " non amo " dicit, amat.
Sed meliore fide paulatim extinguitur ignis
  Quam subito; lente desine, tutus eris.   650
Flumine perpetuo torrens solet acrius ire:
  Sed tamen haec brevis est, illa perennis aqua.

646 ut *MSS.*: dum *edd.*
651 acrius *edd.*: altior *R*; altius *other MSS.* : acrior *Riese.*

THE REMEDIES OF LOVE

was already cured: neighbourhood proved his bane: meeting his mistress was too much for him. The scar ill-healed relapsed to the old wound, and my arts sustained defeat. A fire next door is ill repulsed; 'tis best to avoid the neighbourhood. And frequent not the colonnade that she frequents when walking, nor cultivate the same society. What boots it by remembrance to heat once more a cooling passion? If you can, you must live in another world. With difficulty will you be kept, when hungry, from the appointed feast, and springing water provokes a raging thirst. 'Tis hard to hold the bull when he spies the heifer, the lusty steed ever whinnies at the sight of the mare. When this is done, in order at last to gain the shore, it is not enough to leave her alone behind. Bid farewell to mother and sister, and to the nurse her confidant, and to whoever will be any part of your mistress. Nor let her slave come, nor her handmaid with feigned tears greet you imploringly in her mistress' name. Nor must you ask how she fares, though you wish to know; endure! you will gain by being tongue-tied. You too who relate the cause of ended love, and recount your many complaints against your mistress, cease to complain; thus by silence will you win better revenge, so that she fades away from your regrets. And I would rather you were silent than say you had ceased to love; he who says o'er much "I love not" is in love. But with better surety is the fire gradually extinguished than on a sudden; leave off slowly, and you will be safe. A torrent is wont to flow more fiercely than an unbroken stream: but that is short-lived, this goes on

Fallat, et in tenues evanidus exeat auras,
　　Perque gradus molles emoriatur amor.
Sed modo dilectam scelus est odisse puellam :　　655
　　Exitus ingeniis convenit iste feris.
Non curare sat est : odio qui finit amorem,
　　Aut amat, aut aegre desinet esse miser.
Turpe vir et mulier, iuncti modo, protinus hostes ;
　　Non illas lites Appias ipsa probat.　　660
Saepe reas faciunt, et amant ; ubi nulla simultas
　　Incidit, admonitu liber aberrat amor.
Forte aderam iuveni ; dominam lectica tenebat :
　　Horrebant saevis omnia verba minis.
Iamque vadaturus "lectica prodeat" inquit ;　　665
　　Prodierat : visa coniuge mutus erat.
Et manus et manibus duplices cecidere tabellae,
　　Venit in amplexus, atque "ita vincis" ait.
Tutius est aptumque magis discedere pace,
　　Nec petere a thalamis litigiosa fora.　　670
Munera quae dederas, habeat sine lite, iubeto :
　　Esse solent magno damna minora bono.
Quod si vos aliquis casus conducet in unum,
　　Mente memor tota quae damus arma, tene.
Nunc opus est armis ; hic, o fortissime, pugna :　　675
　　Vincenda est telo Penthesilea tuo.
Nunc tibi rivalis, nunc durum limen amanti,
　　Nunc subeant mediis inrita verba deis.
Nec compone comas, quia sis venturus ad illam,
　　Nec toga sit laxo conspicienda sinu.　　680

---

[1] Venus, because she had a temple near the fountain called
Aqua Appia ; cf. *Ars Am.* 1. 82, 3. 452.
[2] Possibly in the legal sense of "adesse," "to act as
counsel for" ; the "double tablet" (*i.e.* two thin boards
smeared with wax, that were folded together) probably con-
tained his accusation ; for litigation between husbands and

for ever. Let love fail, and vanish into tenuous air, and die by slow degrees. But to hate a woman once loved is a crime: that is an end fitting to savage minds. It is enough to be indifferent: he who ends love by hating, either loves still, or will find it hard to end his misery. Shameful is it that a man and woman lately at one should be foes forthwith; the Appian [1] herself approves not such strife as that. Men often put women in the dock, and love them: where no quarrel comes love unremembered slips away. I happened to be in the company of a youth; [2] his lady was in her litter: all his speech bristled with savage threats. On the point of summoning her on bail, "Let her come forth from the litter," he cried; forth she came: when he saw his wife, he was dumb. His hands dropped, and from his hands the double tablet; he rushed into her arms, and cried, "Thus thou dost conquer." It is safer and more fitting to separate in peace, nor to hurry from marriage chamber to contentious courts. Bid her keep unchallenged the gifts you gave: the loss will be outweighed by the greatness of your gain. But if some chance brings you together, use all your memory and wit to wield the arms I give you. Now have you need of arms; here, brave warrior, must you fight: Penthesilea [3] must fall before your steel. Remember now your rival, the threshold so hard to the lover, the fruitless prayers to witnessing gods. Do not arrange your hair because you are meeting her, nor let your toga's loose folds attract

wives, cf. *Ars Am.* 2. 153, 4.   It seems hardly possible that " conjux" should here mean "mistress," though some editors take it so.

[3] The queen of the Amazons, slain in fight by Achilles.

223

Nulla sit, ut placeas alienae cura puellae;
 Iam facito e multis una sit illa tibi.

Sed quid praecipue nostris conatibus obstat?
 Eloquar, exemplo quemque docente suo.
Desinimus tarde, quia nos speramus amari: 685
 Dum sibi quisque placet, credula turba sumus.
At tu nec voces (quid enim fallacius illis?)
 Crede, nec aeternos pondus habere deos.
Neve puellarum lacrimis moveare, caveto:
 Ut flerent, oculos erudiere suos.   690
Artibus innumeris mens oppugnatur amantum,
 Ut lapis aequoreis undique pulsus aquis.
Nec causas aperi, quare divortia malis:
 Nec dic, quid doleas: clam tamen usque dole.
Nec peccata refer, ne diluat: ipse favebis,   695
 Ut melior causa causa sit illa tua.
Qui silet, est firmus; qui dicit multa puellae
 Probra, satisfieri postulat ille sibi.
Non ego Dulichio furari more sagittas,
 Nec raptas ausim tinguere in amne faces: 700
Nec nos purpureas pueri resecabimus alas,
 Nec sacer arte mea laxior arcus erit.
Consilium est, quodcumque cano: parete canenti,
 Utque facis, coeptis, Phoebe saluber, ades.
Phoebus adest: sonuere lyrae, sonuere pharetrae; 705
 Signa deum nosco per sua: Phoebus adest.
Confer Amyclaeis medicatum vellus aënis
 Murice cum Tyrio; turpius illud erit:
Vos quoque formosis vestras conferte puellas;
 Incipiet dominae quemque pudere suae: 710

699 furari *Housman, Palmer*: furiali *MSS.*

---

[1] *i.e.* when they swear that they love us

remark. Take no trouble to please a woman now estranged; see that she now is one out of many to you.

But what particularly hinders our endeavours? I will speak, though each may learn from his own case. We are slow in breaking off, because we hope that we are loved: while each of us flatters himself, we are a believing crew. But do not you believe that words (what more deceiving than they?) or the eternal gods have weight.[1] And take care not to be moved by women's tears: they have taught their eyes to weep. By innumerable arts are lovers' feelings assailed, as the rock is beaten by waves on every side. Reveal not the reasons why you prefer to separate, nor say what your grievance is: yet, to yourself, keep up the grievance. Nor mention her shortcomings, lest she remove them; yourself will be her advocate, so that her cause will be better than yours. Silence is strength; to reproach a woman often is to ask to be satisfied. I would not dare to pilfer arrows in Dulichian wise,[2] nor to drench in water the stolen torch; I shall not clip the Boy's bright wings, nor by my art unstring the sacred bow. Whate'er I sing is wisdom; obey my song, and thou, health-bringing Phoebus, aid, as thou dost, my enterprise. Phoebus is nigh to aid: his lyres and quivers have resounded; I recognise the god by his own signs: Phoebus is nigh to aid. Compare a fleece that Amyclae's vats have dyed, with Tyrian purple; 'twill be of baser hue: do you too compare your girls with beauties; each will begin to be ashamed of his own mistress:

[2] The reference is to Ulysses, who deceived Philoctetes into giving up the bow which was to take Troy (see l. 111).

I

OVID

Utraque formosae Paridi potuere videri,
 Sed sibi conlatam vicit utramque Venus.
Nec solam faciem, mores quoque confer et artes:
 Tantum iudicio ne tuus obsit amor.
Exiguum est, quod deinde canam; sed profuit illud   715
 Exiguum multis: in quibus ipse fui.
Scripta cave relegas blandae servata puellae:
 Constantes animos scripta relecta movent.
Omnia pone feros, quamvis invitus, in ignes,
 Et dic "ardoris sit rogus iste mei."   720
Thestias absentem succendit stipite natum:
 Tu timide flammae perfida verba dabis?
Si potes, et ceras remove: quid imagine muta
 Carperis?   hoc periit Laodamia modo.
Et loca muta nocent; fugito loca conscia vestri   725
 Concubitus; causas illa doloris habent.
"Hic fuit, hic cubuit; thalamo dormivimus illo:
 Hic mihi lasciva gaudia nocte dedit."
Admonitu refricatur amor, vulnusque novatum
 Scinditur: infirmis culpa pusilla nocet.   730
Ut paene extinctum cinerem si sulpure tangas,
 Vivet et e minimo maximus ignis erit,
Sic, nisi vitaris quidquid renovabit amorem,
 Flamma redardescet, quae modo nulla fuit.
Argolides cuperent fugisse Capharea puppes,   735
 Teque, senex, luctus ignibus ulte tuos.
Praeterita cautus Niseïde navita gaudet:
 Tu loca quae nimium grata fuere, cave.

---

[1] Althaea caused the death of her son Meleager by burning the brand on which his life depended. She was daughter of Thestius.

[2] Laodamia revered the memory of her husband Protesilaus by making an image of him; when forbidden to do this by her father Acastus she burnt herself to death.

[3] Caphareus was a promontory on the Argolic coast where Nauplius showed false lights, and lured Greek vessels returning from Troy to destruction, in revenge for the death of his son

each rival might have seemed fair to Paris, but each rival compared with Venus suffered defeat. Nor compare looks alone, but character and accomplishments as well; only let not your love impede your judgment. My next point is a small one; but, small as it is, it has profited many: and among these was I. Beware of reading again the treasured letters of an alluring mistress; letters read over again move even constant minds. Consign them all, though unwillingly, to the fierce flames, and say, "Let that be my passion's funeral pyre." Thestias burnt in the brand her absent son:[1] will you be cowardly in burning treacherous words? If you can, get rid of her pictures also: why does a mute image affect you? in this way Laodamia perished.[2] Mute places too are harmful; avoid places that know the secret of your unions; they hold the seeds of sorrow. "Here was she, here she lay; in that chamber did we sleep; here did she give me wanton joys at night." Love brought to mind is stung to life, and the wound is rent anew: to the weak the smallest error is hurtful. Just as a cinder nearly spent will live, if you touch it with sulphur, and from a small become a mighty fire, so, save you shun whate'er may renew your passion, the flame that was lately naught will glow once more. Fain would the Argive vessels have shunned Caphareus and thee, old man, who with fires avenged thy grief. The cautious mariner is glad when Nisus' daughter is passed;[3] do you beware of spots that

Palamedes. Nisus' daughter, *i.e.*, Scylla, the famous monster who preyed on Ulysses' crew as he passed between her and the whirlpool Charybdis. But the monster is not usually identified with Nisus' daughter, who was changed into a bird called "ciris" (see n. on l. 67), though the former too was once a maiden.

OVID

Haec tibi sint Syrtes : haec Acroceraunia vita :
  Hic vomit epotas dira Charybdis aquas.   740

Sunt quae non possunt aliquo cogente iuberi,
  Saepe tamen casu facta iuvare solent.
Perdat opes Phaedra, parces, Neptune, nepoti,
  Nec faciet pavidos taurus avitus equos.
Gnosida fecisses inopem, sapienter amasset :   745
  Divitiis alitur luxuriosus amor.
Cur nemo est, Hecalen, nulla est, quae ceperit Iron ?
  Nempe quod alter egens, altera pauper erat.
Non habet, unde suum paupertas pascat amorem :
  Non tamen hoc tanti est, pauper ut esse velis.   750
At tanti tibi sit non indulgere theatris,
  Dum bene de vacuo pectore cedat amor.
Enervant animos citharae lotosque lyraeque
  Et vox et numeris brachia mota suis.
Illic adsidue ficti saltantur amantes :   755
  Quid caveas, actor, quid iuvet, arte docet.
Eloquar invitus : teneros ne tange poetas !
  Summoveo dotes ipsius ipse meas.
Callimachum fugito : non est inimicus Amori :
  Et cum Callimacho tu quoque, Coë, noces.   760
Me certe Sappho meliorem fecit amicae,
  Nec rigidos mores Teïa Musa dedit.
Carmina quis potuit tuto legisse Tibulli,
  Vel tua, cuius opus Cynthia sola fuit ?

---

¹ Phaedra, wife of Theseus, fell in love with her stepson
Hippolytus, and then falsely accused him to Theseus of
attempting her honour ; Theseus called on his father Neptune
to punish Hippolytus, and he sent a sea-monster to frighten the
horses of the youth, who was killed by the upsetting of the
chariot. "Gnosida" : Ariadne. Hecale, an old woman who
showed kindness to Theseus. Irus, the beggar in the Odyssey.

once were all too pleasant. Let these be your Syrtes:
avoid this Acroceraunia: here dire Charybdis spews
forth the water she has swallowed.

Some things there are that no order can compel,
yet happening by chance they often help. Let
Phaedra lose her wealth: Neptune, you will spare
your grandson, nor will his grandsire's bull alarm
the steeds. Hadst thou made the Gnosian poor,
she had loved wisely: wanton love is fed on riches.
Why has no man taken Hecale, no woman Irus?[1]
surely, because she was poor, and he a beggar.
Poverty has no means to feed its passion; yet it
is not worth while to wish to be poor for that.
But let it be worth while to abstain from theatres,
until love ebb quite away from your empty heart.
Zithers and flutes and lyres enervate the mind, and
voices, and arms that move to their own rhythm.[2]
There constantly in the dance are lovers played:
the actor's art teaches what you must shun and
what delights you. Unwillingly I speak: touch
not the poets of love; with my own hand I take
my own gifts from you. Avoid Callimachus: he is
no enemy to love; thou, too, O Coan,[3] with Calli-
machus dost harm. Me certainly did Sappho make
more welcome to my mistress, nor did the Muse of
Teos[4] teach me strictness. Who could have read
unscathed the songs of Tibullus, or thine whose
work was Cynthia alone?[5] Who after reading

[2] Dancing to the ancients was as much an affair of arms
as it is to us of feet; it meant moving the whole body, and
especially the arms, rhythmically and expressively, and
often a character or a story was represented thereby.

[3] The poet Philetas.

[4] Anacreon.

[5] Propertius.

OVID

Quis poterit lecto durus discedere Gallo ?　　　　76
　Et mea nescio quid carmina tale sonant.
Quod nisi dux operis vatem frustratur Apollo,
　Aemulus est nostri maxima causa mali :
At tu rivalem noli tibi fingere quemquam,
　Inque suo solam crede iacere toro.　　　　　　77
Acrius Hermionen ideo dilexit Orestes,
　Esse quod alterius coeperat illa viri.
Quid, Menelae, doles ? ibas sine coniuge Creten,
　Et poteras nupta lentus abesse tua.
Ut Paris hanc rapuit, nunc demum uxore carere　77
　Non potes : alterius crevit amore tuus.
Hoc et in abducta Briseide flebat Achilles,
　Illam Plisthenio gaudia ferre toro ;
Nec frustra flebat, mihi credite : fecit Atrides,
　Quod si non faceret, turpiter esset iners.　　　78
Certe ego fecissem, nec sum sapientior illo :
　Invidiae fructus maximus ille fuit.
Nam sibi quod numquam tactam Briseida iurat
　Per sceptrum, sceptrum non·putat esse deos.
Di faciant, possis dominae transire relictae　　78
　Limina, proposito sufficiantque pedes.
Et poteris ; modo velle tene : nunc fortiter ire,
　Nunc opus est celeri subdere calcar equo.
Illo Lotophagos, illo Sirenas in antro
　Esse puta ; remis adice vela tuis.　　　　　79
Hunc quoque, quo quondam nimium rivale dolebas,
　Vellem desineres hostis habere loco.

---

[1] She married Neoptolemus, son of Achilles.
[2] *i.e.*, of Agamemnon, according to one legend the son o
Plisthenes.　Agamemnon took away Briseis from Achilles

Gallus could go away hard-hearted? My poems
too sound somewhat in that strain. Yet, unless
Apollo, prince of the craft, deceives the bard, a
rival is the chief cause of our malady: but picture
no rival to yourself, and think she lies on her couch
alone. The more ardently did Orestes love Her-
mione, that she had begun to be another's.[1] Why
grievest thou, Menelaus? thou wentest to Crete
without a consort, and wert able to be long absent
from thy bride. Only when Paris bore her off art
thou unable to be without a wife: 'twas another's
love that fired thine own. This too did Achilles
bewail in the loss of Briseis, that she should give
joy to the Plisthenian[2] couch; nor bewailed he
without cause, believe me: Atrides did what he had
been a shameful sluggard not to do. Certainly I
would have done it, nor am I wiser than he: that
was the choicest fruit of their quarrel. For that he
swears by his sceptre that Briseis ne'er was touched,
he deems not his sceptre to be heaven. May the
gods grant you to be able to pass by the threshold of
a deserted mistress, and may your feet avail for your
purpose! Yes, you will be able; only let your will
not fail: now must your course be courageous, now
spur your flying steed. Think that in this cave there
are Lotophagi, in that Sirens;[3] let sails assist your
oars. Him too whose rivalry once pained you I would
have you cease to look on as a foe. Nay, be sure to

when the latter refused to fight for the Greeks, Agamemnon
offered to give her back, and to swear he had not touched
her; see Hom. *Il.* bks. 1 and 9.

[3] The Lotus-eaters and Sirens were both encountered by
Odysseus in his wanderings; the former lulled into forget-
fulness, the latter attracted by song and then destroyed; for
the latter cf. *Ars Am.* 3. 311.

At certe, quamvis odio remanente, saluta ;
  Oscula cum poteris iam dare, sanus eris.

Ecce, cibos etiam, medicinae fungar ut omni   795
  Munere, quos fugias quosque sequare, dabo.
Daunius, an Libycis bulbus tibi missus ab oris,
  An veniat Megaris, noxius omnis erit.
Nec minus erucas aptum vitare salaces,
  Et quicquid Veneri corpora nostra parat.   800
Utilius sumas acuentes lumina rutas,
  Et quidquid Veneri corpora nostra negat.
Quid tibi praecipiam de Bacchi munere, quaeris ?
  Spe brevius monitis expediere meis.
Vina parant animum Veneri, nisi plurima sumas   805
  Et stupeant multo corda sepulta mero.
Nutritur vento, vento restinguitur ignis :
  Lenis alit flammas, grandior aura necat.
Aut nulla ebrietas, aut tanta sit ut tibi curas
  Eripiat ; siqua est inter utrumque, nocet.   810

Hoc opus exegi : fessae date serta carinae ;
  Contigimus portus, quo mihi cursus erat.
Postmodo reddetis sacro pia vota poetae,
  Carmine sanati femina virque meo.

greet him, though hatred linger yet; as soon as you can embrace him, you are healed.

And then there is diet too; that I may perform all a physician's task, I will tell you what to take and what to shun. Onions, be they Daunian [1] or sent from Libyan shores or come they from Megara, all are harmful. Nor less should you avoid salacious rocket, and whatever sets our bodies in trim for Venus. More usefully may you eat rue that sharpens the eyesight, and whatever sets our bodies out of trim for Venus. You ask what is my counsel concerning Bacchus' gift? sooner than you expect will you be quit of my counselling. Wine prepares the heart for love, unless you take o'ermuch and your spirits are dulled and drowned by too much liquor. By wind is a fire fostered, and by wind extinguished; a gentle breeze fans the flame, a strong breeze kills it. Either no drunkenness, or so much as to banish care: aught between these two is harmful.

I have finished my task; hang garlands on the weary vessel; the haven whither my course was set is reached. Soon will you pay your dutiful vows to the inspired poet, made whole, both man and woman, by my song.

[1] *i.e.*, Italian.

THE WALNUT-TREE

NUX

Nux ego iuncta viae cum sim sine crimine vitae,
    A populo saxis praetereunte petor.
Obruere ista solet manifestos poena nocentes,
    Publica cum lentam non capit ira moram :
Nil ego peccavi nisi si peccare docetur   5
    Annua cultori poma referre suo.
At prius arboribus, tum cum meliora fuerunt
    Tempora, certamen fertilitatis erat ;
Tum domini memores sertis ornare solebant
    Agricolas fructu proveniente deos :   10
Saepe tuas igitur, Liber, miratus es uvas,
    Mirata est oleas saepe Minerva suas,
Pomaque laesissent matrem, nisi subdita ramo
    Longa laboranti furca tulisset opem :
Quin etiam exemplo pariebat femina nostro,   15
    Nullaque non illo tempore mater erat.
At postquam platanis sterilem praebentibus umbram
    Uberior quavis arbore venit honor,
Nos quoque frugiferae (si nux modo ponor in illis)
    Coepimus in patulas luxuriare comas.   20
Nunc neque continuos nascuntur poma per annos,
    Uvaque laesa domum laesaque baca venit ;
Nunc uterum vitiat quae volt formosa videri,
    Raraque in hoc aevo est quae velit esse parens.
Certe ego, si nunquam peperissem, tutior essem :   25
    Ista Clytaemestra digna querela fuit.

10 agricolas *Heinsius* (as in Tibullus 1. 1. 14, etc.) : agricolae
MSS.

THE WALNUT-TREE

I, a walnut tree, hard by the roadside, though my
life be blameless, yet am pelted with stones by the
passing folk. 'Tis flagrant sinners that doom is wont
to overwhelm, when the people's wrath brooks not
slow delay: in naught have I sinned, unless it is
taught that to render yearly fruit to the husband-
man is a sin. But of old, when times were better,
trees vied in fruitfulness; then were the mindful
owners wont, as the fruit waxed ripe, to adorn with
garlands the farmer-gods; often, therefore, O Liber,
didst thou marvel at thy grapes, oft did Minerva
marvel at her olives, and the apples would have
hurt the mother tree, had not a long fork placed
beneath the labouring bough brought succour: nay,
by our example did women give birth, and none in
those times was not a mother. But since more
plenteous honour has come to planes that yield a
sterile shade, than to any tree, we fruit-bearers
also (if as a nut tree I am counted among them)
have begun to luxuriate in spreading foliage. Now
apples grow not every year, and injured grapes and
injured berries are brought home: now she that
would seem beautiful harms her womb, and rare in
these days is she who would be a parent. Certainly
I should be safer had I never borne; worthy of
Clytemnestra was that complaint.[1] Should the vine

---

[1] She was killed by Orestes, her own offspring.

Si sciat hoc vitis, nascentes supprimet uvas,
    Orbaque, si sciat hoc, Palladis arbor erit :
Hoc in notitiam veniat maloque piroque :
    Destituent silvas utraque poma suas :   30
Audiat hoc cerasus, bacas exire vetabit ;
    Audiat hoc ficus, stipes inanis erit.
Non equidem invideo : numquid tamen ulla feritur
    Quae sterilis sola conspicienda coma est ?
Cernite sinceros omnes ex ordine truncos,   35
    Qui modo nil quare percutiantur habent.
At mihi saeva nocent mutilatis vulnera ramis,
    Nudaque deiecto cortice ligna patent.
Non odium facit hoc, sed spes inducta rapinae :
    Sustineant aliae poma, querentur idem.   40

Sic reus ille fere est de quo victoria lucro
    Esse potest ; inopis vindice facta carent :
Sic timet insidias qui se scit ferre viator
    Cur timeat : tutum carpit inanis iter :
Sic ego sola petor, solam quia causa petendi est ;   45
    Frondibus intactis cetera turba viret.
Nam quod habent frutices aliquando proxima nostris
    Fragmina, quod laeso vimine multa iacent,
Non istis sua facta nocent : vicinia damno est :
    Excipiunt ictu saxa repulsa meo ;   50
Idque fide careat, si non, quae longius absunt
    Nativum retinent inviolata decus.
Ergo si sapiant et mentem verba sequantur,
    Devoveant umbras proxima quaeque meas.
Quam miserum est, odium damnis accedere nostris 55
    Meque ream nimiae proximitatis agi !

32 Only one *MS.* (*M*) has this reading ; the rest have " audiat
hoc cerasus: stipes inanis erit " as pentameter, and different
lines for the hexameter, *e.g.* " quaeque sibi vario distinguit
poma colore " (which is also found in the margin of *M*).

know this, it will suppress its grapes at birth; and childless, should it know this, will be the tree of Pallas. Let this come to the knowledge of apple or of pear: their orchards will be bereft of either fruit: should the cherry hear this, it will forbid its berries to push forth: should the fig hear this, it will be a barren stump. I do not envy them: yet is any tree struck that is sterile, and admired for its leaves alone? Look at all those uninjured trunks, that have no reason why they should be pelted. But my mutilated boughs are hurt by cruel wounds, and my wood lies bare and open where the bark is stripped away. 'Tis not hatred does this, but the hope of plunder that I inspire: let others carry fruit, they will make the same complaint.

So is he generally accused whose defeat means gain; a poor man's deeds escape censure:[1] so does that traveller fear an ambush who knows that what he bears has cause for fear; but empty pockets travel safe: so am I alone assailed, because I alone give cause for assault; the rest are verdant, and their leaves untouched. For whereas sometimes trees have broken fragments near to mine, and many an injured branch lies low, 'tis not their deeds that harm them; 'tis neighbourhood brings them loss: they receive the stones that strike me and rebound; and that would lack credence did not those which are furthest away retain inviolate their native glory. So, could they think and words follow their thought, all the nearest would execrate my shade. How wretched that hate should be added to my loss, and that I should stand trial for undue proximity!

[1] Men only prosecute when they have something to gain by it.

Sed, puto, magna mea est operoso cura colono !
  Inveniat, dederit quid mihi praeter humum.
Sponte mea facilis contempto nascor in agro,
  Parsque loci, qua sto, publica paene via est.   60
Me sata ne laedam, quoniam et sata laedere dicor,
  Imus in extremo margine fundus habet.
Non mihi falx nimias Saturnia deputat umbras,
  Duratam renovat non mihi fossor humum ;
Sole licet siccaque siti peritura laborem,   65
  Irriguae dabitur non mihi sulcus aquae.
At cum maturas fisso nova cortice rimas
  Nux agit, ad partes pertica saeva venit ;
Pertica dat plenis inmitia vulnera ramis,
  Ne possim lapidum verbera sola queri :   70
Poma cadunt mensis non interdicta secundis
  Et condit lectas parca colona nuces.
Has puer aut certo rectas dilaminat ictu
  Aut pronas digito bisve semelve petit.
Quattuor in nucibus, non amplius, alea tota est,   75
  Cum sibi suppositis additur una tribus.
Per tabulae clivum labi iubet alter et optat
  Tangat ut e multis quaelibet una suam.
Est etiam, par sit numerus qui dicat an impar,
  Ut divinatas auferat augur opes.   80
Fit quoque de creta, qualem caeleste figuram
  Sidus et in Graecis littera quarta gerit.

---

¹ Nuts were common playthings of boys, and Ovid mentions
various games here ; but there is no very clear explanation of
ll. 73, 4. In 75, 6 the idea seems to be building a castle of
three nuts with a fourth on top. In 79, 80 it is guessing "odd
or even," of a number of nuts (cf. Hor. *Sat.* 2. 3. 248.).

² A large triangle would be drawn in chalk, and lines drawn
within it ; a nut is thrown, so as not to go outside the triangle
("quae constitit intus,") and to touch as many lines as possible,
the prize being as many nuts as it touches lines. If "qui

But the toilsome husbandman, I ween, takes great thought for me! let him find aught he has given me save earth alone. Easily and freely do I grow on despised ground, and that part of the place where I stand is almost public road. Lest I harm the crops, for I am even said to harm the crops, the furthest and extremest limit of the estate receives me. Saturn's sickle prunes not my superfluous shade, no digger renews my hardened soil; though I be sick even to death with sun and parching thirst, I shall be given no rill of refreshing water. But when the new nut in due season shows chinks in its splitting rind thither comes the cruel rod; the rod inflicts ruthless wounds on swelling branches, lest I be able to complain of stones alone: down falls my fruit that is not forbidden to dessert, and the thrifty housewife stores the collected nuts. These, as they stand upright, a boy[1] splits with certain aim, or, as they lie on their side, strikes with his finger once or twice. In four nuts, and no more, is all his hazard, when one is added to the three beneath it. Another bids them roll down a sloping board, and prays that one out of many, whiche'er it be, may touch his own. Then there is he who guesses whether the number be odd or even, that the augur may bear away the wealth he has divined. Then too there is drawn in chalk a shape such as a heavenly constellation or the fourth Greek letter bears.[2] When this has

constitit . . . virga . . . ipse" be read, the game would be for a boy to stand inside the triangle and to try to touch with a stick as many nuts as possible arranged inside it. The references in ll. 81–2 are to a triangular arrangement of stars above the head of the constellation Aries, and to the Greek Delta.

Haec ubi distincta est gradibus, quae constitit intus
   Quot tetigit virgas, tot capit ipsa nuces.
Vas quoque saepe cavum spatio distante locatur,   85
   In quod missa levi nux cadat una manu.

Felix, secreto quae nata est arbor in arvo
   Et soli domino ferre tributa potest :
Non hominum strepitus audit, non illa rotarum,
   Non a vicina pulverulenta via est :   90
Illa suo, quaecunque tulit, dare dona colono
   Et plenos fructus annumerare potest.
At mihi maturos nunquam licet edere fetus,
   Ante diemque meae decutiuntur opes.
Lamina mollis adhuc tenero est in lacte, quod intra est,
   Nec mala sunt ulli nostra futura bono :   96
Iam tamen invenio qui me iaculentur et ictu
   Praefestinato munus inane petant.
Si fiat rapti, fiat mensura relicti,
   Maiorem domini parte, viator, habes.   100
Saepe aliquis, foliis ubi nuda cacumina vidit,
   Esse putat Boreae triste furentis opus ;
Aestibus hic, hic me spoliatam frigore credit ;
   Est quoque, qui crimen grandinis esse putet.
At mihi nec grando, duris invisa colonis,   105
   Nec ventus fraudi solve geluve fuit :
Fructus obest, peperisse nocet, nocet esse feracem,
   Quaeque fuit multis, ei mihi, praeda malo est.
Praeda malo, Polydore, fuit tibi, praeda nefandae
   Coniugis Aonidum misit in arma virum.   110
Hesperii regis pomaria tuta fuissent,
   Una sed inmensas arbor habebat opes.

83 quae MSS. : qui *some edd.*
84 virgas *some edd.* : virga MSS. : ipsa MSS. : ipse *some edd.*
95 tenero est *G* : tenet os *M*.

THE WALNUT-TREE

been marked with degrees, the nut that stops within
it gains itself as many nuts as it has touched lines.
Often too a hollow vessel is placed at a distance, into
which a nut flung by a skilful hand may fall.

Happy the tree that grows in a secluded field, and
can pay tribute to its lord alone: it hears not the
clamour of men nor the rumble of wheels, it is not
dusty from the neighbouring road: it can give
whatsoever it bears as a gift to its own husband-
man, and reckon its produce to the full. But I may
never bring forth ripe progeny, and my wealth is
struck off before its prime. My skin is still soft with
the young milk that is within, nor are my ills like to
be anyone's good: yet already do I find men pelting
me, and with o'er-hasty blows seeking a vain prize.
If account were taken of what is stolen, and of
what is left, wayfarer, thou hast a greater share
than my own lord. Often someone, seeing my
summit bare of leaves, deems it the work of furious
Boreas; one thinks that the heat, another that the
frost, has robbed me; another fancies that hailstorms
are to blame. But neither hail, loathed of hardy
husbandmen, nor wind nor sun nor frost has injured
me: my fruit is my bane, it is harmful to bear, it is
harmful to be fertile; gain, which has hurt many,
has hurt me too. Gain hurt thee, Polydorus; his
wicked consort's gain sent her spouse against Aonian
arms. Safe had been the apple orchards of the
Hesperian king, but one tree held unbounded wealth.[1]

[1] Polydorus was a son of Priam, who entrusted him to the
care of Polymestor, king of the Thracian Chersonese, with a
sum of money; Polymestor killed him for the sake of the
gold. Eriphyle was bribed by the gift of a necklace to send
her husband Amphiaraus to the war against Thebes. The
garden of the Hesperides bore trees with golden fruit.

At rubus et sentes tantummodo laedere natae
　　Spinaque vindicta cetera tuta sua est.
Me, quia nec noceo nec obuncis vindicor hamis,　　115
　　Missa petunt avida saxa proterva manu.
Quid si non aptas solem vitantibus umbras,
　　Finditur Icario cum cane terra, darem?
Quid nisi suffugium nimbos vitantibus essem,
　　Non expectata cum venit imber aqua?　　120
Omnia cum faciam, cum praestem sedula cunctis
　　Officium, saxis officiosa petor.
Haec mihi perpessae domini patienda querela est:
　　Causa vocor, quare sit lapidosus ager;
Dumque repurgat humum collectaque saxa remittit, 125
　　Semper habent in me tela parata viae.
Ergo invisa aliis uni mihi frigora prosunt:
　　Illo me tutam tempore praestat hiems.
Nuda quidem tunc sum, nudam tamen expedit esse,
　　Non spolium de me quod petat hostis habet.　　130
At simul induimus nostris sua munera ramis,
　　Saxa novos fructus grandine plura petunt.
Forsitan hic aliquis dicat "quae publica tangunt,
　　Carpere concessum est: hoc via iuris habet."
Si licet hoc, oleas destringite, caedite messes;　　135
　　Improbe, vicinum carpe, viator, holus.
Intret et Urbanas eadem petulantia portas,
　　Sitque tuis muris, Romule, iuris idem:
Quilibet argentum prima de fronte tabernae
　　Tollat et ad gemmas quilibet alter eat;　　140
Auferat hic aurum, peregrinos ille lapillos,
　　Et quascunque potest tangere tollat opes.
Sed neque tolluntur nec, dum regit omnia Caesar,
　　Incolumis tanto praeside raptor erit.

135 scilicet *MSS.* : si licet *G* (first hand) and *edd.*

But brambles and briars, born only to hurt, and other thorns are safe in their own defence. But I, because I harm not, nor am protected by hooked nails, am pelted by wanton stones flung by greedy hands. What if I gave not timely shade to those who flee the sun when the Icarian dog cracks the ground?[1] What were I not a refuge to those who shelter from storms, when comes a downfall of unexpected rain? Though I do all this, though to all I perform untiring service, for all my service I am pelted with stones. And having borne this I must bear the complaining of my master: I am held the cause why his field is stony; and while he clears the ground again, and collects and throws back the stones, the road ever has weapons ready against me. Therefore the cold that others hate is useful to me alone; in that season winter assures my safety. Then indeed am I naked, yet to be naked is an advantage; I have no spoil to tempt an enemy. But as soon as I clothe my branches with their bounty, stones more numerous than hail are aimed at the new fruit. Perchance someone will say here: "What touches public ground it is right to pluck: such right the road can claim." If this is lawful, strip the olives, cut the harvest; pluck neighbouring cabbages, insatiable wayfarer. Let the same impudence even enter the City's gates, and suffer your walls, Romulus, to enjoy the same privilege: let anyone take silver from a shop-front, and his friend lay hand upon the jewels: let one steal gold, another foreign pearls, let him take all the riches he can find. Yet are they not so pilfered, nor, while Caesar governs the world, will a robber be safe under so mighty a prince.

[1] The Dog-star, supposed to be Maera, the dog of Erigone, daughter of Icarius.

At non ille deus pacem intra moenia finit :   145
    Auxilium toto spargit in orbe suum.
Quid tamen hoc prodest, media si luce palamque
    Verberor et tutae non licet esse nuci ?
Ergo nec nidos foliis haerere nec ullam
    Sedibus in nostris stare videtis avem.   150
At lapis in ramo sedit quicunque bifurco
    Haeret, et ut capta victor in arce manet.
Cetera saepe tamen potuere admissa negari,
    Et crimen nox est infitiata suum :
Nostra notat fusco digitos iniuria suco   155
    Cortice contactas inficiente manus.
Ille cruor meus est, illo maculata cruore
    Non profectura dextra lavatur aqua.
O, ego, cum longae venerunt taedia vitae,
    Optavi quotiens arida facta mori !   160
Optavi quotiens aut caeco turbine verti
    Aut valido missi fulminis igne peti !
Atque utinam subitae raperent mea poma procellae,
    Vel possem fructus excutere ipsa meos !
Sic, ubi detracta est a te tibi causa pericli,   165
    Quod superest tutum, Pontice castor, habes.
Quid mihi tunc animi est, ubi sumit tela viator
    Atque oculis plagae destinat ante locum ?
Nec vitare licet moto fera volnera trunco,
    Quem sub humo radix curvaque vincla tenent.   170
Corpora praebemus plagis ut saepe sagittis
    Quem populus manicas deposuisse vetat,
Utve gravem candens ubi tolli vacca securim
    Aut stringi cultros in sua colla videt.

But that god confines not peace within city walls: he sends forth his aid to all the world. Yet what does this avail, if openly in broad day I am beaten, and if a nut tree may not be safe? Therefore you see neither nests clinging to my foliage, nor any bird perching upon my resting-places. But any stone that has wedged in a forked bough is fixed, and abides like a conqueror in a captured citadel. Yet other crimes when committed can often be denied, and night disavows her guilty deed: injury done to me marks the fingers with dark juice, and my bark stains the hands that touch it. That is my blood: the hand that blood has tainted is washed in unavailing water. Ah! how oft, grown weary of my long life, have I wished to wither up and die! How oft have I wished, either to be uprooted by a blind hurricane, or to be struck by the strong flame of a hurled brand! Ay, would that a sudden storm would sweep away all my fruit, or that I myself could shake off all my nuts! So, when the cause of thy peril has been torn from thee, O Pontic beaver, thou keepest safe what is left.[1] What spirit have I then, when the traveller takes his weapons, and his eye picks out the spot for his blow? Nor may I shun the fierce stroke by motion of my trunk, which the curving bonds of the root hold beneath the earth. I offer my body to the stroke, as oft to arrows he whom the folk forbid to lay aside his chains, or as when the white heifer sees the axe uplifted, or the knife drawn across her throat. Oft have you thought

---

[1] The beaver was commonly supposed to escape the hunters by biting off the object of their chase, viz. his testicles, which secreted an oil much used by the ancients in midwifery.

Saepe meas vento frondes tremuisse putastis,　　　175
　　Sed metus in nobis causa tremoris erat.
Si merui videorque nocens, imponite flammae
　　Nostraque fumosis urite membra focis :
Si merui videorque nocens, excidite ferro
　　Et liceat miserae dedoluisse semel.　　　180
Si nec cur urar nec cur excidar habetis,
　　Parcite : sic coeptum perficiatis iter.

180 dedoluisse *Heinsius* : dedecus esse *MSS*

my leaves were trembling in the wind, but fear was the cause of my trembling. If I have deserved it, and am judged guilty, put me on the fire, and burn my limbs on smoky hearths: if I have deserved it, and am judged guilty, cut me down with the steel, and let my wretchedness once for all have an end. If ye have no cause for burning or for cutting down, spare me: so may ye finish the journey ye have begun.

IBIS

IBIS

Tempus ad hoc, lustris bis iam mihi quinque peractis,
    Omne fuit Musae carmen inerme meae;
Nullaque, quae possit, scriptis tot milibus, extat
    Littera Nasonis sanguinolenta legi:
Nec quemquam nostri nisi me laesere libelli,   5
    Artificis periit cum caput Arte sua.
Unus (et hoc ipsum est iniuria magna) perennem
    Candoris titulum non sinit esse mei.
Quisquis is est (nam nomen adhuc utcumque tacebo),
    Cogit inassuetas sumere tela manus.   10
Ille relegatum gelidos aquilonis ad ortus
    Non sinit exilio delituisse meo;
Vulneraque inmitis requiem quaerentia vexat,
    Iactat et in toto nomina nostra foro;
Perpetuoque mihi sociatam foedere lecti   15
    Non patitur vivi funera flere viri.
Cumque ego quassa meae complectar membra carinae,
    Naufragii tabulas pugnat habere mei:
Et qui debuerat subitas extinguere flammas,
    Hic praedam medio raptor ab igne petit.   20
Nititur, ut profugae desint alimenta senectae:
    Heu! quanto est nostris dignior ipse malis!
Di melius! quorum longe mihi maximus ille est,
    Qui nostras inopes noluit esse vias.
Huic igitur meritas grates, ubicumque licebit,   25
    Pro tam mansueto pectore semper agam.

---

[1] He refers to the *Ars Amatoria*; cf. i. 656.

IBIS

Up to this time, when I have already completed fifty years, all the song of my Muse has been harmless; and not a letter of Naso, who wrote so many thousands, exists to be read that is stained with blood : nor have my writings hurt anyone save me, when his own Art proved the artist's bane.[1] One man[2] (and this is itself a mighty wrong) suffers not my title to innocence to endure. Whoever he is (for in any case I shall still be silent of his name), he compels my unaccustomed hands to take up arms. He suffers me not, though banished to the North wind's icy birthplace, to lie hidden in my exile; cruelly he vexes the wounds that crave repose, and shouts my name in all the Forum, nor allows her who is joined to me in the perpetual union of the marriage-bed to weep for her husband's living corpse. And while I embrace the shattered fragments of my bark, he fights to possess my shipwrecked planks; and he who ought to have extinguished the sudden flames seeks plunder like a robber from the midst of the fire. He strives that my exiled old age may lack sustenance : ah ! how much worthier is he himself of my distress ! May the gods forbid ! of whom the greatest far is he, who would not have my voyage destitute.[3] To him, therefore, will I render merited thanks, always wherever I may, for his so kindly heart. Let

<hr>

[2] See Introduction, p. x. [3] *i.e.* Augustus.

Audiat hoc Pontus: faciet quoque forsitan idem,
  Terra sit ut propior testificanda mihi.
At tibi, calcasti qui me, violente, iacentem,
  Qua licet ei misero! debitus hostis ero.   30
Desinet esse prius contrarius ignibus umor,
  Iunctaque cum luna lumina solis erunt;
Parsque eadem caeli zephyros emittet et euros,
  Et tepidus gelido flabit ab axe notus;
Et nova fraterno veniet concordia fumo,   35
  Quem vetus accensa separat ira pyra;
Et ver autumno, brumae miscebitur aestas,
  Atque eadem regio vesper et ortus erit:
Quam mihi sit tecum positis, quae sumpsimus, armis
  Gratia, commissis, improbe, rupta tuis.   40
Pax erit haec nobis, donec mihi vita manebit,   43
  Cum pecore infirmo quae solet esse lupis.
Prima quidem coepto committam proelia versu,   45
  Non soleant quamvis hoc pede bella geri:
Utque petit primo plenum flaventis harenae
  Nondum calfacti militis hasta solum,
Sic ego te nondum ferro iaculabor acuto,
  Protinus invisum nec petet hasta caput;   50
Et neque nomen in hoc nec dicam facta libello,
  Teque brevi, qui sis, dissimulare sinam.
Postmodo, si perges, in te mihi liber iambus
  Tincta Lycambeo sanguine tela dabit.

---

[1] The brothers Eteocles and Polynices, sons of Oedipus, slew
each other in single combat, and so bitter was their hate that
even the flames of the pyre on which their bodies were burnt
would not join together.

[2] This couplet is placed by some editors after ll. 33, 34, as
being more akin in sense than ll. 35, 36.

[3] The couplet (ll. 41, 42) omitted here is the same as ll. 133,
134, and has evidently been inserted in error. It is not found
in two MSS. (GP). After l. 44 Housman would insert ll. 135–140.

Pontus hear these words: perchance too that same
power will cause a nearer land to be called by me
to witness. But thou, thou man of blood, who
didst spurn me fallen, where'er I may, thou wretch,
I shall be thy devoted foe. Sooner shall moisture
cease to be opposed to fire, and the sun's light be
joined to the moon; the same part of heaven
shall send forth western winds and eastern, and
the warm south blow from the cold sky; a strange
concord shall unite the brothers' smoke, which
ancient anger separates on the kindled pyre;[1]
sooner shall spring mingle with autumn, or summer
with midwinter, and the same region be both even-
ing and sunrise,[2] than the arms that we took up
be laid aside, and between thee and me, shameless
wretch, there be that friendship which thy crime
sundered.[3] That peace shall we enjoy, while life
remains to me, which wolves are wont to keep with
the defenceless flock. First will I join battle in the
measure I have begun, although wars are not wont
to be waged in this strain;[4] and as the spear of
the soldier who is not yet fired to battle first
attacks the yellow, sandy soil, so will I not yet
shoot at thee with sharpened steel, nor shall my
javelin seek forthwith thy hateful life; and no
name nor deeds shall I mention in this work, and
I will suffer thee a short while to dissemble who thou
art. Afterwards, if thou dost continue, my satire un-
restrained shall hurl at thee missiles tinged by

[4] The elegiac metre was not usually the metre of satire
or attack; that was the iambic metre, in which Archi-
lochus (fl. 700 B.C.) attacked Lycambes and his daughters,
with such effect that Neobule, whom Lycambes had
promised to the poet and then refused, took her own
life.

Nunc quo Battiades inimicum devovet Ibin,   55
  Hoc ego devoveo teque tuosque modo.
Utque ille, historiis involvam carmina caecis:
  Non soleam quamvis hoc genus ipse sequi.
Illius ambages imitatus in Ibide dicar
  Oblitus moris iudiciique mei.   60
Et quoniam, qui sis, nondum quaerentibus edo,
  Ibidis interea tu quoque nomen habe;
Utque mei versus aliquantum noctis habebunt,
  Sic vitae series tota sit atra tuae.
Haec tibi natali facito, Ianique kalendis   65
  Non mentituro quilibet ore legat.

Di maris et terrae, quique his meliora tenetis
  Inter diversos cum Iove regna polos,
Huc, precor, huc vestras omnes advertite mentes,
  Et sinite optatis pondus inesse meis: 70
Ipsaque tu tellus, ipsum cum fluctibus aequor,
  Ipse meas aether accipe summe preces;
Sideraque et radiis circumdata solis imago,
  Lunaque, quae numquam quo prius orbe micas,
Noxque tenebrarum specie reverenda taurum;   75
  Quaeque ratum triplici pollice netis opus,
Quique per infernas horrendo murmure valles
  Inperiuratae laberis amnis aquae,
Quasque ferunt torto vittatis angue capillis
  Carceris obscuras ante sedere fores;   80
Vos quoque, plebs superum, Fauni Satyrique Laresque
  Fluminaque et nymphae semideumque genus:
Denique ab antiquo divi veteresque novique
  In nostrum cuncti tempus, adeste, chao,

---

[1] Callimachus, who was a native of Cyrene, founded by Battus in the 7th century.

Lycambean blood. Now, in such wise as Battiades [1] calls curses down on his enemy Ibis, so do I call curses down on thee and thine. Like him I will enshroud my song in doubtful story, although I am not wont to pursue this style. His riddlings shall I be said to have imitated, forgetful of my judgment and my custom. And because I reveal not yet to those who ask me, who thou art, bear thou also meanwhile the name of Ibis; and just as my lines have something of the dark, so let thy own life's series all be black. Be this what he offers thee upon thy birthday and upon Janus' Kalends,[2] whosoever reads with lips that shall not lie.

Gods of land and sea, and ye who hold with Jove a better realm than these between the sundered poles, hither, I pray, turn hither all of you your minds, and allow weight to my desires: and thou thyself, O Earth, and thyself, O Sea with thy waves, and thyself, O supreme Air, hear my petition; ye constellations, too, and the sun's ray-encircled image, and thou Moon that never shinest with the orb thou hadst before, and Night, awful in the beauty of thy shadows; and ye who with triple thumb spin your appointed task, and thou river of unperjured water, that with roar terrific flowest through the infernal vales, and ye who, as they tell, your tresses bound by twisted serpents, sit before the dim prison gates, ye too, the host of gods above, Fauns, Satyrs, Lars, streams and nymphs, and the race of demigods: gods lastly old and new from ancient chaos down to our own time, be present all, while dreadful spells are

---

[2] Instead of good wishes, usual on these days, he must bring him Ovid's poem.

Carmina dum capiti male fido dira canuntur   85
    Et peragunt partes ira dolorque suas.
Adnuite optatis omnes ex ordine nostris,
    Et pars sit voti nulla caduca mei.
Quaeque precor, fiant: ut non mea dicta, sed illa
    Pasiphaës generi verba fuisse putet.   90
Quasque ego transiero poenas, patiatur et illas;
    Plenius ingenio sit miser ille meo!
Neve minus noceant fictum execrantia nomen
    Vota, minus magnos commoveantve deos:
Illum ego devoveo, quem mens intellegit, Ibin,   95
    Qui scit se factis has meruisse preces.
Nulla mora est in me: peragam rata vota sacerdos.
    Quisquis ades sacris, ore favete, meis;
Quisquis ades sacris, lugubria dicite verba,
    Et fletu madidis Ibin adite genis: 100
Ominibusque malis pedibusque occurrite laevis,
    Et nigrae vestes corpora vestra tegant!
Tu quoque, quid dubitas ferales sumere vittas?
    Iam stat, ut ipse vides, funeris ara tui.
Pompa parata tibi est: votis mora tristibus absit: 105
    Da iugulum cultris, hostia dira, meis.

Terra tibi fruges, amnis tibi deneget undas,
    Deneget afflatus ventus et aura suos.
Nec tibi sol calidus, nec sit tibi lucida Phoebe,
    Destituant oculos sidera clara tuos.   110
Nec se Vulcanus nec se tibi praebeat aër,
    Nec tibi det tellus nec tibi pontus iter.

---

[1] Theseus, lover of Ariadne, daughter of Minos and Pasiphae, who uttered dreadful threats against Hippolytus.

[2] "ore favere" means "to speak no word inappropriate to the rites in progress"; if the occasion is joyful, to speak no gloomy word, if angry or mournful, to speak no cheerful one.

chanted against that faithless head, and grief and anger play their parts. Give assent all in turn to my desires, and let no part of my supplication fall! And what I pray, may that be done: so that he deem them not my sayings, but the words of the lover of Pasiphae's daughter.[1] And whatever penalties I pass by, may he suffer those as well; let him be richer in misery than my wit can conceive! Nor may vows that doom a feigned name to perdition be less strong to harm, or move less powerful gods: that Ibis do I execrate whom the mind understands, who knows that his deeds have merited these curses. I am in no mood to tarry: as priest I will fulfil the appointed prayers. Whosoever thou art that attendest at my rite, suit thy speech thereto;[2] whosoever thou art that attendest at the rite, utter words of woe, and draw near to Ibis with tear-moistened cheeks; meet him with evil omens and with left feet foremost, and let black raiment hide your bodies! Thou too,[3] why dost thou hesitate to assume the garb of woe? Already thy funeral altar is set up, as thou dost see thyself. The procession is ready for thee; let not my angry prayers be delayed; offer thy throat, O fearful victim, to my knife.

May the earth refuse thee her fruits and the river his waters, may wind and breeze deny their breath. May the sun not be warm for thee, nor Phoebe bright, may the clear stars fail thy vision. May neither Vulcan nor the air lend thee their aid, nor earth nor sea afford thee any path. Mayst

---

[3] *i.e.* the victim, against whom the solemn ritual of execration was about to be performed. The curses follow, 107 *sqq.*

Exul, inops erres, alienaque limina lustres,
    Exiguumque petas ore tremente cibum.
Nec corpus querulo nec mens vacet aegra dolore,   11
    Noxque die gravior sit tibi, nocte dies.
Sisque miser semper, nec sis miserabilis ulli:
    Gaudeat adversis femina virque tuis.
Accedat lacrimis odium, dignusque puteris,
    Qui mala cum tuleris plurima, plura feras.   12
Sitque, quod est rarum, solito defecta favore
    Fortunae facies invidiosa tuae.
Causaque non desit, desit tibi copia mortis:
    Optatam fugiat vita coacta necem:
Luctatusque diu cruciatos spiritus artus   12
    Deserat, et longa torqueat ante mora.

Evenient.   dedit ipse mihi modo signa futuri
    Phoebus, et a laeva maesta volavit avis.
Certe ego, quae voveo, superos motura putabo,
    Speque tuae mortis, perfide, semper alar.   13
Et prius hanc animam, nimium tibi saepe petitam,
    Auferet illa dies, quae mihi sera venit,
Quam dolor hic umquam spatio evanescere possit,
    Leniat aut odium tempus et hora meum.
Pugnabunt arcu dum Thraces, Iazyges hasta,   13
    Dum tepidus Ganges, frigidus Hister erit;
Robora dum montes, dum mollia pabula campi,
    Dum Tiberis liquidas Tuscus habebit aquas,
Tecum bella geram; nec mors mihi finiet iras,
    Saeva sed innocuis manibus arma dabit.   14

thou wander an exile and destitute, and haunt the doors of others, and beg a little food with trembling mouth. May neither thy body nor thy sick mind be free from querulous pain, may night be to thee more grievous than day, and day than night. Mayst thou ever be piteous, but have none to pity thee; may men and women rejoice at thy adversity. May hatred crown thy tears, and mayst thou be thought worthy, having borne many ills, to bear yet more. And (what is rare) may the aspect of thy fortune, though its wonted favour be lost, bring thee but ill-will. Mayst thou have cause enough for death, but no means of dying; may thy life be compelled to shun the death it prays for. May thy spirit struggle long ere it leave thy tortured limbs, and rack thee first with long delaying.

These things shall be. Phoebus himself of late gave me signs of the future, and a bird of sorrow flew from the left.[1] Surely may I think that my prayers will move the gods, and ever, treacherous one, will I feed on the hope of thy death. And sooner will that late-arriving day deprive me of the life too oft assailed by thee, than age ever cause this resentment of mine to fail, or length of time appease my hate. While Thracians fight with the bow and Iazygians with the spear, while Ganges is warm and Danube cold, while oaks are on the mountains and lush pasture on the plains, while Tuscan Tiber holds running waters, I shall wage war with thee; nor shall death end my wrath, but give fierce weapons to my innocuous

---

[1] The left is used here in the Greek sense of being the unlucky side; Ovid rejoices that the omens should be unlucky (for Ibis).

Tunc quoque, cum fuero vacuas dilapsus in auras,
 Exanimis mores oderit umbra tuos,
Tunc quoque factorum veniam memor umbra tuorum,
 Insequar et vultus ossea forma tuos.
Sive ego, quod nollem, longis consumptus ab annis, 14 (?)
 Sive manu facta morte solutus ero :
Sive per inmensas iactabor naufragus undas,
 Nostraque longinquus viscera piscis edet :
Sive peregrinae carpent mea membra volucres :
 Sive meo tinguent sanguine rostra lupi : 15 (?)
Sive aliquis dignatus erit subponere terrae
 Et dare plebeio corpus inane rogo :
Quidquid ero, Stygiis erumpere nitar ab oris,
 Et tendam gelidas ultor in ora manus.
Me vigilans cernes, tacitis ego noctis in umbris 15 (?)
 Excutiam somnos visus adesse tuos.
Denique quidquid ages, ante os oculosque volabo
 Et querar, et nulla sede quietus eris.
Verbera torta dabunt sonitum nexaeque colubrae,
 Conscia fumabunt semper ad ora faces. 16 (?)
His vivus furiis agitabere, mortuus isdem,
 Et brevior poena vita futura tua est.
Nec tibi continget funus lacrimaeque tuorum ;
 Indeploratum proiciere caput ;
Carnificisque manu, populo plaudente, traheris, 16 (?)
 Infixusque tuis ossibus uncus erit.
Ipsae te fugient, quae carpunt omnia, flammae ;
 Respuet invisum iusta cadaver humus.
Unguibus et rostro crudus trahet ilia vultur
 Et scindent avidi perfida corda canes, 17 (?)

169 crudus *Heinsius* : tardus *MSS*.

ghost. Then also when I shall be scattered into
tenuous air my lifeless shade shall detest thy
ways; then too shall I come, a shade that forgets
not thy deeds, and in bony shape shall I assail thy
face. Whether I am consumed (as I fain would not
be) by length of years, or undone by a self-sought
death; whether I am tossed in shipwreck o'er un-
measured waters, and the outlandish fish devours
my flesh; whether foreign fowl prey upon my
limbs, or wolves stain their jaws with my blood;
whether someone deign to put my lifeless corpse
beneath the earth, or to set it upon a common
pyre: whatever I shall be, I shall strive to burst
forth from the Stygian realm, and shall stretch
forth icy hands in vengeance against thy face.
Waking thou shalt behold me, in the silent shadows
of the night I shall appear before thee and drive
away thy slumbers. Finally, whatever thou dost I
shall hover before thine eyes and countenance, and
make complaint, and in no place shalt thou have
repose. Twisted thongs shall crack and twined
serpents hiss, and torches smoke before thy guilty
face. By these furies shalt thou be driven while
living and by these when dead, and thy punishment
shall outlast thy life. Nor shall any funeral fall
to thy lot, nor lamentation of thy kin; thou shalt
be cast forth, a life unmourned. The hand of the
executioner shall drag thee, amid the plaudits of
the mob, and his hook shall be fixed in thy bones.[1]
The very flames, which consume all things, shall
shun thee; the righteous ground shall spurn thy
hated corpse. With beak and talons the cruel
vulture shall pluck at thy loins, and ravening dogs

[1] cf. Juv. 10. 66 : Seianus ducitur unco.

Deque tuo fiet—licet hac sis laude superbus—
    Insatiabilibus corpore rixa lupis.
In loca ab Elysiis diversa vocabere campis,
    Quasque tenet sedes noxia turba, coles.
Sisyphus est illic saxum volvensque petensque,   175
    Quique agitur rapidae vinctus ab orbe rotae,
Quaeque gerunt umeris perituras Belides undas,
    Exulis Aegypti, turba cruenta, nurus.
Poma pater Pelopis praesentia quaerit, et idem
    Semper eget, liquidis semper abundat aquis ;   180
Iugeribusque novem summus qui distat ab imo,
    Visceraque assiduae debita praebet avi.
Hic tibi de Furiis scindet latus una flagello,
    Ut sceleris numeros confiteare tui :
Altera Tartareis sectos dabit anguibus artus :   185
    Tertia fumantes incoquet igne genas.
Noxia mille modis lacerabitur umbra, tuasque
    Aeacus in poenas ingeniosus erit.
In te transcribet veterum tormenta reorum :
    Omnibus antiquis causa quietis eris.   190
Sisyphe, cui tradas revolubile pondus, habebis :
    Versabunt celeres nunc nova membra rotae :
Hic et erit, ramos frustra qui captet et undas :
    Hic inconsumpto viscere pascet aves.
Nec mortis poenas mors altera finiet huius,   195
    Horaque erit tantis ultima nulla malis.
Inde ego pauca canam, frondes ut siquis ab Ida
    Aut summam Libyco de mare carpat aquam.

189 reorum *Heinsius* : virorum *MSS.*

---

[1] Ixion and the Danaids, the latter compelled to carry water
for ever in sieves, for murdering their husbands, the sons of
Aegyptus.

tear thy perfidious heart, and o'er thy body (of such fame mayst thou boast) shall rage the strife of insatiable wolves. To places far removed from Elysian fields shalt thou be summoned, and where the guilty have their dwelling shalt thou abide. Sisyphus is there, rolling his stone and seeking it again, and he who is whirled, fast bound, by the circle of the flying wheel, and the daughters of Belus who bear on their shoulders the water that runs away, the daughters-in-law of exiled Aegyptus, a bloodstained company.[1] Pelops' sire grasps at the fruit before him, and ever lacks yet ever abounds in running waters; and he whose extremities nine acres sunder, who yields his forfeited entrails to the assiduous bird.[2] Here shall one of the Furies tear thy side with a scourge, that thou mayst confess the full measure of thy wickedness; another shall cut up thy limbs for the snakes of Tartarus; a third shall roast thy smoking face with fire. In a thousand ways shall thy noxious shade be mangled, and Aeacus shall use all his art to find thee punishments. To thee shall he transfer the torments of sinners of old; to all the ancients shalt thou bring peace. Sisyphus, thou shalt have one to whom thou mayst give thy revolving weight; the swift wheels now shall turn new limbs; this man shall it be who will grasp in vain at boughs and waves; this man will feed the birds with liver unconsumed. Nor shall another death bring this death's torments to an end, no hour shall be the last for misery so great. Thereof will I sing but little, as though one gathered leaves from Ida, or water from the surface of the Libyan sea. For

[2] Tantalus and Tityus.

Nam neque quot flores Sicula nascantur in Hybla,
   Quotve ferat, dicam, terra Cilissa crocos,   200
Nec cum tristis hiems Aquilonis inhorruit alis,
   Quam multa fiat grandine canus Athos ;
Nec mala voce mea poterunt tua cuncta referri,
   Ora licet tribuas multiplicata mihi.
Tot tibi vae ! misero venient talesque ruinae,   205
   Ut cogi in lacrimas me quoque posse putem.
Illae me lacrimae facient sine fine beatum :
   Dulcior hic risu tunc mihi fletus erit.

Natus es infelix,—ita di voluere—nec ulla
   Commoda nascenti stella levisve fuit.   210
Non Venus affulsit, non illa Iuppiter hora,
   Lunaque non apto solque fuere loco,
Nec satis utiliter positos tibi praebuit ignes
   Quem peperit magno lucida Maia Iovi.
Te fera nec quicquam placidum spondentia Martis   215
   Sidera presserunt falciferique senis.
Lux quoque natalis, ne quid nisi triste videres,
   Turpis et inductis nubibus atra fuit.
Haec est, in fastis cui dat gravis Allia nomen,
   Quaeque dies Ibin, publica damna, tulit.   220
Qui simul impurae matris prolapsus ab alvo
   Cinyphiam foedo corpore pressit humum,
Sedit in adverso nocturnus culmine bubo,
   Funereoque graves edidit ore sonos.
Protinus Eumenides lavere palustribus undis,   225
   Qua cava de Stygiis fluxerat unda vadis,
Pectoraque unxerunt Erebeae felle colubrae,
   Terque cruentatas increpuere manus.

---

[1] Ellis suggests that Mercury would be favourable to Ibis,
as having an affection for the animal of that name: cf. Aelian,
H.N. 10, 27.   A magical papyrus has Ἑρμαϊκὴς Ἴβεως.

neither can I say how many flowers bloom in Sicilian
Hybla, nor how many crocuses the Cilician earth
doth bear, nor, when the fierce storm quivers upon
the wings of the North wind, with how many hail-
stones Athos is made white; nor can all thy sins
be recounted by my speech, though thou give me
voices manifold. So many (woe upon thee!) and
such destructions shall come on thee, that I ween
I too could be compelled to weep. Those tears will
make me happy without end; that weeping will be
sweeter to me than laughter.

Thou wert born unfortunate (so willed the gods),
no star was favourable or kindly at thy birth. Venus
shone not, nor Jupiter in that hour, neither moon
nor sun were fitly placed, nor did he whom shining
Maia bore to mighty Jove set his fires in position to
bring thee aught of profit.[1] The savage star of
Mars that promises naught peaceful bore thee down,
and the star of the aged wielder of the scythe.[2]
Thy natal day too, that thou mightest see naught
save gloom, was foul and black with pall of cloud.
This is the day to which in our Annals deadly Allia
gives her name,[3] and the day which brought Ibis to
birth, brought destruction to our people. So soon
as, fallen from an impure mother's womb, his unclean
body lay on the Cinyphian [4] soil, a nocturnal owl sat
over against him in a tree-top, and uttered dismal
sounds with death-foretelling mouth. Forthwith the
Furies washed him in the waters of the mere, where
flowed a channel from the Stygian stream, and
anointed his breast with poison of a snake of Erebus,
and thrice smote their blood-stained hands together.

[2] *i.e.* Saturn.
[3] The date of the famous battle of the Allia, when the
Romans were defeated by the Gauls, July 18th, 390 B.C.
[4] *i.e.* African, from a small river on the N. coast.

Gutturaque imbuerunt infantia lacte canino:
    Hic primus pueri venit in ora cibus: 230
Perbibit inde suae rabiem nutricis alumnus,
    Latrat et in toto verba canina foro.
Membraque vinxerunt tinctis ferrugine pannis,
    A male deserto quos rapuere rogo:
Et ne non fultum nuda tellure iaceret,   235
    Molle super silices inposuere caput.
Iamque recessurae viridi de stipite factas
    Admorunt oculos usque sub ora faces.
Flebat, ut est infans fumis contactus amaris,
    De tribus est cum sic una locuta soror: 240
"Tempus in inmensum lacrimas tibi movimus istas,
    Quae semper causa sufficiente cadent."
Dixerat; at Clotho iussit promissa valere,
    Nevit et infesta stamina pulla manu;
Et ne longa suo praesagia diceret ore,   245
    "Fata canet vates qui tua," dixit, "erit."
Ille ego sum vates: ex me tua vulnera disces,
    Dent modo di vires in mea verba suas;
Carminibusque meis accedent pondera rerum,
    Quae rata per luctus experiere tuos.   250
Neve sine exemplis aevi cruciere prioris,
    Sint tua Troianis non leviora malis,
Quantaque clavigeri Poeantius Herculis heres,
    Tanta venenato vulnera crure geras.
Nec levius doleas, quam qui bibit ubera cervae,   255
    Armatique tulit vulnus, inermis opem;
Quique ab equo praeceps in Aleïa decidit arva,
    Exitio facies cui sua paene fuit.

257 in Aleïa *Heinsius*: aliena in . . . arva, alienis . . . arvis
MSS.

---

[1] Philoctetes; see note on *Rem. Am.* 111.

His infant throat had they moistened with bitches'
milk : this was the first food to enter the child's
mouth : thence drank the fosterling the madness of
his nurse, and o'er the whole city his snarling voice
is heard.   They swathed his limbs in bands of dusky
hue, snatched from a pyre abandoned as accursed ;
and lest it lie unpropped on the naked earth they
set a flint-stone beneath his baby head.   And now,
about to withdraw, they placed before his eyes, close
by his face, a green-wood torch.   The babe was
weeping, smarting from the pungent smoke, when
one sister of the three thus spake : " Unto endless
ages have we called forth those tears of thine, which,
their cause failing not, shall ever fall." She had done ;
but Clotho bade her promise have power, and with
hostile hand spun dark-hued threads ; and that her
own mouth might not utter the long presage, " There
shall be a bard," said she, " to sing thy fate." That
bard am I ; from me shalt thou learn thy wounds, so
do the gods but lend their strength to my words ;
and the weight of circumstance shall aid my songs,
whose fulfilment thou shalt experience to thy sorrow.
And lest the examples of a former age be lacking to
thy torments, let not thine ills be lighter than those
of Troy, and such wounds as the son of Poeas, heir of
club-wielding Hercules, endured in his envenomed
leg, mayst thou bear in thine.[1]   Nor mayst thou
suffer less grievously than he who drank of the hind's
udders, whom the armed man wounded and the un-
armed succoured ;[2] or than he who from his horse fell
headlong to the Aleian fields, whose face was well-

---

[2] Telephus was suckled by a hind, and was both wounded
and healed by Achilles' spear ; "inermis," *i. e.* Machaon.

OVID

Id quod Amyntorides videas, trepidumque ministro
    Praetemptes baculo luminis orbus iter.   260
Nec plus aspicias quam quem sua filia rexit,
    Expertus scelus est cuius uterque parens :
Qualis erat, postquam est iudex de lite iocosa
    Sumptus, Apollinea clarus in arte senex :
Qualis et ille fuit, quo praecipiente columba   265
    Est data Palladiae praevia duxque rati :
Quique oculis caruit, per quos male viderat aurum,
    Inferias nato quos dedit orba parens :
Pastor ut Aetnaeus, cui casus ante futuros
    Telemus Eurymides vaticinatus erat :   270
Ut duo Phinidae, quibus idem lumen ademit,
    Qui dedit : ut Thamyrae Demodocique caput
Sic aliquis tua membra secet, Saturnus ut illas
    Subsecuit partes, unde creatus erat.
Nec tibi sit melior tumidis Neptunus in undis,   275
    Quam cui sunt subitae frater et uxor aves ;
Sollertique viro, lacerae quem fracta tenentem
    Membra ratis Semeles est miserata soror.
Vel tua, ne poenae genus hoc cognoverit unus,
    Viscera diversis scissa ferantur equis :   280

---

[1] Bellerophon, to whom Sthenoboea, wife of Proetus, king of Corinth, played the part of Potiphar's wife ; after slaying the Chimaera he descended from Pegasus on the Aleian fields in Cilicia (cf. Hom. *Il.* 6. 201).

[2] Phoenix, who was blinded by his father.

[3] Oedipus (261) ; Tiresias (263) was called upon by Jupiter and Juno to say whether sexual intercourse was more pleasing to the man or to the woman ; having decided in favour of the latter he incurred the anger of Juno, who blinded him ; Phineus (265) taught the Argonauts how to sail through the Symplegades ;

nigh his destruction.[1] Mayst thou see what Amyntor's son beheld, and reft of light grope thy timorous path by the service of a stick.[2] Nor mayst thou see more than he whom his daughter guided, whose wickedness both his parents knew; but be as was the old man, famous for Apollo's craft, when he was taken to judge the jesting quarrel; as he, too, by whose precept the dove was made forerunner and guide of the Palladian ship; and also as he who lost those eyes by which to his loss he looked upon the gold, and which the bereft mother gave as death-offering to her son; or as Aetna's shepherd, to whom Telemus, son of Eurymus, foretold what should befall him; as the two sons of Phineus, from whom he reft the light who gave it; as the head of Thamyris or of Demodocus.[3] So may one hack thy limbs, as Saturn cut off those parts that wrought his birth.[4] Nor may Neptune be kinder to thee among the swelling waves than to him whose brother and wife became on a sudden birds; or to the man of guile, whom Semele's sister pitied as he clung to the fragments of his shattered raft.[5] Either (lest one alone [6] know this fashion of punishment) may thy flesh be torn and carried by horses diverse ways; or mayst thou bear

Polymestor (267) stole the gold entrusted to Polydorus, and was blinded by the latter's mother Hecuba; Polyphemus; Plexippus and Pandion, according to Apollodorus, but the names vary; Thamyris and Demodocus, both blind bards.

[4] Saturn (Cronos) mutilated his father Uranus.

[5] Ceyx, king of Trachis, whose brother Daedalion became a hawk, and his wife Alcyone a halcyon or kingfisher: Ino saved Ulysses when flung from his raft by giving him her veil (Hom. *Od.* 5. 333): in Homer, however, the raft is not yet shattered.

[6] Mettius Fufetius, King of Alba, suffered this fate, after breaking a treaty he had made with Rome; see Livy, i. 28.

OVID

Vel quae qui redimi Romano turpe putavit,
  A duce Puniceo pertulit, ipse feras.
Nec tibi subsidio praesens sit numen, ut illi,
  Cui nil Hercei profuit ara Iovis.
Utque dedit saltus de summa Thessalus Ossa,   28
  Tu quoque saxoso praecipitere iugo.
Aut velut Eurylochi, qui sceptrum cepit ab illo,
  Sint artus avidis anguibus esca tui.
Vel tua maturet, sicut Minoïa fata,
  Per caput infusae fervidus umor aquae.   29
Utque operum mitis, sed non impune, Prometheus,
  Aërias volucres compede fixus alas.
Aut ut Erechthides, magno ter ab Hercule victus,
  Caesus in inmensum proiciare fretum.
Aut ut Amyntiaden, turpi dilectus amore   29
  Oderit, et saevo vulneret ense puer.
Nec tibi fida magis misceri pocula possint,
  Quam qui cornigero de Iove natus erat.
More vel intereas capti suspensus Achaei,
  Qui miser aurifera teste pependit aqua.   30

---

282 Puniceo *MSS. (but the word is not otherwise found)*
Cinyphio *later MSS. (see* l. 222).
  284 Hercei *B* : Rhoetei *Merkel.*
  291 operum mitis *Merkel* : parum mitis *MSS.* : parum
inmitis *Owen* : *Housman brackets the couplet.*
  293 Erechthides *Ellis* : ethreclides, echecratides, etracide
MSS. : victus *T* : quintus *MSS.*

₁ Regulus.
  [2] Priam ; cf. Virg. *Aen.* 2. 506 where Priam is slain at th
altar of Zeus in his own courtyard.   Hercei, *i.e.* of the Ἕρκος o
court, where the altar was.
  [3] Apparently a king of Thessaly since Eurylochus was one.
  [4] The fate of Minos, at the hands of the daughters o
Cocalus, when he went to Sicily in search of the escape
Daedalus.

what he bore at the Punic chieftain's hands, who
held it base for a Roman to be ransomed.[1] Nor may
a present deity bring thee aid, as to him whom the
household shrine of Jove availed naught.[2] And as
Thessalus[3] leapt down from Ossa's height, so mayst
thou too be hurled from a rocky ridge. Or like
Eurylochus, who took the sceptre from him, may
thy limbs be food for greedy snakes. Or like Minos'
fate, let the boiling heat of water poured upon thy
head hasten thy death.[4] And like Prometheus,
whose deeds were kindly, yet not unpunished, mayst
thou be fettered and feed the birds of air.[5] Or like
Erechthides, thrice defeated by mighty Hercules,
mayst thou be slain and hurled into the immeasur-
able deep.[6] Or like Amyntas' son, may the boy
thou dost love detest thy shameful wooing, and
wound thee with his angry blade.[7] Nor may cups
more trustworthy be mixed for thee than for him
who was born of horned Jove.[8] Or hanging like
the captive Achaeus mayst thou die, who hung
miserably by the stream that bears the gold.[9] Or

[5] Ellis thinks there may be a play on the Greek word
Μῆτις = Wisdom, and "mitis," and interprets "that failed
in his philanthropy"; there are similar plays on words in
Aesch. *P. V.* 85. and Prop. iii. 5. 7, 8.

[6] Probably Eryx, whom Hercules defeated in wrestling
and flung into the sea; for the genealogy, see Ellis *ad loc.*

[7] Philip of Macedon, son of Amyntas, killed by Pausanias,
whom he had once outraged. Others explain of Archelaus,
king of Macedonia.

[8] Alexander the Great, who declared himself the son of
Zeus Ammon, the horned god, and loved to be represented as
horned himself; according to some he was poisoned, though
this is probably inaccurate.

[9] A rebel against Antiochus the Great, who beheaded him,
sewed him up in an ass's skin and hung him on a cross at
Sardis, by the "golden" river Pactolus (214 B.C.).

Aut ut Achilliden, cognato nomine clarum,
　Opprimat hostili tegula iacta manu.
Nec tua quam Pyrrhi felicius ossa quiescant,
　Sparsa per Ambracias quae iacuere vias.
Nataque ut Aeacidae iaculari moriaris adactis;　　305
　Non licet hoc Cereri dissimulare sacrum.
Utque nepos dicti nostro modo carmine regis,
　Cantharidum sucos dante parente bibas.
Aut pia te caeso dicatur adultera, sicut
　Qua cecidit Leucon vindice, dicta pia est.　　310
Inque pyram tecum carissima corpora mittas,
　Quem finem vitae Sardanapallus habet.
Utque Iovis Libyci templum violare parantes,
　Acta noto vultus condat harena tuos.
Utque necatorum Darei fraude secundi,　　315
　Sic tua subsidens devoret ora cinis.
Aut ut olivifera quondam Sicyone profecto,
　Sit frigus mortis causa famesque tuae.

---

¹ Pyrrhus, king of Epirus, who claimed descent from Achilles
(whose son was also named Pyrrhus), met his death by being
struck by a tile at the siege of Argos (272 B.C.).

² Pyrrhus, son of Achilles, was killed by Orestes at Delphi,
but this is the only reference to Ambracia. It may refer to
some unknown story about the younger Pyrrhus, grandson of
the king of Epirus.

³ A grand-daughter of Pyrrhus, king of Epirus, named
Deidamia, or Laodamia, who was the victim of popular fury,
and was killed in the temple of Ceres (the authorities, however,
say Diana); Ceres cannot shroud this murder in the same
mystery as the rites of Eleusis.

⁴ Pyrrhus, grandson of Pyrrhus, king of Epirus, who was
poisoned with his mistress Tigris by his mother Olympias. For
Spanish fly, cf. Cic. *Tusc.* 5. 40. 117.

⁵ Leucon was a son of Athamas, and was killed in error by
his mother Themisto, who married Athamas, though his wife
Ino unknown to him was still living (therefore a " pia adult-

like Achilles' scion, whose kindred name brings him renown, may a tile flung by an enemy's hand destroy thee.[1] Nor may thy bones rest more blissful than those of Pyrrhus, which lay scattered through Ambracian ways.[2] And like the daughter of Aeacides mayst thou die by the blows of javelins; this rite Ceres may not dissemble.[3] And like the grandson of the monarch named in my song but now, mayst thou drink at thy parent's hand the juice of the Spanish fly.[4] Or may an adulteress be called righteous for slaying thee, as she was called righteous by whose vengeance Leucon fell.[5] And mayst thou send with thee to the pyre the bodies most dear to thee,[6] an end of life that befell Sardanapalus. And like them who prepared to violate the shrine of Libyan Jove,[7] may the sand driven by the South wind o'erwhelm thy face. And like those slain by the fraud of the second Darius, even so may the sinking ashes devour thy countenance.[8] Or like him who once set forth from olive-bearing Sicyon, may cold and hunger be the cause of thy death.[9]

era "); when Athamas wished to bring Ino back, Themisto plotted vengeance: so Ellis, but the schol. explains of a Leucon, king of Pontus, in love with his brother's wife.

[6] His wife and concubines (Athenaeus 529).

[7] Persian soldiers sent by king Cambyses (Hdt. 3. 25).

[8] Darius Ochus devised a punishment to evade an oath he had taken not to kill those taken in a conspiracy against him, which was to contrive that they should fall when asleep into a pit of ashes (presumably red hot); cf. Val. Max. 9. 2. 6, and also Maccabees, 2. 13.5.

[9] Conjectures mentioned by Ellis are: (i) Neocles, during tyranny of Paseas, 252–1 B.C.; (ii) Neophron or Nearchusa, a tragedian; (ii) Adrastus, once king of Sicyon, whose πάθεα were celebrated by the Sicyonians; (iv) Demetrius Poliorcetes, for whose end cf. Plut. *Dem.* 46.

Aut ut Atarnites, insutus pelle iuvenci
    Turpiter ad dominum praeda ferare tuum.   320
Inque tuo thalamo ritu iugulere Pheraei,
    Qui datus est leto coniugis ense suae,
Quosque putas fidos, ut Larisaeus Aleuas
    Vulnere non fidos experiare tuo.
Utque Milo, sub quo cruciata est Pisa tyranno,   325
    Vivus in occultas praecipiteris aquas.
Quaeque in Aphidantum Phylaceïa regna tenentem
    A Iove venerunt, te quoque tela petant.
Aut ut Amastriacis quondam Lenaeus ab oris,
    Nudus Achillea destituaris humo.   330
Utque vel Eurydamas ter circum busta Thrasylli
    Est Larisaeis raptus ab hoste rotis,
Vel qui, quae fuerat tutatus moenia saepe,
    Corpore lustravit non diuturna suo,
Utque novum passa genus Hippomeneïde poenae   335
    Tractus in Actaea fertur adulter humo,
Sic, ubi vita tuos invisa reliquerit artus,
    Ultores rapiant turpe cadaver equi.
Viscera sic aliquis scopulus tua figat, ut olim
    Fixa sub Euboico Graia fuere sinu ;   340
Utque ferox periit et fulmine et aequore raptor,
    Sic te mersuras adiuvet ignis aquas.

---

[1] Hermias, king of Atarne, who rebelled against the Persians about the middle of the 4th cent. B.C.

[2] Alexander, tyrant of Pherae (369–335), slain by his wife Thebe when plotting to slay his sons.

[3] Unknown : he seems to have been treacherously stabbed.

[4] No satisfactory explanation ; see excursus in Ellis, p. 176.

[5] Lycaon, slain by Jove for having feasted him with human flesh.

Or like the Atarnean, mayst thou, sewed in a bullock's
hide, be basely carried as booty to thy lord.[1] And
mayst thou be murdered in thy chamber like him of
Pherae, who was slain by the sword of his own
spouse,[2] and like Aleuas of Larissa mayst thou by
thine own wound find faithless those whom thou
thinkest faithful.[3] And like Milo, under whose
tyranny Pisa groaned, mayst thou be hurled alive
into hidden waters.[4] And may the missiles sped by
Jove against him who held the Phylacian realm of
the Aphidantians seek thee also.[5] Or like Lenaeus
faring once from Amastris' shores mayst thou be left
destitute on Achillean soil.[6] And as either Eurydamas
was thrice dragged round Thrasyllus' tomb by
Larissean wheels, or he who with his own body
purified the walls, so soon to fall, which he had often
saved, or as the adulterer was dragged, they say,
o'er Attic soil, while the daughter of Hippomenes
suffered a new kind of doom, so, when the hated life
has left thy limbs, may avenging steeds pull thy
dishonoured corpse.[7] In such wise may some rock
pierce thy flesh, as the Greeks were pierced in the
Euboean bay ; and as the bold ravisher perished by
thunderbolt and by sea, so may fire aid the waters

[6] Explained either of Mithridates the Great, who was
surnamed Dionysus ("Achillea" being explained either by
two places near the Tauric Chersonese, 'Αχιλλέως δρόμος and
'Αχιλλεῖος κώμη, cf. Bergk, fr. 49), or of Philoctetes, read-
ing "Lemnaeus," when Ellis would read "Echidnaea," of
the viper that bit him.

[7] Eurydamas had killed Thrasyllus, brother of Simon of
Larissa ; Hector's being dragged round the walls is compared
to the solemn lustral processions round city walls ; the
seducer of Limone (see l. 459) was dragged behind a chariot,
while she was shut up with a horse and torn to pieces
(probably related in Callimachus' *Ibis*).

OVID

Mens quoque sic furiis vecors agitetur, ut illi,
    Unum qui toto corpore vulnus habet ;
Utque Dryantiadae Rhodopeïa regna tenenti,   345
    In gemino dispar cui pede cultus erat,
Ut fuit Oetaeo quondam generoque draconum
    Tisamenique patri Callirhoësque viro.
Nec tibi contingat matrona pudicior illa,
    Qua potuit Tydeus erubuisse nuru :   350
Quaeque sui Venerem iunxit cum fratre mariti,
    Locris in ancillae dissimulata nece.
Tam quoque, di faciant, possis gaudere fideli
    Coniuge, quam Talai Tyndareique gener :
Quaeque parare suis letum patruelibus ausae   355
    Belides assidua colla premuntur aqua.
Byblidos et Canaces, sicut facis, ardeat igne,
    Nec nisi per crimen sit tibi fida soror.
Filia si fuerit, sit quod Pelopea Thyesti,
    Myrrha suo patri, Nyctimeneque suo.   360
Neve magis pia sit capitique parentis amica,
    Quam sua vel Pterelae, vel tibi, Nise, fuit :

---

[1] The wreck of Greek vessels returning from Troy on
Caphereus ; Ajax Oileus, who ravished Cassandra, was struck
by a thunderbolt and then drowned.

[2] Ajax, who could only be wounded in his left side ;
Lycurgus, king of Thrace, who had lost one foot ($\mu o\nu o\kappa\rho\eta\pi\tilde{\iota}\delta a$
$\Lambda\nu\kappa o\tilde{\nu}\rho\gamma o\nu$) ; Hercules, burnt on Mt. Oeta ; Athamas, whose wife
Ino was daughter of Cadmus and Harmonia, changed into
snakes ; Orestes ; Alcmaeon, who slew his mother Eriphyle for
causing the death of her husband Amphiaraus : all these were
driven mad in one way or other.

[3] Aegiale, wife of Diomede, who had many lovers.

that will drown thee.[1] Mayst thou in mind too be
as distraught and frenzy-driven as he who in his whole
body has but one wound; or as the son of Dryas who
held the realm of Rhodope, and wore unlike gear on
his two feet; or the Oetean of old, or the son-in-law
of serpents, or Tisamenus' sire, or Callirhoe's hus-
band.[2] Nor may thy mother be more chaste than
she for whom as his daughter-in-law Tydeus might
have blushed:[3] or as the Locrian who joined in love
with her husband's brother, when she had been
disguised in the person of her slaughtered handmaid.[4]
And so, Heaven grant, mayst thou find joy in the
faithfulness of thy spouse, as did Talaus' or Tyndareus'
son-in-law:[5] or as did their husbands in the daughters
of Belus, who dared to plan death for their own cousins,
and whose necks are bowed with constant carrying
of water.[6] May thy sister burn, as with a torch, with
the fire of Byblis and of Canace, nor prove her love
save by a crime.[7] If thou hast a daughter, may she
be what Pelopea was to Thyestes, Myrrha to her
father and Nyctimene to hers.[8] Nor may she be
more dutiful and more considerate to her father's
head than was his daughter to Pterelas, or thine to

[4] Arsinoe, wife of Lysimachus, Ptolemy Ceraunus, Ptolemy
Philadelphus in succession, of whom the two latter were her
brothers, but Ceraunus was still alive when she married
Philadelphus; she escaped from Ephesus when attacked by
Seleucus by disguising a handmaid as herself; the latter was
killed, and she escaped.

[5] Amphiaraus in Eriphyle, daughter of Talaus, who caused
his death, and Agamemnon in Clytemnestra.

[6] The Danaids, who slew their cousin-husbands, sons of
Aegyptus, and had to carry water in sieves as a punish-
ment.

[7] They each fell in love with their own brother.

[8] More instances of incest.

OVID

Infamemque locum sceleris quae nomine fecit,
    Pressit et inductis membra paterna rotis.
Ut iuvenes pereas, quorum vestigia, vultus,   365
    Brachia Pisaeae sustinuere fores:
Ut qui perfusam miserorum saepe procorum
    Ipse suo melius sanguine tinxit humum:
Proditor ut saevi periit auriga tyranni,
    Qui nova Myrtoae nomina fecit aquae: 370
Ut qui velocem frustra petiere puellam,
    Dum facta est pomis tardior illa tribus:
Ut qui tecta novi formam celantia monstri
    Intrarunt caecae non redeunda domus:
Ut quorum Aeacides misit violentus in altum   375
    Corpora cum senis altera sena rogum:
Ut quos, obscuri victos ambagibus oris,
    Legimus infandae Sphinga dedisse neci:
Ut qui Bistoniae templo cecidere Minervae,
    Propter quod facies nunc quoque tecta deaest: 380
Ut qui Threïcii quondam praesepia regis
    Fecerunt dapibus sanguinolenta suis:
Therodamanteos ut qui sensere leones,
    Quique Thoanteae Taurica sacra deae:

---

[1] Comaetho cut off the golden lock that secured Pherelas
immortality; Nisus had a purple lock, which Scylla cut off;
for Tullia, wife of Tarquin the Proud, drove a cart over her
dead father, whence the place was called "vicus sceleratus."

[2] The suitors of Hippodamia, who were so treated by her
father Oenomaus, when he had defeated them in a chariot-race.

[3] Oenomaus himself committed suicide when defeated.

[4] Myrtilus, the treacherous charioteer of Oenomaus, who was
flung into the sea by Pelops, hence called Myrtoan.

[5] Atalanta could only be wooed by racing her on foot:
Milanion by throwing down the apples diverted her attention,
and won the race.

[6] The Labyrinth containing the Minotaur.

[7] The twelve Trojans whom Achilles sacrificed at the pyre of
Patroclus.

280

thee, O Nisus: or than she who made the place
infamous with the mention of her sin, and crushed
her sire's limbs beneath driven wheels.[1] As those
youths mayst thou perish, whose feet and faces and
arms the gates of Pisa held aloft:[2] as he who with his
own blood more profitably stained the ground that
the blood of wretched suitors oft had drenched:[3]
as perished the traitorous charioteer of the fierce
tyrant, giving a new name to the Myrtoan sea:[4] as
they who wooed the fleet-footed girl in vain, until
three apples made her slower;[5] as they who entered
the chambers that hid the monster of strange shape,
the blind dwelling whence there was no return:[6] as
those whose bodies, six with another six again,
Aeacides in fury sent to the lofty pyre:[7] as those
whom, overcome by her mouth's dark riddling, the
Sphinx, we read, sent to unspeakable death:[8] as
those who fell in the shrine of Bistonian Minerva,
wherefore even now the face of the goddess is
veiled:[9] as those who once made the stalls of the
Thracian monarch gory with the feast of their own
flesh:[10] as they who felt the lions of Therodamas, or
knew the Tauric rites of the goddess of Thoas:[11] as

[8] They were hurled from a steep cliff if they failed to
answer the riddles of the Sphinx.

[9] cf. Lycophron, *Alex.* 987 ff. The reference is to a
slaughter of Trojan refugees in a temple of Minerva (Athena)
at Siris in Magna Graecia; the statue of Minerva there was
sometimes claimed to be the real Palladium. "Bistonian,"
because the Siritans were thought to be Thracian in
origin.

[10] The victims of Diomede, king of Thrace, who fed his
mares on human flesh.

[11] Therodamas, a Libyan king who threw strangers to lions
(cf Ov., *Pont.* 1. 2. 119); Thoas, king of the Tauric Cherso-
nese, who practised human sacrifice to Artemis (cf. Eurip.,
Iph. in Taur.).

Ut quos Scylla vorax Scyllaeque adversa Charybdis   385
  Dulichiae pavidos eripuere rati :
Ut quos demisit vastam Polyphemus in alvum :
  Ut Laestrygonias qui subiere manus :
Ut quos dux Poenus mersit putealibus undis
  Et iacto canas pulvere fecit aquas :   390
Sex bis ut Icaridos famulae periere procique,
  Inque caput domini qui dabat arma procis :
Ut iacet Aonio luctator ab hospite fusus,
  Qui, mirum, victor, cum cecidisset, erat :
Ut quos Antaei fortes pressere lacerti :   395
  Quosque ferae morti Lemnia turba dedit :
Ut qui post longum, sacri monstrator iniqui,
  Elicuit pluvias victima caesus aquas :
Frater ut Antaei quo sanguine debuit, aras
  Tinxit, et exemplis occidit ipse suis :   400
Ut qui terribiles pro gramen habentibus herbis
  Impius humano viscere pavit equos :
Ut duo diversis sub eodem vindice caesi
  Vulneribus, Nessus Dexamenique gener :
Ut pronepos, Saturne, tuus, quem reddere vitam   405
  Urbe Coronides vidit ab ipse sua :

---

[1] See *Odyssey*, bk. 12.

[2] *Ibid.*, bk. 9 and bk. 10.

[3] The senate of Acerra (Appian, viii. 63); "white," *i.e.* instead of red with blood.

[4] The handmaidens of Penelope, slain by Odysseus, and the traitor Melanthius (*Od.* 22).

[5] Antaeus, king of Libya, compelled strangers to wrestle with him ; he was thrown by Hercules (born at Thebes, hence Aonian = Boeotian) ; Antaeus renewed his strength so often as he touched the earth. His brothers were Thrasius (or Phrasius) and Busiris ; the former taught the rite of

they whom greedy Scylla or Charybdis facing Scylla
snatched trembling from the Dulichian craft:[1] as
they whom Polyphemus sent down into his vast
paunch, or who suffered Laestrygonian violence:[2] as
they whom the Punic chieftain sank in the waters of
the well, and throwing dust upon them made the
water white:[3] as perished the twice six handmaidens
of Icarius' daughter and her suitors, and he who gave
arms to the suitors against his master's life:[4] as lies
the wrestler whom the Aonian stranger threw, whose
falling, wondrous to tell, brought him victory; as
those whom the strong arms of Antaeus crushed,
and those whom the Lemnian crowd sent to a savage
death: as he who taught a cruel rite, and after long
time, a victim slain, brought rainy showers: as
Antaeus' brother stained the altars with the blood it
was right to shed, and fell by the example of his
own deed:[5] as he who impiously fed the terrible
steeds with human flesh in place of the grass that
holds the grain:[6] as the two slain by different
wounds of the same avenger's hand, Nessus and
Dexamenus' son-in-law:[7] as thy great-grandson,
Saturn, whom from his own city the son of Coronis

human sacrifice, to put an end to a long drought (397, 8); the
latter was slain at the altar on which he practised this rite of
Hercules; with " sanguine" therefore understand "quo" (his
own). "Lemnia turba," if referring to the Lemnian women
who slew their husbands, comes in here oddly out of place :
Housman reads "clava," which would refer to Periphetes,
son of Vulcan the Lemnian, who murdered strangers with a
club : this would certainly fit the context better.

[6] Diomede of Thrace.

[7] The avenger was Hercules, who slew Nessus the Centaur
for trying to outrage Deianira, and Eurytion, also a Centaur,
who had compelled Dexamenus, father of Deianira, to betroth
his daughter to him.

Ut Sinis et Sciron et cum Polypemone natus :
  Quique homo parte sui, parte iuvencus erat :
Quique trabes pressas in humum mittebat in auras,
  Aequoris aspiciens huius et huius aquas :   410
Quaeque Ceres laeto vidit pereuntia vultu
  Corpora Thesea Cercyonea manu.

Haec tibi, quem meritis precibus mea devovet ira,
  Evenient, aut his non leviora malis :
Qualis Achaemenides Sicula desertus in Aetna,   415
  Troica cum vidit vela venire, fuit :
Qualis erat nec non fortuna binominis Iri,
  Quique tenent pontem, spe tibi maior erit.
Filius et Cereris frustra tibi semper ametur,
  Destituatque tuas usque petitus opes :   420
Utque per alternos unda labente recursus
  Subtrahitur presso mollis harena pedi,
Sic tua nescio qua semper fortuna liquescat,
  Lapsaque per medias effluat usque manus.
Utque pater solitae varias mutare figuras,   425
  Plenus inextincta conficiare fame ;
Nec dapis humanae tibi sint fastidia ; quaque
  Parte potes, Tydeus temporis huius eris ;

418 qui *G*: que *MSS.*: spe *Housman*: vae tibi talis erit
Owen.

---

[1] Periphetes, son of Vulcan, son of Jove, slain by Theseus
near Epidaurus, the city of Aesculapius, son of the nymph
Coronis.

[2] The various victims of Theseus : Procrustes was son of
Polypemon ; l. 408, the Minotaur ; Pityocamptes, sometimes
identified with Sinis, lived on the Isthmus of Corinth (410)
and slew strangers by bending down pine trees and fastening
human bodies to them and letting them fly apart, whence his
name, Pine-bender ; Cercyon slew strangers who were on the
way to the festival of Eleusis.

saw expire:[1] as Sinis and Sciron and Polypemon with his son, and he who was part man, part bullock: and as he who let fly into the air the boughs bent down to the earth, and beheld the waters of this sea and of that: and as the body of Cercyon that Ceres with joyful face saw perishing by Theseus' hand.[2]

Such ills shall befall thee whom my anger execrates with merited curses, or ills no less than these! Such a lot as was that of Achaemenides, abandoned on Sicilian Etna, when he saw the Trojan sails approach:[3] and that of Irus the double-named, and of them who haunt the bridge, shall be greater than thou canst hope for.[4] May the son of Ceres be ever loved by thee in vain, and ever for all thy seeking fail thy fortune:[5] and as when the wave by alternate ebbings glides away the soft sand is withdrawn from the foot's pressure, so in some subtle wise may thy fortune ever melt, and glide and flow away ever through thy hands. And like the sire of her who was wont to change from shape to shape though full mayst thou be wasted by inextinguishable hunger;[6] nor mayst thou shrink from human flesh; but where thou art strongest thou shalt be the Tydeus of these

[3] For Achaemenides see Virg., *Aen.* 3. 587 ff. He was a famine-stricken Greek whom Ulysses and his men had forgotten and left behind when they fled from the Cyclops.

[4] Irus was the beggar in the *Odyssey* (bk. 18), also called Arnaeus. Bridges were haunted by beggars (Juv. 4. 116, 14. 134).

[5] Plutus, god of wealth.

[6] Erysichthon, father of Mestra (cf. *Metam.* 8. 847 ff.), whom in order to appease his insatiable hunger he sold to different masters in turn, according as she changed herself into a bird, an ox, etc.

Atque aliquid facias, a vespere Solis ad ortus
    Cur externati rursus agantur equi;   430

Foeda Lycaoniae repetes convivia mensae,
    Temptabisque cibi fallere fraude Iovem;

Teque aliquis posito temptet vim numinis opto,
    Tantalides ut sis tu Teleique puer.

Et tua sic latos spargantur membra per agros,   435
    Tamquam quae patrias detinuere vias.

Aere Perilleo veros imitere iuvencos,
    Ad formam tauri conveniente sono.

Utque ferox Phalaris, lingua prius ense resecta
    More bovis Paphio clausus in aere gemas.   440

Dumque redire voles aevi melioris in annos,
    Ut vetus Admeti decipiare socer.

Aut eques in medii mergare voragine caeni,
    Dummodo sint fati nomina nulla tui.

Atque utinam pereas, veluti de dentibus orti   445
    Sidonia iactis Graia per arva manu.

---

[1] Tydeus gnawed his enemy's skull: "qua parte potes," *i.e.* your mouth.

[2] As did the deed of Atreus, when he served up Thyestes' sons for him to eat.

[3] The sons of Lycaon served up human flesh to Jove, who slew them with a thunderbolt.

[4] Pelops, served up for the gods by his father Tantalus;

days; [1] mayst thou do such a deed as shall make
the horses of the Sun in terror dash from evening to
the East again; [2] thou shalt repeat the foul banquet
of the Lycaonian board, and try to deceive Jove with
counterfeited food; [3] and I pray that someone may
serve thee up and provoke the god to wrath, that
thou mayst be Tantalus' son and the son of Teleus. [4]
And may thy limbs be so scattered o'er the broad
fields as those which stayed a father's march. [5]
Mayst thou imitate real bullocks with the bronze of
Perillus, whilst thy cries match the shape of the
bull.   And like fierce Phalaris, thy tongue first
severed with the sword, mayst thou bellow like an
ox imprisoned in Paphian bronze. [6]   And while thou
wishest to return to years of lustier life, mayst thou
be deceived like the aged father-in-law of Admetus. [7]
Or on horseback mayst thou be sunk in the midst of
a morass of mud, so long as thy fate hath no renown. [8]
And wouldst that thou mightest perish like those
sprung from the teeth that a Sidonian hand
scattered on Grecian fields. [9]   And may the ill-

Harpalyce served up to her father Clymenus, son of Teleus,
the infant son whom she had had by him.

[5] Absyrtus, son of Aeetes, slain by Medea when escaping
with Jason, to delay the pursuit.

[6] Perillus made a brazen bull for Phalaris, tyrant of
Agrigentum, and was himself imprisoned in it; Phalaris
was himself burnt in the bull by the people.   Paphos is in
Cyprus, where bronze was first made.

[7] Pelias, whose daughters were persuaded by Medea that
they could restore him to youth by boiling him in a cauldron;
by this deception he lost his life.

[8] As Curtius, who leapt into the chasm in Rome, and
gained renown thereby.

[9] The famous dragon's teeth sown by Cadmus of Phoe-
nicia.

Et quae Pitthides fecit, de fratre Medusae
   Eveniant capiti vota sinistra tuo:
Et quibus exiguo est volucris devota libello,
   Corpora proiecta quae sua purgat aqua.   450
Vulnera totque feras quot dicitur ille tulisse,
   Cuius ab inferiis culter abesse solet.
Attonitusque seces, ut quos Cybeleïa mater
   Incitat, ad Phrygios vilia membra modos;
Deque viro fias nec femina nec vir, ut Attis,   455
   Et quatias molli tympana rauca manu.
Inque pecus subito Magnae vertare Parentis,
   Victor ut est celeri victaque versa pede.
Solaque Limone poenam ne senserit illam,
   Et tua dente fero viscera carpat equus.   460
Aut ut Cassandreus, domino non mitior illo
   Saucius ingesta contumuleris humo.
Aut ut Abantiades, aut ut Cycneïus heros,
   Clausus in aequoreas praecipiteris aquas.
Victima vel Phoebo sacras macteris ad aras,   465
   Quam tulit a saevo Theudotus hoste necem.

447 Pitthides *Saluagnius*: Penthides, Pentelidis *MSS*.
fratre *MSS*.: fraterque *GPX*.

---

[1] Theseus was grandson of Pittheus by his mother Aethra;
he uttered dire threats against his son Hippolytus, who was
first cousin of Medusa, her father Phorcys being, like Theseus,
a son of Neptune. If "fraterque" be kept, it would refer to
Eurystheus, brother of another Medusa, who uttered curses
against Hercules (Owen, cf. Apollodorus 2. 4. 5).
[2] A reference to the *Ibis* of Callimachus; the ibis was an
Egyptian bird.
[3] Osiris, who was mangled by Typhon; the knife therefore
was naturally objectionable to him.

starred curses that the son of Pittheus uttered concerning Medusa's brother befall thy head:[1] and those too wherewith in a brief volume that bird is execrated which cleanses its body by throwing water on it.[2] And as many wounds mayst thou suffer as he is said to have suffered, from whose rites the knife is wont to be absent.[3] And like those whom the Cybelean mother excites mayst thou in frenzy sever thy slighted parts to Phrygian strains;[4] and from a man mayst thou become nor man nor woman, like Attis, and with soft hand shake the loud timbrels. And mayst thou be suddenly turned into a beast of the Mighty Mother, as he who won and she who lost the race were turned.[5] And lest Limone alone endure that punishment, may thy flesh too be torn by the horse's savage tooth.[6] Or like him of Cassandrea, no gentler than that monarch, mayst thou be wounded and buried beneath high-piled earth.[7] Or like Abantiades or the Cycnean hero mayst thou be hurled, imprisoned, into the sea's waters.[8] Or mayst thou be slain a victim at the altar of sacrifice, as Theodotus suffered death from

[4] The Phrygian priests of Cybele mutilated themselves under the influence of wild pipe-music.

[5] According to one story Hippomenes and Atalanta were turned into a lion and a lioness by Jove for profaning his temple. Lions were supposed to serve the Great Mother, Cybele.

[6] The daughter of Hippomenes referred to in ll. 335, 6.

[7] Ellis explains of Ptolemy Ceraunus, tyrant of Cassandrea (Potidaea), and as cruel as the well-known tyrant of that place, *i.e.* Apollodorus. Housman would avoid the difficulty of "domino illo" by inserting before this couplet ll. 439, 440.

[8] Perseus, great-grandson of Abas, committed to the sea with his mother in a wooden chest; Tenes, son of Cycnus, was similarly treated by his father.

OVID

Aut te devoveat certis Abdera diebus,
  Saxaque devotum grandine plura petant.
Aut Iovis infesti telo feriare trisulco,
  Ut satus Hipponoo, Dexionesque pater,   470
Ut soror Autonoes, ut cui matertera Maia,
  Ut temere optatos qui male rexit equos ;
Ut ferus Aeolides, ut sanguine natus eodem,
  Quo genita est liquidis quae caret Arctos aquis,
Ut Macelo rapidis icta est cum coniuge flammis, 475
  Sic, precor, aetherii vindicis igne cadas.
Praedaque sis illis, quibus est Latonia Delos
  Ante diem rapto non adeunda Traso :
Quique verecundae speculantem labra Dianae,
  Quique Crotopiaden diripuere Linum.   480
Neve venenato levius feriaris ab angue,
  Quam senis Oeagri Calliopesque nurus :
Quam puer Hypsipyles, quam qui cava primus acuta
  Cuspide suspecti robora fixit equi.
Neve gradus adeas Elpenore cautius altos,   485
  Vimque feras vini quo tulit ille modo.
Tamque cadas domitus, quam quisquis ad arma vocantem
  Iuvit inhumanum Thiodamanta Dryops :

---

[1] The "foe" was Apollodorus of Cassandrea (see above, 461),
but authorities give the name of the youth he put to death as
Callimeles.

[2] Seems to refer to a sort of purification by slaying a human
scapegoat, like the φαρμακοί at Athens and an occurrence at
Ephesus related by Philostratus in the life of Apollonius at
Tyana, who advised the Ephesians to get rid of a plague by stoning
an old man.

[3] Capaneus, one of the Seven against Thebes (cf. Statius,
Theb. 10) ; Aesculapius, for restoring a mortal to life ; Semele ;
Iasion, who offered violence to Demeter ; Phaethon ; Salmoneus
(cf. Virg., *Aen.* 6. 585) ; a son of Lycaon, for the sin described
in ll. 431, 2 ; the daughter of L. was Callisto who was turned
into the Great Bear, *i.e.* Arctos ; the allusion in "Macelo" is
unknown (there is another reading, "Macedo," equally obscure).

his ruthless foe.[1]   Or may Abdera call curses upon
thee on certain days, and stones more numerous
than hail seek the object of their cursing.[2]   Or
mayst thou be struck by the triple dart of angry
Jove, like the son of Hipponous and the sire of
Dexione, like the sister of Autonoe and the nephew
of Maia, like him who badly guided the rashly
prayed-for steeds; like the bold son of Aeolus, like
him who was born of that same blood wherefrom was
begotten Arctos who knows not liquid waters, like
as Macelo with her spouse was struck by devouring
flames, so, I pray, mayst thou fall by a heavenly
avenger's fire.[3]   And mayst thou be a prey to them
who, since they slew Trasus ere his time, may not
approach Latonian Delos:[4] to them too who tore
in pieces him who spied on chaste Diana's bath, and
Linus, grandson of Crotopus.[5]   Nor mayst thou be
more lightly stung by poisoned snake than the
daughter-in-law of old Oeager and Calliope: or than
Hypsipyle's babe, or he who first with sharp point of
spear transfixed the hollow wood of the suspected
horse.[6]   Nor mayst thou climb the lofty steps more
cautiously than Elpenor, but bear, as he bore it, the
potency of wine.[7]   So mayst thou fall vanquished,
as fell whoe'er of the Dryopians succoured the
churlish Thiodamas when he called to arms:[8] as

[4] Trasus, or Thasus, was a priest of Diana slain by dogs,
which therefore were not allowed in Delos.

[5] Dogs slew Actaeon, who was changed into a stag for
seeing Diana bathing, and tore in pieces the infant son of
Psamathe and Apollo (Statius, *Theb.* 1. 587 ff.).

[6] Eurydice, wife of Orpheus; Opheltes or Archemorus
(cf. Statius, *Theb.* 4. 719 ff.); Laocoon, Virg., *Aen.* 2. 41 ff.

[7] See Hom., *Od.* 10. 552, 11. 61.

[8] Thiodamas of Dryopia refused help to Hercules when
going to the help of Hyllus his son; the Dryopians were
subsequently subdued by Hercules.

Quam ferus ipse suo periit mactatus in antro
  Proditus inclusae Cacus ab ore bovis :   49
Quam qui dona tulit Nesseo tincta veneno,
  Euboicasque suo sanguine tinxit aquas.
Vel de praecipiti venias in Tartara saxo,
  Ut qui Socraticum de nece legit opus ;
Ut qui Theseae fallacia vela carinae   49
  Vidit, ut Iliaca missus ab arce puer,
Ut teneri nutrix, eadem matertera, Bacchi,
  Ut cui causa necis serra reperta fuit ;
Livida se scopulis ut virgo misit ab altis,
  Dixerat invicto quae mala verba deo.   50
Feta tibi occurrat patrio popularis in arvo,
  Sitque Phalaeceae causa leaena necis.
Quique Lycurgiden letavit, et arbore natum,
  Idmonaque audacem, te quoque rumpat aper.
Ísque vel exanimis faciat tibi vulnus, ut illi,   50
  Ora super fixi quem cecidere suis.
Sivei dem, simili pinus quem morte peremit,
  Phryx et venator sis Berecyntiades.
Si tua contigerit Minoas puppis harenas,
  Te Corcyraeum Cressia turba putet.   51

    492 sanguine tinxit *MSS.* : nomine fecit *G.*
    508 Phryx et *late MSS.* : phitia, frixia, frigia *MSS.*

----

[1] See Virg., *Aen.* 8. 194 ff. Lichas, a servant of Hercules
took the poisoned robe of Nessus from Deianira to Hercules
Euboean, as being in the neighbourhood of Mt. Oeta.
[2] Cleombrotus and the *Phaedo*, see Callimachus *Anth. Pal.*
7. 471, Cic., *Tusc.* 1. 34; Aegeus, father of Theseus; Astyanax,
son of Hector; Íno, mother of Melicertes (Palaemon); Perdix
(Ov., *Metam.* 8. 236 ff.), thrown from the Acropolis at Athens
by his uncle Daedalus, who was jealous of his skill; reading
"livida" the reference is to Aglauros, daughter of Cecrops,
who was jealous of the attentions of Mercury to her sister Herse
but the MSS. have "Lindia" or "Lidia" (Lydia); for ex-
planations of these readings see Ellis *ad loc.*

fierce Cacus himself did perish, slaughtered in his own cave, and betrayed by the voice of the imprisoned cow : or he who took the gifts steeped in the poison of Nessus, and stained the Euboean waters with his blood.[1] Or mayst thou go down to Tartarus from a rock's sheer height, like him who read the Socratic work on death, like him who saw the deceiving sails of Theseus' bark, like the boy flung from Ilium's citadel, like the nurse and aunt of infant Bacchus, like him whose death came from the saw that he invented, or as the jealous maiden threw herself from the high cliffs, who had said angry words to the invincible god.[2] May a lioness of thy land, lately delivered, meet thee in thy native fields, and bring thee the death Phalaecus suffered.[3] And may the boar that slew Lycurgus' son, and him that was born of a tree, and courageous Idmon, tear thee too asunder.[4] And even dying may he wound thee, as him upon whom fell the head of the boar he had transfixed.[5] Or mayst thou be at once that Phrygian whom a pine tree slew with a like fate, and the huntsman son of Berecyntia.[6] If thy ship shall have touched Minoan sands, let the Cretan crowd deem

[3] Phalaecus was a tyrant of Ambracia, slain by a lioness when he was fondling its cub.

[4] Ancaeus the Argonaut, slain in the famous boar hunt in Aetolia; Adonis, son of Myrrha, who was turned into a myrrh tree; Idmon, the prophet of the Argonauts.

[5] The story is told of a hunter who hung up the head of a boar he had killed without dedicating it to Diana, as the custom was, and that he then lay down to sleep under it, and that the head fell down and killed him in his sleep.

[6] The line is corrupt, but the poet seems to be playing on the existence in legend of two persons of the name of Attis, one a hunter slain by a boar, the other the Attis who mutilated himself under a pine tree.

OVID

Lapsuramque domum subeas, ut sanguis Aleuae,
　　Stella Leoprepidae cum fuit aequa viro.
Utque vel Evenus, torrenti flumine mersus
　　Nomina des rapidae, vel Tiberinus, aquae.
Astacidaeque modo decisa cadavere trunco,　　　　　　515
　　Digna feris, hominis sit caput esca tuum,
Quodque ferunt Brotean fecisse cupidine mortis,
　　Des tua succensae membra cremanda pyrae.
Inclususque necem cavea patiaris, ut ille
　　Non profecturae conditor historiae.　　　　　　　520
Utque repertori nocuit pugnacis iambi,
　　Sic sit in exitium lingua proterva tuum.
Utque parum stabili qui carmine laesit Athenas,
　　Invisus pereas deficiente cibo.
Utque lyrae vates fertur periisse severae,　　　　　525
　　Causa sit exitii dextera laesa tui.
Utque Agamemnonio vulnus dedit anguis Oresti,
　　Tu quoque de morsu virus habente cadas.

515 Astacidae *Conrad de Mure*: ytacide, hirtacide *MSS.*
decisa *BH.*: defixa *MSS.*: cadavere *Heinsius*: cadavera
MSS.

---

[1] The Corcyreans tried to prevent the Cretans from bringing
the bones of Minos from Sicily to Crete.

[2] The son of L. was Simonides, the seed of A. was Scopas,
a Thessalian noble ; Simonides, when dining with Scopas, was
summoned out of the room : in the interval the house collapsed,
killing Scopas and the other guests ; " stella," of the Dioscuri,
for two youths were announced to be asking for Sim., but when
he went out he saw nobody (Cic., *de Orat.* 2. 86).

[3] Evenus threw himself into the Lycormas, a river of Aetolia,
which was called after him ; Tiberinus, an early king of Alba,
fell into the Tiber, so called after him.

[4] Menalippus, whose head was gnawed by Tydeus (Statius
Theb. 8 *sub fin.*).

[5] Brotea appears to be the same as Biothea or Axiothea,
wife of Nicocreon, king of Cyprus, who threw herself into

thee a Corcyrean.[1] And mayst thou enter a house doomed to fall, like the seed of Aleuas, when the star was propitious to Leoprepes' famous son.[2] Or like Evenus, drowned in a river torrent, or Tiberinus, mayst thou give thy name to the rapid stream.[3] And like Astacides may thy head be cut from thy truncated corpse, and, though deserving of beasts, be food for a man.[4] And that which they say Brotea did in longing for death, mayst thou give thy limbs to be burnt upon the kindled pyre.[5] And while imprisoned mayst thou suffer a violent death, as he who wrote the history that would profit him naught.[6] And as it hurt the inventor of the quarrelsome iambus, so may a wayward tongue be for thy destruction.[7] And like him who harmed Athens with his halting song mayst thou perish, hated, by failure of food.[8] And as the poet of the austere lyre is said to have perished, may an injured hand be the cause of thy death.[9] And as the serpent wounded Orestes, Agamemnon's son, so mayst thou too fall by a poisoned bite.[10] May the

the fire to die with her husband; but there is considerable doubt, and the reference may be to Broteas, a son of Jove, who threw himself into the fire when blinded by his father, or even Hercules Bruttius.

[6] Callisthenes, a historian of Alexander's wars, suspected by A. of conspiring against him, mutilated and imprisoned, and then given poison.

[7] Archilochus, who, however, is commonly supposed to have been killed in battle.   [8] Reference unknown.

[9] "Dextera laesa" is sometimes taken as = "broken faith," and explained of Timocreon, who accused Themistocles of playing him false in the matter of his exile on the charge of Medism: "exilii" then would be read. Otherwise the point is unknown.

[10] According to one legend Orestes is said to have perished in this way.

Sit tibi coniugii nox prima novissima vitae :
    Eupolis hoc periit et nova nupta modo.   530
Utque cothurnatum cecidisse Lycophrona narrant,
    Haereat in fibris fixa sagitta tuis.
Aut lacer in silva manibus spargare tuorum,
    Sparsus ut est Thebis angue creatus avo.
Perque feros montes tauro rapiente traharis,   535
    Ut tracta est coniunx imperiosa Lyci.
Quodque suae passa est paelex invita sororis,
    Excidat ante pedes lingua resecta tuos.
Conditor ut tardae, laesus cognomine, Myrrhae,
    Orbis in innumeris inveniare locis.   540
Inque tuis opifex, vati quod fecit Achaeo,
    Noxia luminibus spicula condat apis.
Fixus et in duris carparis viscera saxis,
    Ut cui Pyrrha sui filia fratris erat.
Ut puer Harpagides referas exempla Thyestae,   545
    Inque tui caesus viscera patris eas.
Trunca geras saevo mutilatis partibus ense,
    Qualia Mamertae membra fuisse ferunt.
Utque Syracosio praestricta fauce poetae,
    Sic animae laqueo sit via clausa tuae.   550

539 conditor *HT* : cognitor *other MSS.*
548 Mamertae *V* : mimerti, mimnermi *various MSS.* : Mamerci
Owen.

---

[1] Cf. *Anth. Pal.* 7. 298.
[2] The mention of Lycophron as a tragic poet refers to his
Alexandra.
[3] Pentheus, torn by the Bacchanals, grandson of Cadmus,
who was turned into a snake.
[4] Dirce suffered this fate at the hands of the sons of Antiope,
Amphion and Zethus, for the treatment of their mother. Lycus
was a king of Thebes.
[5] Philomela, ravished by Tereus, and sister of his wife Procne.
[6] The reference is to a poem entitled *Smyrna*, written by
C. Helvius Cinna ; its tardy appearance after nine years is men-

first night of wedlock be the last of thy life : in this fashion perished Eupolis and his new bride.[1] And as they relate that buskined Lycophron fell, so in thy flesh may the barb stick fast.[2] Or rent asunder mayst thou be strewn in the woods by thine own kin, as at Thebes he was strewn who was born of the serpent's son.[3] And over wild mountains mayst thou be dragged by a tearing bull, as was dragged the imperious spouse of Lycus.[4] And, what the unwilling rival of her own sister suffered, may thy tongue cut out fall before thy feet.[5] And like the author of tardy Myrrha, whose surname wrought him harm, mayst thou be found in countless places of the world.[6] And may the craftsman bee, as he did to the Achaean seer, bury in thine eyes his noxious dart.[7] And chained on the hard rocks mayst thou have thine entrails torn, as he whose brother's daughter Pyrrha was.[8] Like the young son of Harpagus mayst thou recall the example of Thyestes, and carved in pieces enter thy father's bowels.[9] Mayst thou have limbs maimed and parts mutilated by the savage sword, as they say were those of Mamertas.[10] And as with the Syracusan bard whose throat was strangled, so may a noose stop the way

tioned by Catullus (95). Cinna was torn in pieces by the mob after the death of Julius Caesar, being mistaken for Cornelius Cinna, the conspirator.   [7] Reference unknown.

[8] Epimetheus, father of Pyrrha, was brother of Prometheus.

[9] Harpagus was a friend of Astyages the Mede, who, finding that he had allowed Cyrus to live, against his orders slew his son and served him up for his father to eat.

[10] This Mamertas is thought by Ellis to be the same as the Mamercus who is told of in Plutarch's *Timoleon*, and by other authors ; he was a tyrant of Catana, and an enemy of Timoleon ; being finally captured he was " executed like a pirate," apparently some cruel method of execution.

Nudave derepta pateant tua viscera pelle,
   Ut Phrygium cuius nomina flumen habet.
Saxificae videas infelix ora Medusae,
   Cephenum multos quae dedit una neci.
Potniadum morsus subeas, ut Glaucus, equarum,   555
   Inque maris salias, Glaucus ut alter, aquas.
Utque duobus idem dictis modo nomen habenti,
   Praefocent animae Gnosia mella viam.
Sollicitoque bibas, Anyti doctissimus olim
   Imperturbato quod bibit ore reus.   560
Nec tibi, siquid amas, felicius Haemone cedat:
   Utque sua Macareus, sic potiare tua.
Vel videas, quod iam cum flammae cuncta tenerent,
   Hectoreus patria vidit ab arce puer.
Sanguine probra luas, ut avo genitore creatus,   565
   Per facinus soror est cui sua facta parens.
Ossibus inque tuis teli genus haereat illud,
   Traditur Icarii quo cecidisse gener.
Utque loquax in equo est elisum guttur acerno,
   Sic tibi claudatur pollice vocis iter.   570

558 Gnosia *edd.* : noxia *GVX.*

---

[1] Usually explained of Theocritus, but without any evidence.

[2] Marsyas; see Ov., *Metam.* 6. 400.

[3] Cepheus was the father of Andromeda, and resisted the attempt of Perseus to carry her off; whereupon many of the Cephenians were turned to stone by the Gorgon's head.

[4] Glaucus of Potniae in Boeotia fed mares on human flesh, but was devoured by them; G. of Anthedon was a fisherman, who became a sea-god and a prophet (Ov., *Metam.* 13. 905). G., infant son of Minos, fell into a jar of honey and was suffocated.

[5] Socrates the philosopher was accused by Anytus, and condemned to drink the hemlock.

[6] Haemon was the son of Creon, king of Thebes, who loved Antigone, and slew himself when she was condemned to be buried alive; Macareus and the daughter of Aeolus, who were lovers, slew themselves.

of thy breath.[1] Or may thy flesh be exposed by stripping off the skin, like him whose name a Phrygian river bears.[2] Mayst thou in evil hour see the face of Medusa that turns to stone, who alone gave many of the Cephenians to death.[3] Like Glaucus mayst thou suffer the bites of Potnian mares, and like another Glaucus leap into the waters of the sea. And like him who hath the same name as the two aforesaid may Gnosian honey choke thy breath.[4] And with harassed countenance mayst thou drink what once the learned prisoner of Anytus drank with countenance unperturbed.[5] Nor if thou lovest at all may it turn out more happily for thee than for Haemon, and as Macareus possessed his mistress so mayst thou thine.[6] Or mayst thou see what Hector's son saw from his native citadel, when already the flames were mastering all.[7] Mayst thou atone thy shame with blood, as he whose grandsire was the father that begot him, by whose crime his own parent was made his sister.[8] And in thy bones may that kind of weapon stick fast, whereby Icarius' son-in-law is said to have fallen.[9] And as the chattering throat was crushed in the maple horse, so may a thumb close the passage of thy voice.[10] Or

[7] He was flung from the citadel of Troy.

[8] Adonis was born of Myrrha by her father Cinyras, and killed by a boar.

[9] Odysseus was killed by his son Telegonus (by Circe), by the sting of an "acanthus" or τρυγών (sting ray); there was a play of Sophocles entitled *Odysseus Acanthoplex*. Penelope was daughter of Icarius.

[10] Anticlus was in the wooden horse, and was only prevented from answering Helen when she imitated the voices of the wives of the Greek warriors by Ulysses choking him with his hand (cf. Hom., *Od.* 4. 271 ff.).

Aut ut Anaxarchus pila minuaris in alta,
  Ictaque pro solitis frugibus ossa sonent.
Utque patrem Psamathes, condat te Phoebus in ima
  Tartara, quod natae fecerat ille suae.
Inque tuos ea pestis eat, quam dextra Coroebi   575
  Vicit, opem miseris Argolisinque tulit.
Utque nepos Aethrae, Veneris moriturus ob iram,
  Exul ab attonitis excutiaris equis.
Propter opes magnas ut perdidit hospes alumnum,
  Perdat ob exiguas te tuus hospes opes.   580
Utque ferunt caesos sex cum Damasichthone fratres,
  Intereat tecum sic genus omne tuum.
Addidit ut fidicen miseris sua funera natis,
  Sic tibi sint vitae taedia iusta tuae.
Utve soror Pelopis, saxo dureris oborto,   585
  Et laesus lingua Battus ab ipse sua.
Aëra si misso liquidum iaculabere disco,
  Quo puer Oebalides, ictus ab orbe cadas.
Siqua per alternos pulsabitur unda lacertos,
  Omnis Abydena sit tibi peior aqua.   590

---

[1] Anaxarchus was an enemy of Nicocreon, tyrant of Cyprus,
and falling into his power was pounded in a mortar.

[2] Psamathe was the daughter of Crotopus, king of Argos,
and bore a child to Apollo (cf. l. 480) ; her father is nowhere
else stated to have put his daughter to death. Apollo, angry
at the death of the child, sent a monster to plague Argos, and
many children perished, till Coroebus slew it, and defied the
wrath of Apollo (cf. Statius, *Theb.* 1. 562 ff.).

[3] Hippolytus, son of Theseus, refused the love of Phaedra
his stepmother, and was accused by her of outrage ; Theseus

like Anaxarchus mayst thou be crushed small in a deep mortar, and thy pounded bones sound like the wonted grain.[1] And like Psamathe's sire may Phoebus bury thee in lowest Tartarus, as he had done to his own daughter. And on thy kindred may that pestilence fall, which the might of Coroebus overcame and brought succour to the poor Argive women.[2] And as Aethra's grandson, doomed to die by Venus' wrath, mayst thou be hurled, an exile, from terror-stricken steeds.[3] As the host slew his ward for his great wealth, so for thy little wealth may thy host slay thee.[4] And as they say his six brethren perished with Damasichthon, so may all thy race perish with thee.[5] As the harper completed with his own his wretched children's deaths, so mayst thou with reason grow weary of thy life.[6] Or like Pelops' sister mayst thou harden with a growth of stone, or like Battus harmed by his own tongue.[7] If thou wilt launch the disk and hurl it at the liquid air, mayst thou fall struck by the circle that slew the young Oebalides.[8] If with alternate arm thou wilt beat the wave, may every strait be more dangerous to thee than that of Abydos.[9] As the comic writer

cursed him, and he was killed by his horses taking fright at a sea-monster sent by Neptune.

[4] Polydorus was killed by his host Polymestor for the gold he had.

[5] They were the seven sons of Niobe, slain by Apollo.

[6] Amphion, husband of Niobe, took his own life.

[7] Niobe was sister of Pelops, and daughter of Tantalus; Battus was changed into stone for deceiving Mercury in the matter of some stolen cattle.

[8] Hyacinthus, son of Oebalus, king of Sparta, a favourite of Apollo, was killed by him in error while throwing the discus.

[9] The reference is to Leander.

OVID

Comicus ut mediis periit, dum nabat, in undis,
    Et tua sic Stygius strangulet ora liquor.
Aut ubi ventosum superaris naufragus aequor,
    Contacta pereas, ut Palinurus, humo.
Utque cothurnatum vatem tutela Dianae,   595
    Dilaniet vigilum te quoque turba canum.
Aut ut Trinacrius salias super ora gigantis,
    Plurima qua flammas Sicanis Aetna vomit.
Diripiantque tuos insanis unguibus artus
    Strymoniae matres, Orpheos esse ratae.   600
Natus ut Althaeae flammis absentibus arsit,
    Sic tuus ardescat stipitis igne rogus.
Ut nova Phasiaca comprensa est nupta corona,
    Utque pater nuptae, cumque parente domus;
Ut cruor Herculeos abiit diffusus in artus;   605
    Corpora pestiferum sic tua virus edat.
Qua sua Penteliden proles est ulta Lycurgum,
    Haec maneat teli te quoque plaga novi.
Utque Milo robur diducere fissile temptes,
    Nec possis captas inde referre manus.   610
Muneribusque tuis laedaris, ut Icarus, in quem
    Intulit armatas ebria turba manus.
Quodque dolore necis patriae pia filia fecit,
    Vincula per laquei fac tibi guttur eat.

607 penteliden . . . Lycurgum, pentiladen, penthiden,
Lycinum *MSS.*: Prataliden . . . Lycastum *Ellis* (*Am. Journ.
Phil.* 33. 205).

---

[1] Explained variously of Eupolis, Menander and Terence.
[2] See Virg., *Aen.* 6. 355. P. was the helmsman of Aeneas.
[3] Euripides was said to have perished thus. "Diana's
guardians" are hunting hounds.
[4] Empedocles the philosopher. The volcano was supposed
to cover one of the Giants.
[5] Strymonian, *i.e.* Thracian.
[6] Meleager, son of Althaea, was caused to die by the burning
of a brand, on which his own life depended.

perished in mid-water as he swam, thy mouth too
may the Stygian wave thus stifle.[1] Or when ship-
wrecked thou hast o'ercome the windy sea, mayst
thou die like Palinurus after gaining land.[2] And as
Diana's guardians tore the tragic bard, so may a
crowd of watchful hounds tear thee in pieces.[3] Or
like the Trinacrian mayst thou leap into the giant's
mouth, where in full might Sicanian Aetna vomits
flames.[4] And may Strymonian mothers rend thy
limbs with frenzied nails, deeming them those of
Orpheus.[5] As absent flames consumed Althaea's
son, so may a firebrand kindle thy funeral pile.[6] As
the new bride took fire from the Phasian garland,
and the sire of the bride, and with her sire the
house ; as the gore ran diffused through the limbs of
Hercules, so may pestilent poison devour thy frame.[7]
As his own offspring was revenged upon Lycurgus,
the Pentelid, so may the stroke of a strange weapon
await thee also.[8] And like Milo mayst thou strive to
draw apart the split oak tree, nor be able to draw back
thence thy captured arms.[9] And mayst thou be
hurt by thine own gifts, as Icarus against whom the
drunken crowd brought armed violence. And as
did the loving daughter in grief at her father's death,
make thy throat to enter the rope's noose.[10] And

[7] Creusa, wife of Jason, and Hercules were both destroyed
by poisonous robes, the one purposely by Medea (of Phasian
Colchis), the other in error by Deianira's gift. The blood
was that of Nessus the Centaur.

[8] There is a doubtful reading here ; and no explanation of
the couplet is known.

[9] Milo was a famous wrestler of Croton in S. Italy.

[10] Icarus was slain by a drunken crowd in Attica to whom
he had taught the culture of the vine (Icarius is the usual
form of the name) ; his daughter Erigone in grief for his
death hanged herself.

OVID

Obstructoque famem patiaris limine tecti,   615
    Ut legem poenae cui dedit ipsa parens.
Illius exemplo violes simulacra Minervae,
    Aulidis a portu qui leve vertit iter.
Naupliadaeve modo poenas pro crimine falso
    Morte luas, nec te non meruisse iuvet.   620
Aethalon ut vita spoliavit Isindius hospes,
    Quem memor a sacris nunc quoque pellit Ion :
Utque Melanthea tenebris a caede latentem
    Prodidit officio luminis ipsa parens :
Sic tua coniectis fodiantur pectora telis,   625
    Sic precor auxiliis impediare tuis.
Qualis equos pacto, quos fortis agebat Achilles,
    Acta Phrygi timido, nox tibi talis eat.
Nec tu quam Rhesus somno meliore quiescas,
    Quam comites Rhesi tum necis, ante viae ;   630
Quam quos cum Rutulo morti Ramnete dederunt
    Impiger Hyrtacides Hyrtacidaeque comes.
Cliniadaeve modo circumdatus ignibus atris
    Membra feras Stygiae semicremata neci.

---

[1] Pausanias, king of Sparta, when condemned to death was shut up in the temple of Athene Chalcioecus, and walled in there ; his mother was among the first to bring stones for that purpose.

[2] *i.e.* may you commit sacrilege like Ulysses, who stole the Palladium. No satisfactory explanation of l. 618.

[3] Palamedes, falsely accused of treachery by Ulysses and put to death.

[4] An Isindian (of Isindos, an Ionian city) slew a guest named Aethalos, whence Isindians were barred from the Pan-ionian festival.

[5] See Hom., *Od.* 19. 386. But at this time, when Ulysses was having his legs washed and sat in the gloom to avoid being recognised, he had not yet killed the traitor Melantheus, but was only planning it ; Ovid may have thought he had done the deed. He was nearly betrayed by his mother (see 19. 473).

mayst thou suffer starvation from the blocking of the
door of thy house, as he whose own mother decreed
his punishment.[1] Mayst thou violate Minerva's image
after his example who turned aside the rash journey
from Aulis' haven.[2] Or like the son of Nauplius
mayst thou pay by death the penalty of a false
charge, nor find pleasure in thy innocence.[3] As the
Isindian host deprived Aethalus of life, whom the
unforgetting Ionian debars e'en now from the sacred
rites:[4] and as his own mother by the aid of light
revealed him that lurked in darkness after the slay-
ing of Melantheus,[5] so may hurled weapons pierce
thy breast, so, I pray, may thine own helpers hinder
thee. As passed the night for the timorous Phrygian
who bargained the steeds that valiant Achilles
drove, so may the night pass for thee.[6] Nor mayst
thou repose with better slumber than Rhesus, or
than they who bore Rhesus company, first on the
road, then in death;[7] or than those whom bold
Hyrtacides and the comrade of Hyrtacides slew with
Rutulian Ramnes.[8] Or like the son of Clinias,
surrounded by venomous flames mayst thou take thy
charred limbs to Stygian death.[9] And as with

[6] Dolon (*Il.* 10) made a bargain with Hector that he should
have Achilles' horses if he brought back news from the
Greek camp whether they were planning retreat or not.

[7] Rhesus was a Thracian prince whose camp was raided by
Ulysses and Diomede, himself slain and his horses driven to
the Greek camp; it was while out scouting that Ulysses met
Dolon and heard about Rhesus and his steeds. Twelve of
his comrades were slain in the raid with Rhesus.

[8] Nisus was the son of Hyrtacus; he and his friend
Euryalus are the heroes of an exploit in *Aen.* 9. Ramnes
was one of the Rutulians whom they slew.

[9] Alcibiades perished by being burnt in a cottage in which
he was sleeping.

Utque Remo muros auso transire recentes,   635
  Noxia sint capiti rustica tela tuo.
Denique Sarmaticas inter Geticasque sagittas
  His precor ut vivas et moriare locis.

Haec tibi tantisper subito sint missa libello,
  Inmemores ne nos esse querare tui.   640
Pauca quidem, fateor : sed di dent plura rogatis,
  Multiplicentque suo vota favore mea.
Postmodo plura leges et nomen habentia verum,
  Et pede quo debent acria bella geri.

IBIS

Remus [1] who dared to o'erleap the rising wall, may rustic weapons be hurtful to thy head. Finally, I pray that in these regions,[2] among Sarmatian and Getic arrows, thou mayst live and die.

Receive this message meanwhile that my hasty volume brings, lest thou complain I have forgot thee. Brief is it, I confess; but may the gods give more than they are asked, and by their favour send my prayer manifold increase. Thou shalt read more anon, bearing thine own true name, and writ in a measure wherein bitter wars rightly should be waged.

[1] Remus was killed by his brother Romulus for leaping in contempt over the wall he was building for the city of Rome.

[2] *i.e.* in Tomi (in Scythia), whence Ovid is writing.

ON SEA-FISHING

HALIEUTICON

. . . .
Accepit mundus legem ; dedit arma per omnes
Admonuitque sui.   vitulus sic namque minatur,
Qui nondum gerit in tenera iam cornua fronte,
Sic dammae fugiunt, pugnant virtute leones
Et morsu canis et caudae sic scorpius ictu   5
Concussisque levis pennis sic evolat ales.
Omnibus ignotae mortis timor, omnibus hostem
Praesidiumque datum sentire et noscere teli
Vimque modumque sui.   sic et scarus arte sub undis
Si n 10
Decidit adsumptamque dolo tandem pavet escam,
Non audet radiis obnixa occurrere fronte,
Aversus crebro vimen sed verbere caudae
Laxans subsequitur tutumque evadit in aequor.
Quin etiam si forte aliquis, dum praenatat, arto   15
Mitis luctantem scarus hunc in vimine vidit,
Aversi caudam morsu tenet atque ita <vellit>
Libera ut e nassa quae texit praeda resultet.
Sepia tarda fugae tenui cum forte sub unda
Deprensa est (iam iamque manus timet hilla rapaces), 20

13 sed *edd.* : sub *V.*
18 The above is Vollmer's suggestion for the corrupt reading
of *V.*; Owen reads "atque ligati|tutor servato quem texit
cive resultat."
20 hilla *Birt.* : illa *V.*

---

[1] The parrot-wrasse (scarus cretensis), mentioned by Horace,
Ep. 2. 50, *Sat.* 2. 2. 22, by Pliny, *N.H.* 9. 62 "nunc principatus
scaro datur," and Galen, *De alim. fac.* 3.

ON SEA-FISHING

. . . THE universe received the law ; to all he did
give arms, and reminded them of himself. For thus
threatens the calf, who bears no horns as yet on his
young forehead ; thus do hinds flee, lions fight with
valour, and dogs with their teeth, and the scorpion
with the stroke of his tail, and thus with a light
shaking of his pinions does the bird fly away. In all
is the fear of a death they know not, to all is given
to be aware of their enemy and how to guard against
him, and to know the force and measure of their
own weapon. Thus the Scar,[1] if cunningly (lured)
beneath the waves he has fallen into (a wicker trap)[2]
. . . and only fears the bait when tricked into
seizing it, ventures not with opposing forehead to
dash against the rods, but turning away loosens
the wicker-work with much lashing of his tail, and
wriggling out escapes into the safety of the sea.
Nay too if by chance any kindly Scar, swimming
past, has seen him struggling in the wicker-work,
he grasps with his jaws his tail from behind, and so
pulls him, that the prey may spring clear of the
basket which held him. The Squid, tardy in flight,
when caught perchance beneath the clear water
(and every moment his entrails fear the clutching

---

[2] Pliny's paraphrase of this passage (*N.H.* 32. 2. 11) shows
that there was some mention of a " nassa " or wicker basket ;
the line has been variously filled up, *e.g.* " si nassae in
patulas fraudes de vimine textas " (Owen), or " si nassae in
fraudem pellectus ventris ab ira " (Vollmer).

OVID

Inficiens aequor nigrum vomit illa cruorem
Avertitque vias oculos frustrata sequentes.
Clausus rete lupus quamvis inmitis et acer
Dimotis cauda submissus sidit harenis
. . . . in auras   25
Emicat atque dolos saltu deludit inultus.
Et muraena ferox teretis sibi conscia tergi
Ad laxata magis conixa foramina retis
Tandem per multos evadit lubrica flexus
Exemploque nocet : cunctis iter invenit una.   30
At contra scopulis crinali corpore segnis
Polypus haeret et hac eludit retia fraude :
Et sub lege loci sumit mutatque colorem
Semper ei similis quem contigit : atque ubi praedam
Pendentem saetis avidus rapit, hic quoque fallit,   35
Elato calamo cum demum emersus in auras
Bracchia dissolvit populatumque expuit hamum.
At mugil cauda pendentem everberat escam
Excussamque legit. lupus acri concitus ira
Discursu fertur vario fluctusque ferentes   40
Prosequitur quassatque caput, dum volnere saevus
Laxato cadat hamus et ora patentia linquat.
Nec proprias vires nescit muraena nocendi
Auxilioque sui morsu nec comminus acri
Deficit aut animos ponit captiva minaces   45
. . . .

21 illa cruorem *Sannazarius* : illac *V*.
25 Filled up by Birt thus : " in foveaque iacens, ubi rete leva-tur," "and lying in the hole, when the net is raised."
45 After this line Birt, following Pliny's paraphrase, would insert the line "amplius os hamo vorat eroditque ita linum," " his mouth devours more than the hook, and thus gnaws through the line."

---

[1] *i.e.* injures the fisherman's catch.

hands) vomits dark blood from his mouth and stains
the sea, and turns from his track baffling the eyes
that follow him. The Pike enclosed in a net,
though huge and fierce, sinks down submissive,
parting the sands with his tail . . . darts up into
the air and by his leap mocks with impunity their
guile. The bold Lamprey, too, aware of his smooth
back, struggling with the looser meshes of the net,
at length escapes by many slippery writhings, and
damages by his example:[1] for by himself he finds a
way for all. But the lazy Polypus with his hairy body
clings to the rocks,[2] and by this ruse eludes the nets,
and takes or changes colour as the spot determines,
ever like to that which he has touched; and when
he greedily seizes the prey that hangs from the line,
he also plays his trick, for when the rod is lifted
and he at length emerges into the air, he loosens the
grip of his arms and spews forth the plundered hook.
But the Mullet with his tail strikes off the suspended
bait, and gathers it when it falls. The Pike, stung
to violent wrath, dashes here and there, and follows
the waves that carry him, and tosses his head till
the wound is widened, and the cruel barb falls out
and leaves the gaping mouth. Nor is the Lamprey
ignorant of his own powers of harm, nor fails in his
own defence nor in fierce biting at close quarters,
nor even when captive loses his fighting spirit. . . .
The Anthias uses weapons on his back which he

[2] Oppian uses similar words about the Cuttlefish (sepia):
"with those locks she clings to the rocks even as a ship
fastens her cables to the rocks upon the shore." (*Hal.* ii. 125:
Mair's translation in L.C.L.)

Anthias in tergo quae non videt utitur armis,
Vim spinae novitque suae versoque supinus
Corpore lina secat fixumque intercipit hamum.

Cetera quae densas habitant animalia silvas
Aut vani quatiunt semper lymphata timores   50
Aut trahit in praeceps non sana ferocia mentis :
Ipsa sequi natura monet vel comminus ire.
Impiger ecce leo venantum sternere pergit
Agmina et adversis infert sua pectora telis ;
Quomque venit fidens magis et sublatior ardet   55
Concussitque toros et viribus addidit iram,
Procidit atque suo properat sibi robore letum.
Foedus Lucanis provolvitur ursus ab antris, —
Quid nisi pondus iners stolidaeque ferocia mentis ?
Actus aper saetis iram denuntiat hirtis :   60
Se ruit oppositi nitens in volnera ferri,
Pressus et emisso moritur per viscera telo.
Altera pars fidens pedibus dat terga sequenti
Ut pavidi lepores, ut fulvo tergore dammae
Et capto fugiens cervus sine fine timore.   65
Hic generosus honos et gloria maior equorum ;
Nam capiunt animis palmam gaudentque triumpho :
Seu septem spatiis circo meruere coronam,
Nonne vides victor quanto sublimius altum
Attollat caput et volgi se venditet aurae ?   70
Celsave cum caeso decorantur terga leone,
Quam tumidus quantoque venit spectabilis actu
Compescitque solum generoso concita pulsu
Ungula sub spoliis graviter redeuntis opimis !
Quid laus prima canum ? quibus est audacia praeceps 75

55 quomque *edd.* : quodque *V*.
57 procidit *Burman* : prodedit *V*.
73 compescit *Ries* : conpiscat *V*.

does not see, and knows the power of his spine, and turning upon his back he cuts the twine and cuts off the implanted hook.

The other animals that dwell in the dense forest are either racked and ever maddened by empty fears, or driven headlong by frenzied daring : Nature herself bids them give chase or grapple in close fight. Lo! the impetuous Lion dashes to overthrow the hunters' ranks, and presents his breast to their opposing weapons; and even while he advances with greater boldness and ardour more exultant, and tosses his brawny muscles and adds anger to his might, he falls and his strength but hastens his own death. From his Lucanian den waddles forth the ugly Bear, —what save sluggish weight and stolid fierceness? The hunted Boar proclaims his wrath by his shaggy bristles; he rushes with all his might upon the wounds of the opposing steel, and, checked by a dart sped through his vitals, he dies. Another group trust to their feet and flee before the pursuer, as frightened hares and hinds with tawny bodies and the stag that flees unceasingly once he has known panic. Here is the high-born pride and the nobler glory of the Steeds; for by mettle do they win the prize, and they exult in victory. If in the seven laps of the Circus they have gained the crown, see you not how much higher the victor holds his lofty head, and commends himself to the breeze of popular favour? Or when his tall back is adorned by a slain lion's skin, how swelling his pomp, with what action he courts the eye, while with haughty beat of hoof he tramples the ground, and returns heavily laden with rich spoils! What is the chiefest praise of Hounds? Headlong boldness is theirs, and excellent

Venandique sagax virtus viresque sequendi;
Quae nunc elatis rimantur naribus auras,
At nunc demisso quaerunt vestigia rostro
Et produnt clamore feram dominumque vocando
Increpitant: quem si conlatis effugit armis,⠀⠀⠀⠀⠀⠀80
Insequitur tumulosque canis camposque per omnes. . . .

⠀⠀⠀Noster in arte labor positus, spes omnis in illa.
Nec tamen in medias pelagi te pergere sedes
Admoneam vastique maris temptare profundum:
Inter utrumque loci melius moderabere linum.⠀⠀⠀⠀⠀85
. . . .

Aspera num saxis loca sint (nam talia lentos
Deposcunt calamos, at purum retia litus),
Num mons horrentes demittat celsior umbras
In mare (nam varie quidam fugiuntque petuntque),
Num vada subnatis imo viridentur ab herbis⠀⠀⠀⠀90
Obiectetque moras et molli serviat algae.
Discripsit sedes varie natura profundi
Nec cunctos una voluit consistere pisces.

⠀⠀⠀Nam gaudent pelago quales scombrique bovesque,
Hippuri celeres et nigro tergore milvi⠀⠀⠀⠀⠀⠀95
Et pretiosus elops nostris incognitus undis
Ac durus xiphias ictu non mitior ensis
Et pavidi magno fugientes agmine thynni,
Parva echenais (at est, mirum, mora puppibus ingens)
Tuque comes ratium tractique per aequora sulci⠀⠀⠀100
Qui semper spumas sequeris, pompile, nitentes

⠀⠀85 linum *Merkel*: finem *V.*: funem *Ulitius.* After this
line another lacuna is suspected, *e.g.* (Birt) " pisces observes quid
ament et dona locorum," " you should observe what the fish like
and what the places provide."
⠀⠀91 obiectet (sc. imum) *Heinsius*: oblectet *V.*

sagacity in the chase, and power to pursue. Now with noses raised they sniff the air, now with lowered muzzles seek the track, and drive forth the quarry by their clamour, and calling chide their master; and should the beast escape him when the battle is joined, the hound pursues it o'er every hill and plain. . . .

On skill does our toil depend, all our hope lies therein. Yet I would not bid you go to the midmost regions of the sea, or try the depths of the vast ocean; between either extreme will you guide your line more profitably . . . whether the waters are studded with rocks (for such places need pliant rods, while an open coast admits of nets), or whether a high mountain cast its shivering shadows upon the sea (for in different wise do some fishes shun or seek the bait), or whether the shallows are verdant with grasses that grow at the bottom, and it interpose delays and foster the soft seaweed. In varying wise has Nature designed the dwellings of the deep, nor has she wished all fishes to abide together.

Some rejoice in the open sea, such as Mackerel[1] and Turbot and swift Carp[2] and black-backed Gurnards, and the costly Sturgeon, unknown to our waters, and the cruel Sword-fish, as merciful as a sword-thrust, and frightened Tunnies that flee in large shoals, the tiny Remora (yet, strange to tell, a great hinderer of ships), and thou, companion of vessels and of the furrow traced upon the deep,

---

[1] Pelagic fish, but "they approach the shore at certain seasons in countless multitudes, either prior to, after, or during breeding, or for predaceous purposes" (Day, i, p. 85).

[2] Probably Coryphaena hippurus; mod. Gk. λαμπούγα, μανάλια "popularly but erroneously called dolphins."

OVID

Cercyrosque ferox scopulorum fine moratus,
Cantharus ingratus suco, tum concolor illi
Orphos caeruleaque rubens erythinus in unda,
Ínsignis sargusque notis, insignis iulis   105
Et super aurata sparulus cervice refulgens
Et rutilus phager et fulvi synodontes et ex se
Concipiens channe, gemino sibi functa parente,
Tum viridis squamis, parvo saxatilis ore
Et rarus faber et pictae mormyres et auri   110
Chrysophrys imitata decus, tum corporis umbrae
Liventis rapidique lupi percaeque tragique,
Quin laude insignis caudae melanurus et ardens
Auratis muraena notis merulaeque virentes
Immitisque suae gonger per volnera genti   115
Et captus duro nociturus scorpios ictu
Ac nunquam aestivo conspectus sidere glaucus.

At contra herbosa pisces laetantur harena
Ut scarus, epastas solus qui ruminat escas,
Fecundumque genus maenae lamirosque smarisque   120
Atque immunda chromis, merito vilissima salpa
Atque avium phycis nidos imitata sub undis

116 captus *Ciacconus* : capitis *V*.
122 phycis *Ulitius*, cf. Plin. *N.H.* 9 : dulces *V*.

---

[1] Really Naucrates ductor, one of the horse-mackerels
(carangidae) ; for their love of following ships see Pliny, 9. 51
and Oppian, *Hal.* i. 185 ff.
[2] Merou, or Great sea-perch (serranus gigas), highly esteemed
for its white flesh ; Oppian (i. 142) calls it late-dying, *i.e.*
tenacious of life ; mentioned by Aristophanes, *Vesp.* 493.
[3] Dentex vulgaris, one of the sea-breams. Oppian (*Hal.* iii.
610) says that they travel in separate bands, like soldiers.

Rudder-fish [1] that always followest the shining foam,
and bold Pinnace lurking at the edge of rocks, and
Sea-bream [2] of unpleasing taste, then Stone-brass like
in hue to him, and Mullet glowing red in the blue
wave, and Sargus notable for his markings, notable
too the Rainbow-wrasse, and Bream that shines
with gilded neck, glittering Braize, tawny Synodons,[3]
and self-conceiving Channe [4] that plays the part of
both parents to itself, then Rock-fish green-scaled
and small of mouth, rare Dory, painted Mormyrs,[5]
and Gilt-head [6] that counterfeits the sheen of gold,
Umbers with livid body and swift Pikes and Perch [7]
and Goat-fish,[8] and Black-tail whose tail wins high
renown, and Lamprey glowing with gold markings,
and green Sea-carp, and Conger-eel made cruel by
the wounds of his own tribe, and Scorpion that
when taken will hurt with a fierce sting, and Blue-
fish [9] never seen under summer stars.

But on the other hand are fish that rejoice in
grassy sand, as the Scar who alone chews the cud
of eaten food, and the prolific tribe of Maenae, and
Lamirus and Picarel and unclean Chromis, and Salpa
justly held most worthless, and Phycis that imitates
beneath the waves the nests of birds, and Red

[4] Mentioned by Aristotle, who was aware that the genus
Serranus to which it belongs was hermaphrodite; this fish is
either serranus cabrilla or scriba.

[5] Mentioned in *Anth. Pal.* 6. 304.

[6] It gets its name from its inter-orbital golden bands
(French, "daurade"); mentioned by Martial, 13. 90.

[7] A freshwater fish that sometimes enters salt water
(perca fluviatilis), cf. Ausonius, *Mosella* 115; or else serranus
scriba, a rock-fish.

[8] The male of the maenis, or maena (l. 120).

[9] Oppian says of it that it loves its young beyond all
other fishes that are oviparous, *Hal.* i. 749 ff.

OVID

Et squa\<mas\> tenui suffusus sanguine mullus,
Fulgentes soleae candore et concolor i\<llis\>
Passer et Hadriaco mirandus litore rhombus,   125
Tum lepores lati, tum molles tergore ranae
Extremi pareuc

. . . .
. . . .

Lubricus et spina nocuus non gobius una   130
Et nigrum niveo portans in corpore virus
Lolligo durique sues sinuosaque caris
Et tam deformi non dignus nomine asellus
Tuque peregrinis acipenser nobilis undis . . . . .

123 squamas *Ciacconus*, fr. Oppian, *Hal.* 87 : squa *V.*: squatu
et, squalus et *edd.*
124 concolor illis *Heinsius* : concolori *V.*
127 Filled by Birt thus : "extremi aspectu taeter quibus ori
hiatus," "last those whose gaping mouth is grim to behold."

Mullet whose scales are suffused with tenuous blood, Soles shining bright and Passer of like hue with them and the marvellous Turbot of the Adriatic shore, broad Hares and soft-backed Frog-fish, and last of all . . . the slippery Gudgeon, harmful with not one spine only, the Cuttle-fish that bears black poison in a snow-white body, tough Hogs and sinuous Prawns, and Donkey-fish, undeserving of a name so mean, and thou, Sturgeon, renowned in foreign waters . . .

M

A POEM OF CONSOLATION

CONSOLATIO AD LIVIAM

Visa diu felix, "mater" modo dicta "Neronum,"
    Iam tibi dimidium nominis huius abest;
Iam legis in Drusum miserabile, Livia, carmen,
    Unum qui dicat iam tibi "mater" habes,
Nec tua te pietas distendit amore duorum,   5
    Nec posito fili nomine dicis "uter?"
Et quisquam leges audet tibi dicere flendi?
    Et quisquam lacrimas temperat ore tuas?
Ei mihi, quam facile est, quamvis hic contigit omnes,
    Alterius luctu fortia verba loqui: 10
"Scilicet exiguo percussa es fulminis ictu,
    Fortior ut possis cladibus esse tuis."
Occidit exemplum iuvenis venerabile morum:
    Maximus ille armis, maximus ille toga.
Ille modo eripuit latebrosas hostibus Alpes   15
    Et titulum belli dux duce fratre tulit:
Ille genus Suevos acre indomitosque Sicambros
    Contudit inque fugam barbara terga dedit,
Ignotumque tibi meruit, Romane, triumphum,
    Protulit in terras imperiumque novas.   20
Solvere vota Iovi fatorum ignara tuorum,
    Mater, et armiferae solvere vota deae
Gradivomque patrem donis implere parabas
    Et quoscunque coli est iusque piumque deos,

---

[1] Apparently meant to illustrate l. 10, as a usual common-
place of consolation. At the same time the author suggests that
no one could show more fortitude than Livia.

[2] In 12 B.C.

324

A POEM OF CONSOLATION

TO LIVIA AUGUSTA ON THE DEATH OF HER SON, DRUSUS NERO

O THOU who didst long seem blest, called but of late "the mother of the Neros," now is the half of that title thine no more; now art thou reading a sad plaint to Drusus' memory, now hast thou but one to call thee "mother"; neither does thy affection distract thee between love for two, nor hearing the word "son" dost thou ask "which." And does any dare to tell thee the conditions of mourning? does any check the tears upon thy face? Alas! how easy it is, though this sorrow has touched all, to speak brave words in another's grief! "Lightly, be sure, has the thunderbolt touched thee, that by thy calamities thou mayst be able to be more stout-hearted."[1] A youth is dead, whose life was a pattern that all might reverence; great in arms was he, and great in peace. He wrested of late from the foe their Alpine hiding-places, and won renown, sharing with his brother the captaincy of the war; he crushed the fierce tribe of Suevi and the untamed Sicambri, and turned their barbarous backs to flight, and won for thee, O Roman, a triumph before unknown, and extended thy sway to new lands.[2] Ignorant of thy destinies thou wert preparing, O mother, to pay thy vows to Jove, to pay thy vows to the armed goddess, and to heap with gifts our sire Gradivus, and all the gods whom 'tis right and dutiful to worship; thy

Maternaque sacros agitabas mente triumphos,   25
  Forsitan et curae iam tibi currus erat.
Funera pro sacris tibi sunt ducenda triumphis
  Et tumulus Drusum pro Iovis arce manet.
Fingebas reducem praeceptaque mente fovebas
  Gaudia et ante oculos iam tibi victor erat: 30
" Iam veniet, iam me gratantem turba videbit,
  Iam mihi pro Druso dona ferenda meo.
Obvia progrediar felixque per oppida dicar
  Collaque et osque oculosque illius ore premam.
Talis erit, sic occurret, sic oscula iunget;   35
  Hoc mihi narrabit, sic prior ipsa loquar."
Gaudia magna foves: spem pone, miserrima, falsam;
  Desine de Druso laeta referre tuo.
Caesaris illud opus, voti pars altera vestri,
  Occidit: indignas, Livia, solve comas.   40
Quid tibi nunc mores prosunt actumque pudice
  Omne aevom et tanto tam placuisse viro?
Quidque pudicitia tantum cumulasse bonorum,
  Ultima sit laudes inter ut illa tuas?
Quid, tenuisse animum contra sua saecula rectum,   45
  Altius et vitiis exeruisse caput?
Nec nocuisse ulli et fortunam habuisse nocendi,
  Nec quemquam nervos extimuisse tuos?
Nec vires errasse tuas campove forove
  Quamque licet citra constituisse domum?   50
Nempe per hos etiam Fortunae iniuria mores
  Regnat et incerta est hic quoque nixa rota;

34 Most *MSS.* read " collaque et osque oculos."
43 cumulasse *Molsheim*: inviolata *MSS.*: in tanto inviolata,
Vollmer.

---

[1] Drusus was the " work " of Caesar, who had adopted him
and trained him for his work; he and his brother were the hope
of Caesar and Livia ("vestri").

mother's mind was brooding on the sacred triumph :
perchance thou wert even thinking on the chariot.
A funeral must thou lead in place of the sacred
triumph, and the pyre awaits Drusus before the
citadel of Jove. Thou didst picture him returned,
and cherished in thy heart the joys he bade thee
feel, and already he stood victorious before thine
eyes. "Soon will he come : soon will the throng
behold me giving thanks, soon must I bear gifts for
my Drusus' safety. I shall go forth to meet him,
and through the cities I shall be called fortunate ;
his neck will I embrace and kiss his mouth and
eyes. Even so will he be, so will he meet me, and
so kiss me ; such tale will he tell, thus will I accost
him first." Great are the joys thou art cherishing ;
unhappiest of women, put aside false hopes, cease to
tell joyful tidings of thy Drusus. That achievement
of Caesar, the one half of your hopes,[1] has perished :
undo, Livia, thy undeserving locks. What now avails
thy character, thy whole life chastely lived, thy having
so pleased so mighty a lord ? And what with chastity
to have crowned such a sum of dignities that it is the
last among thy praises ? What avails it to have kept
thy mind upright against thy age, and to have lifted
thy head clear of its vices ? To have harmed none,
yet to have had the power to harm, and that none
feared thy might ? That thy power strayed not to
the Campus or the Forum,[2] and that thou didst order
thy house within the bounds permitted thee ? Ay,
verily o'er such lives too Fortune's injustice reigns ;
here too she rides her shifting wheel ; here too is

[2] *i.e.* to public life, which was not women's business ; the
following line simply means that she kept within the proper
woman's sphere and looked after her household. Other edd.
read " continuisse," understand " vires tuas."

Hic quoque sentitur : ne quid non improba carpat
    Saevit et iniustum ius sibi ubique facit.
Scilicet immunis si luctus una fuisset   55
    Livia, Fortunae regna minora forent.
Quid si non habitu sic se gessisset in omni,
    Ut sua non essent invidiosa bona ?
Caesaris adde domum, quae certe, funeris expers,
    Debuit humanis altior esse malis.   60
Ille vigil, summa sacer ipse locatus in arce,
    Res hominum ex tuto cernere dignus erat,
Nec fleri ipse suis nec quemquam flere suorum
    Nec, quae nos patimur volgus, et ipse pati ;
Vidimus erepta maerentem stirpe sororis :   65
    Luctus, ut in Druso, publicus ille fuit ;
Condidit Agrippam quo te, Marcelle, sepulcro,
    Et cepit generos iam locus ille duos ;
Vix posito Agrippa tumuli bene ianua clausa est,
    Percipit officium funeris ecce soror.   70
Ecce ter ante datis iactura novissima Drusus
    A magno lacrimas Caesare quartus habet.
Claudite iam, Parcae, nimium reserata sepulcra,
    Claudite : plus iusto iam domus ista patet.
Cedis, et incassum tua nomina, Druse, levantur   75
    Ultima : sit fati haec summa querela tui.
Iste potest implere dolor vel saecula tota
    Et magni luctus obtinuisse locum.
Multi in te amissi, nec tu, tot turba bonorum,
    Omnis cui virtus contigit, unus eras,   80

---

70 perficit *MSS.*   79 turba *Scaliger* : verba *MSS.*

---

[1] The bereavements alluded to here are—(i) the death of the
young Marcellus, son of Augustus' sister Octavia by her first
husband, M. Claudius Marcellus, 23 B.C. (cf. Virg. *Aen.* vi.
860 ff.); (ii) that of Agrippa, his son-in-law, statesman and
general, 12 B.C. ; (iii) that of his sister Octavia.

she felt: lest anything escape her insatiate grasp, she rages, and everywhere makes injustice justice for herself. Forsooth, if Livia alone had been immune from grief, then Fortune's realm had suffered! What if she had not so borne herself in all her ways that her blessings stirred no envy? Think too of Caesar's house, which surely should have been exempt from death and higher than human ills. He, our guardian, set consecrated on the highest citadel, was worthy to regard the affairs of men from a place of safety, nor to be wept for by his own, nor weep for any of his kin, nor to endure himself what we, the common folk, endure; we have seen him mourning for his sister's offspring snatched away: that grief, as in Drusus' case, was shared by all; he buried Agrippa in thy sepulchre, Marcellus, and already that place held his two sons-in-law; scarce was the tomb's door fast closed upon Agrippa's corpse, lo! his sister receives the rites of death.[1] Lo! thrice has the tribute been paid,[2] and Drusus, the latest loss, is the fourth to draw tears from mighty Caesar. Shut now, ye Fates, shut the tomb too oft unlocked! more already than is right has that house of yours been opened. Drusus, thou goest; and fruitlessly is thy name called for the last time:[3] let this be the last complaining for thy fate. Sorrow for thee can fill whole ages, and take rank as a mighty mourning: many men were lost in thee, nor wert thou, so great a multitude of virtues, the only one in whom all excellence was found,[4]

[2] *i.e.* of tears, "ter datis lacrimis."

[3] The name of the dead man was called aloud three times before the body was placed on the pyre (cf. 219).

[4] He refers to Drusus' brother, of whom he now proceeds to speak.

Nec genetrice tua fecundior ulla parentum,
   Tot bona per partus quae dedit una duos.
Heu, par illud ubi est totidem virtutibus aequom
   Et concors pietas nec dubitatus amor?
Vidimus attonitum fraterna morte Neronem   85
   Pallida promissa flere per ora coma,
Dissimilemque sui, voltu profitente dolorem:
   Ei mihi, quam toto luctus in ore fuit!
Tu tamen extremo moriturum tempore fratrem
   Vidisti, lacrimas vidit et ille tuas,   90
Affigique suis moriens tua pectora sensit
   Et tenuit voltu lumina fixa tuo,
Lumina caerulea iam iamque natantia morte,
   Lumina fraternas iam subitura manus.
At miseranda parens suprema neque oscula legit,   95
   Frigida nec fovit membra tremente sinu;
Non animam apposito fugientem excepit hiatu
   Nec sparsit caesas per tua membra comas.
Raptus es absenti, dum te fera bella morantur,
   Utilior patriae quam tibi, Druse, tuae.   100
Liquitur, ut quondam zephyris et solibus ictae
   Solvuntur tenerae vere tepente nives;
Te queritur casusque malos irrisaque vota
   Accusatque annos ut diuturna suos.
Talis in umbrosis, mitis nunc denique, silvis   105
   Deflet Threicium Daulias ales Ityn;
Alcyonum tales ventosa per aequora questus
   Ad surdas tenui voce sonantur aquas;
Sic plumosa novis plangentes pectora pennis
   Oeniden subitae concinuistis aves;   110

103 **vota** *Heinsius*: tales *MSS*.

---

[1] *i.e.* after having put her own son to death as a revenge upon Tereus.

nor was any mother more fruitful than thine, who
alone by two births brought forth so many virtues.
Alas! where is that pair well-matched in every
excellence, devotion of heart to heart and love un-
doubted? We beheld Nero dazed by his brother's
death, and weeping pale-faced with dishevelled hair,
unlike himself in his grief-proclaiming countenance;
alas, how that grief was shown in every line! Yet
thou didst see thy brother in death's last hour, and
he saw thy tears, and dying he felt thy breast
pressed close to his, and kept his eyes fixed upon
thy face, his eyes, all but merged in darksome
death, his eyes, soon to be closed by his brother's
hand. But thy unhappy mother neither imprinted
her last kisses nor cherished the cold limbs in her
trembling bosom; she caught not the flying life on
open lips set near to thine, nor scattered her shorn
tresses o'er thy limbs. In her absence wert thou
torn away, while savage war detained thee, more
useful to thy country, Drusus, than to thyself. She
melts away, as melt the soft snows, what time the
suns and zephyrs smite them, and the spring is
warm; of thee she complains, of thy misfortune
and her slighted vows, and blames her years as one
who has lived too long. Even so in the shady woods
the Daunian bird, now gentle at last,[1] laments the
Thracian Itys, even such the plaints that o'er the
windy seas the piping Halcyons utter to the un-
hearing waves; so, beating plumy bosoms with new
wings, did ye chant together of Oeneus' son, ye

Sic flevit Clymene, sic et Clymeneides, alte
    Quom iuvenis patriis excidit ictus equis.
Congelat interdum lacrimas duratque tenetque
    Suspensasque, oculis fortior, intus agit :
Erumpunt iterumque lavant gremiumque sinusque, 115
    Effusae gravidis uberibusque genis.
In vires abiit flendi mora : plenior unda
    Defluit, exigua siqua retenta mora.

Tandem ubi per lacrimas licuit, sic flebilis orsa est
    Singultu medios impediente sonos :   120
" Nate, brevis fructus, duplicis sors altera partus,
    Gloria confectae, nate, parentis, ubi es ?
Sed neque iam ' duplicis ' nec iam ' sors altera partus,'
    Gloria confectae nunc quoque matris, ubi es ?
Heu, modo tantus, ubi es ? tumulo portaris et igni. 125
    Haec sunt in reditus dona paranda tuos ?
Sicine dignus eras oculis occurrere matris ?
    Sic ego te reducem digna videre fui ?
Caesaris uxori si talia dicere fas est,
    Iam dubito, magnos an rear esse deos.   130
Nam quid ego admisi ? quae non ego numina cultu,
    Quos ego non potui demeruisse deos ?
Hic pietatis honos ? artus amplector inanes :
    Et vorat hos ipsos flamma rogusque sinus.
Tene ego sustineo positum scelerata videre ?   135
    Tene meae poterunt ungere, nate, manus ?
Nunc ego te infelix summum teneoque tuorque
    Effingoque manus oraque ad ora fero ?

125 qui modo tantus eras *two MSS*.
134 evocat . . . suus *MSS*. : Vollmer keeps this, explaining
"evocat" as "calls away from my embrace" and "suus" as
"artubus paratus."

unexpected birds;[1] so Clymene wept, so Clymene's daughters, when the stricken youth[2] fell from his father's chariot on high. Sometimes she makes her tears congeal and harden, restrains them, and, braver than her eyes, drives them within, just quivering to fall: yet forth they burst, and once more flood her lap and bosom, pouring out from laden and ne'er-failing eyelids. Weeping gains strength from tarrying; the stream flows fuller, if even a brief delay has held it back.

At length, when her tears allowed, thus dolefully she began, though sobbing checked her in mid-utterance: "O son, brief fruit, and half the fortune of a twofold birth, glory of thy aged mother, O son, where art thou? No more a 'twofold birth,' no more 'one-half its fortune,' yet still the glory of thy aged mother, where art thou? Ah, late so mighty, where art thou? to the flame and to the pyre art thou borne. Are these the gifts prepared for thy return? Deservedst thou thus to meet thy mother's eyes, deserved I thus to behold thee on thy return? If Caesar's consort may speak thus, I doubt now whether to think the gods are great. For what sin have I done? what powers, what gods have I failed to win by my devotion? Is this piety's reward? I clasp lifeless limbs, and flame and pyre devour this very womb. Can I bear to see thee lying there, cursed that I am? will my hands bring themselves to anoint thee, O my son? Now for the last time do I grasp thee and behold thee, wretched that I am? and stroke thy hands and set my lips to

[1] The sisters of Meleager, son of Oeneus, who were turned into guinea-fowl ("meleagrides.")

[2] Phaethon, son of Clymene.

Nunc primum aspiceris consul victorque parenti?
  Sic mihi, sic miserae nomina tanta refers? 140
Quos primum vidi fasces, in funere vidi,
  Et vidi eversos indiciumque mali.
Quis credat? matri lux haec carissima venit,
  Qua natum in summo vidit honore suum?
Iamne ego non felix? iam pars mihi rapta Neronum, 145
  Materni celeber nomine Drusus avi?
Iamne meus non est nec me facit ille parentem?
  Iamne fui Drusi mater et ipse fuit?
Nec quom victorem referetur adesse Neronem,
  Dicere iam potero 'maior an alter adest?' 150
Ultima contigimus: ius matris habemus ab uno,
  Unius est munus quod tamen orba negor.
Me miseram, extimui frigusque per ossa cucurrit:
  Nil ego iam possum certa vocare meum.
Hic meus ecce fuit: iubet hic de fratre vereri; 155
  Omnia iam metuo: fortior ante fui.
Sospite te saltem moriar, Nero: tu mea condas
  Lumina et excipias hanc animam ore pio.
Atque utinam Drusi manus altera et altera fratris
  Formarent oculos comprimerentque meos. 160
Quod licet, hoc certe tumulo ponemur in uno,
  Druse, neque ad veteres conditus ibis avos;
Miscebor cinerique cinis atque ossibus ossa:
  Hanc lucem celeri turbine Parca neat."
Haec et plura refert: lacrimae sua verba sequuntur 165
  Oraque nequiquam per modo questa fluunt.

---

[1] For the idea of the life escaping through the open mouth
and being received on the lips of the loving friend or relative
(cf. l. 97), cf. *Ars Am.* 3. 745, Statius, *Silvae*, 5. 1. 195.
[2] He would be buried among the Julian house, not the
Claudian.

thine? Now first art thou seen as consul and as
victor by thy mother? Is it so, is it so thou bringest
me home (woe is me!) these mighty names? The
rods that I see for the first time, I see when thou
art dead; I see them reversed, significant of evil.
Who would believe it? can this be the gladdest day
that has dawned for thy mother, that whereon she
sees her son in highest honour? Can I be no longer
blest? can the half of the Neros now be taken from
me, Drusus renowned for the name of his mother's
sire? Can he be mine no more, nor make me any
more a parent? Am I no more the mother of
Drusus? lives he now no more? No more, when it
is told me that victorious Nero is at hand, shall I be
able to say, 'Is it the elder or the other that is
here?' I have touched the depths: I hold the
rights of a mother from one alone; of one alone
is it the gift that nevertheless I am not called
childless. Ah, wretched me! I am afraid, a chill
runs through my bones: naught can I surely call
any more my own. Lo! he was mine: he bids me
fear for his brother; now fear I all things; ere now
I was braver. At least, O Nero, may I die before
thee, mayst thou shut my eyes, and may thy
devoted mouth receive this life.[1] Ah, would that
one hand of Drusus and one hand of his brother
could set and close my eyelids! This at least is
possible—in this tomb shall we be laid together,
Drusus, nor buried shalt thou go to the sires of
old;[2] I shall be mingled with thee, ashes with ashes,
bone with bone: may Fate with swift wheel spin
that day!"

This and more does she say: tears follow her
words, and flow unavailing o'er the face that late

Quin etiam corpus matri vix vixque remissum
 Exequiis caruit, Livia, paene suis.
Quippe ducem arsuris exercitus omnis in armis,
 Inter quae periit, ponere certus erat :   170
Abstulit invitis corpus venerabile frater
 Et Drusum patriae quod licuitve dedit.
Funera ducuntur Romana per oppida Drusi,
 (Heu facinus) per quae victor iturus erat,
Per quae deletis Raetorum venerat armis :   175
 Ei mihi, quam dispar huic fuit illud iter.
Consul init fractis maerentem fascibus Urbem :
 Quid faceret victus, sic ubi victor init ?
Maesta domus plangore sonat, cui figere laetus
 Parta sua dominus voverat arma manu.   180
Urbs gemit et voltum miserabilis induit unum—
 Gentibus adversis forma sit illa, precor !
Incerti clauduntque domos trepidantque per Urbem,
 Hic illic pavidi clamque palamque dolent.
Iura silent mutaeque tacent sine vindice leges ; 185
 Aspicitur toto purpura nulla foro.
Dique latent templis neque iniqua ad funera voltus
 Praebent nec poscunt tura ferenda rogo :
Obscuros delubra tenent ; pudet ora colentum
 Aspicere invidiae, quam meruere, metu.   190
Atque aliquis de plebe pius pro paupere nato
 Sustulerat timidas sidera ad alta manus,
Iamque precaturus " quid ego autem credulus " inquit
 " Suscipiam in nullos irrita vota deos ?

---

   183 trepidantque *edd.* : strepitantque *MSS.*

336

lamented. Nay, too, the corpse, hardly, ay hardly
given up to his mother, almost, O Livia, lacked its
proper rites. For the whole host was resolved to lay
its chief on the pyre to burn in the harness wherein
he perished; but his brother against their will
snatched away the sacred body, and gave Drusus (or
all that he could give [1]) to his native land. Drusus'
funeral train proceeds through the Roman towns (ah,
dreadful thought!), through which he was to pass in
triumph, through which he had come after crushing
Rhaetian arms; [2] how unlike, alas! was this march
to that! The consul enters a mourning city with
broken rods: what should the vanquished do when
the conqueror enters thus? With mournful wailing
resounds the house whereon its master had joyfully
vowed to fix the arms his hand had won. The
City groans, and puts on one countenance of woe—
be such, I pray, the aspect of our foes! In un-
certainty they close their houses and tremble
throughout the city; hither and thither they go in
fear, openly and in secret they make moan. The
Courts are silent, and the laws unchampioned are
mute and still; no purple is seen in all the Forum.
The gods are hidden in their temples, nor show
their faces at this unrighteous death, nor demand
the incense needed by the pyre; they lurk obscure
in their shrines, and feel shame to look on the faces
of their worshippers, in fear of the hatred they have
earned. And a man of the people had devoutly
raised to the high stars his timid hand, in his needy
son's behalf, and now was about to pray; "But
why," he said, "should I credulously make vain
vows to gods who are not? Livia moved them not,

_____
[1] _i.e._ the corpse of Drusus.   [2] In 16, 15 B.C.

Livia, non illos pro Druso Livia movit :   195
    Nos erimus magno maxima cura Iovi ? "
Dixit et iratus vota insuscepta reliquit
    Duravitque animum destituitque preces.

Obvia turba ruit lacrimisque rigantibus ora
    Consulis erepti publica damna refert.   200
Omnibus idem oculi, par est concordia flendi :
    Funeris exequiis adsumus omnis eques ;
Omnis adest aetas, maerent iuvenesque senesque,
    Ausoniae matres Ausoniaeque nurus.
Auctorisque sui praefertur imagine maesta   205
    Quae victrix templis debita laurus erat.
Certat onus lecti generosa subire iuventus
    Et studet officio sedula colla dare.
Et voce et lacrimis laudasti, Caesar, alumnum,
    Tristia cum medius rumperet orsa dolor.   210
Tu letum optasti, dis aversantibus omen,
    Par tibi, si sinerent te tua fata mori.
Sed tibi debetur caelum, te fulmine pollens
    Accipiet cupidi regia magna Iovis.
Quod petiit tulit ille, tibi ut sua facta placerent,   215
    Magnaque laudatus praemia mortis habet.
Armataeque rogum celebrant de more cohortes :
    Has pedes exequias reddit equesque duci.
Te clamore vocant iterumque iterumque supremo ;
    At vox adversis collibus icta redit.   220
Ipse pater flavis Tiberinus adhorruit undis,
    Sustulit et medio nubilus amne caput.

---

[1] The writer was of equestrian family.

[2] The "decursio" consisted of a solemn march three times
round the pyre (cf. Virg., *Aen.* xi. 188). Suetonius tells us
that this honour was paid every year by the army to the tomb
of Drusus in the Campus Martius (Claud. 1).

even Livia, in behalf of Drusus : shall I be the chiefest care of Mighty Jove?" He spoke, and in anger left his vows unuttered, and hardened his soul and abandoned all his prayer.

The crowd rush forward, and with tears bedewing their cheeks tell of the consul's death and the public loss. All eyes are the same, there is an equal harmony of weeping ; we[1] knights are all present at the funeral rites : every age is there, young men and old alike lament, Ausonian matrons and Ausonian daughters. Before the sad image of its chief is borne the victorious laurel owed to the temples. High-blooded youths vie in bearing the burden of the bier, and in offering willing necks for the duty. With voice and tears, O Caesar, thou didst praise thy foster-son, though sorrow checked the course of thy sad words. Thou didst ask a like death for thyself (though the gods averted the omen) did thy fates but suffer thee to die. But to thee heaven is owing ; thee the great hall of eager Jove, strong in the thunderbolt, will welcome. What he sought— that his deeds should please thee—that he won ; in thy praise he wins great recompense for death. Armed cohorts duly pay reverence to the pyre, horsemen and infantry perform the obsequies of their chief.[2] With a shout they call thee, and once again, and again the last time of all, but their voices re-echo back from yonder hills. Father Tiber himself shuddered in his yellow waves, and from mid-stream raised his cloudy head.[3] Then with huge

[3] It is possible to see an imitation of this passage in Milton's *Lycidas*, "Next Camus reverend sire," etc. Cf. also Statius, *Theb.* 9. 404 sqq.

OVID

Tum salice implexum muscoque et arundine crinem
    Caeruleum magna legit ab ore manu
Uberibusque oculis lacrimarum flumina misit :   225
    Vix capit adiectas alveus altus aquas.
Iamque rogi flammas extinguere fluminis ictu,
    Corpus et intactum tollere certus erat ;
Sustentabat aquas cursusque inhibebat ad aequor,
    Ut posset toto proluere amne rogum ;   230
Sed Mavors, templo vicinus et accola Campi,
    Tot dixit siccis verba neque ipse genis :
" Quamquam amnes decet ira, tamen, Tiberine, quiescas:
    Non tibi, non ullis vincere fata datur.
Iste meus periit : periit arma inter et enses   235
    Et dux pro patria : funere causa latet.
Quod potui tribuisse, dedi : victoria parta est :
    Auctor abit operis, sed tamen extat opus.
Quondam ego tentavi Clothoque duasque sorores,
    Pollice quae certo pensa severa trahunt,   240
Ut Remus Iliades et frater conditor Urbis
    Effugerent aliqua stagna profunda via.
De tribus una mihi 'partem accipe quae datur'
      inquit
    'Muneris ; ex istis quod petis alter erit.
Hic tibi, mox Veneri Caesar promissus uterque :   245
    Hos debet solos Martia Roma deos.'
Sic cecinere deae : nec tu, Tiberine, repugna,
    Irrite nec flammas amne morare tuo,
Nec iuvenis positi supremos destrue honores.
    Vade age et immissis labere pronus aquis."   250
Paret et in longum spatiosas explicat undas
    Structaque pendenti pumice tecta subit.

229 ad aequor *Heinsius* : equorum *MSS.*
236 funere *edd.* : funera *MSS.*

hand he lifted from his cerulean face the tresses
interwoven with willow and reed and moss, and sent
forth streams of tears from brimming eyes; the deep
channel scarce holds the added waters. Already
was he resolved to extinguish the flames upon the
pyre with the impact of the stream, and take away
the corpse unharmed; he was checking his waters, and
staying their course to the sea, that he might flood
the pyre with his whole river; but Mavors in his
neighbouring shrine, near dweller to the Campus,
spoke thus, his own cheeks also wet: "Though
anger becomes rivers, yet, Tiber, keep thou still;
not to thee, not to any is it given to conquer Fate.
He died my votary: among arms and swords he
died, a captain in his country's service; his cause is
forgotten in his death. Such tribute as I could pay,
I have paid: the victory has been won; gone is the
author of the work, yet the work remains. Once
did I assail Clotho and her two sisters, who draw
with sure thumb the inexorable threads, that Remus,
Ilia's son, and his brother, founder of the City,
might by some way escape the depths below. Of
the three one said to me: 'Take that part of the
gift which is given thee; one of the two shall be
according to thy prayer. He to thee is promised,
to Venus hereafter Caesars twain:[4] these gods
alone are owed by Martian Rome.' Thus sang the
goddesses; and thou, O Tiber, struggle not in vain,
nor with thy river stay the flames, nor spoil the last
honours of the dead youth. Go now, glide on thy
way with unchecked current." He obeys, and
lengthwise unfolds his watery mass, and enters his
house wrought out of hanging rock. The flame long

---

[1] Julius and Augustus; "owed," *i.e.* to heaven.

Flamma diu cunctata caput contingere sanctum
　Erravit posito lenta sub usque toro.
Tandem ubi complexa est silvas alimentaque sumpsit,
　Aethera subiectis lambit et astra comis,　　　　　256
Qualis in Herculeae colluxit collibus Oetae,
　Quom sunt imposito membra cremata deo.
Uritur heu decor ille viri generosaque forma
　Et facilis voltus, uritur ille vigor　　　　　　　260
Victricesque manus facundaque principis ora
　Pectoraque, ingenii magna capaxque domus.
Spes quoque multorum flammis uruntur in isdem ;
　Iste rogus miserae viscera matris habet.
Facta ducis vivent operosaque gloria rerum :　　　365
　Haec manet, haec avidos effugit una rogos.
Pars erit historiae totoque legetur in aevo
　Seque opus ingeniis carminibusque dabit.
Stabis et in rostris tituli speciosus honore,
　Causaque dicemur nos tibi, Druse, necis.　　　　270

At tibi ius veniae superest, Germania, nullum :
　Postmodo tu poenas, barbare, morte dabis.
Aspiciam regum liventia colla catenis
　Duraque per saevas vincula nexa manus
Et tandem trepidos voltus inque illa ferocum　　275
　Invitis lacrimas decidere ora genis.
Spiritus ille minax et Drusi morte superbus
　Carnifici in maesto carcere dandus erit.
Consistam lentisque oculis laetusque videbo
　Strata per obscaenas corpora nuda vias.　　　　280
Hunc Aurora diem spectacula tanta ferentem
　Quam primum croceis roscida portet equis !

342

hesitating to touch the sacred head strayed slowly yet beneath the standing pyre. At length it embraced the timber and gained nourishment, and towered o'er the foliage and licked the stars of heaven, even as it glowed on the hills of Oeta, of Herculean fame, when the limbs of the god who lay there were consumed. Burning, alas! is the hero's comeliness, his noble beauty, his kindly features; burning is that vigour, those victorious hands, the chieftain's eloquent mouth, his breast, that great and spacious home of wisdom. In those same flames burn the hopes of many; that pyre holds his unhappy mother's flesh and blood. The chieftain's deeds will live, and the hard-won glory of his exploits; this abides, this alone escapes the greedy pyres. It will be a part of history, and will be read in every age, and will be a theme for writers and for poets. And on the Rostra shalt thou stand, glorious with thy roll of honours,[1] and we shall be called the cause of thy death, O Drusus.

But for thee, Germania, no right of pardon remains; thou shalt atone hereafter, barbarian, by thy death. I shall see the necks of kings livid with chains, and ruthless fetters entwining cruel hands, and faces cowed at last, and the tears falling down unwilling, haughty cheeks. That threatening spirit, exulting in Drusus' death, must be given to the executioner in the gloomy cell. I will stop, and leisurely with glad eyes gaze on naked bodies strewn on the unsightly roads. The day that brings so great a spectacle—let dewy Aurora speed it hither on her saffron car!

---

[1] A list of the honours that the man had won was usually inscribed on the base of a statue.

Adice Ledaeos, concordia sidera, fratres
    Templaque Romano conspicienda foro.
Quam parvo numeros implevit principis aevo,   285
    In patriam meritis occubuitque senex !
Nec sua conspiciet (miserum me) munera Drusus
    Nec sua prae templi nomina fronte leget.
Saepe Nero inlacrimans summissa voce loquetur
    " Cur adeo fratres heu sine fratre deos ? "   290
Certus eras numquam nisi victor, Druse, reverti ;
    Haec te debuerant tempora : victor eras.
Consule nos, duce nos, duce iam victore caremus :
    Invenit tota maeror in Urbe locum.
At comitum squalent immissis ora capillis,   295
    Infelix, Druso sed pia turba suo.
Quorum aliquis tendens in te sua bracchia dixit
    " Cur sine me, cur sic incomitatus abis ? "

Quid referam de te, dignissima coniuge Druso
    Atque eadem Drusi digna parente nurus ?   300
Par bene compositum : iuvenum fortissimus alter,
    Altera tam forti mutua cura viro.
Femina tu princeps, tu filia Caesaris illi
    Nec minor es magni coniuge visa Iovis.
Tu concessus amor, tu solus et ultimus illi,   305
    Tu requies fesso grata laboris eras.
Te moriens per verba novissima questus abesse
    Et mota in nomen frigida lingua tuum.
Infelix recipis non quem promiserat ipse,
    Nec qui missus erat, nec tuus ille redit,   310

---

[1] " Add," *i.e.* to the honours already mentioned.   Drusus
had erected or at least dedicated a temple to Castor and Pollux.

344

A POEM OF CONSOLATION

Add too the Ledaean brethren, concordant stars,
and the temples conspicuous in the Roman Forum.[1]
In how short a time did he fulfil the office of a
leader, and by his services to his country died an
old man! Yet—woe is me!—Drusus will never see
his bounty, nor read his name upon the temple's
front. Often will Nero weeping humbly say:
"Why brotherless, alas! do I approach the brother
gods?" Thou wast resolved, O Drusus, ne'er to
return save victorious; times such as these owed
thee to us; victorious thou wert. 'Tis a consul, a
leader, a leader already victorious we have lost!
Lo! in all Rome has mourning found a home. But
his comrades are unsightly to behold with hair un-
kempt, a hapless crowd, but faithful to their Drusus.
And one of them, stretching out his arms towards
thee, cried: "Why goest thou without me, why
thus companionless?"

What shall I say of thee, most worthy consort of
thy Drusus, worthy daughter-in-law of Drusus'
mother?[2] A pair well suited: the one a hero
among youths, the other that hero's darling, as she
was his. Queen among women wert thou to him,
and daughter of Caesar, nor didst thou seem less than
the wife of mighty Jove. Thou wert his freely
given, his last and only love, thou wert his pleasant
repose from weary toil. Thy absence did he, dying,
in his last words bewail, and his tongue, though
cold, strove to pronounce thy name. Hapless one,
thou receivest not him whom he himself did promise,
not him who was sent forth: that spouse of thine

[2] She was Antonia, mother by Drusus of Germanicus and
Claudius the Emperor, and daughter of Mark Antony and
Octavia. Her elder sister was grandmother of the Emperor
Nero.

Nec tibi deletos poterit narrare Sicambros,
  Ensibus et Suevos terga dedisse suis,
Fluminaque et montes et nomina magna locorum
  Et siquid miri vidit in orbe novo.
Frigidus ille tibi corpusque refertur inane,   315
  Quemque premat sine te sternitur ecce torus.
Quo raperis laniata comas similisque furenti?
  Quo ruis? attonita quid petis ora manu?
Hoc fuit Andromache, cum vir religatus ad axem
  Terruit admissos sanguinolentus equos;   320
Hoc fuit Euadne tunc cum ferienda coruscis
  Fulminibus Capaneus impavida ora dedit.
Quid mortem tibi maesta rogas amplexaque natos
  Pignora de Druso sola relicta tenes,
Et modo per somnos agitaris imagine falsa   325
  Teque tuo Drusum credis habere sinu,
Et subito temptasque manu sperasque receptum,
  Quaeris et in vacui parte priore tori?
Ille pio, si non temere haec creduntur, in arvo
  Inter honoratos excipietur avos,   330
Magnaque maternis maioribus, aequa paternis
  Gloria quadriiugis aureus ibit equis,
Regalique habitu curruque superbus eburno
  Fronde triumphali tempora vinctus erit.
Accipient iuvenem Germanica signa ferentem   335
  Consulis imperio conspicuumque decus,
Gaudebuntque suae merito cognomine gentis,
  Quod solum domito victor ab hoste tulit.
Vix credent tantum rerum cepisse tot annos,
  Magna viri latum quaerere facta locum.   340

---

[1] One of the Seven against Thebes; for his death see Statius,
Thebaid. x (*sub fin.*)
[2] *i.e.* this was the only prize of victory for him.

returns not, nor can he tell thee of the Sicambri's ruin, nor how the Suevi turned their backs to his swordsmen, nor of the rivers and the mountains and the mighty names of places, and of all the wonders that he saw in that new world. Cold he returns to thee, a lifeless corpse, and a couch is strewn for him to press without thee. Whither rushest thou, tearing thy hair and like to a mad woman? Whither hastenest? Why marrest thou thy face with frenzied hand? Such a sight was Andromache, when her husband bound all bloody to the axle frightened the galloping steeds; such was Evadne, when Capaneus[1] offered his unaffrighted countenance to be struck by the flashing brand. Why dost thou sadly pray for death, and embracing thy children hold the only pledges left thee in place of Drusus? and now in thy dreams art haunted by false visions, and believest thou hast thy Drusus in thy arms? and suddenly dost feel with thy hand and hope he is thine once more, and search the desolate couch where once he lay? He in the fields of bliss, if such belief is not vain, will be welcomed by his honoured forefathers, and, high renowned among his mother's ancestors, and no less among his sire's, will ride all golden in a four-horsed chariot, and in royal dress, proud in his ivory car, will have his temples bound with triumphal sprays. They will receive the hero who bears the standards of Germany and the illustrious fame of consular command, and they will rejoice in the well-won surname of their house, which alone[2] he bore in triumph from the conquered foe. Scarce will they believe that so great achievement filled years so few, they will think a hero's mighty deeds demand an ample space. These

Haec ipsum sublime ferent, haec, optima mater,
  Debuerint luctus attenuare tuos.
Femina digna illis quos aurea condidit aetas,
  Principibus natis, principe digna viro,
Quid deceat Drusi matrem matremque Neronis   345
  Aspice, quo surgas, aspice, mane toro.
Non eadem volgusque decent et lumina rerum :
  Est quod praecipuum debeat ista domus.
Imposuit te alto Fortuna locumque tueri
  Iussit honoratum : Livia, perfer onus.   350
Ad te oculos auresque trahis, tua facta notamus,
  Nec vox missa potest principis ore tegi.
Alta mane supraque tuos exurge dolores
  Infragilemque animum, quod potes, usque tene.
An melius per te virtutum exempla petemus,   355
  Quam si Romanae principis edis opus ?
Fata manent omnes, omnes expectat avarus
  Portitor et turbae vix satis una ratis.
Tendimus huc omnes, metam properamus ad unam,
  Omnia sub leges Mors vocat atra suas.   360
Ecce necem intentam caelo terraeque fretoque
  Casurumque triplex vaticinantur opus :
I nunc et rebus tanta impendente ruina
  In te solam oculos et tua damna refer.
Maximus ille quidem iuvenum spes publica vixit   365
  Et qua natus erat gloria summa domus ;
Sed mortalis erat : nec tu secura fuisti
  Fortia progenie bella gerente tua.
Vita data est utenda, data est sine faenore nobis
  Mutua nec certa persoluenda die.   370

exploits will exalt him on high, these exploits, best
of mothers, should have made thy sorrow less. O
woman worthy of those men whom the age of gold
brought forth, worthy of thy princely sons, thy
princely consort, see what becomes the mother of
Drusus and Nero's mother, see from whose couch
thou risest in the morning! The same behaviour
becomes not common folk and our country's lights;
a special duty that house of thine doth owe. Fortune
placed thee high, and bade thee guard an honoured
station; bear thy burden, Livia, to the end. Thou
drawest to thee ears and eyes, we mark thy doings,
nor can the voice a ruler's mouth doth utter be
concealed. Remain exalted and rise above thy grief,
and keep (thou canst) a spirit aye unbroken. Can
we find better patterns of virtues in thee than when
thou dost the work of a Roman queen? Fate awaits
all; all doth the greedy ferryman await, and the one
bark that scarce holds all the crowd. Hither we all
are bound, we hurry to one goal; black Death
summons all beneath its laws. Lo! the prophets
sing that destruction threatens sky and earth and
sea, and that the triple fabric is doomed to fall: go
now, and while so vast a ruin o'erhangs the world,
bring back all eyes to thee alone and to thy loss!
Mightiest was he of youths, his people's hope, while
yet he lived, and supreme glory of the house that
gave him birth; but he was mortal, nor wert thou
free from care while thy son waged valiant wars.
Life is given to be used:[1] 'tis lent to us without
interest, nor to be paid back on any appointed day.

---

[1] An obvious reminiscence of Lucretius' famous line,
"vitaque mancipio nulli datur, omnibus usu," 3. 971.

Fortuna arbitriis tempus dispensat iniquis:
　　Illa rapit iuvenes, sustinet illa senes,
Quaque ruit furibunda ruit totumque per orbem
　　Fulminat et caecis caeca triumphat equis.
Regna deae immitis parce irritare querendo,　　　　375
　　Sollicitare animos parce potentis erae.
Quae tamen hoc uno tristis tibi tempore venit,
　　Saepe eadem rebus favit amica tuis.
Nata quod alte es quodque es fetibus aucta duobus,
　　Quodque etiam magno consociata Iovi,　　　　380
Quod semper domito rediit tibi Caesar ab orbe,
　　Gessit et invicta prospera bella manu,
Quod spes implerunt maternaque vota Nerones,
　　Quod pulsus totiens hostis utroque duce —
Rhenus et Alpinae valles et sanguine nigro　　　　385
　　Decolor infecta testis Isargus aqua,
Danuviusque rapax et Dacius orbe remoto
　　Apulus (huic hosti perbreve Pontus iter)
Armeniusque fugax et tandem Dalmata supplex
　　Summaque dispersi per iuga Pannonii;　　　　390
Et modo Germanus Romanis cognitus orbis:
　　Aspice quam meritis culpa sit una minor.
Adde quod est absens functus nec cernere nati
　　Semineces oculos sustinere tui,
Qui dolor et menti lenissimus influit aegrae,　　　　395
　　Accipere es luctus aure coacta tuos,

---

[1] Apulum was in the centre of the Dacian mountains; Dacia
was bordered on the east by the Black Sea.
[2] Besides the campaigns of Drusus and his brother in the
Alps, Tiberius advanced to the Danube in 12 B.C., while Drusus
fought in Germany. The relations between Rome and Persia
were settled by negotiation in 20 B.C., after Tiberius had
marched into Armenia and set a client of Rome upon the throne.

A POEM OF CONSOLATION

Fortune ordains the time at her own unjust will:
youths she carries off, the aged she supports; her
onset, when she makes it, is furious, through all the
world her lightnings flash, and she triumphs blindly
on blind steeds. Offend not with thy complaints
the sway of the stern goddess, vex not the spirit of
that powerful queen. Yet the same power that at
this one time has visited thee in wrath has oft been
friendly and shown favour to thy fortunes. For that
thou wert born in lofty state, blest with two sons,
ay and made the partner of great Jove, that Caesar
ever returned from mastering the world to thee, and
with invincible might waged prosperous wars, that
the Neros fulfilled thy hopes and mother's prayers,
that under either's captaincy the foe was routed so
oft—witness the Rhine and Alpine valleys and
Isargus, whose waters the dark stain of gore dis-
colours, and rapacious Danube, and the Dacian
Apulian [1] in his far-off world (for this foe Pontus is
a very short march away), and the Armenian, ready
to flee, and the Dalmatian, at last a suppliant, and the
Pannonians scattered over their mountain summits,
and the German world that Romans but late have
known: [2] see how many the merits that outweigh
a single fault. Add that he died far away, nor had
thine eyes to endure the sight of thy son's eyes clos-
ing in death, and that (most gently thus doth sorrow
steal into a sick mind) 'twas with thine ears thou
wast compelled to receive thy sorrows; while amid

The allusion to Pannonia and Dalmatia can hardly be to the
great Pannonian revolt of A.D. 6, fifteen years after Drusus'
death, but rather to the operations of Tiberius mentioned
above.

Praevertitque metus per longa pericula luctum,
　　Tu quibus auditis anxia mentis eras :
Non ex praecipiti dolor in tua pectora venit,
　　Sed per mollitos ante timore gradus.　　　　　　　400
Iuppiter ante dedit fati mala signa cruenti,
　　Flammifera petiit cum tria templa manu :
Iunonisque gravis nocte impavidaeque Minervae
　　Sanctaque et immensi Caesaris icta domus.
Sidera quin etiam caelo fugisse feruntur,　　　　　405
　　Lucifer et solitas destituisse vias :
Lucifer in toto nulli comparuit orbe
　　Et venit stella non praeeunte dies :
Sideris hoc obitum terris instare monebat
　　Et mergi Stygia nobile lumen aqua.　　　　　　　410

At tu, qui superes maestae solacia matri,
　　Comprecor, illi ipsi conspiciare senex.
Perque annos diuturnus eas fratrisque tuosque
　　Et vivat nato cum sene mater anus.
Eventura precor : deus excusare priora　　　　　　415
　　Dum volet, a Druso cetera laeta dabit.
Tu tamen ausa potes tanto indulgere dolori,
　　Longius ut nolis (heu male fortis) ali.
Vix etiam fueras paucas vitalis in horas,
　　Obtulit invitae quom tibi Caesar opem ;　　　　420
Admovitque preces et ius immiscuit illis
　　Aridaque affusa guttura tinxit aqua.
Nec minor est nato servandae cura parentis :
　　Hic adhibet blandas, nec sine iure, preces.
Coniugis et nati meritum pervenit ad omnis ;　　425
　　Coniugis et nati, Livia, sospes ope es.
Supprime iam lacrimas : non est revocabilis istis,
　　Quem semel umbrifera navita lintre tulit.

409 obitus MSS.

long perils, the hearing of which kept thy mind anxious, fear anticipated thy mourning; not abruptly did sorrow burst into thy heart, but by steps that fear had already made gentle. Jupiter before gave the baleful sign of bloody fate, when he assailed three temples with fire-bearing hand; and on a night grave Juno's shrine and that of fearless Minerva and the sacred palace of all-powerful Caesar were struck. Nay, stars also are said to have fled the sky, and Lucifer to have left his wonted path: Lucifer in all the world was seen of none, and the day came unheralded by any star: this gave warning that a star's destruction threatened the earth, and that a noble light should be sunk in Stygian waters.

But thou who dost survive to console thy sorrowing mother, live, I pray, that she herself may see thy old age. Live long, and pass thy brother's and thine own allotted years, and let thine aged mother live with her aged son. My prayer shall be fulfilled; heaven, while it would fain excuse the past, will make all else happy after Drusus. Yet thou canst dare to indulge so violent a grief that thou refusest with unwise courage to take food. Scarce hadst thou been like to live for even a few hours, when Caesar brought thee succour against thy will; he urged thee with prayers, and mingled claims of right therein, and pouring water he moistened thy parched throat. Nor had thy son less care to save his parent: he made persuasive entreaty, and with good right. The merit of thy consort and of thy son hath reached to all: by the aid of thy consort and of thy son, O Livia, thou didst survive. Refrain at last thy tears: they will not call him back whom once the ferryman has borne in the ghost-laden skiff.

Hectora tot fratres, tot deflevere sorores
    Et pater et coniux Astyanaxque puer   430
Et longaeva parens : tamen ille redemptus ad ignes
    Nullaque per Stygias umbra renavit aquas.
Contigit hoc etiam Thetidi : populator Achilles
    Iliaca ambustis ossibus arva premit.
Illi caeruleum Panope matertera crinem   435
    Solvit et immensas fletibus auxit aquas,
Consortesque deae centum longaevaque magni
    Oceani coniux Oceanusque pater
Et Thetis ante omnes : sed nec Thetis ipsa neque omnes
    Mutarunt avidi tristia iura dei.   440
Prisca quid huc repeto ? Marcellum Octavia flevit
    Et flevit populo Caesar utrumque palam.
Sed rigidum ius est et inevitabile Mortis,
    Stant rata non ulla fila tenenda manu.
Ipse tibi emissus nebulosum litus Averni,   445
    Si liceat, forti verba tot ore sonet :
" Quid numeras annos ? vixi maturior annis :
    Acta senem faciunt : haec numeranda tibi,
His aevom fuit implendum, non segnibus annis :
    Hostibus eveniat longa senecta meis.   450
Hoc atavi monuere mei proavique Nerones
    (Fregerunt ambo Punica bella duces),
Hoc domus ista docet, per te mea, Caesaris alti :
    Exitus hic, mater, debuit esse meus.
Nec meritis (quamquam ipsa iuvant magis) afuit illis,
    Mater, honos : titulis nomina plena vides.   456

For Hector all his many brothers, all his sisters wept,
and his sire and wife and child Astyanax and aged
mother : yet was he ransomed but for the pyre,
and no ghost swam back across the Stygian pools.
This befell Thetis also : Achilles the destroyer rests
his charred bones upon the Ilian fields.   For him
Panope, his mother's sister, loosed her cerulean
hair, and swelled the boundless waters with her
tears, and a hundred comrades of the goddess, and
mighty Ocean's aged spouse, and father Ocean, and
Thetis before all ; but not Thetis herself nor all of
them could change the stern laws of the greedy
god.   Why do I tell old stories here ? Octavia wept
Marcellus, and each in the sight of the people did
Caesar weep.   But fixed and inevitable is death's
law, unswerving are the threads, not to be checked
by any hand.   He himself escaping (were it lawful)
the misty shore of Acheron, would with brave mouth
proclaim these words : "Why dost thou number
years ? I have lived to a riper age than years can
show.   'Tis deeds make old : these must thou
number : with these was my life fulfilled, not with
tardy years ; let a long old age befall my foes.
This lesson my grandsires taught, and the Neros
who were before them (both chieftains[1] shattered
the Punic hosts), this is the lesson of lofty Caesar's
house, that is mine through thee : such an end, O
mother, was mine by right.   Nor to those my merits
(though by themselves they better please) has
honour been wanting : thou seest my name decked

[1] They were Appius Claudius and C. Claudius Nero :
the former began the invasion of Sicily and the first
Punic war, the latter fought in the battle of Metaurus,
207 B.C.

Consul et ignoti victor Germanicus orbis,
 Cui fuit heu mortis publica causa, legor:
Cingor Apollinea victricia tempora lauro
 Et sensi exequias funeris ipse mei,   460
Decursusque virum notos mihi donaque regum
 Cunctaque per titulos oppida lecta suos,
Et quo me officio portaverit illa iuventus,
 Quae fuit ante meum tam generosa torum.
Denique laudari sacrato Caesaris ore   465
 Emerui, lacrimas elicuique deo.
Et cuiquam miserandus ero? iam comprime fletus.
 Hoc ego qui flendi sum tibi causa rogo."
Haec sentit Drusus, si quid modo sentit in umbra,
 Nec tu de tanto crede minora viro.   470
Est tibi (sitque precor) multorum filius instar
 Parsque tui partus sit tibi salva prior;
Est coniux, tutela hominum, quo sospite vestram,
 Livia, funestam dedecet esse domum.

with titles; as 'consul' dost thou read of me, as conqueror of Germany, a world unknown, who died, alas! in his country's cause: my victorious temples are wreathed in Apollo's laurel, and I have felt the obsequies of my own funeral, and the familiar solemn march of men, and the gifts of kings, and all the cities read upon their placards[1]; and with what dutifulness those youths carried me, who stood so nobly born before my pyre. Last, I have meed of praise from Caesar's sacred lips, and drew tears from a god. And shall I need any's pity? Refrain at last thy weeping. This I ask, who am thy weeping's cause." This does Drusus feel, if he feels aught in the shadows, nor believe thou less of so great a hero. Thou hast, and mayst thou ever have, I pray, a son who is a pattern to many; may the elder part of thy offspring be preserved to thee. Thou hast a spouse, the guardian of mankind, and while he lives, it becomes not thy house, O Livia, to mourn.

---

[1] Placards on which were inscribed the names of captured cities were carried in the triumphal procession.

APPENDIX

ON CURSING IN ANCIENT TIMES

THE extraordinary outburst of the *Ibis*, a piece of writing probably unique in literature, may seem to justify some remarks of a more general nature concerning curses in ancient times. It is a natural instinct to call upon divine powers to hear and to support any expression of ill-will against an enemy, and consequently we find imprecations assuming a highly solemn character from this association; all readers of Greek Tragedy are familiar with the Ἀρά, for instance, pronounced against Polynices by Oedipus in Sophocles' "Oedipus Coloneus":

1383–1396 : " And thou—begone, abhorred of me and unfathered!—begone, thou vilest of the vile, and with thee take these my curses which I call down on thee—never to vanquish the land of thy race, no, nor ever return to hill-girt Argos, but by a kindred hand to die, and slay him by whom thou hast been driven out. Such is my prayer, and I call the paternal darkness of dread Tartarus to take thee unto another home,—I call the spirits of this place,—I call the destroying God, who hath set that dreadful hatred in you twain. Go, with these words in thine ears—go, and publish it to the Cadmeans all, yea, and to thine own staunch allies, that Oedipus hath divided such honours to his sons."
(Jebb's translation.)

359

APPENDIX

Such a curse was felt to have a sort of living force, and was, in fact, personified, as in Soph. *Electra*, 111, where Agamemnon's curse is invoked as πότνια 'Αρά, and distinguished from the Erinyes, or ministers of vengeance that fulfil it. Hence the idea of a curse as something that endures from one generation to another.

Again, the State could pronounce an 'Αρά against individuals or generally against all who acted treasonably or sacrilegiously, the usual formula being "let him be utterly ruined (ἐξώλη) himself and all his race"; such a curse had force in Greek Law, see Ziebarth in *Hermes*, xxx. p. 57: "Der Fluch im griechischen Recht." It was not the custom, however, to invoke gods in such oaths, at least in such as were purely political; in curses pronounced against violators of shrines they would naturally be invoked. In Latin "devotio" means rather the offering of *oneself* to the anger of the gods for the good of the community, as in Livy, 7. 6, 8. 9, 25. 14, where "exsecratus" is the word used (cf. too the story of Caligula in Suet. *Cal.* 27), although it was felt that he who so devoted himself carried the curse with him into the enemy's ranks, as in Livy, 10. 28:

"Quom secundum sollennes precationes adiecisset, 'prae se agere sese formidinem ac fugam, caedemque ac cruorem, caelestium, inferorum iras: contacturum funebribus diris signa tela arma hostium; locumque eundem suae pestis et Gallorum ac Samnitium fore'; haec exsecratus in se hostesque, etc."

In Livy, 10. 38, the Samnites take a dreadful oath and bind themselves on pain of awful penalties to fight the Romans: this is called "exsecratio" or

APPENDIX

" detestatio." For " devotio" meaning simply calling down a curse on a foe, cf. Macrobius, 3. 13, who speaks of Carthage, Corinth and other towns as having been cursed (" devota ").

When we turn to individual or private imprecations, we find that the need of supernatural support, or perhaps rather of the certainty of that support, is very much greater. If you can compel, rather than simply ask, the powers to back your curse, you are obviously in a much stronger position ; hence magic, which is exactly that, the compelling or binding of supernatural power. The words used express that, in Greek καταδεσμός, lit. a binding-down, in Latin, " defixio," a fixing- or fastening-down, with reference rather to nailing down; Audollent is probably right in comparing the nails of Necessity in Horace, *Odes*, 1. 35, 17. 3, 24. 5. Magic, of course, was used very widely in the ancient world ; its uses were necromantic, or the evocation of supernatural powers to gain knowledge of the future or counsel in some matter, amatory, or the gaining of the affections of some man or woman, medicinal, or healing of some wound or disease, and indeed for the fulfilment of almost any wish or purpose whatever. One important class is that of cursing : cursing by magic, says R. Wünsch, was known in Europe from the 4th cent. B.C. down to the 6th cent. after Christ. Egyptian papyri have been found containing proper formulae for use in magic of all kinds, while the favourite method of delivering the curse was to write it on a lead tablet, and insert the tablet in some tomb ; in this way the curse was, as it were, " posted " to the powers below. Large numbers of these have been discovered, and may be read in the

APPENDIX

editions of Wünsch (*C. I. A.* vol. iii, Appendix, 1897, Sethianische Fluchungstafeln aus Rom, 1898, Antike Fluchtafeln, 1907), Audollent (*Defixionem Tabellae*, 1904), etc.

Curses and threats are often directed against the deity invoked, to make the compulsion more effective, as in the passage in Lucan, 6. 507 sqq., where Erichtho threatens the Furies, or in Statius, *Theb.* 4. 470 sqq.; or against the disease, for instance, as in the charm " Recede ab illo Gaio Seio, Solomon te sequitur " (see R. Heim, *Incantamenta Magica*, pp. 479–82). Threatening directed against deities frequently forms part of ancient ritual, *e.g.* the cursing at the sacrifice of Heracles, βουθοίνας, at Lindos, when the Dorians prayed for a bad hay-harvest; cf. too the advice in Stobaeus, " Blaspheme when sowing cummin; that is the way to make it grow well." The idea is that the gods are hostile on principle, and so you must ask the opposite of what you want. The gods, in fact, are σχέτλιοι, act out of " pure cussedness," cf. Homer, *Il.* 2. 112, 24. 33, etc., and must be treated as the peasant treats his pig when he pulls it backwards to get it into the stye (S. Eitrem, *Papyri Osloenses*, p. 36 sqq.).

One feature of magic cursings is what is known as the ἀδύνατον, *i.e.* the appeal to something impossible: the magician prays that the order of nature may be inverted unless the deities do what he wants, the point being that, as a magician, he is able to bring this about, and can therefore really put pressure upon them. This became a recognised literary ornament; perhaps the most famous example of it is Euripides, *Medea*, 410: Ἄνω ποταμῶν ἱερῶν χωροῦσι παγαί, etc., " Back streams the wave on the

362

APPENDIX

ever-running river" (G. Murray); cf. Horace, *Odes*, 1. 29. 10; *Epod.* 5. 78; Ovid, *Trist.* 1. 8. 1; *Ibis*, 31–40; Virgil, *Ecl.* 1. 60; Propertius, 1. 15. 29, 2. 15. 30, ps.; Virgil, *Dirae*, 4–8, 98–101. Eitrem (*op. cit.* p. 70) gives a parallel from "a very impressive poem from the old Norse and Icelandic literature (? 13th cent.) which is a real magic imprecation in the style of the *Dirae* and the *Ibis*, viz. the Busluboen (F. Jonsson, *Norskislandsk Skjaldedigtning*, B. ii. p. 350 ff.). Here the old woman Busla invokes all sorts of evils upon the king Ring, who is going to kill his two sons: May the invisible genii lose their way, may things unheard of happen, rocks be shaken, worlds be confused, the weather be worsened, tumult rise—unless thou, king Ring, givest mercy to Heriod and safety to Bagas Bose. Busla goes on calling down all sorts of bodily evils upon the king (may vipers gnaw thy heart), also evils when sailing, riding, dwelling at home or in his bed (may dogs gnaw thee to death and thy soul sink into hell).

We may now look at some magical curses taken from the lead tablets discovered in various places in Europe and North Africa:

1. From Megara (*C. I. A.* iii. App. = *Defixionum Tabellae Atticae*, ed. Wünsch, p. xiii: *Antike Fluchtafeln*, 1: Audollent, *Defixionum Tabellae*, p. 75)—1st or 2nd cent. p. Chr.

. . . we doom them and anathematize them. Althaia Kore, who huntest on the mountains, Hecate, Selene . . . these we anathematize. Body spirit soul understanding mind perception life heart with Hecatean words with abraic (= magical) oaths . . . bidden by the sacred names and abriac oaths . . .

hairs head brain visage ears eyebrows nostrils . . .
teeth jaws . . . blood flesh to burn . . . which may
he suffer.

2. From Carthage (*D. T. A.* p. xvii: Audollent,
p. 323), ? 3rd cent. p. Chr. The writing is surrounded
with letters and magic signs.

Semesilam damatameneus lesnnallelam laikam
ermoubele iakoub ia ioerbeth iopakerbeth eomaltha-
beth allasan. Curse: I cast a spell upon you by
the mighty names that ye bind every limb and every
sinew of Victoricus whom earth bore, mother of every
living thing, the charioteer of the Blues, and of his
horses which he will drive, Juvenis and Advocatus
and Bubalus, belonging to Secundinus, and Pompei-
anus and Baianus and Victor and Eximius, belonging
to Victoricus, and Dominator, belonging to the
Messallae, and all that are yoked with them: bind
their legs and their speed and their leaping and
their running, dim their eyes that they may not see,
constrict their life and heart that they may not
breathe. As this cock is bound in arms and feet
and head, so bind the legs and the arms and the
head and the heart of Victoricus, the Blue charioteer,
to-morrow, and the horses that he will drive, Juvenis
and Advocatus and Baibalus and Laureatus, belong-
ing to Secundinus, and Pompeianus and Baianus and
Victor and Eximius, belonging to Victoricus, and
Dominatus, belonging to Messallae, and all that are
yoked with them. Further, I cast a spell on you in
the name of the heavenly god above, who sitteth
upon the Cherubim, who set bounds to the earth
and parted the sea, Iao Abriao Arbathiao Adonai
Sabao, that ye bind Victoricus, the Blue charioteer,

and the horses that he will drive, Juvenis and Advocatus, belonging to Secundinus, and Pompeianus and Baianus and Victor and Eximius, belonging to Victoricus, and Dominatus, belonging to Messalla, that they come not to victory in the Circus to-morrow. Now! now! quickly! quickly!

3. From the amphitheatre at Carthage (*Ant. Fluchtaf.* 4, Audollent, p. 336), *circ.* 200 p. Chr. Latin.

The lines of the following are written over the picture of a serpent-headed man (? Typhon-Seth, the evil demon of magic) with a spear in his right hand and a thunderbolt in his left.

Slay exterminate wound Gallicus son of Prima in this hour in the ring of the amphitheatre . . . bind his feet his limbs his senses his inward parts. Bind Gallicus son of Prima that he slay nor bear nor bull with one stroke, nor slay with two strokes, nor slay bear or bull with three strokes. In the name of the living omnipotent God perform this. Now! now! quickly! quickly! let the bear crush him and wound him!

4. From Puteoli (*Ant. Fluchtaf.* 2). With reference to this "hymn of hate," it may be noticed that Michael has the duty of bringing curses to the notice of infernal powers.

Iao El Michael Nephtho. May Gaius Stalcius Liberarius (acc. to Wünsch = Stlaccius Liberalis) son of Philista be hated by Lollia Rufina, be hated by Haplus (= Simplex), be hated by Eutychus, be hated by Celer, be hated by Rufus, be hated by the whole household of Rufina, be hated by Polybius, be hated by Anomis, be hated by Thebe.

5. From Athens (Audollent, p. 83) *circ.* 300 p.
Chr. This tablet had been pierced five times with
a nail.

I bind Theagenes, tongue and soul and the word
(*i.e.* the evidence) which he is devising; and I bind
Pyrrhias the cook, his tongue and soul, and the
word which he is devising; and I bind the wife of
Pyrrhias, tongue and soul; and I bind Kerkyon the
cook and Dokimos the cook, tongue and soul and
the word which they are devising; and I bind
Kineas, tongue and soul and the word which he is
devising with Theagenes; and I bind Seuthes,
tongue and soul and the word which he is devising,
feet and hands, eyes and mouth; and I bind
Lamprias, tongue and soul and the word which
he is devising; hands and feet, eyes and mouth;
all these I bind, cause to disappear, entomb, defix;
that they shall never appear in the court and before
the judge, should they work against me, neither in
word nor deed.

It will be seen that what is done to the tablet
containing the spell is thought of as happening to
the victims of it: hence the piercing of the tablet
with the nail.

6. From Santones (Audollent, p. 168), A.D. 172.
Latin.

I call down upon the persons written below,
Lentinus and Tasgillus, that they go to Pluto and
go hence to Proserpine. Just as this pup has hurt
nobody, so . . . nor may they be able to win this
lawsuit: just as the mother of this pup could not
defend it, so neither may their advocates be able to

defend them ; so may these enemies be turned away from the suit; as this pup is turned away and cannot rise, so neither may they ; so may they be transfixed as it is ; as in this tomb the animals (explained by Aud. as the corpses in the tomb) are dumb and cannot rise, so neither they . . . Altracatetracati gallara precata egdarata, etc.

7. From Cyprus (Audollent, p. 54). One of a large number that all begin with the same formula, four hexameter lines ; a great part consists of names of deities, or of the mysterious words and sounds known as Ἐφέσια γράμματα, what Lucian describes as βαρβάρικά τινα καὶ ἄσημα ὀνόματα καὶ πολυσύλλαβα, Menippus, 9 (" barbaric and senseless and many-syllabled names ").

Deities that are beneath the earth and deities that are fathers of our fathers and mothers equal to men, ye who lie here and ye who are set there having first taken the grievous soul from the heart, take away from Krateros the fierceness that he hath against me Kallias and the wrath, and rob him of his power and might and make him weak and voiceless and breathless, weak toward me Kallias. I conjure you by the great gods Masomasimablaboio Eumazo, etc., etc. . . . . . . gods of the underworld, take Krateros . . . the fierceness and the anger, etc., and deliver him to the doorkeeper of Hades Mathyruphramenon and him that is set over the gate and the bars of heaven Sterxerx, etc. . . . . . I invoke upon you the king of the dumb demons; hear ye the great name, for the great Sisochor who bringeth out the gates of Hades commandeth you, and bind my adversary Krateros and put to sleep his tongue his fierceness, etc., that Krateros may not be able to oppose me in any matter. I conjure you, demons multitudinous and slain by violence and untimely dead and unprovided with burial, by the earth-shatterer (*i.e.* Hecate) who brought down the limbs of the limb-bearer and the limb-bearer himself. I conjure you by Achelomorphoth who is the only god upon earth Osous oisornophris ousrapio do that which is written herein . . . gods of the underworld and Hecate of the underworld and Hermes of the underworld and Pluto and the Erinyes beneath the earth and ye who lie here below untimely and nameless Eumazon, take away the voice of Krateros against me Kallias Masomacho; we entrust to you the muzzling of Krateros, give up his name to the gods of the underworld. . . . These will wholly accomplish for me and will muzzle my adversary Krateros; wake up for me, thou that holdest the subterranean kingdom of all the Erinyes. I conjure you by the gods in Hades . . . Aothiomos iioieioegooeoiphri he that in heaven hath his ethereal kingdom Miothilamps in heaven Iao . . . Eablephauben thanatopoutoer. I conjure Bathumia, etc. . . I conjure the gods from Kronos onward Ablanathanalba sisopetron take Krateros the adversary of me Kallias. . . .

8. From Attica (Audollent, p. 102).

I doom and devote to the messengers of the underworld Hermes of the underworld Hecate of the underworld to Pluto and Kore and Persephone and to the Fates of the underworld and to all the gods and to Kerberos, guardian . . . and to shivering and to the daily fever of him that holds and

releases not; I doom them to be senseless . . .
I doom all things . . . mouth shoulders arms breast
stomach back abdomen thighs . . . Paulos the
stone-mason . . .

9. From Carthage (Audollent, p. 341; Wünsch,
Neue Fluchtafeln, Rhein. Mus. 1900, p. 260–5).
Latin.

Bachachuch . . . who art a great deity in Egypt,
bind, utterly bind Maurussus the hunter whom
Felicitas bore; Iekri, take away his sleep, let not
Maurussus sleep whom Felicitas bore; Parpaxin, god
almighty, bring to the infernal abodes Maurussus
whom Felicitas bore; Noktoukit who possessest the
regions of Italy and Campania, who wert drawn
through the Acherusian lake, bring to the Tartarean
abodes within seven days Maurussus whom Felicitas
bore; Butubachk deity who possessest Spain and
Africa who alone passest through the sea, pass
through the soul and spirit of Maurussus whom
Felicitas bore; pass through every remedy and
every phylactery and every safeguard and every
anointing of oil; and bring him, bind him, bind him
utterly . . . carry off, take away consume (*apsumatis
desumatis consumatis*) the heart limbs inward parts
entrails of Maurussus whom Felicitas bore; and
thee I adjure whoever art the demon of the under-
world by these holy binding names:

Maskellei Maskello Phnoukentabaoth that huntest
upon the mountains and cleavest the earth . . . . . .
kerderosandale kataneikandale seize him and make
him pale mournful sad . . . dumb not controlling
himself Maurussus whom Felicitas bore; in every
contest in every fight may he faint and fall . . .

APPENDIX

Maurussus whom Felicitas bore; in the ring of the amphitheatre in the same hour may Maurussus suffer whom Felicitas bore; may he not be able to . . . may he be misguided, utterly misguided, Maurussus whom Felicitas bore; nor may he be able to fling his lasso over the bear, nor bind it . . . may his arms and strength and feet be bound, may he not be able to run, may he grow weary and lose his breath and spirit for every battle, in all conflicts may he be torn, beaten and wounded . . . then may he be transfixed dragged and go forth, Maurussus whom Felicitas bore; . . . swiftly depress fix transfix consume . . . Maurussus whom Felicitas bore; slackly may he . . . the bites of the wild beasts . . . bulls boars and lions . . .

Besides other enemies, the chief objects of these imprecations were adversaries at law and performers in the Circus; there are also a number of love charms extant. Those quoted will suffice to show the general character of such denunciations: a solemn invocation of deities with names that are sometimes Greek, sometimes Hebraic (Adonai, Iao, Michael, etc.), sometimes a mere jumble of words and syllables with any or no meaning: the curse, usually of an exhaustive character, and often containing phrases repeated over and over again; in some cases there is reference to a magical action, as in the sympathetic magic of tying down the cock and the puppy.

References to magic and description of magical proceedings are not uncommon in ancient literature; the subject has recently been excellently treated in a book entitled *Magic in Greek and Latin Literature*,

APPENDIX

by J. E. Lowe (Blackwell), who considers that the
Romans regarded magic much more seriously than
the Greeks; "the Greek temperament was to a
great extent self-sufficing, and did not need to have
recourse to such extraneous means of satisfying
spiritual wants as were provided by the black arts.
The Romans, on the other hand, combined in a
curious manner the cold and calculating character
of the Stoics with the quick passions and emotions
typical of all southern people. It was at the meeting
of these extremes that magic stepped in." We
must refer the reader to this book for information
upon magical practices as reflected in literature;
here we are only concerned with imprecations,
and must conclude with some remarks upon two
examples of that literary type (if it can be so
called), the *Dirae* and the *Ibis*.

Both contain a series of curses directed against
an offending object, in the one case a personal
enemy, in the other an estate from which the writer
has been evicted and which has passed into the
hands of a stranger. In the *Ibis* there is a solemn
appeal to deities, 67–86: this is lacking in the
Dirae: both have the figure referred to above as
ἀδύνατον, *Ib*. 31–40, *Dir*. 4–8, 98–101: the *Dirae* has
something in the nature of a refrain, lacking in the
Ibis: the refrain is familiar in literature from pieces
such as Theocritus' second Idyll and Catullus, lxiv,
and we have seen from the "defixiones" quoted
above that repetition of a phrase is a feature of
magic spells; cf. also the chant of the Furies in
the *Eumenides* of Aeschylus, 321–346. Of the two
pieces, however, it is the *Ibis* that breathes more
of the bitter, relentless spirit of the magical im-

371

precations; we do not, of course, know how closely it was copied from the *Ibis* of Callimachus, in which he attacked his literary enemy, Apollonius, but it is impossible to forget that the scene of that earlier feud was Egypt, the true home of magic of all kinds, that the ibis was a bird used in magic rites (see the Paris Papyrus, pp. 45, 47–49, ed. Wessely, 1888), and that the enemy whom Ovid attacks was also a native of N. Africa, where magic specially flourished.

It is true that one passage in the *Ibis* does not altogether bear out the parallel with the magical imprecation: in ll. 97–106 he refers to himself as a " sacerdos " and to Ibis as his victim, for whom the altar is prepared and all the circumstances of sacrifice are ready. It is not likely that " sacerdos " would ever have been used to express a magician, and again in l. 130 it is the " superi " whom his prayers will move; the occasion is here rather that of a public denunciation, a " devotio " in the sense referred to above, rather than in the sense which it often does bear, that of a magic spell-binding; Audollent says (p. xl.), " tibi audire videaris Romanorum imperatorem Karthagini diras minitantem," though the rest of the poem can hardly be thought to maintain the dignity of a Roman general; it is much too personal, too obviously inspired by personal hostility and resentment. There is another mark of the magical incantation, viz. the reference to the " feigned name," l. 93; magicians would always take care that there was no doubt as to the identity of the person attacked, even if his name were not given, for it would always be expressed in some riddling way (cf. quem mens intelligit, 95); of this Audollent gives instances on pp. xl. and l.

INDEX OF NAMES

(A. = *Ars Amatoria*, C. = *Consolatio ad Liviam*, H. = *Halieuticon*, I. = *Ibis*,
M. = *de Medicamine Faciei*, N. = *Nux*, R. = *Remedia Amoris*.)

INDEX OF NAMES

374

INDEX OF NAMES

INDEX OF NAMES

INDEX OF NAMES

INDEX OF NAMES

INDEX OF SUBJECTS

(*Note :* the first line only of any passage is quoted.)

381

INDEX OF SUBJECTS

PRINTED IN GREAT BRITAIN BY
RICHARD CLAY AND COMPANY, LTD.,
BUNGAY, SUFFOLK.

THE LOEB CLASSICAL LIBRARY

VOLUMES ALREADY PUBLISHED

Latin Authors

AMMIANUS MARCELLINUS. Translated by J. C. Rolfe.
3 Vols. (Vols. I. and II. *2nd Imp. revised.*)

APULEIUS: THE GOLDEN ASS (METAMORPHOSES).
W. Adlington (1566). Revised by S. Gaselee. (*7th Imp.*)

ST. AUGUSTINE, CONFESSIONS OF. W. Watts (1631).
2 Vols. (*5th Imp.*)

ST. AUGUSTINE, SELECT LETTERS. J. H. Baxter.

AUSONIUS. H. G. Evelyn White. 2 Vols.

BEDE. J. E. King. 2 Vols.

BOETHIUS: TRACTS AND DE CONSOLATIONE PHILO-
SOPHIAE. Rev. H. F. Stewart and E. K. Rand. (*4th Imp.*)

CAESAR: CIVIL WARS. A. G. Peskett. (*4th Imp.*)

CAESAR: GALLIC WAR. H. J. Edwards. (*9th Imp.*)

CATO AND VARRO: DE RE RUSTICA. H. B. Ash and
W. D. Hooper. (*2nd Imp.*)

CATULLUS, F. W. Cornish; TIBULLUS. J. B. Postgate;
AND PERVIGILIUM VENERIS. J. W. Mackail. (*11th Imp.*)

CELSUS: DE MEDICINA. W. G. Spencer. 3 Vols. (Vol.
I. *2nd Imp. revised.*)

CICERO: BRUTUS, AND ORATOR. G. L. Hendrickson and
H. M. Hubbell. (*2nd Imp.*)

CICERO: DE FINIBUS. H. Rackham. (*3rd Imp. revised.*)

CICERO: DE NATURA DEORUM AND ACADEMICA. H.
Rackham.

CICERO: DE OFFICIIS. Walter Miller. (*4th Imp.*)

CICERO: DE ORATORE. 2 Vols. E. W. Sutton and H.
Rackham.

CICERO: DE REPUBLICA AND DE LEGIBUS. Clinton
W. Keyes. (*2nd Imp.*)

CICERO: DE SENECTUTE, DE AMICITIA, DE DIVI-
NATIONE. W. A. Falconer. (*5th Imp.*)

CICERO: IN CATILINAM, PRO FLACCO, PRO MURENA,
PRO SULLA. Louis E. Lord. (*2nd Imp. revised.*)

CICERO: LETTERS TO ATTICUS. E. O. Winstedt.
3 Vols. (Vol. I. *6th Imp.*, Vol. II. *3rd Imp.* and Vol. III.
3rd Imp.)

O (OVID, A.L.)

1

CICERO: LETTERS TO HIS FRIENDS. W. Glynn Williams. 3 Vols. (Vols. I. and II. *2nd Imp. revised.*)
CICERO: PHILIPPICS. W. C. A. Ker. (*2nd Imp. revised.*)
CICERO: PRO ARCHIA, POST REDITUM, DE DOMO, DE HARUSPICUM RESPONSIS, PRO PLANCIO. N. H. Watts. (*2nd Imp.*)
CICERO: PRO CAECINA, PRO LEGE MANILIA, PRO CLUENTIO, PRO RABIRIO. H. Grose Hodge. (*2nd Imp.*)
CICERO: PRO MILONE, IN PISONEM, PRO SCAURO, PRO FONTEIO, PRO RABIRIO POSTUMO, PRO MARCELLO, PRO LIGARIO, PRO REGE DEIOTARO. N. H. Watts.
CICERO: PRO QUINCTIO, PRO ROSCIO AMERINO, PRO ROSCIO COMOEDO, CONTRA RULLUM. J. H. Freese. (*2nd Imp. revised.*)
CICERO: TUSCULAN DISPUTATIONS. J. E. King. (*2nd Imp.*)
CICERO: VERRINE ORATIONS. L. H. G. Greenwood. 2 Vols.
CLAUDIAN. M. Platnauer. 2 Vols.
COLUMELLA: DE RE RUSTICA. H. B. Ash. 3 Vols. Vol. I.
CURTIUS, QUINTUS: HISTORY OF ALEXANDER. Translated by J. C. Rolfe. 2 Vols.
FLORUS. E. S. Forster, and CORNELIUS NEPOS. J. C. Rolfe. (*2nd Imp.*)
FRONTINUS: STRATAGEMS AND AQUEDUCTS. C. E. Bennett and M. B. McElwain.
FRONTO: CORRESPONDENCE. C. R. Haines. 2 Vols.
GELLIUS. J. C. Rolfe. 3 Vols. (Vols. I and II. *2nd Imp.*)
HORACE: ODES AND EPODES. C. E. Bennett. (*12th Imp. revised.*)
HORACE: SATIRES, EPISTLES, ARS POETICA. H. R. Fairclough. (*7th Imp. revised.*)
JEROME: SELECTED LETTERS. F. A. Wright.
JUVENAL AND PERSIUS. G. G. Ramsay. (*6th Imp.*)
LIVY. B. O. Foster, F. G. Moore, Evan T. Sage, and A. C. Schlesinger. 13 Vols. Vols. I.–VII., IX.–XII. (Vol. I. *3rd Imp.*, Vols. II., III. and IX. *2nd Imp. revised.*)
LUCAN. J. D. Duff. (*2nd Imp.*)
LUCRETIUS. W. H. D. Rouse. (*6th Imp. revised.*)
MARTIAL. W. C. A. Ker. 2 Vols. (Vol. I. *5th Imp.*, Vol. II. *3rd Imp. revised.*)
MINOR LATIN POETS: from PUBLILIUS SYRUS to RUTILIUS NAMATIANUS, including GRATTIUS, CALPURNIUS SICULUS, NEMESIANUS, AVIANUS, and others with "Aetna" and the "Phoenix." J. Wight Duff and Arnold M. Duff. (*2nd Imp.*)
OVID: THE ART OF LOVE AND OTHER POEMS. J. H. Mozley. (*3rd Imp.*)
OVID: FASTI. Sir James G. Frazer.
OVID: HEROIDES AND AMORES. Grant Showerman. (*4th Imp.*)

2

OVID: METAMORPHOSES. F. J. Miller. 2 Vols. (Vol.
I. 9th Imp., Vol. II. 7th Imp.)
OVID: TRISTIA AND EX PONTO. A. L. Wheeler. (2nd Imp.)
PERSIUS. Cf. JUVENAL.
PETRONIUS. M. Heseltine; SENECA: APOCOLOCYN-
TOSIS. W. H. D. Rouse. (7th Imp. revised.)
PLAUTUS. Paul Nixon. 5 Vols. (Vols. I. and II. 4th Imp.,
Vol. III. 3rd Imp.)
PLINY: LETTERS. Melmoth's Translation revised by
W. M. L. Hutchinson. 2 Vols. (5th Imp.)
PLINY: NATURAL HISTORY. H. Rackham and W. H. S.
Jones. 10 Vols. Vols. I–V. H. Rackham. (Vol. I. 3rd Imp.
Vols. II. and III. 2nd Imp.)
PROPERTIUS. H. E. Butler. (5th Imp.)
QUINTILIAN. H. E. Butler. 4 Vols. (2nd Imp.)
REMAINS OF OLD LATIN. E. H. Warmington. 4 Vols.
Vol. I. (ENNIUS AND CAECILIUS.) Vol. II. (LIVIUS,
NAEVIUS, PACUVIUS, ACCIUS.) Vol. III. (LUCILIUS
AND LAWS OF XII TABLES.) Vol. IV. (ARCHAIC
INSCRIPTIONS.)
SALLUST. J. C. Rolfe. (3rd Imp. revised.)
SCRIPTORES HISTORIAE AUGUSTAE. D. Magie. 3
Vols. (Vol. I. 2nd Imp. revised.)
SENECA: APOCOLOCYNTOSIS. Cf. PETRONIUS.
SENECA: EPISTULAE MORALES. R. M. Gummere. 3
Vols. (Vol. I. 3rd Imp., Vols. II. and III. 2nd Imp. revised.)
SENECA: MORAL ESSAYS. J. W. Basore. 3 Vols. (Vols.
II. and III. 2nd Imp. revised.)
SENECA: TRAGEDIES. F. J. Miller. 2 Vols. (Vol. I.
3rd Imp., Vol. II. 2nd Imp. revised.)
SIDONIUS: POEMS AND LETTERS. W. B. Anderson.
2 Vols. Vol. I.
SILIUS ITALICUS. J. D. Duff. 2 Vols. (Vol. II. 2nd Imp.)
STATIUS. J. H. Mozley. 2 Vols.
SUETONIUS. J. C. Rolfe. 2 Vols. (Vol. I. 6th Imp., Vol. II.
5th Imp. revised.)
TACITUS: DIALOGUS. Sir Wm. Peterson. AGRICOLA
AND GERMANIA. Maurice Hutton. (6th Imp.)
TACITUS: HISTORIES AND ANNALS. C. H. Moore and
J. Jackson. 4 Vols. (Vols. I. and II. 2nd Imp.)
TERENCE. John Sargeaunt. 2 Vols. (Vol. I. 6th Imp.,
Vol. II. 5th Imp.)
TERTULLIAN: APOLOGIA AND DE SPECTACULIS.
T. R. Glover. MINUCIUS FELIX. G. H. Rendall.
VALERIUS FLACCUS. J. H. Mozley. (2nd Imp. revised.)
VARRO: DE LINGUA LATINA. R. G. Kent. 2 Vols.
(2nd Imp.)
VELLEIUS PATERCULUS AND RES GESTAE DIVI
AUGUSTI. F. W. Shipley.
VIRGIL. H. R. Fairclough. 2 Vols. (Vol. I. 16th Imp.,
Vol. II. 13th Imp. revised.)

VITRUVIUS : DE ARCHITECTURA. F. Granger. 2 Vols. (Vol. I. 2nd *Imp.*)

Greek Authors

ACHILLES TATIUS. S. Gaselee. (2nd *Imp.*)

AENEAS TACTICUS, ASCLEPIODOTUS AND ONASANDER. The Illinois Greek Club.

AESCHINES. C. D. Adams. (2nd *Imp.*)

AESCHYLUS. H. Weir Smyth. 2 Vols. (Vol. I. 5th *Imp.*, Vol. II. 4th *Imp.*)

ANDOCIDES, ANTIPHON. Cf. MINOR ATTIC ORATORS.

APOLLODORUS. Sir James G. Frazer. 2 Vols. (2nd *Imp.*)

APOLLONIUS RHODIUS. R. C. Seaton. (4th *Imp.*)

THE APOSTOLIC FATHERS. Kirsopp Lake. 2 Vols. (Vol. I. 6th *Imp.*, Vol. II. 5th *Imp.*)

APPIAN'S ROMAN HISTORY. Horace White. 4 Vols. (Vol. I. 3rd *Imp.*, Vols. II., III. and IV. 2nd *Imp.*)

ARATUS. Cf. CALLIMACHUS.

ARISTOPHANES. Benjamin Bickley Rogers. 3 Vols. Verse trans. (4th *Imp.*)

ARISTOTLE : ART OF RHETORIC. J. H. Freese. (3rd *Imp.*)

ARISTOTLE : ATHENIAN CONSTITUTION, EUDEMIAN ETHICS, VICES AND VIRTUES. H. Rackham. (2nd *Imp.*)

ARISTOTLE : GENERATION OF ANIMALS. A. L. Peck.

ARISTOTLE : METAPHYSICS. H. Tredennick. 2 Vols. (3rd *Imp.*)

ARISTOTLE : MINOR WORKS. W. S. Hett. On Colours, On Things Heard, On Physiognomies, On Plants, On Marvellous Things Heard, Mechanical Problems, On Indivisible Lines, On Position and Names of Winds.

ARISTOTLE : NICOMACHEAN ETHICS. H. Rackham. (5th *Imp. revised.*)

ARISTOTLE : OECONOMICA AND MAGNA MORALIA. G. C. Armstrong; (with Metaphysics, Vol. II.). (3rd *Imp.*)

ARISTOTLE : ON THE HEAVENS. W. K. C. Guthrie. (2nd *Imp. revised.*)

ARISTOTLE : ON THE SOUL, PARVA NATURALIA, ON BREATH. W. S. Hett. (2nd *Imp. revised.*)

ARISTOTLE : ORGANON. H. P. Cooke and H. Tredennick. 2 Vols. Vol. I.

ARISTOTLE : PARTS OF ANIMALS. A. L. Peck; MOTION AND PROGRESSION OF ANIMALS. E. S. Forster. (2nd *Imp. revised.*)

ARISTOTLE : PHYSICS. Rev. P. Wicksteed and F. M. Cornford. 2 Vols. (Vol. II. 2nd *Imp.*)

ARISTOTLE : POETICS AND LONGINUS. W. Hamilton Fyfe; DEMETRIUS ON STYLE. W. Rhys Roberts. (4th *Imp. revised.*)

ARISTOTLE : POLITICS. H. Rackham. (3rd *Imp. revised.*)

ARISTOTLE : PROBLEMS. W. S. Hett. 2 Vols.

ARISTOTLE: RHETORICA AD ALEXANDRUM (with PROBLEMS, Vol. II.). H. Rackham.
ARRIAN: HISTORY OF ALEXANDER AND INDICA. Rev. E. Iliffe Robson. 2 Vols. (Vol. I. *2nd Imp.*)
ATHENAEUS: DEIPNOSOPHISTAE. C. B. Gulick. 7 Vols. (Vols. V. and VI. *2nd Imp.*)
ST. BASIL: LETTERS. R. J. Deferrari. 4 Vols.
CALLIMACHUS AND LYCOPHRON. A. W. Mair; ARATUS. G. R. Mair.
CLEMENT OF ALEXANDRIA. Rev. G. W. Butterworth. (*2nd Imp.*)
COLLUTHUS. Cf. OPPIAN.
DAPHNIS AND CHLOE. Thornley's Translation revised by J. M. Edmonds; AND PARTHENIUS. S. Gaselee. (*3rd Imp.*)
DEMOSTHENES: DE CORONA AND DE FALSA LEGATIONE. C. A. Vince and J. H. Vince. (*2nd Imp. revised.*)
DEMOSTHENES: MEIDIAS, ANDROTION, ARISTOCRATES, TIMOCRATES AND ARISTOGEITON, I. AND II. Translated by J. H. Vince.
DEMOSTHENES: OLYNTHIACS, PHILIPPICS AND MINOR ORATIONS: I.–XVII. AND XX. J. H. Vince.
DEMOSTHENES: PRIVATE ORATIONS. A. T. Murray. 3 Vols. (Vol. I. *2nd Imp.*)
DIO CASSIUS: ROMAN HISTORY. E. Cary. 9 Vols. (Vols. I. and II. *2nd Imp.*)
DIO CHRYSOSTOM. J. W. Cohoon and H. Lamar Crosby. 5 Vols. Vols. I.–IV.
DIODORUS SICULUS: THE LIBRARY. 12 Vols. Vols. I.–IV. translated by C. H. Oldfather. Vol. IX. translated by C. H. Geer.
DIOGENES LAERTIUS. R. D. Hicks. 2 Vols. (Vol. I. *3rd Imp.*, Vol. II. *2nd Imp.*)
DIONYSIUS OF HALICARNASSUS: ROMAN ANTIQUITIES. Spelman's translation revised by E. Cary. 7 Vols. Vols. I.–VI. (Vol. I. *2nd Imp.*)
EPICTETUS. W. A. Oldfather. 2 Vols. (Vol. I. *2nd Imp.*)
EURIPIDES. A. S. Way. 4 Vols. (Vols. I., II. and IV. *6th Imp.*, Vol. III. *5th Imp.*) Verse trans.
EUSEBIUS: ECCLESIASTICAL HISTORY. Kirsopp Lake and J. E. L. Oulton. 2 Vols. (Vol. I. *2nd Imp.*, Vol. II. *3rd Imp.*)
GALEN: ON THE NATURAL FACULTIES. A. J. Brock. (*3rd Imp.*)
THE GREEK ANTHOLOGY. W. R. Paton. 5 Vols. (Vols. I. and II. *4th Imp.*, Vols. III. and IV. *3rd Imp.*)
GREEK ELEGY AND IAMBUS WITH THE ANACREONTEA. J. M. Edmonds. 2 Vols. (Vol. I. *2nd Imp.*)
THE GREEK BUCOLIC POETS (THEOCRITUS, BION, MOSCHUS). J. M. Edmonds. (*6th Imp. revised.*)
GREEK MATHEMATICAL WORKS. Ivor Thomas. 2 Vols.

HERODES. Cf. THEOPHRASTUS : CHARACTERS.
HERODOTUS. A. D. Godley. 4 Vols. (Vol. I. *4th Imp.*, Vols. II. IV. *3rd Imp.*)
HESIOD AND THE HOMERIC HYMNS. H. G. Evelyn White. (*6th Imp., revised and enlarged.*)
HIPPOCRATES AND THE FRAGMENTS OF HERACLEITUS. W. H. S. Jones and E. T. Withington. 4 Vols. (Vols. I., II. and IV. *2nd Imp.*, Vol. III. *3rd Imp.*)
HOMER : ILIAD. A. T. Murray. 2 Vols. (*5th Imp.*)
HOMER : ODYSSEY. A. T. Murray. 2 Vols. (*7th Imp.*)
ISAEUS. E. W. Forster. (*2nd Imp.*)
ISOCRATES. George Norlin. 3 Vols.
ST. JOHN DAMASCENE : BARLAAM AND IOASAPH. Rev. G. R. Woodward and Harold Mattingly. (*2nd Imp. revised.*)
JOSEPHUS. H. St. J. Thackeray and Ralph Marcus. 9 Vols. Vols. I.–VII. (Vol. V. *2nd Imp.*)
JULIAN. Wilmer Cave Wright. 3 Vols. (Vols. I. and II. *2nd Imp.*)
LUCIAN. A. M. Harmon. 8 Vols. Vols. I.–V. (Vols. I. and II. *3rd Imp.*, Vol. III. *2nd Imp.*)
LYCOPHRON. Cf. CALLIMACHUS.
LYRA GRAECA. J. M. Edmonds. 3 Vols. (Vol. I. and III. *3rd Imp.*, Vol. II. *2nd Ed. revised and enlarged.*)
LYSIAS. W. R. M. Lamb. (*2nd Imp.*)
MANETHO. W. G. Waddell : PTOLEMY : TETRABIBLOS. F. E. Robbins. (*2nd Imp.*)
MARCUS AURELIUS. C. R. Haines. (*3rd Imp. revised.*)
MENANDER. F. G. Allinson. (*2nd Imp. revised.*)
MINOR ATTIC ORATORS (ANTIPHON, ANDOCIDES, DEMADES, DEINARCHUS, HYPEREIDES). K. J. Maidment and J. O. Burtt. 2 Vols. Vol. I. K. J. Maidment.
NONNOS. W. H. D. Rouse. 3 Vols. (Vol. III. *2nd Imp.*)
OPPIAN, COLLUTHUS, TRYPHIODORUS. A. W. Mair.
PAPYRI. NON-LITERARY SELECTIONS. A. S. Hunt and C. C. Edgar. 2 Vols. LITERARY SELECTIONS. Vol. I. (Poetry). D. L. Page. (*2nd Imp.*)
PARTHENIUS. Cf. DAPHNIS AND CHLOE.
PAUSANIAS : DESCRIPTION OF GREECE. W. H. S. Jones. 5 Vols. and Companion Vol. (Vols. I. and III. *2nd Imp.*)
PHILO. 10 Vols. Vols. I.–V.; F. H. Colson and Rev. G. H. Whitaker. Vols. VI.–IX.; F. H. Colson. (Vol. IV. *2nd Imp.*)
PHILOSTRATUS : THE LIFE OF APOLLONIUS OF TYANA. F. C. Conybeare. 2 Vols. (Vol. I. *3rd Imp.*, Vol. II. *2nd Imp.*)
PHILOSTRATUS : IMAGINES; CALLISTRATUS : DESCRIPTIONS. A. Fairbanks.
PHILOSTRATUS AND EUNAPIUS : LIVES OF THE SOPHISTS. Wilmer Cave Wright.
PINDAR. Sir J. E. Sandys. (*7th Imp. revised.*)

PLATO: CHARMIDES, ALCIBIADES, HIPPARCHUS, THE LOVERS, THEAGES, MINOS AND EPINOMIS. W. R. M. Lamb.

PLATO: CRATYLUS, PARMENIDES, GREATER HIPPIAS, LESSER HIPPIAS. H. N. Fowler. (*3rd Imp.*)

PLATO: EUTHYPHRO, APOLOGY, CRITO, PHAEDO, PHAEDRUS. H. N. Fowler. (*9th Imp.*)

PLATO: LACHES, PROTAGORAS, MENO, EUTHYDEMUS. W. R. M. Lamb. (*2nd Imp. revised.*)

PLATO: LAWS. Rev. R. G. Bury. 2 Vols. (*2nd Imp.*)

PLATO: LYSIS, SYMPOSIUM, GORGIAS. W. R. M. Lamb. (*4th Imp. revised.*)

PLATO: REPUBLIC. Paul Shorey. 2 Vols. (Vol. I. *4th Imp.*, Vol. II. *3rd Imp.*)

PLATO: STATESMAN, PHILEBUS. H. N. Fowler; ION. W. R. M. Lamb. (*3rd Imp.*)

PLATO: THEAETETUS AND SOPHIST. H. N. Fowler. (*3rd Imp.*)

PLATO: TIMAEUS, CRITIAS, CLITOPHO, MENEXENUS, EPISTULAE. Rev. R. G. Bury. (*2nd Imp.*)

PLUTARCH: MORALIA. 14 Vols. Vols. I.–V. F. C. Babbitt; Vol. VI. W. C. Helmbold; Vol. X. H. N. Fowler.

PLUTARCH: THE PARALLEL LIVES. B. Perrin. 11 Vols. (Vols. I., II., III., VI., VII., and XI. *2nd Imp.*)

POLYBIUS. W. R. Paton. 6 Vols.

PROCOPIUS: HISTORY OF THE WARS. H. B. Dewing. 7 Vols. (Vol. I. *2nd Imp.*)

PTOLEMY: TETRABIBLOS. Cf. MANETHO.

QUINTUS SMYRNAEUS. A. S. Way. Verse trans. (*2nd Imp.*)

SEXTUS EMPIRICUS. Rev. R. G. Bury. 4 Vols. (Vol. I. *2nd Imp.*)

SOPHOCLES. F. Storr. 2 Vols. (Vol. I. *8th Imp.*, Vol. II. *5th Imp.*) Verse trans.

STRABO: GEOGRAPHY. Horace L. Jones. 8 Vols. (Vols. I., V. and VIII. *2nd Imp.*)

THEOPHRASTUS: CHARACTERS. J. M. Edmonds; HERODES, etc. A. D. Knox. (*2nd Imp.*)

THEOPHRASTUS: ENQUIRY INTO PLANTS. Sir Arthur Hort, Bart. 2 Vols.

THUCYDIDES. C. F. Smith. 4 Vols. (Vol. I. *3rd Imp.*, Vols. II., III. and IV. *2nd Imp. revised.*)

TRYPHIODORUS. Cf. OPPIAN.

XENOPHON: CYROPAEDIA. Walter Miller. 2 Vols. (Vol. I. *2nd Imp.*, Vol. II. *3rd Imp.*)

XENOPHON: HELLENICA, ANABASIS, APOLOGY, AND SYMPOSIUM. C. L. Brownson and O. J. Todd. 3 Vols. (*3rd Imp.*)

XENOPHON: MEMORABILIA AND OECONOMICUS. E. C. Marchant. (*2nd Imp.*)

XENOPHON: SCRIPTA MINORA. E. C. Marchant. (*2nd Imp.*)

IN PREPARATION

Greek Authors

ALCIPHRON. A. R. Benner and F. Fobes.
ARISTOTLE : DE MUNDO.
ARISTOTLE : HISTORY OF ANIMALS. A. L. Peck.
ARISTOTLE : METEOROLOGICA. H. P. Lee.
DEMOSTHENES : EPISTLES, etc. N. W. and N. J. De Witt.
PLOTINUS.

Latin Authors

ST. AUGUSTINE : CITY OF GOD. W. S. Maguinness.
[CICERO] : AD HERENNIUM. H. Caplan.
CICERO : DE INVENTIONE, etc. H. M. Hubbell.
CICERO : PRO SESTIO, IN VATINIUM, PRO CAELIO,
  DE PROVINCIIS CONSULARIBUS, PRO BALBO. J. H.
  Freese and R. Gardner.
PHAEDRUS AND OTHER FABULISTS. B. E. Perry.
PRUDENTIUS. J. H. Thomson.

DESCRIPTIVE PROSPECTUS ON APPLICATION

London   -   WILLIAM HEINEMANN LTD
Cambridge, Mass.   HARVARD UNIVERSITY PRESS